Frommer's

Boston

2004

by Marie Morris

La Familigia 112 Salem

Here's what the critics say about Frommer's:

"Amazingly easy to use. Very portable, very complete."
— *Booklist*

"Detailed, accurate, and easy-to-read information for all price ranges."
— *Glamour Magazine*

"Hotel information is close to encyclopedic."
— *Des Moines Sunday Register*

"Frommer's Guides have a way of giving you a real feel for a place."
— *Knight Ridder Newspapers*

WILEY

Wiley Publishing, Inc.

About the Author

Marie Morris grew up in New York and graduated from Harvard, where she studied history. She has worked for the *Boston Herald, Boston* magazine, and the *New York Times*. She's the author of *Boston For Dummies,* and she covers Boston for *Frommer's New England*. She lives in Boston, not far from Paul Revere.

Published by:

Wiley Publishing, Inc.

111 River St.
Hoboken, NJ 07030

ISBN 0-7645-3884-5
ISSN 0899-322X

Editor: Paul Prince
Production Editor: M. Faunette Johnston
Photo Editor: Richard Fox
Cartographer: Roberta Stockwell
Production by Wiley Indianapolis Composition Services

For information on our other products and services or to obtain technical support, please contact our Customer Care Department within the U.S. at 800-762-2974, outside the U.S. at 317-572-3993 or fax 317-572-4002.

Wiley also publishes its books in a variety of electronic formats. Some content that appears in print may not be available in electronic formats.

Manufactured in the United States of America

5 4 3 2 1

Contents

6 Where to Dine

7 What to See & Do in Boston

8 Boston Strolls

List of Maps

Acknowledgments

Many thanks to my research assistants and cheerleaders, Kristin Goss, Sue Costello, Joie Watson, Michael Dobler, Betsy Bates, Debbie and Neil Goldfine, Kelly Wallace, and Matthew Saal. And special thanks to my favorite dinner companions, Pete Christmann and Will Christmann.

—Marie Morris

An Invitation to the Reader

In researching this book, we discovered many wonderful places—hotels, restaurants, shops, and more. We're sure you'll find others. Please tell us about them so that we can share the information with your fellow travelers in upcoming editions. If you were disappointed with a recommendation, we'd love to know that, too. Please write to:

Frommer's Boston 2004
Wiley Publishing, Inc. • 111 River St. • Hoboken, NJ 07030

An Additional Note

Please be advised that travel information is subject to change at any time—and this is especially true of prices. We therefore suggest that you write or call ahead for confirmation when making your travel plans. The authors, editors, and publisher cannot be held responsible for the experiences of readers while traveling. Your safety is important to us, however, so we encourage you to stay alert and be aware of your surroundings. Keep a close eye on cameras, purses, and wallets, all favorite targets of thieves and pickpockets.

Other Great Guides for Your Trip:

Frommer's New England
Frommer's Portable Boston
Frommer's Best-Loved Driving Tours: New England
Frommer's Irreverent Guide to Boston

Frommer's Star Ratings, Icons & Abbreviations

Every hotel, restaurant, and attraction listing in this guide has been ranked for quality, value, service, amenities, and special features using a **star-rating system.** In country, state, and regional guides, we also rate towns and regions to help you narrow down your choices and budget your time accordingly. Hotels and restaurants are rated on a scale of zero (recommended) to three stars (exceptional). Attractions, shopping, nightlife, towns, and regions are rated according to the following scale: zero stars (recommended), one star (highly recommended), two stars (very highly recommended), and three stars (must-see).

In addition to the star-rating system, we also use **seven feature icons** that point you to the great deals, in-the-know advice, and unique experiences that separate travelers from tourists. Throughout the book, look for:

Finds	Special finds—those places only insiders know about
Fun Fact	Fun facts—details that make travelers more informed and their trips more fun
Kids	Best bets for kids and advice for the whole family
Moments	Special moments—those experiences that memories are made of
Overrated	Places or experiences not worth your time or money
Tips	Insider tips—great ways to save time and money
Value	Great values—where to get the best deals

The following **abbreviations** are used for credit cards:

AE	American Express	DISC	Discover	V	Visa
DC	Diners Club	MC	MasterCard		

Frommers.com

Now that you have the guidebook to a great trip, visit our website at **www.frommers.com** for travel information on more than 3,000 destinations. With features updated regularly, we give you instant access to the most current trip-planning information available. At Frommers.com, you'll also find the best prices on airfares, accommodations, and car rentals—and you can even book travel online through our travel booking partners. At Frommers.com, you'll also find the following:

- Online updates to our most popular guidebooks
- Vacation sweepstakes and contest giveaways
- Newsletter highlighting the hottest travel trends
- Online travel message boards with featured travel discussions

What's New in Boston

A casual observer might suspect that nothing in Boston is new. It's a relatively old place, with a rich history that informs every aspect of the present-day city. Look a little closer, though. Widespread construction—of highways and a dramatic new bridge as well as buildings—is altering the face of the city. Add the security-conscious national mood and the uncertain economy (which has led to widespread state budget cuts), and you might expect to arrive in a city on edge. But Boston rolls with the punches—having come through revolution, war, and social upheaval in its nearly 400 years, the city will adjust to the latest changes, too.

In fact, you might say change is in the air: In 2003 Boston enacted a **smoking ban** in all workplaces, including restaurants, bars, and nightclubs. At press time, Cambridge was more lenient, but the prohibition may be statewide by the time you visit.

Also in 2003, the **"Big Dig"** highway-construction project entered its final phase. The connection from the Massachusetts Turnpike (I-90) to Logan International Airport opened, the northbound lanes of the I-93 tunnel beneath downtown handled their first traffic, and the gorgeous **Leonard P. Zakim Bunker Hill Bridge** opened.

Another grand opening, of the $800 million, 1.6-million-square-foot **Boston Convention & Exhibition Center** in South Boston, will take place in June 2004.

Here's a look at some other developments.

PLANNING YOUR TRIP The **U.S. Olympic Gymnastics Trials** will return to the FleetCenter in June 2004. In July, after the traditional weeklong Fourth of July blowout, **Harborfest,** are **SailBoston,** which attracts hundreds of ships and millions of spectators; the **Macworld Conference & Expo** (at the new convention center); and the **Democratic National Convention,** at the FleetCenter. See chapter 2.

GETTING TO KNOW BOSTON Check to make sure that budget cuts have spared **Night Owl** bus service before you launch a night on the town. The MBTA (© **617/222-3200;** www.mbta.com) operates the popular service on Friday and Saturday nights between subway closing time (12:30–1am) and 2:30am. See chapter 4.

ACCOMMODATIONS The go-go 1990s left behind more than worthless stock certificates. Hotels that were in the planning stages during the dot-com boom are opening or under construction now.

The **Hotel Marlowe,** 25 Edwin H. Land Blvd., Cambridge (© **800/ 825-7040;** www.hotelmarlowe.com), is the first Kimpton property in the Northeast. The 236-unit hotel exudes the chic style guests expect from the San Francisco–based chain.

The 188-room **Brookline Courtyard by Marriott,** 40 Webster St. (© **800/321-2211;** www.brooklinecourtyard.com), is convenient to the Longwood Medical Area.

The **Hampton Inn Boston/Cambridge,** 191 Msgr. O'Brien Hwy. (✆ **800/426-7866;** www.hamptoninn.com), is in a handy location in East Cambridge.

The original **Ritz-Carlton,** 15 Arlington St. (✆ **800/241-3333** or 617/536-5700; www.ritzcarlton.com), reopened in late 2002 after a $50 million overhaul.

The six-story **Hotel Commonwealth,** 650 Beacon St. (✆ **800/784-4000** or 617/927-4445; www.hotelcommonwealth.com), a 150-unit lodging in Kenmore Square, was scheduled to open in mid-2003 after lengthy construction delays. See chapter 5.

DINING Davio's (✆ **617/357-4810**) has relocated from Newbury Street to 75 Arlington St. It's just a few blocks away, but this is already one of the best moves since Babe Ruth switched to the outfield.

One of Cambridge's premier special-occasion destinations, Upstairs at the Pudding, has reopened in a new location as **Upstairs on the Square,** 91 Winthrop St. (✆ **617/864-1933**).

Also in Cambridge, **Jasper White's Summer Shack,** 149 Alewife Brook Pkwy. (✆ **617/576-2433**), is a cavernous place that serves everything from corn dogs to gourmet lobster. See chapter 6.

WHAT TO SEE & DO The **Museum of Fine Arts** (✆ **617/267-9300;** www.mfa.org) has begun work on a $180 million expansion that incorporates a new East Wing. Check out the plans, by celebrated architect Norman Foster, when you visit the existing galleries.

Suffolk Downs racetrack, 111 Waldemar Ave., East Boston (✆ **617/567-3900;** www.suffolkdowns.com), could have slot machines by 2004. Check at your hotel to see whether the legislation permitting them has passed.

The **Boston Tea Party Ship & Museum** (✆ **617/338-1773;** www.

bostonteapartyship.com) closed indefinitely after a fire in 2001; if you hope to visit, call ahead to see whether it has reopened.

Two popular attractions reopened in 2002 after extensive renovations: The **Longfellow National Historic Site,** 105 Brattle St., Cambridge (✆ **617/876-4491;** www.nps.gov/long), and the **Mapparium,** which is now a featured exhibit at the Mary Baker Eddy Library, 200 Mass. Ave., Boston (✆ **888/222-3711;** www.marybakereddylibrary.org). See chapter 7.

SHOPPING Is it Boston or Paris? The white-blouse emporium Anne Fontaine blazed the trail, and now you can feed your friends, light your home, and paint your face in *haute* French style without leaving the Back Bay. Head to **Oliviers & Co.,** 161 Newbury St. (✆ **866/828-6620**), for gourmet olive oil; **Diptyque,** 123 Newbury St. (✆ **617/351-2430**), for scented candles; and **Sephora,** Shops at the Prudential Center, 800 Boylston St. (✆ **617/262-4200**), for a dizzying array of makeup, perfume, and skin-care products.

And as long as you're dizzy and thinking about your skin, explore the face and body preparations at **Kiehl's,** 112 Newbury St. (✆ **617/247-1777**). See chapter 9.

BOSTON AFTER DARK In 2004, James Levine will replace Seiji Ozawa as music director of the **Boston Symphony Orchestra** (✆ **617/266-1492** or 617/CONCERT for program information; www.bso.org). Ozawa has already moved on; expect guest conductors—including Levine—to be striking up the band during your visit.

The **Emerson Majestic Theatre,** 219 Tremont St. (✆ **617/824-8000;** www.maj.org), has reopened after an extensive restoration.

Finale, a Theater District dining favorite that serves mostly desserts, has opened a branch at 30 Dunster St., Harvard Square (© **617/441-9797**). See chapter 10.

SIDE TRIPS FROM BOSTON Salem's **Peabody Essex Museum,** East India Sq. (© **800/745-4054** or 978/ 745-9500; www.pem.org), opened a new wing in 2003 after a $100 million expansion project. The highlight is an 18th-century house imported from China and reassembled here. See chapter 11.

1

The Best of Boston

Visitors to Boston in 2004 will find a city that's hitting its stride. Boston has always responded to uncertain times with great resolve, and the early 21st century is no different. Rerouting an interstate highway, opening a dramatic bridge and a gargantuan convention center, asking sailors from around the world and Democrats from around the country to stop by for a visit—Bostonians are getting on with their lives and inviting millions of out-of-towners to watch.

The $14.6 billion "Big Dig" will be near completion when you visit. The largest construction project in the world, which is moving an elevated expressway underground, has dominated the downtown waterfront for much of a decade. A breathtaking white bridge over the Charles River between Boston and Cambridge opened to traffic in 2003. And the end is near, with the entire project hurtling toward completion in early 2005.

The new highway will run beneath a modern metropolis that's also a relentlessly historic destination. An ongoing building boom may overshadow the famous 18th- and 19th-century architecture, but even rampant development can't change the colonial character of the central city.

It's not perfect, of course. Nightmarish traffic, daredevil drivers, and grating accents don't help any city's reputation. Although Boston is the biggest college town in the world, there isn't much of a late-night scene. And far from gone is the inferiority complex epitomized by the description "like New York, but smaller." Still, as it has for centuries, Boston offers cosmopolitan sophistication on a comfortable scale, balancing celebration of the past with pursuit of the future.

Here's hoping your experience is memorable and delightful.

1 Frommer's Favorite Boston Experiences

- **A Sky Full of Fireworks.** Twice during Independence Day festivities and again as the new year begins, the firmament flashes in celebration. The Fourth of July fireworks are over the Charles River; the Harborfest display (in early July) and the First Night exhibition explode above the Inner Harbor. See "Boston Calendar of Events" in chapter 2.
- **A Meal at Durgin-Park.** Dinner at this Boston institution (it opened in 1827) might start with oysters. It might also start with a waitress slinging a handful of napkins over your shoulder, dropping a pile of cutlery in front of you, and saying, "Here, give these out." The surly service usually seems to be an act, but it's so much a part of the legend that some people are disappointed when the waitresses are nice (as they often are). See p. 115.
- **A Lunch Break with a Water View.** Head for thze harbor or the river, perch on a park bench or a patch of grass, put away your watch, relax, and enjoy the spectacular scene. Whether it's sailboats or ocean liners, seagulls or scullers,

there's always something worth watching. See chapter 6.

- **A Ride on a Duck.** A Duck Tour, that is. Board a reconditioned amphibious World War II landing craft (on Boylston St. in front of the Prudential Center) for a sightseeing ride that includes a dip in the river—for the Duck, not you. See p. 182.

- **A "Ride" Indoors.** The Mugar Omni Theater (at the Museum of Science) and the 3-D Simons IMAX Theatre (at the New England Aquarium) offer intrepid visitors hair-raising experiences in the safety of a comfortable auditorium. The large-format films concentrate on the natural world. See chapter 7.

- **A Few Hours (at Least) at the Museum of Fine Arts.** Whether you're into Egyptian art or contemporary photography, furniture and decorative arts or the Impressionists, you're sure to find something at the MFA that tickles your interest. See p. 150.

- **An Afternoon Red Sox Game.** Since 1912, baseball fans have made pilgrimages to Fenway Park, the "lyric little bandbox of a ball park" (in John Updike's words) off Kenmore Square. The seats are uncomfortable and expensive, the Red Sox last won the World Series in 1918, and you won't care a whit about either as you soak up the atmosphere and bask in the sun. See p. 192.

- **A Vicarious Thrill.** Without so much as lacing up a sneaker, you can participate in the world-famous Boston Marathon. Stretch a little, so you won't cramp up. Drink plenty of fluids. Stake out a slice of sidewalk on Commonwealth Avenue and cheer as the runners thunder past. Then put your feet up—you've earned it. See p. 194.

- **A Walk Around the North End.** Boston's Little Italy (but don't call it that!) has an old-world flavor you won't want to miss. Explore the shops on Salem Street, wander the narrow side streets, enjoy some pasta, and be sure to stop for coffee and a pastry at a Hanover Street *caffè*. See "Welcome to the North End" on p. 163.

- **A Spring Fling in the Public Garden.** Eight square blocks of paradise await you, filled with flowers, ornamental greenery, and flowering trees and shrubs. Pass through for a quick pick-me-up, take to the lagoon for a swan boat ride, or just enjoy the ducklings. They're on view in the flesh seasonally and in bronze year-round. See chapters 7 and 8.

- **A Newbury Street Safari.** From the genteel Arlington Street end to the cutting-edge Mass. Ave. end, Newbury Street—Boston's legendary shopping destination—is 8 blocks of pure temptation: galleries, boutiques, jewelry and gift shops, bookstores, and more. See chapter 9.

- **A Visit to Faneuil Hall Marketplace.** Specialty shops, an enormous food court, street performers, bars, restaurants, and crowds from all over the world make Faneuil Hall Marketplace (you'll also hear it called Quincy Market) Boston's most popular destination. See chapter 9.

- **A Free Friday Flick.** Families, film buffs, and impoverished culture hounds flock to the lawn in front of the Hatch Shell on the splanade for free movies (*The Wizard of Oz* or *Tarzan,* for example) on Friday nights in the summer. Bring something to sit on, and maybe a sweater. See p. 246.

- **A Concert Alfresco.** Summer nights swing to the beat of outdoor music by amateurs and professionals. A great spot for free jazz is Christopher Columbus Park, on the waterfront, where performances take place Fridays at 7pm. See p. 237.

- **A Concert Indoors.** The lights go down, the crowd falls silent—you get a little thrill even if you're waiting for an Adam Sandler movie. If you're waiting for the Boston Symphony Orchestra, the thrill is as big as the group's string

section. See section 1, "The Performing Arts" in chapter 10.

- **An Off-Season Day Trip.** Destinations that abound with out-of-towners in the summer and fall become more manageable when the weather turns cold. Don't let the CLOSED FOR THE SEASON signs put you off: Under a cloudless sky, against the indigo Atlantic, an all-but-deserted suburban town has a unique appeal. See chapter 11.

2 Best Hotel Bets

- **Best Historic Hotel:** The **Fairmont Copley Plaza Hotel,** 138 St. James Ave. (© 800/441-1414; www.fairmont.com/copleyplaza), opened in 1912 on the original site of the Museum of Fine Arts. Designed by Henry Janeway Hardenbergh (also the architect of the Plaza in New York), it has entertained presidents and celebrities since the day its magnificent gilded lobby opened. See p. 87.
- **Best for Business Travelers:** The **Boston Harbor Hotel,** Rowes Wharf (© 800/752-7077; www.bhh.com), is just far enough from the Financial District (across the street) to buy you some peace at the end of a busy day. And its rooms are so well outfitted that you may not have to go out at all. See p. 74.
- **Best for a Romantic Getaway:** The intimate atmosphere and elegant furnishings make a suite at the **Eliot Hotel,** 370 Commonwealth Ave. (© 800/44-ELIOT; www.eliothotel.com), a great spot for a rendezvous. If you and your beloved need some time apart, close the French doors—you can be in separate rooms yet still maintain eye contact. See p. 87.
- **Best for Families:** The **Doubletree Guest Suites,** 400 Soldiers Field Rd. (© 800/222-TREE; www.doubletree.com), offer two

rooms for the price of one, with two TVs and a refrigerator, and a nice pool. The location, straddling Boston and Cambridge, is especially good if you're driving from the west—you leave the turnpike before downtown traffic shatters the peace in the back of the minivan. See p. 92.

- **Best for Travelers with Disabilities:** The **Royal Sonesta Hotel,** 5 Cambridge Pkwy., Cambridge (© 800/SONESTA; www.sonesta.com/boston), trains its staff in disability awareness and offers 18 rooms (some of which adjoin standard units) equipped for the hearing, ambulatory, and vision impaired. A wheelchair ramp for use in conference rooms is available. Across the river, 48 fully accessible rooms at the **Westin Copley Place Boston,** 10 Huntington Ave. (© 800/WESTIN-1; www.westin.com/copleyplace), adjoin standard units. See p. 98 and 90, respectively.
- **Best Value:** The **Newbury Guest House,** 261 Newbury St. (© 800/437-7668; www.newburyguesthouse.com), would be a good deal even if it weren't ideally located in the heart of the Back Bay. Room prices even include continental breakfast. See p. 91.
- **Best Value for Motorists:** Room rates at **The MidTown Hotel,**

220 Huntington Ave. (© **800/ 343-1177**; www.midtownhotel. com), include parking for one car—a savings of as much as $35— in a handy location. See p. 90.

- **Best Lobby for Pretending That You're Rich:** The Edwardian wonderland that is the street level of the **Fairmont Copley Plaza Hotel** (see the earlier entry "Best Historic Hotel"), is the perfect place for indulging your upper-crust fantasies.
- **Best Service:** Hands down, the **Four Seasons Hotel,** 200 Boylston St. (© **800/332-3442;** www.four seasons.com). The chain's standards

are sky-high, and the friendly and efficient staff here meets and exceeds them. See p. 84.

- **Best Pool:** The **Sheraton Boston Hotel,** 39 Dalton St. (© **800/ 325-3535;** www.sheraton.com/ boston), has a great indoor-out-door pool with a retractable dome. See p. 90.
- **Best Views:** Several hotels offer impressive views of their immedi-ate surroundings, but for a pic-ture-postcard panorama of Boston and Cambridge, head to the upper floors of the **Westin Copley Place Boston** (see the earlier entry "Best for Travelers with Disabilities").

3 Best Dining Bets

- **Best, Period:** If you have only one meal during your visit, make it dinner at **Rialto,** in the Charles Hotel, 1 Bennett St., Cambridge (© **617/661-5050**). See p. 134.
- **Best Spot for Romance:** Soaring ceilings, colorful decor, and (sea-sonally) a roaring fire make the atmosphere in the Monday Club Bar at **Upstairs on the Square,** 91 Winthrop St., Cambridge (© **617/864-1933**), perfect for a rendezvous. See p. 134.
- **Best Spot for a Business Lunch:** Plenty of deals go down at private clubs and formal restaurants, but that can take hours. Leave an impression with your no-nonsense approach and a quick but deli-cious meal at **Cosí Sandwich Bar,** 53 State St. (© **617/723-4447**), 14 Milk St. (© **617/426-7565**), or 133 Federal St. (© **617/ 292-2674**). See p 116.
- **Best Spot for a Celebration:** Cool your heels at the bar at **Dalí,** 415 Washington St., Somerville (© **617/661-3254**), and toast your good news with sangria while you wait for a table. (Finally, a restaurant that makes you glad it

doesn't take reservations.) The dishes on the tapas menu are perfect for sharing, and the atmos-phere is lively and festive. See p. 137.

- **Best Decor:** The luxurious ban-quettes, gorgeous paintings and flowers, and picture windows over-looking the Public Garden make **Aujourd'hui,** in the Four Seasons Hotel, 200 Boylston St. (© **617/ 351-2037**), feel like an extremely elegant treehouse. See p. 123.
- **Best View:** The dining room at the **Bay Tower,** 60 State St. (© **617/723-1666**), isn't the highest in Boston, but its view is the most impressive. From the palatial 33rd floor, everyone in the room (not just people near the windows) can see what's afoot on the harbor and at the airport. See p. 114.
- **Best Wine List:** Organized by characteristics (from light to rich) rather than by vintage or prove-nance, the excellent offerings at the **Blue Room,** 1 Kendall Sq., Cam-bridge (© **617/494-9034**), are arranged in the most user-friendly way imaginable. See p. 137.

- **Best Service:** The waitstaff at **Troquet,** 140 Boylston St. (© **617/695-9463**), answers more questions than the parents of a toddler. Your server will graciously walk you through the wine-oriented menu or graciously leave you to your own devices. See p. 119.
- **Best Value:** At the **Midwest Grill,** 1122 Cambridge St., Cambridge (© **617/354-7536**), the hits just keep on coming. The sword-wielding waiters bring succulent grilled meats until you ask (or beg) them to stop. Arrive hungry and you'll definitely get your money's worth. See p. 139.
- **Best for Kids:** The wood-fired brick ovens of the **Bertucci's** chain are magnets for little eyes, and the pizza that comes out of them is equally enthralling. Picky parents will be happy here, too. Try the locations at Faneuil Hall Marketplace (© **617/227-7889**), 43 Stanhope St., Back Bay (© **617/247-6161**), and 21 Brattle St., Harvard Square, Cambridge (© **617/864-4748**). See p. 126.
- **Best Raw Bar:** After just a few moments of gobbling fresh seafood and being hypnotized by the shuckers at **Ye Olde Union Oyster House,** 41 Union St. (© **617/227-2750**), you might find yourself feeling sorry for the people who wound up with the pearls instead of the oysters. See p. 115.
- **Best Place for a Classic Boston Experience: Durgin-Park,** 340 Faneuil Hall Marketplace (© **617/227-2038**), has packed 'em in since 1827. From tycoon to tourist, everyone is happy here except the famously crotchety waitresses. It's a classic, not a relic. See p. 115.
- **Best American Cuisine:** It's not quite "cuisine," but what's more American than a burger? **Mr. Bartley's Burger Cottage,** 1246 Massachusetts Ave. (© **617/354-6559**),

is famous for its burgers, its onion rings, and a down-to-earth atmosphere that's increasingly rare in Harvard Square. See p. 136.
- **Best French Cuisine: Sel de la Terre,** 255 State St. (© **617/720-1300**). Technically, it's Provençal. Not so technically, it's delicious. Fresh New England ingredients go into the thoroughly French end product. Try as many different breads as you can without ruining your meal. See p. 107.
- **Best Bistro:** A friend who knows both Paris and Boston swears by **Les Zygomates,** 129 South St. (© **617/542-5108**), where you can enjoy the flavor of the Left Bank in a congenial American setting. See p. 114.
- **Best Italian Cuisine:** By far the best restaurant in the North End, **Mamma Maria,** 3 North Sq. (© **617/523-0077**), is one of the best in town. In a lovely setting, it offers remarkable regional Italian fare in a spaghetti-and-meatballs neighborhood. See p. 110.
- **Best Seafood: Legal Sea Foods,** 800 Boylston St., in the Prudential Center (© **617/266-6800**), and other locations, does one thing and does it exceptionally well. It's a chain for a great reason: People can't get enough of the freshest seafood around. See p. 128.
- **Best Pizza:** Considering how well pizza travels, it's surprising that the branches of **Pizzeria Regina** can't seem to get it quite right. For the real thing, head to the North End original, at 11½ Thacher St. (© **617/227-0765**). See p. 114.
- **Best Investment (of Time and Money):** Dinner at **L'Espalier,** 30 Gloucester St. (© **617/262-3023**), is an event. As you enter, you might hear the valet-parking attendant say, "Enjoy your evening." Thanks to the grand cuisine and

solicitous service, you certainly will. See p. 124.

- **Best Outdoor Dining: Oleana,** 134 Hampshire St., Cambridge (℃ **617/661-0505**), offers a serendipitous combination of food and setting. The superb Mediterranean cuisine makes a good match for the peaceful patio. See p. 138.

- **Best Brunch:** The insane displays at many of the top hotels are well worth the monetary and caloric compromises. If you're looking for a delicious meal that won't destroy your budget and waistline, join the throng at the **S&S Restaurant,** 1334 Cambridge St., Cambridge (℃ **617/354-0777**). See p. 140.

- **Best for Pretheater Dinner:** Snappy service is the rule all over Chinatown. Start your evening at **East Ocean City,** 25–29 Beach St. (℃ **617/542-2504**), and you'll be both prompt and well fed for your theater engagement. See p. 120.

2

Planning Your Trip
to Boston

This chapter addresses the practical issues that arise after you select a destination. Now that you've decided to visit Boston, how do you get there? How much will it cost? When should you go? How can you learn more? You'll find answers here, along with information about the climate and the events, festivals, and parades you might want to attend.

1 Visitor Information

The **Greater Boston Convention & Visitors Bureau,** 2 Copley Place, Suite 105, Boston, MA 02116-6501 (© **888/SEE-BOSTON** or 617/536-4100; 0171/431-3434 in the U.K.; fax 617/424-7664; www.boston usa.com), offers a comprehensive visitor information kit ($10.25) and a *Kids Love Boston* guide ($5). The kit includes a travel planner, a guidebook, a map, pamphlets, and coupons for shopping, dining, attraction, and nightlife discounts. Smaller guides to specific seasons or events often are available free.

For information about Cambridge, contact the **Cambridge Office for Tourism,** 18 Brattle St., Cambridge,

MA 02138 (© **800/862-5678** or 617/441-2884; fax 617/441-7736; www.cambridge-usa.org).

The **Massachusetts Office of Travel and Tourism,** 10 Park Plaza, Suite 4510, Boston, MA 02116 (© **800/227-6277** or 617/973-8500; fax 617/973-8525; www.massvacation. com), distributes information about the whole state. Its free *Getaway Guide* magazine includes information about attractions and lodgings, a map, and a calendar.

For visitor center and information desk locations after you arrive, see "Visitor Information" in chapter 4.

Also see the box "Online Traveler's Toolbox" on p. 27.

2 Money

Monetary descriptions and currency exchange information for international travelers appear in chapter 3.

Like other large American cities, Boston can be an expensive destination. At the high end, it's nearly as costly as New York. At the thrifty end, an abundance of reasonably priced establishments cater to the area's large student population.

ATMS
The easiest and best way to get cash away from home is from an ATM (automated teller machine). They're widely available throughout Boston and eastern Massachusetts. Even the smallest towns usually have at least one ATM. The **Cirrus** (© **800/424-7787;** www.mastercard.com) and **PLUS** (© **800/843-7587;** www.visa.com) networks span the globe. Another

Destination Boston: Red Alert Checklist

- Have you booked tickets for concerts and plays, limited-run museum shows, and special-interest tours? If you're planning far enough ahead, you may be able to book a hotel package that includes the tickets you want (to Boston Ballet's *Nutcracker,* for instance). Did you make a reservation at that hot restaurant you read about recently?

- Did you make sure your favorite attraction is open? Security concerns may affect access to some attractions, such as the Prudential Center Skywalk and the Boston area's many federal properties. For example, the Charlestown Navy Yard, home of the USS *Constitution* ("Old Ironsides"), closes to visitors at the first indication of a threat to Boston Harbor. Call ahead to confirm opening and closing times.

- If you use traveler's checks, have you recorded the check numbers, and stored the documentation separately from the checks?

- Did you pack your camera, an extra set of camera batteries, and enough film? Is your film in your carry-on baggage (to keep it away from airport security X-rays)? Most photo supply stores sell protective pouches that should shield film and loaded cameras from X-rays in checked baggage, but may raise alarms and result in a hand inspection.

- Do you have a safe, accessible place to store money?

- Did you bring ID cards that could entitle you to discounts, such as AAA and AARP cards, student and military IDs, and the like?

- Did you bring drug prescriptions and extra glasses or contact lenses?

- Did you find out your daily ATM withdrawal limit?

- Do you have your credit card personal identification numbers (PINs)? Is there a daily withdrawal limit on credit card cash advances?

- If you have an E-ticket, do you have documentation?

- Did you leave a copy of your itinerary and a set of keys with someone reliable at home? Did you stop newspaper and mail delivery?

widespread system, the **NYCE** network (www.nycenet.com), operates primarily in the eastern United States. Look at the back of your bankcard to see which network you're on, then call or check online for ATM locations in the Boston area.

Be sure you know your personal identification number (PIN) before you leave home, and be sure to find out your daily withdrawal limit before you depart. Also keep in mind that many banks impose a fee every time a card is used at a different bank's ATM. On top of this, the bank from which you withdraw cash may charge its own fee. At Massachusetts banks, a message should appear on the screen to warn you that you're about to be charged and then offer you the chance to cancel the transaction. To compare banks' ATM fees within the U.S., use www.bankrate.com.

You can also get cash advances on your credit card at an ATM. Keep in mind that credit card companies try to protect themselves from theft by imposing withdrawal limits, so call

> ### (Tips Cutting Back on ATM Fees
>
> Those charges of a dollar or two (or more) every time you use a "foreign" ATM can really start to add up. To avoid some or all of them, check with your home bank to see whether your debit card works in your destination. You can then ask for cash back with a purchase at most drugstores and supermarkets, and at many convenience stores.

your credit card company to check its limit before you leave home.

TRAVELER'S CHECKS

Traveler's checks are something of an anachronism from the days before the ATM made cash accessible at any time. Traveler's checks used to be the only sound alternative to traveling with dangerously large amounts of cash. They were as reliable as currency, but, unlike cash, could be replaced if lost or stolen.

These days, traveler's checks are less necessary because most cities have 24-hour ATMs that allow you to withdraw small amounts of cash as needed. However, keep in mind that you will likely pay an ATM fee if the bank is not your own, so if you're withdrawing money every day, you might be better off with traveler's checks—provided that you don't mind showing identification every time you want to cash one.

You can get traveler's checks at almost any bank. **American Express** offers denominations of $20, $50, $100, $500, and (for cardholders only) $1,000. You'll pay a service charge ranging from 1% to 4%. You can also get American Express traveler's checks over the phone by calling ⓒ **800/ 221-7282;** Amex gold and platinum cardholders who use this number are exempt from the 1% fee. AAA members can obtain checks without a fee at most AAA offices.

Visa offers traveler's checks at Citibank locations nationwide, as well as at several other banks. The service charge ranges between 1.5% and 2%; checks come in denominations of $20, $50, $100, $500, and $1,000. Call ⓒ **800/732-1322** for information. **MasterCard** also offers traveler's checks. Call ⓒ **800/223-9920** for a location near you.

If you choose to carry traveler's checks, be sure to keep a record of their serial numbers *separate from your checks* in the event that they are stolen or lost. You'll get a refund faster if you know the numbers.

CREDIT CARDS

Credit cards are a safe way to carry money, and they provide a convenient record of your expenses. You can make cash advances on your credit cards at banks or ATMs, provided you know your PIN (personal identification number). If you've forgotten yours, or didn't even know you had one, call the number on the back of your credit card and ask the bank to send it to you. It usually takes 5 to 7 business days, though some banks will provide the number over the phone if you tell them your mother's maiden name or some other personal information.

For tips and telephone numbers to call if your wallet is stolen or lost, go to "Lost or Stolen Wallet" in the "Fast Facts: Boston" section of chapter 4.

3 When to Go

Under normal conditions, Boston attracts throngs of visitors year-round. Even allowing for the uncertain travel scene, you'll still want to make reservations as early as possible if you plan to visit during traditionally busy periods. Between April and November, there are hardly any slow times.

The periods around college graduation (May and early June) and major citywide events (listed later in this section) are especially busy. Spring and fall are popular times for conventions. Families pour into the area in July and August, creating long lines at many attractions. Summer isn't the most expensive time to visit, though: Foliage season (mid-Sept to early Nov), when many leaf-peepers stay in the Boston area or pass through on the way to northern New England, is a huge draw. December is less busy but still a convention time—be on the lookout for weekend bargains.

The "slow" season is January through March, when many hotels offer great deals, especially on weekends. However, this is when unpredictable weather plagues the Northeast (often affecting travel schedules), and when some suburban attractions close for the winter.

Boston's Average Temperatures & Rainfall

	Jan	Feb	Mar	Apr	May	June	July	Aug	Sept	Oct	Nov	Dec
Temp. (°F)	30	31	38	49	59	68	74	72	65	55	45	34
Temp. (°C)	-1	-1	3	9	15	20	23	22	18	13	7	1
Rainfall (in.)	4.0	3.7	4.1	3.7	3.5	2.9	2.7	3.7	3.4	3.4	4.2	4.9

WEATHER

You've probably heard the saying about New England weather: "If you don't like it, wait 10 minutes." Variations from day to day (if not minute to minute) can be enormous. You can roast in March and freeze in June, shiver in July and sweat in November. Dressing in layers is always a good idea.

Spring and fall are the best bets for moderate temperatures, but spring (also known as mud season) is brief. It doesn't usually settle in until early May, and snow sometimes falls in April. Summers are hot, especially in July and August, and can be uncomfortably humid. Fall is when you're most likely to catch a comfortable run of dry, sunny days and cool nights. Winters are cold and usually snowy—bring a warm coat and sturdy boots.

BOSTON CALENDAR OF EVENTS

The **Greater Boston Convention & Visitors Bureau** (© 800/SEE-BOSTON or 617/536-4100; www.bostonusa.com) operates a regularly updated hot line that describes ongoing and upcoming events. The **Mayor's Office of Special Events, Tourism & Film** (© 617/635-3911; www.cityofboston.gov/calendar) can provide information about specific happenings. If you're planning at the last minute, the "Calendar" section of the Thursday *Boston Globe* and the "Scene" section of the Friday *Boston Herald* are always packed with ideas.

(**Fun Fact** **Poetry 101 (Degrees)**

In Boston, you can check the weather forecast by looking up at the short column of lights on top of the old John Hancock building in the Back Bay. (The new Hancock building is the 60-story glass tower next door.) It has its own poem: *Steady blue, clear view; flashing blue, clouds due; steady red, rain ahead; flashing red, snow instead.* During the summer, flashing red means that the Red Sox game is canceled.

January

Martin Luther King Jr. Birthday Celebration, various locations. Events include musical tributes, gospel celebrations, museum displays and programs, readings, speeches, and panel discussions. Check special listings in the Thursday *Boston Globe* "Calendar" section for specifics. Third Monday in January.

Chinese New Year, Chinatown. The dragon parade (which draws a big crowd no matter how cold it is), fireworks, and many raucous festivals. Special programs at the **Children's Museum** (℗ **617/426-8855;** www. bostonkids.org). Depending on the Chinese lunar calendar, the holiday falls between January 21 and February 19. In 2004, it's January 22.

Boston Cooks, various locations. Restaurants throughout the area entertain celebrity chefs and cookbook authors, who design special dinners and take turns behind the stove. Other events include classes, demonstrations, and book signings. Call the Convention & Visitors Bureau (℗ **888/SEE-BOSTON**) or visit www.bostoncooks.com. End of January.

Boston Wine Festival, Boston Harbor Hotel and other locations. Tastings, classes, lectures, receptions, and meals provide a lively liquid diversion throughout winter. Call the festival reservation line (℗ **888/660-WINE** or 617/330-9355; www.bostonwinefestival.net) for details. January to early April.

February

Black History Month, various locations. Programs include special museum exhibits, children's activities, concerts, films, lectures, discussions, readings, and tours of the Black Heritage Trail led by National Park Service rangers (℗ **617/742-5415;** www.nps.gov/boaf). All month.

School Vacation Week, also known as Boston Kids Week, various locations. The slate of activities includes special exhibitions and programs, plays, concerts, and tours. Contact individual attractions for information on programs and extended hours. Third week in February.

March

St. Patrick's Day/Evacuation Day. Parade, South Boston. Celebration, Faneuil Hall Marketplace. The 5-mile parade salutes the city's Irish heritage and the day British troops left Boston in 1776. Head to Faneuil Hall Marketplace for music, dancing, and food. March 17.

New England Spring Flower Show, Bayside Expo Center, Dorchester. This annual harbinger of spring, presented by the **Massachusetts Horticultural Society** (℗ **617/536-9280;** www.masshort. org), draws huge crowds starved for a glimpse of green. Plan to take public transit. Second or third week in March.

April

Big Apple Circus (www.bigapple circus.org), near the South Boston waterfront. The New York–based "one-ring wonder" performs in a heated tent with all seating less than 50 feet from the ring. Proceeds support the Children's Museum. Visit the museum box office, or contact Ticketmaster (℗ **617/931-ARTS;** www.ticketmaster.com). Early April to early May.

Red Sox Opening Day, Fenway Park. Even if your concierge is a magician, this is an extremely elusive ticket. Check with the ticket office (℗ **617/267-1700;** www.red sox.com) when tickets for the season go on sale in January, or try to see the **Patriots Day** game (3rd Mon in Apr), which begins at 11am. Beginning of April.

Swan Boats Return to the Public Garden. Since their introduction in 1877, the swan boats (© 617/ 522-1966; www.swanboats.com) have been a symbol of Boston. Like real swans, they go away for the winter. Saturday before Patriots Day.

Patriots Day, North End, Lexington, and Concord. The events of April 18 and 19, 1775, are commemorated and reenacted. Lanterns are hung in the steeple of the **Old North Church** (© 617/ 523-6676; www.oldnorth.com). Participants dressed as Paul Revere and William Dawes ride from the **Paul Revere House** (© 617/ 523-2338; www.paulreverehouse. org) in the North End to Lexington and Concord to warn the Minutemen that "the regulars are out" (not that "the British are coming"—most colonists considered themselves British). Battles are staged on the town green in Lexington and then at the Old North Bridge in Concord. Contact the **Lexington Chamber of Commerce Visitor Center,** 1875 Massachusetts Ave., Lexington, MA 02173 (© 781/ 862-1450), or the **Concord Chamber of Commerce,** 100 Main St., Suite 310-2, Concord, MA 01742 (© 978/369-3120; www.concord machamber.org), for information on battle reenactments. Third Monday in April (in 2004, it's Apr 19, the actual anniversary).

Boston Marathon, Hopkinton, Massachusetts, to Boston. International stars and local amateurs join in the world's oldest and most famous marathon. The noon start means that elite runners hit Boston around 2pm; weekend warriors stagger across the Boylston Street finish line as much as 6 hours later. Patriots Day (3rd Mon in Apr).

Freedom Trail Week, various locations in Boston, Cambridge, Lexington, and Concord. Another school vacation week, with plenty of crowds and diversions. Family-friendly events include tours, concerts, talks, and other programs related to Patriots Day, the Freedom Trail, and the American Revolution. Third week in April.

May

Museum-Goers' Month, various locations. Contact individual museums for details and schedules of special exhibits, lectures, and events. See chapter 7. All month.

Boston Kite & Flight Festival, Franklin Park (© 617/635-4505). Kites of all shapes and sizes take to the air above a celebration that includes kite-making clinics, music, competitions, and other entertainment. (T: Orange Line to Forest Hills, then no. 16 bus.) Mid-May.

Lilac Sunday, Arnold Arboretum, Jamaica Plain. The only day of the year that the arboretum(© 617/ 524-1717; www.arboretum.harvard. edu) allows picnicking. From sunrise to sunset, wander the grounds and enjoy the sensational spring flowers, including more than 400 varieties of lilacs in bloom. Usually the third Sunday in May.

Street Performers Festival, Faneuil Hall Marketplace. Everyone but the pigeons gets into the act as musicians, magicians, jugglers, sword swallowers, and artists strut their stuff. End of May.

June

Boston Pride March, Back Bay to Beacon Hill (© 617/262-9405; www.bostonpride.org). The largest gay pride parade in New England is the highlight of a weeklong celebration of diversity. The parade, on the second Sunday of the month, starts at Copley Square and ends on Boston Common. Early June.

Dragon Boat Festival, Charles River near Harvard Square, Cambridge (© **617/349-4380;** www. bostondragonboat.org). Teams of paddlers synchronized by a drummer propel boats with dragon heads and tails as they race 500m (1,640 ft.). The winners go to the national championships; the spectators go to a celebration of Chinese culture and food on the shore. Second or third Sunday in June.

Central Square World's Fair, Cambridge (© **617/868-3247**). A celebration of unity and diversity, with the usual food, crafts, and kids' activities—and a twist that elevates this event far above the usual street festival: local and national musicians (rock, jazz, and blues). Early to mid-June.

Cambridge River Festival (© **617/ 349-4380;** www.ci.cambridge.ma. us/~CAC), Memorial Drive from John F. Kennedy Street to Western Avenue. A salute to the arts, with live music, dancing, children's activities, crafts and art exhibits, and international food on the banks of the Charles. Mid-June.

U.S. Olympic Gymnastics Trials, FleetCenter (© **617/624-1000;** www.fleetcenter.com). Tiny tumblers will compete for the right to represent the United States at the Athens Games. Their media entourage will take up a lot of hotel space, so book early if you must visit over this weekend. June 24 to 27, 2004.

Boston Globe **Jazz & Blues Festival,** various locations, indoors and outdoors. Big names and rising stars put on lunchtime, after-work, evening, and weekend performances, some of which are free. Venues include the Hatch Shell on the Esplanade, Newbury Street, and Copley Square. Call the festival

hot line (© **617/267-4301;** www. boston.com/jazzfestival) or pick up a copy of the paper for a schedule when you arrive in town. Some events require advance tickets. Late June.

July

Boston Harborfest, downtown, the waterfront, and the Harbor Islands. The city puts on its Sunday best for the Fourth of July, which has become a gigantic weeklong celebration of Boston's maritime history and an excuse to get out and have fun. Events surrounding **Harborfest** (© **617/227-1528;** www. bostonharborfest.com) include concerts, children's activities, cruises, fireworks, the Boston Chowderfest, guided tours, talks, and the annual turnaround of USS *Constitution.* Beginning of the month (June 29–July 5, 2004).

Boston Pops Concert and Fireworks Display, Hatch Shell, on the Esplanade. Spectators start showing up at dawn (overnight camping is not permitted) for a good spot on the lawn and spend all day waiting for it to get dark enough for fireworks. Others show up at the last minute—the Cambridge side of the river, near Kendall Square, and the Longfellow Bridge are good spots to watch the spectacular aerial show. The program includes the *1812 Overture,* with real cannon fire. For details, check the website (www. july4th.org). July 4.

SailBoston 2004, the harbor and the waterfront from Charlestown to South Boston. Millions of spectators flock to see hundreds of beautiful sailing ships of all sizes. The international vessels arrive and depart in two glorious maritime parades. The piers where the ships berth are open to the public, and activities include festivals and tours. For more information, visit www.sailboston.com or check with the Convention & Visitors Bureau. July 10 to 15, 2004.

Macworld Conference & Expo, Boston Convention & Exhibition Center, South Boston. Tens of thousands of Apple polishers (the computer kind) return to Boston after a 6-year hiatus. Because the brand-new convention center won't have an on-site hotel until at least 2005, expect high demand at existing lodgings. For event details, visit www.mac worldexpo.com. July 12 to 15, 2004.

Puerto Rican Festival, Franklin Park. The 5-day event, instituted in 1967, is part street fair, part cultural celebration, with plenty of live music. (T: Orange Line to Forest Hills, then no. 16 bus.). Late July.

Democratic National Convention, FleetCenter (*©* **617/624-1000;** www.democrats.org). How can a mere 3,000 delegates cause such chaos? Well, they travel with 27,000 other people. Hotels and restaurants were booked months ago, and every attraction in town will be packed. Do yourself a favor and visit at another time. July 26 to 29.

August

Italian-American Feasts, North End. These weekend street fairs begin in July and end in late August with the two biggest: the Fishermen's Feast and the Feast of St. Anthony. The sublime (fresh seafood prepared while you wait, live music, dancing in the street) mingles with the ridiculous (carnival games, fried-dough stands) to leave a lasting impression of fun and indigestion. Visit www.fishermansfeast.com or www.saintanthonysfeast.com for a preview. Weekends throughout August.

August Moon Festival, Chinatown. A celebration of the harvest and the coming of autumn. Activities include the "dragon dance" through the crowded streets, and demonstrations of crafts and martial arts. Mid-August.

September

Boston Film Festival (*©* **781/925-1373;** www.bostonfilmfestival.org), various locations. Independent films continue on the festival circuit or make their premiere, sometimes accompanied by a lecture by an actor or a filmmaker. Most screenings are open to the public without advance tickets. Mid-September.

October

Salem Haunted Happenings, various locations. Parades, parties, a special commuter-rail ride from Boston, fortune-telling, cruises, and tours lead up to a ceremony on Halloween. Contact **Destination Salem** (*©* **877/SALEM-MA**) or check the website (www.hauntedhappenings.org) for specifics. All month.

Columbus Day Parade, downtown and the North End. Beginning with a ceremony on City Hall Plaza at 1pm, the parade winds up in the city's Italian neighborhood, following Hanover Street to the Coast Guard station on Commercial Street. Second Monday in October.

Ringling Brothers and Barnum & Bailey Circus, FleetCenter (*©* **617/624-1000;** www.fleetcenter.com). The Greatest Show on Earth makes its annual 2-week visit. Mid-October.

Head of the Charles Regatta, Boston and Cambridge. High school, college, and postcollegiate rowing teams and individuals—some 4,000 in all—race in front of hordes of fans along the banks of the Charles River and on the bridges spanning it. The Head of the Charles (*©* **617/864-8415;** www.hocr.org) has an uncanny tendency to coincide with a crisp, picturesque weekend. End of October.

Tips   July 2004: A Red Flag

Four major events and the accompanying huge crowds will take over Boston in July 2004: Harborfest, Macworld, SailBoston, and the Democratic National Convention. For details, see the "Calendar of Events" under "July." Make reservations early, try not to visit during the convention, and don't say I didn't warn you.

An Evening with Champions, Bright Athletic Center, Allston. World-class ice-skaters and promising local students stage three performances to benefit the Jimmy Fund, the children's fund-raising arm of the Dana-Farber Cancer Institute. Sponsored by Harvard's **Eliot House** (© 617/493-8172; www.hcs.harvard.edu/~ewc). End of October or early November.

November

Thanksgiving Celebration, Plymouth (© 800/USA-1620; www.visit-plymouth.com). Plymouth observes the holiday with a "stroll through the ages," showcasing 17th- and 19th-century Thanksgiving preparations in historic homes. **Plimoth Plantation,** which re-creates the colony's first years, serves a Victorian Thanksgiving feast. Reservations (© 800/262-9356 or 508/746-1622) are required and are accepted beginning in August. Thanksgiving Day.

December

The Nutcracker, Wang Center for the Performing Arts. Boston Ballet's annual holiday extravaganza is one of the country's biggest and best. This is *the* traditional way to expose young Bostonians (and visitors) to culture, and the spectacular sets make it practically painless. Call **Tele-charge** (© 800/447-7400 or TTY 888/889-8587; www.telecharge.com) as soon as you plan your trip, ask whether your hotel offers a *Nutcracker* package, or cross your fingers and visit the box office

at 270 Tremont St. when you arrive. All month.

Christmas Tree Lighting and **Newbury Street Stroll,** Back Bay and Boston Common. Carol singing precedes the lighting of the city's magnificent tree on Saturday on the Common. It's an annual gift from Nova Scotia—an expression of thanks from the people of Halifax for Bostonians' speedy help in fighting a devastating fire there in 1917. On Sunday, music, holiday activities, and window-shoppers take over Newbury Street. First weekend in December.

Boston Tea Party Reenactment, Old South Meeting House, downtown (© 617/482-6439; www.oldsouthmeetinghouse.org), and Tea Party Ship and Museum, Congress Street Bridge (© 617/338-1773; www.bostonteapartyship.com). Chafing under British rule, the colonists rose up on December 16, 1773, to strike a blow where it would cause real pain—in the pocketbook. A re-creation of the pre-party rally takes place at the meetinghouse; call ahead to see whether the ship has reopened during your visit. Mid-December.

Black Nativity, Converse Hall, Tremont Temple Baptist Church, 88 Tremont St. (© 617/723-3486; www.blacknativity.org). Poet Langston Hughes wrote the "gospel opera," and a cast of more than 100 brings it to life. Most weekends in December.

4 Travel Insurance

Check your existing insurance policies and credit card coverage before you buy travel insurance. You may already have coverage for lost luggage, canceled tickets, or medical expenses. The price of travel insurance varies widely, depending on the cost and length of your trip, your age, your health, and the type of trip you're taking.

TRIP-CANCELLATION INSURANCE Trip-cancellation insurance helps you get your money back if you have to back out of a trip, if you have to go home early, or if your travel supplier goes bankrupt. Allowed reasons for cancellation can range from sickness to natural disasters to the State Department's declaring your destination unsafe for travel. (Insurers usually won't cover vague fears, though, as many travelers discovered when they tried to cancel their trips in Oct 2001 because they were wary of flying after the Sept. 11, 2001, terrorist attacks.) In this unstable world, trip-cancellation insurance is a good buy if you're getting tickets well in advance—who knows what the state of the world, or of your airline, will be in 9 months?

Insurance policy details vary, so read the fine print, and make especially sure that your airline or cruise line is on the list of carriers covered in case of bankruptcy. Don't buy trip-cancellation insurance from the tour operator that may be responsible for the cancellation; buy it only from a reputable travel insurance agency. For information, contact one of the following insurers: **Access America** (ℂ 800/284-8300; www.access america.com), **Travel Guard International** (ℂ 800/826-1300; www. travelguard.com), **Travel Insured International** (ℂ 800/243-3174; www.travelinsured.com), or **Travelex Insurance Services** (ℂ 800/228-9792; www.travelex-insurance.com).

MEDICAL INSURANCE Most health insurance policies cover you if you get sick away from home—but check, particularly if you're insured by an HMO. If you require additional medical insurance, try **MEDEX International** (ℂ 800/527-0218 or 410/453-6300; www.medexassist.com), **Travel Assistance International** (ℂ 800/821-2828; www.travel assistance .com), or **Worldwide Assistance Services** (ℂ 800/777-8710; www. worldwideassistance.com).

LOST-LUGGAGE INSURANCE On domestic flights, checked baggage is covered up to $2,500 per ticketed passenger. On international flights (including U.S. portions of international trips), coverage is limited to approximately $9.05 per pound, up to approximately $635 per checked bag. If you plan to check items more valuable than the standard liability, see if your homeowner's policy covers your valuables, get baggage insurance as part of your comprehensive travel-insurance package, or buy Travel Guard's "BagTrak" product. Don't buy insurance at the airport, where it's usually overpriced. Be sure to take any valuables or irreplaceable items with you in your carry-on luggage, because airline policies don't cover many valuables (including books, money and electronics).

If your luggage is lost, immediately file a lost-luggage claim at the airport, detailing the luggage contents. For most airlines, you must report delayed, damaged, or lost baggage within 4 hours of arrival. The airlines are required to deliver luggage, once found, directly to your house or destination free of charge.

5 Health & Safety

STAYING HEALTHY

Here's hoping you won't need to evaluate Boston's reputation for excellent medical care. The greatest threat to your health is the same as in most other North American cities: overexposure to the summer sun. Be sure to pack sunscreen, sunglasses, and a hat, and don't forget to keep yourself hydrated.

WHAT TO DO IF YOU GET SICK AWAY FROM HOME

In most cases, your existing health plan will provide the coverage you need. But double-check; you may want to buy **travel medical insurance** instead. (See the section on insurance above.) Bring your insurance ID card with you when you travel.

If you suffer from a chronic illness, consult your doctor before your departure. For conditions like epilepsy, diabetes, or heart problems, wear a **Medic Alert Identification Tag** (© 888/633-4298; www.medic alert.org), which will immediately alert doctors to your condition and give them access to your records through Medic Alert's 24-hour hot line.

Pack **prescription medications** in your carry-on luggage, never in your checked baggage, and carry prescription medications in their original containers, with pharmacy labels—

otherwise they won't make it through airport security. Also bring along copies of your prescriptions in case you lose your pills or run out. Don't forget an extra pair of contact lenses or prescription glasses.

If you get sick, consider asking your hotel concierge to recommend a local doctor—even his or her own. Also see "Doctors" in the "Fast Facts: Boston" section in chapter 4.

STAYING SAFE

Boston is a generally safe city, especially in the areas you're likely to visit. Nevertheless, you should take the same precautions you would in any other large North American city. In general, trust your instincts—a dark, deserted street is probably deserted for a reason.

As in any city, stay out of parks (including Boston Common, the Public Garden, and the Esplanade) at night unless you're in a crowd. Specific areas to avoid at night include Boylston Street between Tremont and Washington streets, and Tremont Street from Stuart to Boylston streets. Try not to walk alone late at night in the Theater District and around North Station. Public transportation in the areas you're likely to visit is busy and safe, but service stops between 12:30 and 1am.

6 Specialized Travel Resources

TRAVELERS WITH DISABILITIES

Most disabilities shouldn't stop anyone from traveling. There are more options and resources out there than ever before.

Boston, like all other U.S. cities, has taken the required steps to provide access for people with disabilities. Hotels must provide accessible rooms; museums and street curbs have ramps

for wheelchairs. Some smaller accommodations, including most B&Bs, have not been retrofitted. In older neighborhoods (notably Beacon Hill and the North End), you'll find many narrow streets, cobbled thoroughfares, and brick sidewalks. Near the Big Dig, you'll have to negotiate many uneven road surfaces and pedestrian detours.

Newer stations on the Red, Blue, and Orange lines of the **subway** are wheelchair-accessible; the transit authority is converting the Green Line (which uses trolleys). Contact the **MBTA** (✆ **800/392-6100** outside Mass. or 617/222-3200; www.mbta.com) to see if the stations you need are accessible. All MBTA **buses** have lifts or kneelers; call ✆ **800/LIFT-BUS** for more information. Some bus routes are wheelchair-accessible at all times, but you might have to make a reservation as much as a day in advance for others. To learn more, contact the **Office for Transportation Access,** 145 Dartmouth St., Boston, MA 02116 (✆ **617/222-5976** or TTY 617/222-5854).

One taxi company with wheelchair-accessible vehicles is **Boston Cab** (✆ **617/536-5010**); advance notice is recommended. In addition, an **Airport Accessible Van** (✆ **617/561-1769**) operates within Logan Airport.

An excellent resource is **VSA Arts Massachusetts,** 2 Boylston St., Boston, MA 02116 (✆ **617/350-7713;** TTY 617/350-6836; www.vsamass.org). Its comprehensive website includes general access information and specifics about more than 200 cultural facilities.

The U.S. National Park Service offers a **Golden Access Passport** that gives free lifetime entrance to all properties administered by the National Park Service—national parks, monuments, historic sites, recreation areas, and national wildlife refuges—for persons who are blind or with permanent disabilities, regardless of age. You may pick up a Golden Access Passport at any NPS entrance fee area by showing proof of a medically determined disability and eligibility for receiving benefits under federal law. For more information, go to www.nps.gov/fees_passes.htm or call ✆ **888/467-2757.**

Many travel agencies offer customized tours and itineraries for travelers with disabilities. **Flying Wheels Travel** (✆ **507/451-5005;** www.flyingwheelstravel.com) offers escorted tours and cruises that emphasize sports and private tours in minivans with lifts. **Accessible Journeys** (✆ **800/846-4537** or 610/521-0339; www.disabilitytravel.com) caters specifically to slow walkers and wheelchair travelers and their families and friends.

Organizations that offer assistance to travelers with disabilities include the **Moss Rehab Hospital** (www.mossresourcenet.org), which provides a library of accessible-travel resources online; the **Society for Accessible Travel and Hospitality** (✆ 212/447-7284; www.sath.org; annual membership fees: $45 adults, $30 seniors and students), which offers a wealth of travel resources for all types of disabilities and informed recommendations on destinations, access guides, travel agents, tour operators, vehicle rentals, and companion services; and the **American Foundation for the Blind** (✆ **800/232-5463;** www.afb.org), which provides information on traveling with Seeing Eye dogs.

For more information specifically targeted to travelers with disabilities, the community website **iCan** (www.icanonline.net/channels/travel/index.cfm) has destination guides and several regular columns on accessible travel. Also check out the quarterly magazine **Emerging Horizons** ($14.95 per year, $19.95 outside the U.S.; www.emerginghorizons.com); **Twin Peaks Press** (✆ 360/694-2462; http://disabilitybookshop.virtualave.net/blist84.htm), offering travel-related books for travelers with special needs; and *Open World Magazine,* published by the Society for Accessible Travel and Hospitality (see above; subscription: $18 per year, $35 outside the U.S.).

GAY & LESBIAN TRAVELERS

Overall, Boston is a gay- and lesbian-friendly destination, with a live-and-let-live attitude that long ago replaced the city's legendary Puritanism.

The **Gay and Lesbian Helpline** (© **617/267-9001**) offers information Monday through Friday from 6 to 11pm, and Saturday and Sunday from 5 to 10pm. *Bay Windows* (© **617/266-6670;** www.baywindows. com) is a weekly newspaper that covers New England and publishes cultural listings. The weekly *Boston Phoenix* publishes a monthly supplement, "One in 10," and has a gay-interest area on its website (www. bostonphoenix.com).

An excellent guide to local gay- and lesbian-owned and gay-friendly businesses is the *Pink Pages,* 66 Charles St., Boston, MA 02114 (© **800/ 338-6550;** www.pinkweb.com/boston. index.html). Visit the comprehensive website, or order a copy for $11, including postage. You can also contact the **Boston Alliance of Gay and Lesbian Youth** (© **800/422-2459;** www.bagly.org) and the **Bisexual Resource Center** (© **617/424-9595;** www.biresource.org).

The International Gay & Lesbian Travel Association (© **800/448-8550** or 954/776-2626; www.iglta. org) is the trade association for the gay and lesbian travel industry, and offers an online directory of gay- and lesbian-friendly travel businesses; go to the website and click on "Members."

Many agencies offer tours and travel itineraries specifically for gay and lesbian travelers. **Above and Beyond Tours** (© **800/397-2681;** www.abovebeyondtours.com) is the exclusive gay and lesbian tour operator for United Airlines. **Now, Voyager** (© **800/255-6951;** www.nowvoyager. com) is a well-known San Francisco–based gay-owned and -operated travel service.

The following travel guides are available at most travel bookstores and gay and lesbian bookstores, or you can order them from **Giovanni's Room** bookstore, 1145 Pine St., Philadelphia, PA 19107 (© **215/923-2960;** www.giovannisroom.com): *Out and About* (© **800/929-2268** or 415/ 644-8044; www.outandabout.com), which offers guidebooks and a newsletter 10 times a year packed with solid information on the global gay and lesbian scene; *Spartacus International Gay Guide* and *Odysseus,* both good, annual English-language guidebooks focused on gay men; the *Damron* guides, with separate, annual books for gay men and lesbians; and *Gay Travel A to Z: The World of Gay & Lesbian Travel Options at Your Fingertips,* by Marianne Ferrari (Ferrari Publications; Box 35575, Phoenix, AZ 85069), a very good guidebook series.

SENIOR TRAVEL

Mention that you're a senior citizen when you make your travel reservations. Although the major U.S. airlines except America West have cancelled their senior discount and coupon-book programs, many hotels still offer senior discounts. Boston-area businesses offer many discounts to seniors with identification (a driver's license, passport, or other document that shows your date of birth). The cut-off age is usually 65, sometimes 62. Hotels, restaurants, museums, and movie theaters offer special deals. Restaurants and theaters usually offer discounts only at off-peak times, but museums and other attractions offer reduced rates at all times.

Members of **AARP** (formerly the American Association of Retired Persons), 601 E St. NW, Washington, DC 20049 (© **800/424-3410** or 202/434-2277; www.aarp.org), get discounts on hotels, airfares, and car rentals. AARP offers members a wide range of benefits, including *Modern Maturity* magazine and a monthly newsletter. Anyone 50 or older can join.

With the **Senior Pass,** seniors can ride the MBTA **subways** for 25¢ (a 75¢ savings) and **local buses** for 15¢

(a 60¢ savings). On zoned and express buses and on the commuter rail, the senior fare is half the regular fare. The Senior Pass is available for 50¢ on weekdays from 8:30am to 5pm at the Back Bay MBTA station, or by mail from the Office for Transportation Access, 145 Dartmouth St., Boston, MA 02116 (℗ **617/222-5976** or TTY 617/222-5854). Enclose a 1-by-1-inch photo and a check or money order for 50¢.

The **U.S. National Park Service** offers a **Golden Age Passport** that gives seniors 62 years or older lifetime entrance to all properties administered by the National Park Service—national parks, monuments, historic sites, recreation areas, and national wildlife refuges—for a one-time processing fee of $10, which must be paid in person at any NPS facility that charges an entrance fee. For more information, go to www.nps.gov/fees_passes.htm or call ℗ **888/467-2757.**

Many reliable agencies and organizations target the 50-plus market. **Elderhostel** (℗ **877/426-8056;** www.elderhostel.org) arranges study programs for those 55 and over (and a spouse or companion of any age) in the U.S. and in more than 80 countries around the world. Most courses last 5 to 7 days in the U.S. (2 to 4 weeks abroad), and many include airfare, accommodations in university dormitories or modest inns, meals, and tuition.

Recommended publications offering travel resources and discounts for seniors include: the quarterly magazine *Travel 50 & Beyond* (www.travel50and beyond.com); *Travel Unlimited: Uncommon Adventures for the Mature Traveler* (Avalon); *101 Tips for Mature Travelers,* available from Grand Circle Travel (℗ **800/221-2610** or 617/350-7500; www.gct.com); *The 50+ Traveler's Guidebook* (St. Martin's Press); and *Unbelievably Good Deals and Great Adventures That You Absolutely Can't Get Unless You're Over 50* (McGraw Hill).

FAMILY TRAVEL

Boston is a top-notch family destination, with tons of activities that appeal to children and relatively few that don't. Every hotel and most restaurants in the area have extensive experience meeting kids' needs.

Children (usually under 18, sometimes under 12) can stay free in their parents' hotel room when using existing bedding. Most hotels charge for cots, and some charge for cribs. Always ask whether the hotel you're considering has special offers for families. Many hotels offer family packages that include a room or a suite, breakfast, and parking, plus discount coupons for museums and restaurants. Some discount the price of a kid's room that adjoins the parent's; at others, a suite may give you as much space as—and cost less than—two standard rooms.

When you book your flight, see if your airline offers half-price tickets for children under 3 traveling in car seats.

The **Greater Boston Convention & Visitors Bureau** (℗ **888/SEE-BOSTON;** www.bostonusa.com) sells a *Kids Love Boston* guide ($5) filled with travel information for families.

Throughout this book, the "Kids" icon flags destinations that are especially welcoming and interesting to youngsters. Also consult the boxes on "Family-Friendly Hotels" (p. 88) and "Family-Friendly Restaurants" (p. 126), and the section "Especially for Kids" (p. 178).

Familyhostel (℗ **800/733-9753;** www.learn.unh.edu/familyhostel) takes the whole family, including kids ages 8 to 15, on moderately priced domestic and international learning vacations. A team of academics guides lectures, field trips, and sightseeing.

You can find good family-oriented vacation advice on the Internet from sites like the **Family Travel Network** (www.familytravelnetwork.com); **Traveling Internationally with Your Kids** (www.travelwithyourkids.com), a comprehensive site offering sound advice for long-distance and international travel with children; and **Family Travel Files** (www.thefamilytravelfiles.com), which offers an online magazine and a directory of off-the-beaten-path tours and tour operators for families.

The Unofficial Guide to New England & New York with Kids (Wiley Publishing), a Frommer's publication, is an excellent family resource. *How to Take Great Trips with Your Kids* (The Harvard Common Press) is full of good general advice that can apply to travel anywhere.

STUDENT TRAVEL

Students don't actually rule Boston— it just feels that way sometimes. Many museums, theaters, concert halls, and other establishments offer discounts for college and high school students with valid identification. Some restaurants near college campuses offer student discounts or other deals. Visiting students might want to check campus bulletin boards; many events are open to them. The weekly *Boston Phoenix* also lists activities for students.

STA Travel (© 800/781-4040; www.statravel.com) is the biggest student travel agency in the world, and its deals are available to travelers of all ages. *Note:* In 2002, STA Travel bought competitors **Council Travel** (© 800/226-8624; www.council travel.com) and **USIT Campus** after they went bankrupt.

Travel CUTS (© 800/667-2887 or 416/614-2887; www.travelcuts.com) caters to both Canadian and U.S. students. Irish students should turn to **USIT** (© 01/602-1600; www.usit now.ie).

The Hanging Out Guides (www.frommers.com/hangingout), published by Frommer's, comprise the top travel series for students, covering everything from adrenaline sports to the hottest club and music scenes.

7 Planning Your Trip Online

SURFING FOR AIRFARES

The "big three" online travel agencies, **Expedia.com**, **Travelocity.com**, and **Orbitz.com**, sell most of the air tickets bought on the Internet. (Canadian travelers should try Expedia.ca and Travelocity.ca; U.K. residents can go to Expedia.co.uk and Opodo.co.uk.) Each has different deals with the airlines and may offer different fares on the same flights, so it's wise to shop around. Expedia and Travelocity will also send you **e-mail notification** when a cheap fare becomes available to your favorite destination. Of the smaller travel agency websites, **SideStep** (www.sidestep.com) gets the best reviews from Frommer's authors. It's a browser add-on that purports to "search 140 sites at once," but in reality it beats competitors' fares only as often as other sites do.

Also remember to check **airline websites,** especially those for low-fare carriers such as Southwest, JetBlue, AirTran, WestJet, or Ryanair, whose fares are often misreported or simply missing from travel agency websites. Even with major airlines, you can often shave a few bucks from a fare by booking directly through the airline and avoiding a travel agency's transaction fee. But you'll get these discounts only by **booking online.** Most airlines now offer online-only fares that even their phone agents know nothing about. For the websites of airlines that fly to and from your destination, go to "Getting There" later in this chapter.

Great **last-minute deals** are available through free weekly e-mail services provided directly by the airlines. Most of these are announced on Tuesday or Wednesday and must be purchased online. Most are only valid for travel that weekend, but some (such as Southwest's) can be booked weeks or months in advance. Sign up for weekly e-mail alerts at airline websites or check mega-sites that compile comprehensive lists of last-minute specials, such as **Smarter Living** (smarterliving.com). For last-minute trips, **Site59.com** in the U.S. and **Lastminute.com** in Europe often have better deals than the major-label sites.

If you're willing to give up some control over your flight details, use an **opaque fare service** like **Priceline** (www.priceline.com; www.priceline. co.uk for Europeans) or **Hotwire** (www.hotwire.com). Both offer rock-bottom prices in exchange for travel on a "mystery airline" at a mysterious time of day, often with a mysterious change of planes en route. The mystery airlines are all major, well-known carriers—and the possibility of being sent from Philadelphia to Chicago via Tampa is remote; the airlines' routing computers have gotten a lot better than they used to be. But your chances of getting a 6am or 11pm flight are pretty high. Hotwire tells you flight prices before you buy; Priceline usually has better deals than Hotwire, but you have to play the "name your price" game. If you're new at this, the helpful folks at **BiddingForTravel** (www.biddingfor-travel.com) do a good job of demystifying Priceline's prices. Priceline and Hotwire are great for flights within North America and between the U.S. and Europe. But for flights to other parts of the world, consolidators will almost always beat their fares.

For much more about airfares and savvy air-travel tips and advice, pick up a copy of *Frommer's Fly Safe, Fly Smart* (Wiley Publishing).

SURFING FOR HOTELS

Shopping online for hotels is much easier in the U.S., Canada, and certain parts of Europe than it is in the rest of the world. However, many smaller hotels and B&Bs don't show up on websites at all. Of the "big three" sites, **Expedia** may be the best choice, thanks to its long list of special deals. **Travelocity** runs a close second. Hotel specialist sites **Hotels.com** and **Hotel discounts.com** are also reliable. An excellent free program, **TravelAxe** (www.travelaxe.net), can help you search multiple hotel sites at once, even ones you may never have heard of.

Before you book, always check prices offered directly by the hotel and (if applicable) the chain, both online and over the phone. Any of these options may undercut the price available through a third party.

Priceline and Hotwire are even better for hotels than for airfares; with both, you're allowed to pick the neighborhood and quality level of your hotel before offering up your money. Priceline's hotel product even covers Europe and Asia, though it's much better at getting five-star lodging for three-star prices than at finding anything at the bottom of the scale. *Note:* Hotwire overrates its hotels by one star—what Hotwire calls a four-star is a three-star anywhere else.

SURFING FOR RENTAL CARS

Don't automatically reserve a car when you book your flight and hotel; if you plan to visit only Boston and Cambridge, a car is far more trouble than it's worth.

For booking rental cars online, the best deals are usually through rental-car company websites, although all the major online travel agencies also offer rental-car reservations services. Priceline and Hotwire work well for rental cars, too; the only "mystery" is which major rental company you get, but for most travelers, the difference between Hertz, Avis, and Budget is negligible.

Frommers.com: The Complete Travel Resource

For an excellent travel-planning resource, we highly recommend Frommers.com (www.frommers.com). We're a little biased, of course, but we guarantee that you'll find the travel tips, reviews, monthly vacation giveaways, and online-booking capabilities indispensable. Among the special features are our popular **Message Boards,** where Frommer's readers post queries and share advice (sometimes we authors even show up to answer questions); **Frommers.com Newsletter,** for the latest travel bargains and insider travel secrets; and the **Frommer's Destinations Section,** where you'll get expert travel tips, hotel and dining recommendations, and advice on the sights to see for more than 3,000 destinations around the globe. When your research is done, the **Online Reservations System** (www.frommers.com/book_a_trip/) takes you to our preferred online partners for booking your vacation at affordable prices.

8 The 21st-Century Traveler

INTERNET ACCESS AWAY FROM HOME

Travelers have any number of ways to check their e-mail and surf the Internet on the road. Of course, using your own laptop—or even a PDA or electronic organizer with a modem—gives you the most flexibility. But even if you don't have a computer, you can still gain access to your e-mail and even your office computer from cybercafes.

WITHOUT YOUR OWN COMPUTER

It's hard nowadays to find a city that *doesn't* have a few cybercafes. Although there's no definitive directory for cybercafes—these are independent businesses, after all—three places to start looking are at **www.cybercaptive.com**, **www.netcafeguide.com**, and **www. cybercafe.com**.

Boston is a wired city that, paradoxically, doesn't have many cybercafes. Your best bet if you're away from your hotel and just want to check e-mail is probably Kinko's (for locations, see "Internet Access" under "Fast Facts: Boston" in chapter 4). One business that offers access by the hour is **Tech Superpowers,** 252

Newbury St., 3rd floor (© 617/267-9716; www.newburyopen.net). In its neighborhood, known as "upper Newbury Street," many businesses offer free Wi-Fi access.

Aside from formal cybercafes, most **public libraries** across the world offer Internet access free or for a small charge. **Hotels** that cater to business travelers usually have **in-room dataports** and **business centers,** but the charges can be exorbitant. Also, most **youth hostels** have at least one computer with Internet access.

Most major airports have **Internet kiosks** scattered throughout their gates. These kiosks, which you'll also see in shopping malls, hotel lobbies, and tourist information offices around the world, give you basic Web access for a per-minute fee that's usually higher than cybercafe prices. The kiosks' clunkiness and high price means they should be avoided whenever possible.

To retrieve your e-mail, ask your Internet Service Provider (ISP) if it has a **Web-based interface** tied to your existing e-mail account. If your ISP doesn't have such an interface, you can use the free **Mail2web** service (www.mail2web.com) to view, but not reply

Online Traveler's Toolbox

Veteran travelers usually carry some essential items to make their trips easier. Before I share a few of my favorite websites, here's a crucial piece of advice: Double-check information that you find on websites. No matter how well maintained a site seems, it's as subject to human error as anything else produced by humans. If you find a description of an establishment or event that you know will make or break your trip, a quick phone call to ensure that the information is up-to-date can save you a lot of trouble. Following is a selection of online tools to bookmark and use.

- **Boston.com (www.boston.com):** The *Boston Globe* operates this site, one of the most comprehensive in the region. Besides newspaper content, it offers access to a virtual forest of listings and links. The most helpful area for out-of-towners, the arts and entertainment section (**http://ae.boston.com**), covers dining, movies, music, and the arts.

- **National Park Service (www.nps.gov):** This invaluable site, packed with information about hundreds of places, is especially useful in a history-rich area like eastern Massachusetts. It's subject to occasional budget-related shutdowns, so start surfing early. Click on the state for site listings, which incorporate directions and loads of photos.

- **Massachusetts Bay Transportation Authority (www.mbta.com):** Look here for schedules and route maps for T subways, trolleys, buses, ferries, and commuter trains. You can also buy visitor passes online (subject to a service charge).

- **Citysearch (boston.citysearch.com):** Events and nightlife listings, plus traveler-friendly info on the arts, shopping, and dining, with a significant interactive component. Before you jump at the featured entertainment options, remember that Citysearch is part of Ticketmaster.

- **The Big Dig (www.bigdig.com):** Why would a construction project need a website? After you get a load of this one, you'll know.

- **Boston Online (www.boston-online.com/glossary.html):** This highly entertaining Boston-to-English dictionary both mocks and celebrates local accents.

- **Visa ATM Locator** (www.visa.com), for locations of Plus ATMs worldwide, and **MasterCard ATM Locator** (www.mastercard.com), for locations of Cirrus ATMs worldwide.

- **Intellicast** (www.intellicast.com) and **Weather.com** (www.weather.com). Weather forecasts for all 50 states and for cities around the world.

- **Mapquest** (www.mapquest.com). This best of the mapping sites lets you choose a specific address or destination, and in seconds it will return a map and detailed directions.

- **Universal Currency Converter** (www.xe.com/ucc). See what your dollar or pound is worth in more than 100 other countries.

to, your home e-mail. For more flexibility, you may want to open a free Web-based e-mail account with **Yahoo! Mail** (mail.yahoo.com) or Microsoft's **Hotmail** (www.hotmail.com). Your home ISP may be able to forward your e-mail to the Web-based account automatically.

If you need to view files on your office computer, look into a service called **GoToMyPC** (www.gotomypc.com). The service provides a Web-based interface for you to access and manipulate a distant PC from anywhere—even a cybercafe—provided your "target" PC is on and has an always-on Internet connection. The service offers top-quality security, but if you're worried about hackers, use your own laptop rather than a cybercafe when tapping into the GoToMyPC system.

WITH YOUR OWN COMPUTER

Major Internet Service Providers (ISPs) have **local access numbers** around the world, allowing you to go online by simply placing a local call. Check your ISP's website or call its toll-free number and ask how you can use your current account away from home, and how much it will cost.

Most business-class hotels throughout the world offer dataports for laptop modems, and a few thousand hotels in the U.S. and Europe now offer high-speed Internet access using an Ethernet network cable. You'll have to bring your own cables either way, so **call your hotel in advance** to find out what the options are.

Many business-class hotels in the U.S. also offer a form of computer-free Web browsing through the room TV set. We've successfully checked Yahoo! Mail, but not Hotmail, on these systems.

If you have an 802.11b/**Wi-Fi** card for your computer, several commercial companies have made wireless service available in airports, hotel lobbies, and coffee shops. **T-Mobile Hotspot** (www.t-mobile.com/hotspot) serves up wireless connections at more than 1,000 Starbucks coffee shops nationwide. **Boingo** (www.boingo.com) and **Wayport** (www.wayport.com) have set up networks in airports and high-class hotel lobbies. Best of all, you don't need to be staying at the Four Seasons to use the hotel's network; just set yourself up on a nice couch in the lobby. Unfortunately, the companies' pricing policies are byzantine, with a variety of monthly, per-connection, and per-minute plans.

Community-minded individuals have also set up **free wireless networks** in major cities around the U.S., Europe, and Australia. These networks are spotty, but you get what you (don't) pay for. Each network has a home page explaining how to set up your computer for their particular system; start your explorations at www.personaltelco.net/index.cgi/wirelesscommunities.

USING A CELLPHONE ACROSS THE U.S.

Just because your cellphone works at home doesn't mean it'll work elsewhere in the country (thanks to our nation's fragmented cellphone system). It's a good bet that your phone will work in major cities, but check your wireless company's coverage map on its website before heading out. T-Mobile, Sprint, and Nextel are particularly weak in rural areas. If you need to stay in touch at a destination where you know your phone won't work, **rent** a phone that does from **InTouch USA** (✆ 800/872-7626; www.intouchglobal.com) or a rental-car location, but be aware that you'll pay $1 a minute or more for airtime.

If you're not from the U.S., you'll be appalled at the poor reach of our **GSM (Global System for Mobiles) wireless network.** Your phone will probably work in most major U.S. cities; it definitely won't work in many rural areas. (To see where GSM phones work in the U.S., check out www.t-mobile.com/coverage/national_popup.asp). And you may or may not be able to send SMS (text messaging) home. Assume nothing—call your wireless provider and get the full scoop. In a worst-case scenario, you can always rent a phone; InTouch USA delivers to hotels.

9 Getting There

BY PLANE

The major domestic carriers that serve Boston's **Logan International Airport** (usually just called "Logan"; airport code BOS) are **AirTran** (✆ 800/247-8726; www.airtran.com), **American** (✆ 800/433-7300; www.aa.com), **America West** (✆ 800/235-9292; www.americawest.com), **Continental** (✆ 800/525-0280; www.continental.com), **Delta** (✆ 800/221-1212; www.delta.com), **Frontier** (✆ 800/432-1359; www.frontierairlines.com), **Midwest Express** (✆ 800/452-2022; www.midwestexpress.com), **Northwest** (✆ 800/225-2525; www.nwa.com), **United** (✆ 800/241-6522; www.ual.com), and **US Airways** (✆ 800/428-4322; www.usairways.com). Many international carriers also fly into Boston; see chapter 3.

Logan is in East Boston at the end of the Sumner, Callahan, and Ted Williams tunnels, 3 miles across the harbor from downtown. For a preview and real-time flight arrival and departure information, visit the website (www.massport.com/logan).

One of the airport's five terminals (Terminal A) is closed for construction through at least 2005. (Construction on airport roads, a companion project to the Big Dig, should be wrapping up when you visit.) Each of the remaining terminals has ATMs, Internet kiosks, pay phones with data-ports, fax machines, and an information booth (near baggage claim). Terminals C and E have bank branches that handle currency exchange. Terminal C has a children's play space, and its information booth is a visitor service center. Staff members have gone through concierge training and can help make hotel and restaurant reservations, plan tours, provide convention information, and buy theater and sports tickets.

See the "Let's Make a Deal" box for information on flying into Providence, Rhode Island, and Manchester, New Hampshire.

GETTING INTO TOWN FROM THE AIRPORT

The Massachusetts Port Authority, or **MassPort** (✆ 800/23-LOGAN; www.massport.com), coordinates airport transportation. The toll-free line provides information about getting to the city and to many nearby suburbs. It's available 24 hours a day and is staffed weekdays from 8am to 7pm.

The ride into town takes 10 to 45 minutes, depending on traffic, your destination, and the time of day.

Impressions

The Denver airport is nice but should be moved to the same state as Denver. The Boston airport should also be moved to the same state as Denver; that way, it would be easier to get to it from downtown Boston than it is now.

—Syndicated columnist Dave Barry, 1999

Tips Let's Make a Deal

The domestic discount airline **Southwest** (© 800/435-9792; www.south west.com) doesn't serve Boston. But by redefining "Boston-area airport," it has helped create two magnets for budget-conscious travelers. They're not nearly as convenient as Logan (bus service into Boston can be slow), but fares to either of these airports—on Southwest and other national carriers—can be considerably cheaper than those to Logan.

T. F. Green Airport (© 888/268-7222; www.pvd-ri.com; airport code PVD) is in the Providence suburb of Warwick, Rhode Island, about 60 miles south of Boston. **Bonanza** (© 888/751-8800; www.bonanza bus.com) offers bus service between the airport and Boston's South Station 15 times a day; the fare is $19 one-way, $34 round-trip. Allow at least 90 minutes.

Manchester International Airport (© 603/624-6556; www.fly manchester.com; airport code MHT) is in southern New Hampshire, about 56 miles north of Boston. **Vermont Transit** (© 800/552-8737; www.vermonttransit.com) runs buses to Boston's South Station eight times a day; three continue to Logan Airport. The trip takes 60 to 90 minutes and costs $11 one-way, $22 round-trip

Except at off hours, such as early on weekend mornings, driving is the slowest way to get into central Boston. Because of the Big Dig, it's also the mode of transportation most likely to leave you stranded in a mysterious traffic tie-up. If you must travel during rush hours or on Sunday afternoon, allow plenty of extra time, or plan to take the subway or water shuttle (and pack accordingly).

You can get into town by subway (the T), cab, van, or boat. The **subway** is fast and cheap—Government Center is just 10 minutes away, and a token (good for 1 ride) costs $1. Free **shuttle buses** run from each terminal to the Airport station on the Blue Line of the T from 5:30am to 1am every day, year-round. The Blue Line stops at the New England Aquarium, State Street, and Government Center, downtown points where you can exit or transfer to the other lines.

Because of government fees, just getting into a **cab** at the airport costs $7.50. The total fare to downtown or the Back Bay runs $19 to $26.

Depending on traffic, the driver might use the Ted Williams Tunnel for destinations outside downtown, such as the Back Bay. On a map, this doesn't look like the fastest route, but often it is. You can also try the **Share-A-Cab booths** at each terminal and save up to half the fare.

Back Bay Coach (© 888/BACK-BAY or 617/746-9909; www.backbaycoach.com) operates **van** service between the airport and Boston proper, plus many suburbs. One-way prices start at $9 per person. Call or surf ahead for reservations and fares.

The trip to the downtown waterfront in a weather-protected **boat** takes 7 minutes, dock to dock. The free no. 66 shuttle bus connects the airport terminals to the Logan ferry dock. The **Airport Water Shuttle** (© 617/330-8680) runs to Rowes Wharf every 15 minutes from 6am to 8pm on weekdays and every 30 minutes from 10am to 8pm on Saturday, Sunday, and national holidays (except Jan 1, July 4, Thanksgiving, and Dec 25). The one-way fare is $12 for

Boston & Surrounding Areas

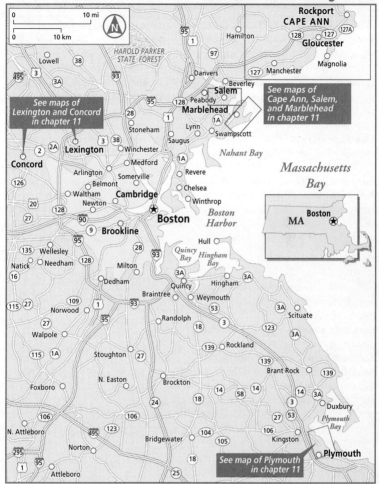

adults, $10 for seniors, $2 for children 5 to 11, and free for children under 5.

Harbor Express (© **617/376-8417;** www.harborexpress.com) runs from the airport to Long Wharf. On weekdays during the morning rush and in the evening, it runs from Long Wharf to Logan. (At other times, the Long Wharf–Logan trip goes through suburban Quincy, so the Airport Water Shuttle is much faster.) It operates 21 times a day on weekdays between 6:30am and 9pm (Fri until 11pm), and less frequently on weekends. There's no service on Thanksgiving and December 25. The one-way fare is $10 for adults, $2 for children 5 to 11, and free for children under 5.

From April through mid-October, the **City Water Taxi** (© **617/422-0392;** www.citywaterztaxi.com) connects about a dozen stops on the harbor, including the airport ferry dock. The flat fare is $10, and children under 13 ride free. Call ahead from the dock for pickup.

Some hotels have their own **shuttles** or **limousines;** ask about them when you make your reservation. To arrange private limo service, call ahead for a reservation, especially at busy times. Your hotel can recommend a company, or try **Carey Limousine Boston** (© **800/336-4646** or 617/ 623-8700), **Commonwealth Limousine Service** (© **800/558-LIMO** outside Mass. or 617/787-1110), or **Dav-El of Boston** (© **800/343-2071** outside Mass. or 617/884-2600).

Unless you need it right away, seriously consider waiting to pick up your **rental car** until you're starting a day trip or other excursion. You'll avoid airport rental fees, hotel parking charges, and, most important, Boston traffic.

GETTING THROUGH THE AIRPORT

With the federalization of airport security, security procedures at U.S. airports are more stable and consistent than ever. Generally, you'll be fine if you arrive at the airport **1 hour** before a domestic flight and **2 hours** before an international flight; if you show up late, tell an airline employee and he or she'll probably whisk you to the front of the line.

Bring a **current, government-issued photo ID** such as a driver's license or passport. If you have an E-ticket, print out the **official confirmation page;** you'll need to show your confirmation at the security checkpoint, and your ID at the ticket counter or the gate. (Children under 18 do not need photo IDs for domestic flights, but the adults checking in with them do.)

Security lines are getting shorter than they were during 2001 and 2002, but some doozies remain. If you have trouble standing for long periods, tell an airline employee; the airline will provide a wheelchair. Speed up security by **not wearing metal objects** such as big belt buckles or earrings. If

you have metal body parts, a note from your doctor can prevent a long chat with the security screeners. Keep in mind that only **ticketed passengers** are allowed past security, except for folks escorting passengers with disabilities, or children.

Federalization has stabilized **what you can carry on** and **what you can't.** The general rule is that sharp things are out, nail clippers are okay, and food and beverages must pass through the X-ray machine—but that security screeners can't make you drink from your coffee cup. Bring food in your carry-on rather than checking it; explosive-detection machines used on checked luggage have been known to mistake food (especially chocolate, for some reason) for bombs. Travelers in the U.S. are allowed one carry-on bag, plus a "personal item" such as a purse, briefcase, or laptop bag. Carry-on hoarders can stuff all sorts of things into a laptop bag; as long as it has a laptop in it, it's still considered a personal item. The Transportation Security Administration (TSA) has issued a list of restricted items; check its website (http://www.tsa.gov/public/index. jsp) for details.

In 2003, the TSA phased out **gate check-in** at all U.S. airports. Passengers with E-tickets and without checked bags can still beat the ticket-counter lines by using **electronic kiosks** or **online check-in.** Ask your airline which alternatives are available, and if you're using a kiosk, bring the credit card you used to book the ticket. If you're checking bags, you will still be able to use most airlines' kiosks; again, call your airline for up-to-date information. **Curbside check-in** is also a good way to avoid lines, although a few airlines still ban curbside check-in entirely; call before you go.

At press time, the TSA is also recommending that you **not lock your checked luggage,** so screeners can search it by hand if necessary. The

---

(Tips **Don't Stow It—Ship It**

If ease of travel is your main concern and money is no object, you can ship your luggage with one of the growing number of luggage-service companies that pick up, track, and deliver your luggage (often through companies such as FedEx) with minimum hassle for you. Traveling luggage-free may be ultra-convenient, but it's not cheap: One-way overnight shipping can cost $100 to $200, depending on what you're sending. Still, for some people, especially the elderly or the infirm, it's a sensible solution to lugging heavy baggage. Specialists in door-to-door luggage delivery are **Virtual Bellhop** (www.virtualbellhop.com), **SkyCap International** (www.skycapinternational.com), and **Luggage Express** (www.usxpluggageexpress.com).

---

agency says to use plastic "zip ties," which are for sale at hardware stores and can be easily cut off.

FLYING FOR LESS: TIPS FOR GETTING THE BEST AIRFARE

Passengers sharing the same airplane cabin rarely pay the same fare. If you purchase tickets at the last minute, change your itinerary at a moment's notice, or fly one-way, you'll likely get stuck paying the premium rate. Here are some ways to keep your airfare costs down:

- You'll pay a fraction of the full fare if you book your ticket **far in advance,** can **stay over Saturday night,** or **fly midweek** or **at less-busy hours.** If your schedule is flexible, say so, and ask if you can secure a cheaper fare by changing your flight plans.
- Keep an eye out in local newspapers for **promotional specials** or **fare wars,** when airlines lower prices on their most popular routes. You rarely see fare wars during peak travel times, but if you can travel in the off season, you may snag a bargain.
- Search **the Internet** for cheap fares (see "Planning Your Trip Online" earlier in this chapter).
- **Consolidators,** also known as bucket shops, are great sources for

international tickets, although they usually can't beat the Internet on fares within North America. Start by looking in Sunday newspaper travel sections; U.S. travelers should focus on the *New York Times, Los Angeles Times,* and *Miami Herald.* **Beware:** Bucket shop tickets usually are nonrefundable or carry stiff cancellation penalties, often as high as 50% to 75% of the ticket price, and some put you on charter airlines with questionable safety records. Several reliable consolidators are worldwide and available on the Net. **STA Travel** (© 800/781-4040; www.statravel.com) is now the world's leader in student travel, thanks to its purchase of Council Travel. It also offers good fares for travelers of all ages. **Flights.com** (© 800/TRAV-800; www.flights.com) started in Europe and has excellent fares worldwide, but particularly to that continent. It also has "local" websites in 12 countries. **FlyCheap** (©800/FLY-CHEAP; www.1800 flycheap.com) is owned by package-holiday megalith MyTravel and so has especially good access to fares for sunny destinations. **Air Tickets Direct** (© 800/778-3447; www.airticketsdirect.com) is based in Montreal and leverages

Travel in the Age of Bankruptcy

At press time, two major U.S. airlines were struggling in bankruptcy court, and most of the rest weren't doing very well, either. To protect yourself, **buy your tickets with a credit card.** The Fair Credit Billing Act guarantees that you can get your money back from the credit card company if a travel supplier goes under (and if you request the refund within 60 days of the bankruptcy). **Travel insurance** can also help, but make sure it covers "carrier default" for your specific travel provider. And be aware that if a U.S. airline goes bust midtrip, a 2001 federal law requires other carriers to take you to your destination (albeit on a space-available basis) for a fee of no more than $25, provided you rebook within 60 days of the cancellation.

the currently weak Canadian dollar for low fares; it'll also book trips to places that U.S. travel agents won't touch, such as Cuba.

- **Join frequent-flier clubs.** Accrue enough miles and you'll be rewarded with free flights and elite status. It's free, and you'll get the best choice of seats, faster response to phone inquiries, and prompter service if your luggage is stolen, your flight is canceled or delayed, or if you want to change your seat. You don't need to fly to build frequent-flier miles—**frequent-flier credit cards** can provide thousands of miles for doing your everyday shopping.

- For many more tips about air travel, including a rundown of the major frequent-flier credit cards, pick up a copy of *Frommer's Fly Safe, Fly Smart* (Wiley Publishing).

LONG-HAUL FLIGHTS: HOW TO STAY COMFORTABLE

Long flights can be trying; stuffy air and cramped seats can make you feel as if you're being sent parcel post in a small box. But with a little planning, you can make an otherwise unpleasant experience almost bearable.

- Your choice of airline and airplane will definitely affect your legroom. Among U.S. airlines, American Airlines has the best average seat pitch (the distance between a seat and the row in front of it). Find

more details at **www.seatguru. com**, which has extensive details about almost every seat on six major U.S. airlines. For international airlines, research firm **Sky-trax** has posted a list of average seat pitches at www.airlinequality.com.

- Emergency-exit seats and bulkhead seats typically have the most legroom. Emergency-exit seats are usually held back to be assigned the day of a flight (to ensure that the seat is filled by someone ablebodied); it's worth getting to the ticket counter early to snag one of these spots for a long flight. Keep in mind that bulkheads are where airlines often put bassinets, so you may be sitting next to an infant.

- To have two seats for yourself, try for an aisle seat in a center section toward the back of coach. If you're traveling with a companion, book an aisle and a window seat. Middle seats are usually booked last, so chances are good you'll end up with three seats to yourselves. And in the event that a third passenger is assigned the middle seat, he or she will probably be more than happy to trade for a window or an aisle.

- Ask about entertainment options. Many airlines offer seatback video systems where you get to choose your movies or play video games—but only on some of their planes. (Boeing 777s are your best bet.)

- To sleep, avoid the last row of any section or a row in front of an emergency exit; these seats are the least likely to recline. Avoid seats near highly trafficked toilet areas. You also may want to reserve a window seat so that you can rest your head and avoid being bumped in the aisle.
- Get up, walk around, and stretch every 60 to 90 minutes to keep your blood flowing. This helps avoid deep-vein thrombosis, or "economy-class syndrome," a rare and deadly condition that can be caused by sitting in cramped conditions for too long.
- Drink water before, during, and after your flight to combat the lack of humidity in airplane cabins—which can be drier than the Sahara. Bring a bottle of water onboard. Avoid alcohol, which will dehydrate you.
- If you're flying with kids, don't forget to carry on toys and books, as well as pacifiers, and chewing gum to help them relieve ear pressure buildup during ascent and descent. Let each child pack his or her own backpack with favorite items.

BY CAR

Driving to Boston is not difficult. (Driving *in* Boston is another story.) But parking is expensive and scarce, and downtown traffic is terrible. The **Big Dig** highway construction project dominates downtown. If you're thinking of driving to Boston only because you want to use the car to get around town, think again.

If you have to drive, try to book a hotel or a special package that offers free parking (see chapter 5 for information). If you pay for parking, expect it to cost at least $22 a day, and build that into your budget.

Three major highways converge in Boston. **I-90,** also known as the Massachusetts Turnpike ("Mass. Pike," to the locals), is an east-west toll road that originates at Logan Airport and links up with the New York State Thruway. **I-93/U.S. 1** extends north to Canada. **I-93/Route 3,** the Southeast Expressway, connects Boston with the south, including Cape Cod. I-93 in downtown Boston is the **Central Artery,** or John F. Fitzgerald Expressway, which was confusing enough even before the Big Dig. To avoid Big Dig construction, exit the Mass. Pike at Cambridge/Allston or at the Prudential Center in the Back Bay. **I-95** (Massachusetts Route 128) is a beltway about 11 miles from downtown that connects Boston to highways in Rhode Island, Connecticut, and New York to the south, and New Hampshire and Maine to the north.

The approach to Cambridge is **Storrow Drive** or **Memorial Drive,** which run along either side of the Charles River. Storrow Drive has a Harvard Square exit that leads across the Anderson Bridge to John F. Kennedy Street and into the square. Memorial Drive intersects with Kennedy Street; turn away from the bridge to reach the square.

Tips **Lights, Camera, Security**

Airport equipment that scans carry-on bags will not damage **videotape** in video cameras, but the magnetic fields emitted by the walk-through security gateways and handheld inspection wands will. Always place your loaded camcorder on the screening conveyor belt or have it hand-inspected. Be sure your batteries are charged—you will probably be required to turn the device on to ensure that it's what it appears to be.

Boston is 218 miles from New York; driving time is about 4½ hours. The 992-mile drive from Chicago to Boston should take around 21 hours; from Washington, D.C., it takes 8 to 9 hours to cover the 468 miles.

The **American Automobile Association** (② 800/AAA-HELP; www.aaa.com) provides members with maps, itineraries, and other travel information, and arranges free towing if you break down. At press time, the Mass. Pike was a privately operated road that arranged its own towing, but the state highway department may be taking over. If you break down there, ask the AAA operator for advice.

It's impossible to say this often enough: **When you reach your hotel, leave your car in the garage** and walk or use public transportation. Use the car for day trips, and before you set out, ask at the front desk for a route that avoids the construction area.

BY TRAIN

Boston has three rail centers: **South Station** on Atlantic Avenue at Summer Street, near the Waterfront and the Financial District; **Back Bay Station** on Dartmouth Street between Huntington and Columbus avenues, across from the Copley Place mall; and **North Station,** on Causeway Street near the FleetCenter. **Amtrak** (② 800/USA-RAIL or 617/482-3660; www.amtrak.com) serves all train stations, which are also linked to the MBTA **subway.** At South Station you can take the Red Line to Cambridge or to Park Street, the system's hub, where you can make connections to the Green, Blue, and Orange lines. The Orange Line connects Back Bay Station with Downtown Crossing, where there's a walkway to Park Street station, and to other points. North Station is a Green and Orange Line stop.

Amtrak runs to South Station from New York and points south and in between, with stops at Route 128 and Back Bay Station. Its Downeaster service (www.thedowneaster.com) connects North Station to Portland, Maine, with several stops en route. The MBTA **commuter rail** runs to Ipswich, Rockport, and Fitchburg from North Station; it runs to points south of Boston, including Plymouth, from South Station.

Bear in mind that the train might not be cheaper than flying, especially for long trips. As with airline ticket prices, train fares are subject to change and can fluctuate depending on the time of year, so plan as far ahead as possible to get the lowest fares. Discounts are never available Friday or Sunday afternoon. Always remember to ask for the discounted rate.

Standard service from New York takes 4½ hours to just under 6 hours; round-trip fares at press time were $98 to $148. From Washington, D.C., count on 7½ to 8½ hours and a round-trip fare of $150 to $208.

High-speed **Acela Express** trains run as fast as 150 mph and are scheduled to cover the 218 miles between Boston and New York in just over 3 hours, though they often take longer. At press time, the price (about $120 one-way) was less than two-thirds of the walk-up plane fare. The trip time between Washington, D.C., and Boston is just under 6 hours, and the one-way fare is about $160. Call Amtrak or check the website (www.amtrak.com/trains/acelaexpress.html) for exact fares, schedules, and reservations.

BY BUS

With one exception, consider long-distance bus travel a last resort. (The bus is the only way out of many small New England towns.) The exception is the **New York** route, which is so desirable that Greyhound and Peter Pan have upgraded service. It's frequent and relatively fast (4–4½ hr.), and the price is about half the regular train fare. If you can catch an express bus, which makes only one stop, it's worth the extra $5 or so.

The bus terminal, formally the **South Station Transportation Center,** is on Atlantic Avenue next to the train station. It's served by the following bus lines: **Greyhound** (© 800/231-2222 or 617/526-1800; www.greyhound.com), **American Eagle** (© 800/453-5040 or 508/993-5040), **Bonanza** (© 888/751-8800 or 617/720-4110; www.bonanzabus.com),

Brush Hill Tours (© 800/343-1328 or 781/986-6100; fax 781/986-0167; www.brushhilltours.com), **Concord Trailways** (© 800/639-3317 or 617/426-8080; www.concordtrailways.com), **Peter Pan** (© 800/343-9999; www.peterpanbus.com), **Plymouth & Brockton** (© 617/773-9401 or 508/746-0378; www.p-b.com), and **Vermont Transit** (© 800/552-8737; www.vermonttransit.com).

10 Packages for the Independent Traveler

Before you start your search for the lowest airfare, you may want to consider booking your flight as part of a travel package. Package tours are not the same thing as escorted tours. Package tours are simply a way to buy the airfare, accommodations, and other elements of your trip (such as car rentals, airport transfers, and sometimes even activities) at the same time and often at discounted prices—kind of like one-stop shopping. Tour operators buy packages in bulk and resell them to the public at a cost that usually undercuts standard rates.

One good source of package deals is the airlines themselves. Several major airlines offer air-land packages to Boston, including **American Airlines Vacations** (© 800/321-2121; www.aavacations.com), **Midwest Express Vacations** (© 800/452-2022; www.midwestexpressvac.com), **United Vacations** (© 888/854-3899; www.unitedvacations.com), and **US Airways Vacations** (© 800/455-0123 or 800/422-3861; www.usairwaysvacations.com). Several big **online travel agencies**—Expedia, Travelocity, Orbitz, Site59, and Lastminute.com—also do a brisk business in packages. If you're unsure about the pedigree of a smaller packager, check with the Better Business Bureau in the city where the company is based, or visit www.bbb.org. If a packager won't tell you where it's based, don't fly with it.

Trolley tour companies (see "Organized Tours" in chapter 7) play a prominent role in Boston tourism. The sightseeing portion of a package is often a free or discounted 1-day trolley tour. **Brush Hill Tours** (© 800/343-1328 or 781/986-6100; fax 781/986-0167; www.brushhilltours.com) is Gray Line's New England incarnation. Its 3-night "Boston City Package" includes lodging, airport or train station transfers, and a tour on the Beantown Trolley (which it owns). Prices start at about $300 per person, based on double occupancy. Brush Hill also offers a variety of half- and full-day escorted tours to destinations such as Plymouth, Salem, Cape Cod, and Newport, Rhode Island.

Another possibility is *Yankee* magazine's **Best of New England Vacations** (© 877/481-5986; www.newengland.com/vacations). Its 3-night packages include a 1-day tour and a copy of the magazine's travel guide; prices start at about $200 per person.

One often-overlooked option, if you live close enough to take advantage of it, is **Amtrak Vacations** (© 800/654-5748; www.amtrak.com/services/vacations.html). Prices are competitive and can undercut air-land packages from many destinations. The train definitely isn't for everyone, though. Sleepers are available on long routes, but if you're paying extra for a berth, an air package might be cheaper and certainly will be less time-consuming.

Travel packages are also listed in the travel section of your local Sunday newspaper. Or check ads in the national travel magazines such as *Arthur Frommer's Budget Travel Magazine, Travel & Leisure, National Geographic Traveler,* and *Condé Nast Traveler.*

Package tours can vary enormously. Some offer a better class of hotels than others. Some offer the same hotels for lower prices. Some offer flights on scheduled airlines, while others book charters. Some limit your choice of accommodations and travel days. You are often required to make a large payment up front. On the plus side, packages can save you money, offering group prices but allowing for independent travel. Some even let you add on a few guided excursions or escorted day trips (also at prices lower than if you booked them yourself) without booking an entirely escorted tour.

Before you invest in a package tour, get some answers. Ask about the **accommodation choices** and prices for each. Then look up the hotels' reviews in a Frommer's guide and check their rates for your specific dates of travel online.

Finally, look for **hidden expenses.** Ask whether airport departure fees and taxes, for example, are included in the total cost.

11 Escorted Tours

Escorted tours are structured group tours, with a group leader. The price usually includes everything: airfare, hotels, meals, tours, admission costs, and local transportation.

Hundreds of companies offer tours that stop in Boston, especially during foliage season, when 5- to 10-day tours of New England are wildly popular. Few spend more than 2 days in Boston, however, meaning that you'll be rushing around trying to cram maximum action into minimum time, or skipping sights and activities you were looking forward to.

If a quick stop is all you can manage, most major tour operators can accommodate you. They include **Liberty Travel** (© 888/271-1584; www.libertytravel.com), **Collette Vacations** (© 800/340-5158; www.collettevacations.com), **Globus and Cosmos** (© 800/851-0728; www.globusandcosmos.com), **Maupintour** (© 800/255-4266; www.maupintour.com), and **Tauck World Discovery** (© 800/788-7885; www.tauck.com).

Many people derive a certain ease and security from escorted trips. Escorted tours—whether by bus, motor coach, train, or boat—let travelers sit back and enjoy their trip without having to spend lots of time behind the wheel. All the little details are taken care of, you know your costs up front, and there are few surprises. Escorted tours can take you to the maximum number of sights in the minimum amount of time with the least amount of hassle—you don't have to sweat over the plotting and planning of a vacation schedule. Escorted tours are particularly convenient for people with limited mobility.

On the downside, an escorted tour often requires a big deposit up front, and lodging and dining choices are predetermined. As part of a cloud of tourists, you'll get little opportunity for serendipitous interactions with locals. The tours can be jam-packed with activities, leaving little room for individual sightseeing, whim, or adventure—plus they also often focus only on the heavily touristed sites, so you miss out on the lesser-known gems.

Before you invest in an escorted tour, ask about the **cancellation**

policy: Is a deposit required? Can the company cancel the trip if it doesn't get enough people? Do you get a refund if it cancels? If *you* cancel? How late can you cancel if you are unable to go? When do you pay in full? *Note:* If you choose an escorted tour, think strongly about purchasing trip-cancellation insurance, especially if the tour operator asks you to pay up front. See the "Travel Insurance" section earlier in this chapter.

You'll also want to get a complete **schedule** of the trip to find out how much sightseeing is planned each day and whether enough time has been allotted for relaxing or wandering solo.

The **size** of the group is also important to know up front. Generally, the smaller the group, the more flexible the itinerary, and the less time you'll spend waiting for people to get on and off the bus. Find out the **demograph-**ics of the group as well. What is the age range? What is the gender breakdown? Is this mostly a trip for couples or singles?

Discuss what the **price** includes. You may have to pay for transportation to and from the airport. A box lunch may be included in an excursion, but drinks might cost extra. Tips may not be included. Find out if you will be charged if you decide to opt out of certain activities or meals.

Before you invest in a package tour, get some answers. Ask about the **accommodation choices** and prices for each. Then look up the hotels' reviews in a Frommer's guide and check their rates for your specific dates of travel online.

Finally, if you plan to travel alone, you'll need to know if the company charges a **single supplement,** and if it can match you up with a roommate.

12 Recommended Books & Films

A list of authors with ties to Boston could fill a book of its own and still only scratch the surface. To get in the mood for Boston before visiting, let the impulse that inspired you to make the trip guide you around the bookstore or library. Here are some suggestions.

For children, *Make Way for Duck-lings,* by Robert McCloskey, is a classic that tells the story of Mrs. Mallard and her babies on the loose in the Back Bay. Once your kids love this book (and they will), you can thrill them with a trip to the Public Garden, where bronze statues of the family occupy a place of honor.

Slightly older kids might know the Public Garden as the setting of part of *The Trumpet of the Swan,* by E. B. White. After reading it, a turn around the lagoon on a swan boat is mandatory.

An excellent historical title is *Johnny Tremain,* by Esther Forbes, a fictional boy's account of the Revolutionary War era. The book vividly describes scenes from the American Revolution, many of which take place along the Freedom Trail.

For adults, two splendid Pulitzer Prize winners chronicle the city's history. *Paul Revere and the World He Lived In* is Forbes's look at Boston before, during, and after the Revolution. *Common Ground: A Turbulent Decade in the Lives of Three American Families,* by J. Anthony Lukas, is the definitive account of the busing crisis of the 1970s.

Architecture buffs will enjoy *Cityscapes of Boston,* by Robert Campbell and Peter Vanderwarker; *Lost Boston,* by Jane Holtz Kay; and *A.I.A. Guide to Boston,* by Susan and Michael Southworth.

The Proper Bostonians, by Cleveland Amory, and *The Friends of Eddie Coyle,* by George V. Higgins, offer looks at wildly different strata of Boston society.

"Paul Revere's Ride," Henry Wadsworth Longfellow's classic but historically inaccurate poem about the events of April 18 to 19, 1775, is collected in many anthologies. It's a must if you plan to walk the Freedom Trail or visit Lexington and Concord.

If you're venturing to Gloucester (or even if you're not), Sebastian Junger's *The Perfect Storm* makes an excellent introduction. The movie version, though heavy on the special effects, was a better-than-average effort. Both tell the story of a fishing boat caught in historically bad weather—and will change the way you look at fish on a menu for a long time after you finish reading or watching.

Television has done more than any movie to make Boston familiar to international audiences, but film is gaining fast. The Boston area is hardly Hollywood, but don't be surprised to stumble upon a crew or hear about a location shoot.

If you have time to see only one movie before your trip, make it *Good Will Hunting.* It makes Boston and Cambridge look sensational, perceptively explores the town-gown divide, *and* (Robin Williams's brogue notwithstanding) pulls off the nearly impossible feat of rendering local accents accurately. Coauthors and costars Ben Affleck and Matt Damon are boyhood friends from Cambridge, and Damon is a couple of semesters short of his Harvard degree.

Good Will Hunting and *The Perfect Storm* are among the best movies with Boston-area backdrops, but there are an awful lot of bad ones out there. Recent releases that are worth renting for more than just the locations include *A Civil Action, The Spanish Prisoner, Next Stop Wonderland* (all Boston), *State and Main* (Manchester-by-the-Sea), and *The Love Letter* (Rockport). At press time, the jury was out on the forthcoming *Mystic River* (Boston) and *Mona Lisa Smile* (Wellesley).

Some older movies are worth setting the VCR for. They include *Blown Away* (especially the scenes when the action first shifts to Boston), *The Verdict* (Boston), *Glory* (a stylish rendition of 19th-century Beacon Hill), *The Witches of Eastwick* (Cohasset), and the sentimental favorite, *Love Story* (Cambridge).

3

For International Visitors

American fads and fashions have spread across the world, making the United States seem familiar long before you arrive. Nevertheless, any international visitor will encounter many peculiarities and uniquely American situations. In our newly security-conscious world, just getting into the country may be more complicated than it once was, but you might also encounter a new attitude: gratitude toward out-of-towners who are willing to make the trip.

Be sure to consult chapter 2 for general advice, too.

1 Preparing for Your Trip

ENTRY REQUIREMENTS

Check at any U.S. embassy or consulate for current information and requirements. You can also obtain a visa application and other information online at the **U.S. State Department's** website, **travel.state.gov**. Click on "Visas for Foreign Citizens" for the latest entry requirements; "Foreign Consular Offices and Links to Foreign Embassies" will provide you with contact information for U.S. embassies and consulates worldwide.

DOCUMENTS

The State Department's **Visa Waiver Pilot Program** allows citizens of some countries to enter the United States without a visa for stays of up to 90 days. At press time, those countries included Andorra, Australia, Austria, Belgium, Brunei, Denmark, Finland, France, Germany, Iceland, Ireland, Italy, Japan, Liechtenstein, Luxembourg, Monaco, the Netherlands, New Zealand, Norway, Portugal, San Marino, Singapore, Slovenia, Spain, Sweden, Switzerland, the United Kingdom, and Uruguay. Citizens of these countries need a valid, machine-readable passport and a round-trip air or cruise ticket in their possession on arrival; before arriving or at the port of entry, they must complete form I-94W. If they first enter the United States, they may then visit Mexico, Canada, Bermuda, and the Caribbean islands and return to the United States without a visa. Further information is available from any U.S. embassy or consulate.

Canadian citizens may enter the United States without visas; they need only proof of residence.

Citizens of all other countries must have a **tourist visa,** available from any U.S. consulate, and a valid passport that expires at least 6 months after the scheduled end of the visit to the United States. **To obtain a visa,** you must submit, in person or by mail, a completed application form with two 1½-inch-square (37mm-sq.) photos and a US$100 fee, and you must demonstrate binding ties to a residence abroad. When you request the application, ask how long processing usually takes; your visa may be available at once, but with stepped-up security now in place, the process may take longer. If you cannot go in person, contact the nearest U.S. embassy or consulate for directions on applying by mail. Your travel agent or airline office also might be able to provide you with visa applications and instructions.

The U.S. consulate or embassy that issues your visa will determine whether you will be issued a multiple- or single-entry visa and will specify any restrictions regarding the length of your stay.

To inquire about visa cases and the application process, call © 202/663-1225. British subjects can call the **U.S. Embassy Visa Information Line** (© **0891/200-290**) or the **London Passport Office** (© 0990/210-410 for recorded information).

Massachusetts recognizes other countries' **driver's licenses,** but you might want to carry an international driver's license if your home license is not written in English.

MEDICAL REQUIREMENTS

Inoculations or vaccinations are not required unless you're arriving from an area known to be suffering from an epidemic (particularly cholera or yellow fever). If you have a disease that requires treatment with a controlled substance or syringe-administered medications, carry a valid signed prescription from your physician to allay suspicions that you might be smuggling narcotics.

Upon entering the United States, foreign nationals are required to declare any dangerous contagious diseases that they carry, which includes infection with HIV, the AIDS virus. Anyone who has such a disease is excluded from entry as a tourist. However, you might be able to apply for a waiver if you are attending a conference or have another compelling nontourism reason for your visit. Call the **INS** (© **800/375-5283**) to inquire. Doubtless many HIV-positive visitors come in without declaring their condition, their way of dealing with an archaic law that was originally intended to halt the spread of tuberculosis and the like.

CUSTOMS
WHAT YOU CAN BRING IN

Every visitor over 21 years old may bring into the United States, free of duty, 1 liter of wine, beer, or hard liquor; 200 cigarettes or 50 cigars (but none from Cuba) or 4.4 pounds of smoking tobacco; and $100 worth of gifts. The exemptions apply to travelers who spend at least 72 hours in the United States and who have not claimed them within the preceding 6 months.

Visitors may not bring plants (vegetables, seeds, tropical plants, and the like) or most foodstuffs (particularly fruit and meat) into the United States.

Declare any medicines that you are carrying, and be prepared to present a letter or prescription from your doctor demonstrating that you need the drugs; you may bring in no more than you would normally use in the duration of your visit.

International tourists may bring in or take out up to $10,000 in U.S. or foreign currency with no formalities. Larger sums must be declared to Customs on entering or leaving, which includes filing form 4790.

For many more details on what you can and cannot bring, check the U.S. Customs website (www.customs.gov; click "Travel"), or call © **202/927-1770.**

WHAT YOU CAN TAKE HOME

Rules governing what you can bring back duty-free vary from country to country and are subject to change, but they're generally posted on the Web. **Canadians** should check the booklet *I Declare,* which you can download or order from Revenue Canada (© **613/993-0534;** www.ccra-adrc. gc.ca). **British** citizens should contact HM Customs & Excise (© **020/7202-4227;** www.hmce.gov. uk). **Australians** can contact the Australian Customs Service (© **1-300/ 363-263** within Australia, 61-2/ 6275-6666 from outside Australia; www.customs.gov.au). **New Zealand** citizens should contact New Zealand Customs (© **09/359-6655;** www. customs.govt.nz).

INSURANCE

The United States has no national health system. Because the cost of medical care is extremely high, we strongly advise every international traveler to secure health insurance coverage before setting out. Doctors and hospitals are expensive and, in most cases, require payment or proof of coverage before providing services.

Travel-insurance policies can cover the loss or theft of your baggage, trip cancellation, and the guarantee of bail in case you're arrested. Good policies will also cover the cost of an accident, repatriation, or death. See "Travel Insurance" on p. 19 for more information. Automobile clubs and travel agencies sell packages such as **Europ Assistance** (www.europ-assistance. com) in Europe at attractive rates. **Worldwide Assistance Services** (© **800/777-8710;** www.worldwide assistance.com) is the agent for Europ Assistance in the United States.

Although lack of insurance might prevent you from being admitted to a hospital except in an emergency, don't worry about being left on a street corner to die: The American way is to fix you now and bill you (over and over, if necessary) later.

FOR BRITISH TRAVELERS

Most big travel agents offer their own insurance and will probably try to sell you a package when you book a holiday. Think before you sign. **Britain's Consumers' Association** recommends that you insist on seeing the policy and reading the fine print before buying travel insurance. **The Association of British Insurers** (© **0171/600-3333;** www.abi.org.uk) gives advice by phone and publishes *Holiday Insurance,* a free guide to policy provisions and prices. You might also shop around for better deals. Try **Columbus Travel Insurance Ltd.** (© **020/7375-0011;** www.columbus direct.net).

FOR CANADIAN TRAVELERS

Check with your provincial health-plan offices, or call **Health Canada** (© **613/957-2991;** www.health canada.ca) to find out the extent of coverage and what documentation and receipts you must take home if you are treated in the U.S.

MONEY
CURRENCY

The American monetary system has a decimal base: 1 U.S. **dollar** ($1) = 100 **cents** (100¢).

The most common **bills** (all ugly, all green) are the $1 (colloquially, a "buck"), $5, $10, and $20 denominations. There are also $2 bills (seldom encountered), $50 bills, and $100 bills; the last two are usually not welcome as payment for small purchases and are not accepted at subway token booths or in most taxis or fast-food restaurants. The slang term "break" (as in "Can you break a 20?") means "make change for."

Two designs of each bill larger than $1 are in circulation. The newer versions have larger, off-center portraits on their "faces" and are identical to old-style money in value and negotiability, with one exception: Some vending machines don't recognize the new designs and bear signs warning you not to use them.

There are six coin denominations: 1¢ (1 cent, or a penny), 5¢ (5 cents, or a nickel), 10¢ (10 cents, or a dime), 25¢ (25 cents, or a quarter), the rarely seen 50¢ piece (50 cents, or a half-dollar), and two $1 designs (1 gold-colored, 1 silver-colored). Dollar coins are not common, and are typically dispensed only by change machines at bus stops and by post office vending machines.

CURRENCY EXCHANGE

The foreign exchange bureaus so common in Europe are rare in the United States and nonexistent outside major

---

Tips In Case of Emergency

Keep copies of all your travel papers separate from your wallet or purse, and leave a copy with someone at home in case you need something faxed to you in an emergency.

---

cities. It's difficult to change foreign money (or traveler's checks in currency other than U.S. dollars) at small-town bank branches. In the Boston area, many banks and some hotels offer currency exchange. At the airport, **Citizens** (© **800/922-9999**) and **Fleet** (© **800/841-4000**) banks and **Travelex** (© **617/567-1087**) have outlets. For more information, see "Currency Exchange" under "Fast Facts: Boston" at the end of this chapter.

CREDIT CARDS

Credit cards are the most widely used form of payment in the United States. The most common are **Visa** (Barclay-Card in Britain), **MasterCard** (Euro-Card in Europe, Access in Britain, Chargex in Canada), **American Express, Discover,** and **Diners Club.** Some stores and restaurants do not accept credit cards, though, so be sure to ask in advance. Most businesses display a sticker near the entrance to let you know which cards they accept.

Note: Some businesses require a minimum purchase, usually around $10, to use a credit card.

We strongly recommend that you travel with at least one major credit card. In an emergency, a credit card can be invaluable. Hotels, car-rental companies, and airlines usually require a credit card imprint as a deposit against expenses, and you need a credit card to rent a car in Massachusetts.

ATMS

You'll find **automated teller machines** (ATMs) all over Boston (and the rest of the U.S.). Most ATMs will allow you to draw U.S. currency against your own bank account. It's even possible to draw against your credit cards if you have a personal identification number (PIN, or "secret code"), but you should do this only in an emergency. The transaction will be treated as a cash advance, and you'll pay dearly for the privilege.

Check with your bank before leaving home, and ask if you'll need to reprogram your PIN before using your ATM card in the United States. Rather than taking out small denominations repeatedly, it makes sense to withdraw larger amounts every 2 or 3 days. Expect to be charged up to $3 per transaction if you're not using your own bank's ATM. One way around these fees is to make a purchase and ask for cash back at stores that accept ATM cards and don't charge usage fees. These include most grocery and drugstores, and some convenience stores.

TRAVELER'S CHECKS

Traveler's checks are widely accepted, especially in cities, but you'll probably find credit cards cheaper and faster. **Make sure your traveler's checks are denominated in U.S. dollars,** because foreign-currency checks are often difficult to exchange. The three most widely recognized issuers are **American Express, Thomas Cook,** and **Visa.** Be sure to record the numbers of the checks and keep that information separate from the checks in case they are lost or stolen. Most businesses take traveler's checks, but you're better off cashing them in at a bank (in small amounts) and paying in cash. You need identification, such as a driver's license or passport, to change a traveler's check.

SAFETY

Tourist areas are generally safe, but U.S. urban areas tend to be less safe than those in Europe or Japan. Visitors should always stay alert, particularly in large cities such as Boston. Although the crime rate is near its lowest point in a generation, that's no consolation if you're the victim. Ask at your hotel's front desk or at a tourist office if you plan to visit an unfamiliar area and aren't sure whether it's safe.

Avoid deserted areas, especially at night. Don't go into any city park at night, even to jog or skate, unless there is an event that attracts crowds—for example, concerts and movies on Boston's Esplanade. Generally speaking, you can feel safe in areas where there are many people and many open establishments.

Avoid carrying valuables with you on the street, and don't display expensive cameras or electronic equipment. Try not to stop in the middle of the sidewalk and unfurl your map—consult it inconspicuously, or ask another pedestrian for directions. Sling your pocketbook diagonally across your body and keep a hand on it, and place your wallet or billfold in an inside pocket. Make sure that your wallet and other valuables are not easily accessible; if possible, keep them on your person. Never, ever, stow anything valuable in the outside pocket of a backpack. In theaters, restaurants, and other public places—especially airports and train and bus terminals—keep your possessions in sight at all times.

Remember that hotels are open to the public; in a large hotel, security might not be able to screen everyone entering. Always lock your room door—don't assume that once inside the hotel you are automatically safe and no longer need to be on guard.

DRIVING

If you must drive—and there's no need to if you're visiting only Boston and Cambridge—the best way to protect yourself is to be aware of your surroundings. Question your rental agency about personal safety, or request a brochure of traveler safety tips when you pick up your car. Ask for written directions or a map with the route clearly marked, showing how to get to your destination. Some agencies will rent you a cellphone along with the car—ask when you make your reservation. If possible, arrive and depart during daylight hours.

Whenever possible, park in well-lighted, well-traveled areas. Always keep your car doors locked, whether the car is attended or not. Look around you before you get out of your car, and never leave any packages or valuables in sight.

If someone attempts to rob you or steal your car, do not try to resist—immediately report the incident to the police by dialing *C* **911.** This is a free call, even from pay phones.

If you drive off a highway into a doubtful neighborhood, leave the area as quickly as possible. If you have an accident, even on the highway, stay in your car with the doors locked until you assess the situation or until the police arrive. If you are bumped from behind on the street or are involved in a minor accident with no injuries and the situation appears to be suspicious, motion to the other driver to follow you to the nearest police precinct, well-lighted service station, or all-night store. *Never* get out of your car in such situations.

If you see someone on the road who indicates a need for help, *do not* stop. Note the location, drive to a well-lighted area, and telephone the police.

2 Getting to the United States

Boston is an increasingly popular direct destination, although many itineraries from overseas still go through another American city.

⎛Tips Planning Pointer

"But New York and Boston look so close on the map," says the thrifty international traveler. No matter how cheap airfare to New York is, make sure that you budget enough time and money to continue to Boston. The transfer from airport to airport (or from airport to train or bus station) in the New York area can be complicated, expensive, or both.

Because of fluctuating demand in these uncertain times, routes and schedules are subject to change; double-check details (especially if you're traveling in the winter) well in advance.

From Canada, **Air Canada** (© 888/247-2262; www.aircanada.ca) flies directly from Halifax, Montréal, and Toronto.

From London, there's direct service from Heathrow on **American** (© 0345/789-789 in the U.K., 800/433-7300 in the U.S.; www.aa. com), **British Airways** (© 0345/ 222-111 or 0845/77-333-77 in the U.K., 800/AIRWAYS in the U.S.; www.britishairways.com), **Delta** (© 0800/414-767 in the U.K., 800/241-4141 in the U.S.; www. delta.com), **United** (© 0845/844-4777 in the U.K., 800/538-2929 in the U.S.; www.ual.com), and **Virgin Atlantic** (© 01293/747-747 in the U.K., 800/862-8621 in the U.S.; www.fly.virgin.com). Some airlines also fly out of Gatwick. From Ireland, **Aer Lingus** (© 3531/886-8844 in Dublin, 800/IRISH-AIR in the U.S.; www.aerlingus.ie) operates frequent flights from Dublin, and U.S. Airways flies seasonally (May–Oct) from Dublin and Shannon. **Lufthansa** (© 01803-803-803 in Germany, 800/645-3880 in the U.S.; www. lufthansa.com) serves Boston from Frankfurt.

From France, **American** (© 0-801-872-872 in France, 800/433-7300 in the U.S.; www.aa.com) and **Air France** (© 0-820-820-820 in France, 800/237-747 in the U.S.; www.airfrance.com) fly from Paris.

From other countries, Northwest/KLM (© 474-7747 in Holland, 800/374-7747 in the U.S.; www. klm.com) flies from Amsterdam; **Alitalia** (© 06/6563-4793 in Italy, 800/223-5730 in the U.S.; www. alitalia.it) flies from Milan; **Icelandair** (© 800/223-5500 in the U.S.; www. icelandair.com) flies from Reykjavik; and **Swiss International Air Lines** (© 0848-85-2000 in Switzerland, 877/359-7947 in the U.S.; www. swiss.com) flies from Geneva and Zurich; **Olympic** (© 0801-44444 in Greece, 800/223-1226 in the U.S.; www.olympic-airways.gr) has weekly flights from Athens. **Qantas** (© 13-13-13 in Australia, 800/227-4500 in the U.S.; www.qantas.com.au) flies to the West Coast of the United States and can provide connecting service to Boston.

AIRLINE DISCOUNTS

Overseas visitors can take advantage of the APEX (Advance Purchase Excursion) reductions offered by all major U.S. and European carriers. For more money-saving airline advice, see p. 33, in the "Getting There" section in chapter 2. For the best rates, compare fares and be flexible about dates and times of travel.

Operated by the European Travel Network, **www.discount-tickets.com** is a great online source for regular and discounted airfares to Boston and other destinations around the world. You can also use this site to compare rates and book accommodations, car rentals, and tours. Click on "Special Offers" for the latest package deals.

IMMIGRATION & CUSTOMS CLEARANCE

Visitors arriving by air, no matter what the port of entry, should cultivate a good measure of patience. Expect to encounter stringent security measures in every American airport at all times. Getting through immigration control might take as long as 2 hours on some days, especially on summer weekends. Add in the time it takes to clear Customs and you'll see that you should allow for long delays when you plan connections between international and domestic flights—an average of 2 to 3 hours at least.

Travelers arriving by car or rail from Canada find border-crossing formalities streamlined almost to the vanishing point. Air travelers from Canada, Bermuda, and some places in the Caribbean can sometimes save time by going through Customs and Immigration at the point of departure.

3 Getting Around the United States

BY PLANE

For a list of domestic carriers that serve Boston, see p. 29.

Some major American carriers—including Delta and Continental—offer travelers on their transatlantic or transpacific flights special low-price tickets on flights in the continental United States under the **Discover America** program (sometimes called **Visit USA**). Offering one-way travel between U.S. destinations at significantly reduced prices, this coupon-based airfare program is the best and easiest way to tour the United States at low cost. These discounted fare coupons are not on sale in the United States; you must buy them abroad in conjunction with your international ticket. Ask your travel agent or the airline reservations agent about this program well in advance of your departure—preferably when you buy your international ticket—because the regulations might govern your trip planning, and conditions can change without notice.

BY CAR

This is the best way to see the country outside the major cities, especially if you have time to explore. Renting a car just to drive around Boston, however, is not advisable.

National car-rental companies with offices in Boston include **Alamo** (© 800/327-9633; www.alamo.com), **Avis** (© 800/331-1212; www.avis.com), **Budget** (© 800/527-0700; www.budget.com), **Dollar** (© 800/800-4000), **Enterprise** (© 800/726-8222; www.enterprise.com), **Hertz** (© 800/654-3131; www.hertz.com), **National** (© 800/227-7368; www.nationalcar.com), and **Thrifty** (© 800/367-2277; www.thrifty.com).

BY TRAIN

International visitors can buy a **USA Rail Pass,** good for 15 or 30 days of unlimited travel on **Amtrak** (© 800/USA-RAIL; www.amtrak.com). Prices in 2003 for a 15-day pass were $295 off-peak (early Sept to late May) and $440 during peak travel periods; for a 30-day pass, $385 off-peak and $550 peak. Passes good only in certain regions are also available; a 5-day Northeast pass goes for $149 year-round.

Passes are available through many foreign travel agents. With a foreign passport, you can also buy passes at Amtrak offices in some U.S. cities, including Boston, San Francisco, Los Angeles, Chicago, New York, Miami, and Washington. Reservations are generally required, and you should make them for each part of your trip when you buy the pass (you can change them later at no cost).

Visitors should be aware of the limitations of long-distance rail travel in the United States. With a few notable exceptions—for instance, the Northeast Corridor between Boston and Washington, D.C.—service is rarely up to European standards. Delays are common, routes are limited and often infrequently served, and fares are rarely significantly lower than discount airfares.

BY BUS

This is the cheapest way to travel in the United States, but it is also often slow and uncomfortable. Still, if you have the time and don't mind the conditions, it is cost-effective. The nationwide line **Greyhound/Trailways** (© **800/231-2222;** www.greyhound. com) offers an Ameripass for 4 to 60 days of unlimited travel. Prices in 2003 ranged from $135 for 4 days, to $324 for 21 days, to $494 for 60 days. Ameripasses good only for travel in certain regions of the country and passes for all of the United States and Canada are also available.

 FAST FACTS: **For the International Traveler**

Also see "Fast Facts: Boston" in chapter 4 for more information.

Automobile Organizations Auto clubs supply members with maps, suggested routes, guidebooks, accident and bail-bond insurance, and emergency road service. The major auto club in the United States, with offices nationwide, is the **American Automobile Association,** or **AAA** (© **800/ 222-4357;** www.aaa.com). If you belong to an auto club at home, inquire about reciprocal arrangements before you leave. AAA can provide you with an International Driving Permit validating your home country's license. Some rental-car agencies provide the same services; inquire when you reserve your car.

Business Hours Banks are open weekdays from 8:30 or 9am to 4 or 5pm, and sometimes Saturday morning; most offer 24-hour access to automated teller machines (ATMs). Business offices generally are open weekdays from 9am to 5 or 6pm. Stores and other businesses are open 6 days a week, and usually on Sunday as well; department stores usually stay open until 9pm at least 1 night a week.

Climate See "When to Go" in chapter 2.

Currency Exchange **Fleet** (© **800/841-4000;** www.fleet.com) offers currency exchange at many locations, including Logan Airport Terminal C (© **617/569-1172**) and Terminal E (© **617/567-2313**), and 1414 Massachusetts Ave., Harvard Square, Cambridge (© **617/556-6050**). Other reliable choices are **Thomas Cook Currency Services** (© **800/287-7362**), 160 Franklin St. and 399 Boylston St.; the **Boston Bank of Commerce,** 133 Federal St. (© **617/457-4400**); and **Ruesch International,** 225 Franklin St. (© **617/482-8600**). Many hotels offer currency exchange; check when you make your reservation.

For the latest market conversion rates, visit **www.oanda.com** or **www.x-rates.com**.

Drinking Laws The legal drinking age in Massachusetts is 21; be ready to show proof of age when you buy or consume alcohol. In many bars, particularly near college campuses, you may be asked for identification if you appear to be under 30 or so. Some bars and clubs "card" (check the ID of) everyone who enters. Beer, wine, and liquor are for sale only in liquor stores and in the liquor sections of supermarkets, which, by law, are closed on Sunday. Bars, taverns, and restaurants may serve alcohol any day of the week. Last call is at 1am on weekdays, 2am on Saturdays.

Do not carry open containers of alcohol in your car or any public area that isn't zoned for alcohol consumption. The police can—and probably will—fine you on the spot. And nothing will ruin your trip faster than getting a citation for DUI (driving under the influence), so don't even think about driving while intoxicated.

Electricity Like Canada, the United States uses 110 to 120 volts, 60 cycles, compared with 220 to 240 volts, 50 cycles, in most of Europe, Australia, and New Zealand. Besides a converter that changes 110–120 volts to 220–240 volts, small appliances of non-American manufacture, such as hair dryers or shavers, require a plug adapter with two flat, parallel pins.

Embassies & Consulates Embassies are in Washington, D.C.; some consulates are in Boston.

The embassy of **Australia** is at 1601 Massachusetts Ave. NW, Washington, DC 20036 (© **202/797-3000**; www.austemb.org). There is no consulate in Boston.

The embassy of **Canada** is at 501 Pennsylvania Ave. NW, Washington, DC 20001 (© **202/682-1740**; www.canadianembassy.org). The **Canadian consulate in Boston** is at 3 Copley Place, Suite 400, Boston, MA 02116 (© **617/262-3760**).

The embassy of the **Republic of Ireland** is at 2234 Massachusetts Ave. NW, Washington, DC 20008 (© **202/462-3939**; www.irelandemb.org). The **Irish consulate in Boston** is at 535 Boylston St., Boston, MA 02116 (© **617/ 267-9330**).

The embassy of **Japan** is at 2520 Massachusetts Ave. NW, Washington, DC 20008 (© **202/238-6700**; www.embjapan.org). The **Japanese consulate in Boston** is at Federal Reserve Plaza, 600 Atlantic Ave., 14th Floor, Boston, MA 02210 (© **617/973-9772**).

The embassy of **New Zealand** is at 37 Observatory Circle NW, Washington, DC 20008 (© **202/328-4800**; www.nzemb.org). There is no consulate in Boston.

The embassy of the **United Kingdom** is at 3100 Massachusetts Ave. NW, Washington, DC 20008 (© **202/462-1340**; http://britain-info.org). The **Boston-area U.K. consulate** is at 1 Memorial Dr., Cambridge, MA 02142 (© **617/248-9555**).

If you come from another country, check the "Consulate Offices" listings in the White Pages (at the end of the Blue Pages government listings in the middle of the telephone directory) to see whether your country has a Boston representative, or call Washington, D.C., directory assistance (© **202/555-1212**) for your embassy's telephone number.

Emergencies Call © **911** for fire, police, and ambulance. This is a free call from public phones. If you encounter such traveler's problems as sickness, an accident, or lost or stolen baggage, call or visit the **Travelers Aid Society,** 17 East St., Boston, MA 02111 (© **617/542-7286**), near South Station. The nonprofit international agency, which specializes in helping travelers in distress, also has a branch at Logan Airport's Terminal E (© **617/567-5385**).

If you have a medical emergency that doesn't require an ambulance, you can walk into a hospital's 24-hour emergency room (usually a separate entrance). For a list of hospitals, see "Fast Facts" in chapter 4.

Gasoline (Petrol) Most service stations sell several grades of gasoline, or "gas." Posted prices are per gallon and include tax. They fluctuate widely and can be as low as half what you would pay in Europe. Each company has a different name for the various levels of octane; most rental cars take the least expensive, regular unleaded. One U.S. gallon equals 3.8 liters or .85 Imperial gallon.

Holidays All banks, government offices, and post offices close on the following national holidays: **New Year's Day** (Jan 1), **Martin Luther King Jr. Day** (3rd Mon in Jan), **Presidents Day** (3rd Mon in Feb), **Memorial Day** (last Mon in May), **Independence Day** (July 4), **Labor Day** (1st Mon in Sept), **Columbus Day** (2nd Mon in Oct), **Veterans Day** (Nov 11), **Thanksgiving** (4th Thurs in Nov), and **Christmas** (Dec 25). Some stores and restaurants and many museums close on national holidays. The Tuesday following the first Monday in November is **Election Day** and is a legal holiday in presidential election years (next in 2004).

In Massachusetts, state offices close for **Patriots Day** on the third Monday in April, and Suffolk County offices (including Boston City Hall) close on March 17 for **Evacuation Day.**

Legal Aid The well-meaning international traveler will probably never become involved with the American legal system. However, you should know a few things just in case. While driving, if you are "pulled over"— stopped by the police—for a minor infraction (for example, of the highway code, such as speeding), *never* attempt to pay the fine directly to a police officer. You might wind up being arrested on the much more serious charge of attempted bribery. Pay fines by mail or directly to the clerk of the court. If you're accused of a more serious offense, you have the right to remain silent—say and do nothing before consulting a lawyer. Under U.S. law, an arrested person is allowed one telephone call to a party of his or her choice. Call your embassy or consulate.

Mail Post offices are scattered throughout the city. Postcard stamps cost 23¢ for delivery in the United States, 50¢ for Mexico or Canada, and 70¢ for other international addresses. Letter stamps for up to 1 ounce cost 37¢ in the United States, 60¢ to Mexico or Canada, and 80¢ to other international addresses. A preprinted postal aerogramme costs 70¢.

Medical Emergencies If you become ill, consult your hotel staff for referral to a physician. For an ambulance, dial 🕐 **911.** Also see "Doctors" in the "Fast Facts" section in chapter 4.

Newspapers & Magazines National newspapers include the *New York Times, USA Today,* and the *Wall Street Journal.* National newsweeklies include *Newsweek, Time,* and *U.S. News & World Report.* The major newspapers in Boston are the *Boston Globe,* the *Boston Herald,* and the weekly *Boston Phoenix.*

Newsstands with good selections of international periodicals include **Out of Town News,** Zero Harvard Square, Cambridge (🕐 **617/354-7777**); **Nini's Corner,** across the street at 1394 Massachusetts Ave. (🕐 **617/547-3558**); and the outdoor newsstand at the corner of Boylston and Dartmouth streets at the Copley T stop on the Green Line.

Passports **For Residents of Canada:** Applications are available at travel agencies throughout Canada or from the central **Passport Office,** Department of Foreign Affairs and International Trade, Ottawa, ON K1A 0G3 (✆ **800/567-6868;** www.dfait-maeci.gc.ca/passport).

For Residents of the United Kingdom: To pick up an application for a standard 10-year passport (5-yr. passport for children under 16), visit your nearest passport office, major post office, or travel agency, or contact the **United Kingdom Passport Service** (✆ **0870/521-0410;** www.ukpa.gov.uk).

For Residents of Ireland: You can apply for a 10-year passport at the **Passport Office,** Setanta Centre, Molesworth St., Dublin 2 (✆ **01/671-1633;** www.irlgov.ie/iveagh). Those under age 18 and over 65 must apply for a 12€ 3-year passport. You can also apply at 1A South Mall, Cork (✆ **021/ 272-525**) or at most main post offices.

For Residents of Australia: You can pick up an application from your local post office or any branch of Passports Australia, but you must schedule an interview at the passport office to present your application materials. Call the **Australian Passport Information Service** at ✆ **131-232,** or visit the government website at www.passports.gov.au.

For Residents of New Zealand: You can pick up an application at any **New Zealand Passports Office** (✆ **0800/225-050** in New Zealand or 04/474-8100) or download it from www.passports.govt.nz.

Radio & Television Nationally, there are six commercial over-the-air television networks—ABC, CBS, NBC, Fox, UPN, and WB—along with the Public Broadcasting System (PBS) and the cable news network CNN. Most hotels have at least basic cable, and many offer access to "premium" movie channels that show uncut theatrical releases. For the major radio and television stations in Boston, see "Fast Facts" in chapter 4.

Safety See "Safety" in the section "Preparing for Your Trip" earlier in this chapter.

Smoking Don't count on being able to light up indoors anywhere in Boston. A 2003 law forbids smoking in workplaces, including bars and clubs, and the ban may have extended statewide by the time you visit.

Taxes The United States imposes no value-added tax (VAT) or other indirect national tax. Every state, county, and city may levy its own tax on purchases, including hotel bills, restaurant checks, and so on. The 5% state sales tax in Massachusetts does not apply to food, prescription drugs, newspapers, or clothing costing less than $175, but there seems to be a tax on everything else. The tax on restaurant meals and takeout food is 5%. The lodging tax in Boston and Cambridge is 12.45%.

Telephone & Fax Private corporations run the U.S. telephone system. Rates, especially for long-distance service and operator-assisted calls, can vary widely, even on calls made from public phones. Local calls in the Boston area usually cost 35¢. Pay phones do not accept pennies, and few will take anything larger than a quarter. If you expect to make a lot of phone calls, **prepaid calling cards** are convenient, if not necessarily economical. They're available at visitor information centers and many stores, usually in multiples of $5. Many public phones at airports accept credit cards.

Most hotels impose hefty surcharges on long-distance and local calls. Hotels that include local calls in the room rate usually advertise it; if you don't hear otherwise, assume that the charge for any call will be astronomical. You are usually better off using public pay phones, which are clearly marked in many private establishments (including hotel lobbies), in most public buildings, and on the street. Outside metropolitan areas, public phones are harder to find. Stores, gas stations, and bars are your best bet.

You can dial most long-distance and international calls directly from any phone. **For calls to other parts of the United States and to Canada,** dial 1 followed by the area code and the seven-digit number. **For other international calls,** dial 011 followed by the country code, city code, and telephone number. Some country and city codes are as follows: **Australia** 61, Melbourne 3, Sydney 2; **Ireland** 353, Dublin 1; **New Zealand** 64, Auckland 9, Wellington 4; **United Kingdom** 44, Belfast 232, Birmingham 21, Glasgow 41, London 71 or 81. If you're calling the **United States** from another country, the country code is 01.

For reversed-charge or **collect** calls, and for person-to-person calls, dial 0 (zero, not the letter *O*) followed by the area code and number. An operator will come on the line, and you should specify that you are calling collect, or person to person, or both. If your operator-assisted call is international, ask for the overseas operator.

Calls to area codes **800, 888, 877,** and **866** are toll-free. However, calls to numbers in area codes **700** and **900** (chat lines, bulletin boards, "dating" services, and so on) can be very expensive—usually 95¢ to $3 or more per minute, sometimes with minimum charges as high as $15 or more.

For directory assistance ("information"), dial *①* **411.**

Most hotels have **fax machines** available for guests' use (be sure to ask if there's a charge), and some hotel rooms have their own fax machines. It might be less expensive to send and receive faxes at a photocopy shop or a store such as **Mail Boxes Etc.,** a national chain of packing service shops (look in the Yellow Pages telephone directory under "Packaging Services"), or **Kinko's,** a national chain of copy shops offering business services.

Telephone Directories The general directory is the **White Pages,** which lists private households and businesses (separately) in alphabetical order. The first page lists emergency numbers. The first section includes a guide to long-distance and international calling, complete with country codes and area codes. Government numbers appear on the Blue Pages (on blue or blue-bordered paper) within the White Pages.

The **Yellow Pages** directory, printed on yellow paper, lists local services, businesses, and industries by type of activity. The listings also cover drugstores (pharmacies) and restaurants by geographical location. The directory includes a condensed city guide, postal ZIP codes, and maps of public transportation routes.

Time Noon in Boston or New York City (Eastern Standard Time) is 5pm in London, 6pm in Cape Town, 11am in Chicago (Central Standard Time),

10am in Denver (Mountain Standard Time), 9am in Vancouver and Los Angeles (Pacific Standard Time), 8am in Anchorage (Alaska Standard Time), 7am in Honolulu (Hawaii-Aleutian Standard Time), and—1 day ahead—5am in Auckland and 3am in Sydney.

Daylight saving time is in effect from the first Sunday in April through the last Saturday in October (starting at 2am), except in Arizona, Hawaii, part of Indiana, and Puerto Rico. Daylight saving time moves the clock 1 hour ahead of Standard Time.

Tipping This is part of the American way of life. Many service employees—waiters and waitresses in particular—rely on tips for the bulk of their earnings. Here are some guidelines. If you receive extraordinary service, consider tipping a bit more.

In hotels, tip bellhops at least $1 per piece, $5 or more for a lot of baggage, and housekeeping $1 to $2 a day. Tip the doorman or concierge only if he or she has provided a service (for example, calling a cab or obtaining difficult-to-get theater tickets). Tip valet parking attendants $1 or $2 each time they get your car.

In restaurants, bars, and nightclubs, tip service staff 15% to 20% of the check. Many restaurants automatically add a 15% to 18% gratuity to the total tab for large parties (usually 6 or more); double-check so that you don't accidentally tip extra. Tip bartenders 10% to 15%, checkroom attendants $1 per garment, and valet-parking attendants $1 to $2 per vehicle. Tipping is not expected at cafeterias, fast-food restaurants, or gas stations.

Tip cab drivers 15% to 20% of the fare. Tip skycaps at airports and redcaps at train stations at least $1 per bag ($5 or so if you have a lot of luggage), and hairdressers and barbers 15% to 20%.

Tipping ushers at movies and theaters and tipping gas-station attendants is not expected.

Toilets International visitors often complain that public toilets are hard to find in the United States. True, there are hardly any on the streets, but you can usually find one in a visitor information center, shopping center, bar, restaurant, hotel, museum, or department store—and it will probably be clean. The cleanliness of toilets at railroad and bus stations and at gasoline service stations varies widely. Some restaurants and bars, including those in Boston's tourist areas, display a sign saying that toilets are for the use of patrons only. Paying for a cup of coffee or a soft drink qualifies you as a patron. Many branches of fast-food restaurants and coffee bars have reliably clean restrooms.

Boston has freestanding, self-cleaning pay toilets in kiosks in eight high-traffic areas downtown, including City Hall Plaza (near the Government Center T stop) and Commercial Street near Snowhill Street, off the Freedom Trail. Entrance costs 25¢. Check carefully before using these toilets—reports of drug use in the enclosed kiosks have led to increased maintenance, but you can't be too careful.

4

Getting to Know Boston

Boston bills itself as "America's Walking City," and walking is by far the easiest way to get around. Legend has it that the street pattern originated as a network of cow paths, but the layout owes more to 17th-century London and to Boston's original shoreline. To orient yourself, it helps to look at the big picture.

This chapter provides an overview of the city's layout and neighborhoods, and lists information and resources that you might need while you're away from home. As you familiarize yourself with Boston's geography, it might help to identify the various neighborhoods and landmarks on the free map provided with this guide.

1 Orientation

VISITOR INFORMATION

You'll probably want to begin exploring at a **visitor information center.** The staff members are knowledgeable and helpful, and you can pick up free maps, brochures, listings of special exhibits, and other materials.

The **Boston National Historic Park Visitor Center,** 15 State St. (© 617/242-5642; www.nps.gov/bost), across the street from the Old State House and the State Street T station, is a good place to start your excursion. National Park Service rangers staff the center, dispense information, and lead free tours of the Freedom Trail. The audiovisual show about the trail provides basic information on 16 historic sites. The center is accessible by stairs and ramps and has restrooms and comfortable chairs. Open daily from 9am to 5pm except January 1, Thanksgiving Day, and December 25.

The Freedom Trail, a line of red paint or painted brick on or in the sidewalk, begins at the **Boston Common Information Center,** 146 Tremont St., on the Common. The center is open Monday through Saturday from 8:30am to 5pm, Sunday from 9am to 5pm. The **Prudential Information Center,** on the main level of the Prudential Center, 800 Boylston St., is open Monday through Friday from 8:30am to 6pm, Saturday and Sunday from 10am to 6pm. The **Greater Boston Convention & Visitors Bureau** (© 888/SEE-BOSTON or 617/536-4100; www.bostonusa.com) operates both centers.

There's a small information booth at **Faneuil Hall Marketplace** between Quincy Market and the South Market Building. It's outdoors and staffed in the spring, summer, and fall Monday through Saturday from 10am to 6pm, Sunday from noon to 6pm.

In Cambridge, there's an information kiosk (© 800/862-5678 or 617/497-1630) in the heart of **Harvard Square,** near the T entrance at the intersection of Massachusetts Avenue, John F. Kennedy Street, and Brattle Street. It's open Monday through Saturday from 9am to 5pm, Sunday from 1 to 5pm.

PUBLICATIONS

The city's newspapers offer the most up-to-date information about events in the area. The "Calendar" section of the Thursday *Boston Globe* lists festivals, concerts, dance and theater performances, street fairs, films, and speeches. The Friday *Boston Herald* has a similar, smaller insert called "Scene." Both papers briefly list events in their weekend editions. The arts-oriented *Boston Phoenix,* published on Thursday, has extensive entertainment and restaurant listings.

Where, a monthly magazine available free at most hotels throughout the city, lists information about shopping, nightlife, attractions, and current shows at museums and art galleries. Newspaper boxes around both cities dispense free copies of the weekly *Tab,* which lists neighborhood-specific event information; *Stuff@Night,* a *Phoenix* offshoot with selective listings and arts coverage; and the *Improper Bostonian,* with extensive event and restaurant listings. Available on newsstands, *Boston* magazine is a lifestyle-oriented monthly with cultural and restaurant listings.

CITY LAYOUT

When Puritan settlers established Boston in 1630, it was one-third the size it is now. Much of the city reflects the original layout, a seemingly haphazard plan that can disorient even longtime residents. Old Boston abounds with alleys, dead ends, one-way streets, streets that change names, and streets named after extinct geographical features. On the plus side, every "wrong" turn **downtown,** in the **North End,** or on **Beacon Hill** is a chance to see something interesting that you might otherwise have missed.

The most prominent feature of downtown Boston is **Boston Common.** Its borders are **Park Street,** which is 1 block long (but looms large in the geography

 It's a Big, Big, Big, Big Dig

In a city with glorious water views, historic architecture, and gorgeous parks, the most prominent physical feature is a giant highway construction project. The Central Artery/Third Harbor Tunnel Project, better known as the Big Dig, is a $14.6 billion (yes, billion!) undertaking. It's in the process of moving I-93 underground—without closing the road through downtown Boston. The first major phase of the Big Dig connected the Massachusetts Turnpike (I-90) directly to the airport. It also encompasses the lovely new Leonard P. Zakim Bunker Hill Memorial Bridge, over the Charles River north of North Station.

If it stays on schedule, the Big Dig will be completed in early 2005. The timeline for 2004 includes demolition of the existing elevated highway. Meanwhile, it's causing countless traffic nightmares, fulfilling millions of Tonka truck fantasies, and making engineering history. Many of the techniques are so unusual that construction professionals come from all over the world just to see them in action. To learn more, visit the website (www.bigdig.com), or just walk around downtown. Complete and ongoing work near the surface is often visible from the street, causing pedestrian and automotive gridlock. Soon you'll see why I want you to leave the car at home.

Boston Orientation

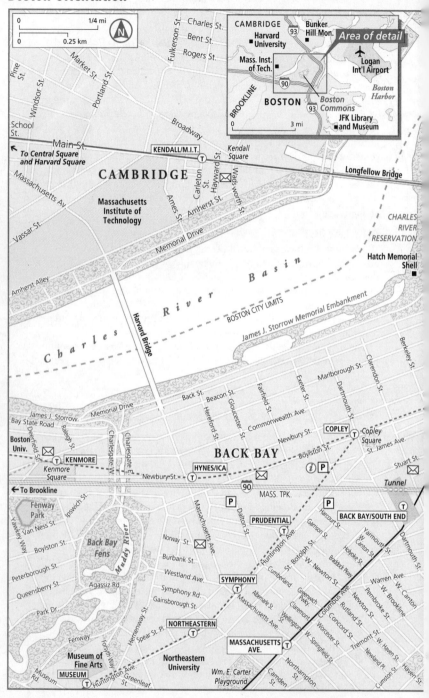

0   1/4 mi
0   0.25 km

CAMBRIDGE   Bunker
   Harvard   Hill Mon.
   University
               Area of detail
   Mass. Inst.
   of Tech.   Logan
                   Int'l Airport
                    Boston
BROOKLINE   Harbor
BOSTON   Boston
          Commons
              JFK Library
0   3 mi   and Museum

Charles St.
Bent St.
Rogers St.
Fulkerson St.
Market St.
Portland St.
Pine St.
Windsor St.
School St.

Main St.
← To Central Square
and Harvard Square
KENDALL/M.I.T.   Kendall
               Square

CAMBRIDGE
Massachusetts Ave.
Broadway

Massachusetts
Institute of
Technology

Carleton St.
Hayward St.
Ames St.
Amherst St.
Wadsworth St.

Longfellow Bridge

Vassar St.

Memorial Drive

CHARLES
RIVER
RESERVATION

Amherst Alley

Charles   River   Basin

Hatch Memorial
Shell

Harvard Bridge

BOSTON CITY LIMITS

James J. Storrow Memorial Embankment

Charles

Berkeley St.

Marlborough St.
Clarendon St.

Back St.
Beacon St.
Exeter St.
Dartmouth St.

James J. Storrow
Bay State Road
Memorial Drive

Back St.
Hereford St.
Gloucester St.
Fairfield St.
Commonwealth Ave.
Newbury St.
COPLEY   Copley
        Square
        St. James Ave.

Boston
Univ.
Deerfield St.
Raleigh St.
KENMORE
Kenmore
Square
Charlesgate W.
Charlesgate

BACK BAY

Boylston St.

HYNES/ICA

COPLEY

Stuart St.

Tunnel

← To Brookline
Newbury St.

90   MASS. TPK.

Fenway
Park
Van Ness St.
Ipswich St.

Yawkey Way
Boylston St.

Back Bay
Fens

Muddy River

Norway St.
Burbank St.
Westland Ave.

Dalton St.

PRUDENTIAL

Harcourt St.
Garrison St.

Yarmouth St.
Canton St.
Holyoke St.

BACK BAY/SOUTH END

Dartmouth St.

Peterborough St.

Queensberry St.

Agassiz Rd.

Park Dr.

Symphony Rd.
Gainsborough St.

SYMPHONY

Massachusetts Ave.

Huntington Ave.
Cumberland
W. Newton St.
W. Brookline
Newton St.
Pembroke St.

Warren Ave.
W. Canton

Fenway

Museum
Rd.

Museum of
Fine Arts
MUSEUM

Huntington Ave.
Greenleaf St.
Forsyth Way
Henenway Ave.
Spear St. Pl.

NORTHEASTERN

Northeastern
University
Wm. E. Carter
Playground

Albemarle St.
Greenwich Pkwy.
Claremont St.
Wellington
W. Springfield St.
Worcester St.
Concord St.
Rutland St.
Columbus Ave.
Braddock Pkwy.

MASSACHUSETTS
AVE.

Northampton St.
Camden St.
Tremont St.
W. Haven St.
Newland Pl.
Cumston St.
Haven St.

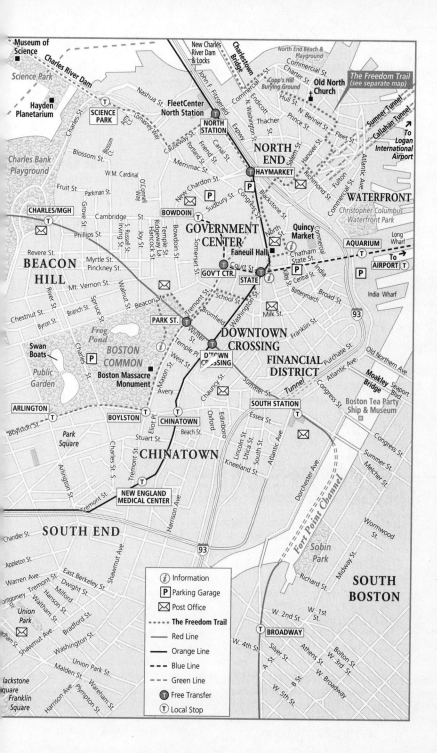

Finding an Address

There's no rhyme or reason to the street pattern, compass directions are virtually useless, and there aren't enough street signs. The best way to find an address is to call ahead and ask for directions, including landmarks, or leave extra time for wandering around. If the directions involve a T stop, be sure to ask which exit to use—most stations have more than one.

---

of the T), and Beacon, Charles, Boylston, and Tremont streets. Another important street is **Massachusetts Avenue,** or "Mass. Ave.," as it's almost always called. Mass. Ave. covers 9 miles, from Roxbury through the South End, the Back Bay, Cambridge, and Arlington, ending in Lexington.

Nineteenth-century landfill projects transformed much of the city's landscape, altering the shoreline and creating the **Back Bay,** where the streets proceed in orderly parallel lines. After you've spent some frustrating time in the older part of the city, that simple plan will seem ingenious. The streets even go in alphabetical order, starting at the Public Garden with Arlington, then Berkeley, Clarendon, Dartmouth, Exeter, Fairfield, Gloucester, and Hereford (and then Mass. Ave.).

STREET MAPS

In addition to the map provided with this guide, free maps of downtown Boston and the rapid-transit lines are available at visitor information centers around the city. *Where* magazine, available free at most hotels, contains maps of central Boston and the T.

Streetwise Boston ($6.95) and *Artwise Boston* ($6.95) are sturdy, laminated maps available at most bookstores. Less detailed but more fun is MapEasy's *GuideMap to Boston* ($6.95), a hand-drawn map of the central areas and major attractions.

THE NEIGHBORHOODS IN BRIEF

These are the areas visitors are most likely to frequent. When Bostonians say **"downtown,"** they usually mean the first six neighborhoods defined here; there's no "midtown" or "uptown." The numerous neighborhoods outside central Boston include the Fenway, South Boston, Dorchester, Roxbury, West Roxbury, and Jamaica Plain. With a couple of exceptions (noted here), Boston is generally safe, but you should still take the precautions you would in any large city, especially at night.

The Waterfront This narrow area runs along the Inner Harbor, on **Atlantic Avenue** and **Commercial Street** from the North Washington Street bridge (the route to Charlestown) to South Station. Once filled with wharves and warehouses, today it abounds with luxury condos, marinas, restaurants, offices, and hotels. Also here are the New England Aquarium and embarkation points for harbor cruises and whale-watching expeditions.

The North End Crossing under (or over, if the Big Dig has progressed enough) **I-93** as you head east toward the Inner Harbor brings you to one of the city's oldest neighborhoods. Home to waves of immigrants in the course of its history, it was predominantly Italian for most of the 20th century. It's now less than half Italian American; many newcomers are young professionals who walk to work in the Financial District. Nevertheless, you'll hear

Italian spoken in the streets and find a wealth of Italian restaurants, *caffès,* and shops. The main street is **Hanover Street.**

North Station Technically part of the North End, but just as close to Beacon Hill, this area around **Causeway Street** is home to the **FleetCenter.** You'll find plenty of nightspots and restaurants, but wandering alone at night (especially on the side streets away from the arena) is not a good idea.

Faneuil Hall Marketplace Employees aside, Boston residents tend to be scarce at Faneuil Hall Marketplace (also called Quincy Market, after its central building). An irresistible draw for out-of-towners and suburbanites, this cluster of restored market buildings— bounded by the Waterfront, the North End, Government Center, and **State Street**—is the city's most popular attraction. You'll find restaurants, bars, a food court, specialty shops, and Faneuil Hall itself. **Haymarket,** off I-93 on **Blackstone Street,** is home to an open-air produce market on Fridays and Saturdays.

Government Center Love it or hate it, Government Center introduced modern design into the staid facade of traditional Boston architecture. Flanked by Beacon Hill, Downtown Crossing, and Faneuil Hall Marketplace, it's home to state and federal offices, City Hall, and a major T stop. The redbrick wasteland of City Hall Plaza lies between **Congress** and **Cambridge streets.**

The Financial District Bounded loosely by Downtown Crossing, **Summer Street, Atlantic Avenue,** and **State Street,** the Financial District is the banking, insurance, and legal center of the city. Aside from

some popular after-work spots, it's quiet at night.

Downtown Crossing The intersection that gives Downtown Crossing its name is at **Washington Street** where **Winter Street** becomes **Summer Street.** The Freedom Trail runs through this shopping and business district between Boston Common, Chinatown, the Financial District, and Government Center. Most of this neighborhood hops during the day and slows down in the evening. The onetime "Combat Zone" (red-light district) has been the object of a massive PR campaign pushing the **Ladder District** designation for the newly spruced-up side streets between Tremont and Washington streets opposite the Common.

Beacon Hill Narrow tree-lined streets and architectural showpieces, mostly in the Federal style, make up this residential area in the shadow of the State House. Louisburg (pronounced "Lewis-burg") Square and Mount Vernon Street, two of the loveliest and most exclusive spots in Boston, are on Beacon Hill. Bounded by Government Center, Boston Common, the Back Bay, and the river, it's also home to Massachusetts General Hospital, on the nominally less tony north side of the neighborhood. **Charles Street,** which divides the Common from the Public Garden, is the main street of Beacon Hill. Other important thoroughfares are **Beacon Street,** on the north side of the Common, and **Cambridge Street.**

Charlestown One of the oldest areas of Boston is where you'll see the Bunker Hill Monument and USS *Constitution* ("Old Ironsides"), as well as one of the city's best-known restaurants, Olives. Yuppification has brought some diversity

---

(*Fun Fact* **By George!**

Washington Street, the most "main" street downtown, has another distinction: As a tribute to the first president, street names (except Mass. Ave.) change when they cross Washington. For example, Bromfield becomes Franklin, Winter becomes Summer, Stuart becomes Kneeland.

---

to what was once an almost entirely white residential neighborhood, but pockets remain that have earned their reputation for insularity.

South Boston Waterfront/Seaport District Across the Fort Point Channel from the Waterfront neighborhood, this district is home to the World Trade Center, the Seaport Hotel, the Fish Pier, a federal courthouse, Museum Wharf, and a lot of construction. Scheduled to open in 2004, the **Boston Convention & Exhibition Center** should bring new vitality to this area. **Seaport Boulevard** and **Northern Avenue** are the main drags.

Chinatown The fourth-largest Chinese community in the country is a small but growing area jammed with Asian restaurants, groceries, and gift shops. Chinatown now fills the area between Downtown Crossing and the Mass. Pike extension. Chinatown's main streets are **Washington Street, Kneeland Street,** and **Beach Street.** The tiny **Theater District** extends about 1½ blocks from the intersection of Tremont and Stuart streets in each direction; be careful there at night after the crowds thin out. (The "Combat Zone," or red-light district between Chinatown and Downtown Crossing, has nearly disappeared under pressure from the business community, which has mounted a campaign to rename the area the "Ladder District," but the name hasn't really caught on.)

The South End Cross **Stuart Street** or **Huntington Avenue** heading south from the Back Bay, and you'll find yourself in a landmark district packed with Victorian row houses and little parks. Known for its ethnic, economic, and cultural diversity, the South End has a large gay community and some of the city's best restaurants. With the gentrification of the 1980s, **Tremont Street** (particularly the end closest to downtown) gained a cachet that it hadn't known for almost a century. *Note:* Don't confuse the South End with South Boston, a residential neighborhood on the other side of I-93.

The Back Bay Fashionable since its creation out of landfill more than a century ago, the Back Bay overflows with gorgeous architecture and chic shops. It lies between the Public Garden, the river, Kenmore Square, and either **Huntington Avenue** or **St. Botolph Street,** depending on who's describing it. Students dominate the area near **Mass. Ave.** but grow scarce as property values rise near the Public Garden. This is one of the best neighborhoods in Boston for aimless walking. Major thoroughfares include **Boylston Street,** which starts at Boston Common and runs into the Fenway; largely residential **Beacon Street** and **"Comm. Ave."** (Commonwealth Avenue); and boutique central, **Newbury Street.**

Huntington Avenue The honorary "Avenue of the Arts" (or, with a Boston accent, "Otts"), though not a formal neighborhood, is where you'll find the Christian Science Center, Symphony Hall (at the corner of Mass. Ave.), Northeastern University, and the Museum of Fine Arts. It begins at Copley Square and touches on the Back Bay, the Fenway, and the Longwood Medical Area before heading into the suburbs. Parts of Huntington can be a little risky, so if you're leaving the museum at night, stick to the car, a cab, or the Green Line, and travel in a group.

Kenmore Square The white-and-red CITGO sign that dominates the skyline above the intersection of **"Comm. Ave."** (Commonwealth Avenue), **Beacon Street,** and **Brookline Avenue** tells you that you're approaching Kenmore Square. Its shops, bars, restaurants, and clubs attract students from adjacent Boston University. The college-town atmosphere goes out the window when the Red Sox are in town, and baseball fans pour into the area on the way to historic Fenway Park, 3 blocks away.

Cambridge Boston's neighbor across the Charles River is a separate city. The areas you're likely to visit are along the MBTA Red Line. **Harvard Square** is a magnet for students, sightseers, and well-heeled shoppers. It's an easy walk along Mass. Ave. southeast to **Central Square,** a rapidly gentrifying area dotted with ethnic restaurants and clubs. North along Mass. Ave. is **Porter Square,** a mostly residential neighborhood with some quirky shops like those that once characterized Harvard Square. Around **Kendall Square** you'll find MIT and many technology-oriented businesses.

2 Getting Around

ON FOOT

If you can manage a fair amount of walking, this is the way to go. You can best appreciate Boston at street level, and walking the narrow, picturesque streets takes you past many gridlocked cars.

Even more than in a typical large city, be alert. Look both ways before crossing, even on one-way streets, where many bicyclists and some drivers blithely go against the flow. The "walk" cycle of many downtown traffic signals lasts only 7 seconds, and a small but significant part of the driving population considers red lights optional anyway. Keep a close eye on the kids, especially in crosswalks.

BY PUBLIC TRANSPORTATION

The **Massachusetts Bay Transportation Authority,** or MBTA (© **800/392-6100** outside Mass. or 617/222-3200; www.mbta.com), is known as the T, and

---

Tips **Late-Night Transit**

After decades of complaints about the T's early closing time, the MBTA introduced "Night Owl" bus service in September 2001. It operates Friday and Saturday nights until 2:30am on popular bus routes and on supplemental bus routes that parallel the subway lines. Originally a 1-year experimental program, it proved so successful that it should (budget permitting) still be operating when you visit. The fare is $1 in coins or a token. For more information and schedules, contact the MBTA (© **800/392-6100** outside Mass. or 617/222-3200; www.mbta.com).

Value Ride & Save

The MBTA's **Boston Visitor Pass** (© **877/927-7277** or 617/222-5218; www. mbta.com) can be a great deal. You get unlimited travel on subway lines and local buses, in commuter rail zones 1A and 1B, and on two ferries. The cost is $6 for 1 day, $11 for 3 consecutive days, and $22 for 7 consecutive days. If the timing works, the $13 **weekly combo pass** might be a better deal. It covers subways and buses but not ferries, and is good from Sunday to Saturday only.

You can order passes in advance over the phone or the Web (there's a fee for shipping), or buy them when you arrive at the Airport T stop, South Station, Back Bay Station, or North Station. They're also for sale at the Government Center and Harvard T stations; the Boston Common, Prudential Center, and Faneuil Hall Marketplace information centers; and some hotels.

its logo is the letter in a circle. It runs subways, trolleys, buses, and ferries in Boston and many suburbs, as well as the commuter rail, which extends as far as Providence, Rhode Island.

For information on services and discounts for seniors and travelers with disabilities, see the "Specialized Travel Resources" section in chapter 2.

BY SUBWAY

Subways and trolleys take you around Boston faster than any other mode of transportation except walking. The oldest system in the country, locally referred to as the T, dates to 1897, and recent and ongoing improvements have made it generally reliable. The trolleys on the ancient Green Line are the most unpredictable—leave extra time if you're taking them to a vital appointment. The system is generally safe, but always watch out for pickpockets, especially during the holiday shopping season. And remember, downtown stops are so close together that it's often faster to walk.

The subways are color-coded and are called the Red, Green, Blue, and Orange lines. (The commuter rail to the suburbs is purple on system maps and is sometimes called the Purple Line.) The local fare is **$1**—you'll need a token—and can be as much as $2.50 for some surface-line extensions on the Green and Red lines. Transfers are free. Route and fare information and timetables are available through the website (www.mbta.com) and at centrally located stations.

Service begins at around 5:15am and ends around 12:30am. The exception is New Year's Eve, or First Night, when closing time is 2am and service is free after 8pm. A sign in every station gives the time of the last train in either direction. For information about Night Owl service, see the box "Late-Night Transit" above.

BY BUS

The MBTA runs buses and "trackless trolleys" (buses with electric antennae) that provide service around town and to and around the suburbs. The local routes that you'll most likely need are **no. 1,** along Mass. Ave. from Dudley Square in Roxbury through the Back Bay and Cambridge to Harvard Square; **no. 92** and **no. 93,** which connect Haymarket and Charlestown; and **no. 77,** along Mass. Ave. north of Harvard Square to Porter Square, North Cambridge, and Arlington.

Boston Transit

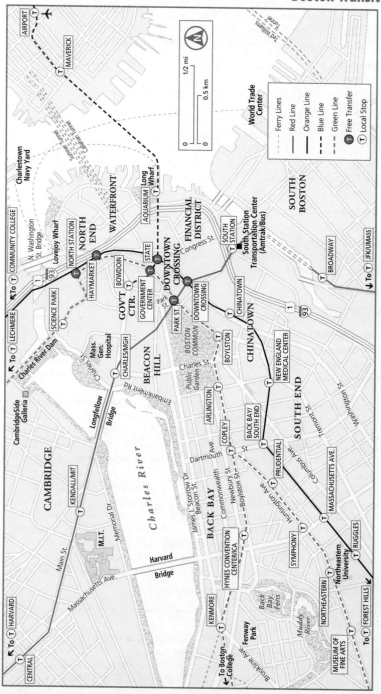

Legend:
- Ferry Lines
- Red Line
- Orange Line
- Blue Line
- Green Line
- Ⓣ Free Transfer
- Ⓣ Local Stop

1/2 mi
0.5 km

Locations and stations:

AIRPORT Ⓣ · MAVERICK Ⓣ · Ted Williams Tunnel · World Trade Center · SOUTH BOSTON · Summer Tunnel · Callahan Tunnel · Charlestown Navy Yard · COMMUNITY COLLEGE Ⓣ · N. Washington St. Bridge · Lovejoy Wharf · NORTH STATION Ⓣ · WATERFRONT · NORTH END · Long Wharf · AQUARIUM Ⓣ · FINANCIAL DISTRICT · SOUTH STATION Ⓣ · South Station Transportation Center (Amtrak/Bus) · BROADWAY Ⓣ · To Ⓣ JFK/UMASS · To Ⓣ LECHMERE · To Ⓣ COMMUNITY COLLEGE · SCIENCE PARK Ⓣ · HAYMARKET Ⓣ · BOWDOIN Ⓣ · STATE Ⓣ · GOV'T CTR. · GOVERNMENT CENTER Ⓣ · Congress St. · DOWNTOWN CROSSING Ⓣ · Park St. · PARK ST. Ⓣ · CHINATOWN Ⓣ · NEW ENGLAND MEDICAL CENTER · Charles River Dam · Mass. Gen. Hospital · CHARLES/MGH Ⓣ · Charles St. · BEACON HILL · BOSTON COMMON · Public Garden · BOYLSTON Ⓣ · SOUTH END · Washington St. · CambridgeSide Galleria · Longfellow Bridge · Embankment Rd. · ARLINGTON Ⓣ · BACK BAY/SOUTH END · Tremont St. · CAMBRIDGE · KENDALL/MIT Ⓣ · Charles River · James J. Storrow Dr. · Beacon St. · Dartmouth St. · COPLEY Ⓣ · Newbury St. · Boylston St. · Commonwealth Ave. · PRUDENTIAL Ⓣ · Columbus Ave. · Main St. · M.I.T. · Memorial Dr. · Harvard Bridge · Massachusetts Ave. · BACK BAY · HYNES CONVENTION CENTER/ICA Ⓣ · Huntington Ave. · SYMPHONY Ⓣ · MASSACHUSETTS AVE. Ⓣ · Northeastern University · RUGGLES Ⓣ · To Ⓣ HARVARD · CENTRAL Ⓣ · KENMORE Ⓣ · Fenway Park · Back Bay Fens · Muddy River · NORTHEASTERN Ⓣ · To Boston College · MUSEUM OF FINE ARTS · To Ⓣ FOREST HILLS · Brookline Ave.

The local bus fare is **75¢;** express bus fares are $1.50 and up. Exact change is required. You can use a token, but you won't get change back. For information about Night Owl service, see the box "Late-Night Transit" above.

BY FERRY

Two popular and useful routes (both included in the MBTA visitor pass) run on the Inner Harbor. The first connects **Long Wharf** (near the New England Aquarium) with the **Charlestown Navy Yard**—it's a good way to get back downtown from "Old Ironsides" and the Bunker Hill Monument. The other runs between **Lovejoy Wharf,** off Causeway Street behind North Station and the FleetCenter, and the **World Trade Center,** on Northern Avenue in South Boston near the Fish Pier and the Seaport Hotel, with a stop at the **Moakley Federal Courthouse.** The fare is $1.25. Call ⓒ **617/227-4321** for more information.

BY WATER TAXI

From April to mid-October, **City Water Taxi** (ⓒ **617/422-0392;** www.city watertaxi.com) offers on-call service in small boats that connect a dozen stops on the Inner Harbor, including the airport. It operates daily from 7am to 7pm. The flat fare is $10, free for kids under 13. Call ahead from the dock for service.

BY TAXI

Taxis are expensive and not always easy to find—seek out a cabstand or call a dispatcher. Always ask for a receipt in case you have a complaint or lose something and need to call the company.

Cabstands are usually near hotels. There are also busy ones at Faneuil Hall Marketplace (on North St.), South Station, and Back Bay Station, and on either side of Mass. Ave. in Harvard Square, near the Harvard Coop bookstore and Au Bon Pain.

To call ahead for a cab, try the **Independent Taxi Operators Association,** or ITOA (ⓒ 617/426-8700); **Boston Cab** (ⓒ 617/536-5010 or 617/262-2227); **Town Taxi** (ⓒ 617/536-5000); or **Metro Cab** (ⓒ 617/242-8000). In Cambridge, call **Ambassador Brattle** (ⓒ 617/492-1100) or **Yellow Cab** (ⓒ 617/ 547-3000). Boston Cab will dispatch a wheelchair-accessible vehicle upon request; advance notice is recommended.

The fare structure: The first ¼ mile (when the flag drops) costs $1.75, and each additional ⅛ mile is 30¢. Wait time is extra, and the passenger pays all tolls, as well as a total of $6 in fees on trips leaving Logan Airport. Charging a flat rate is not allowed within the city; the police department publishes a list (available on the Logan website, www.massport.com/logan) of distances to the suburbs that establishes the flat rate for those trips. If you want to report a problem or have lost something in a cab, call the police department's **Hackney Hotline** (ⓒ **617/536-8294).**

Impressions

Boston's freeway system was insane. It was clearly designed by a person who had spent his childhood crashing toy trains. Every few hundred yards I would find my lane vanishing beneath me and other lanes merging with it from the right or left, or sometimes both. This wasn't a road system, it was mobile hysteria.

—Bill Bryson, *The Lost Continent* (1989)

BY CAR

If you plan to visit only Boston and Cambridge, there's absolutely no reason to have a car. Between the Big Dig, the pricey parking, and the narrow, one-way streets, Boston in particular is a motorist's nightmare. If you arrive by car, park at the hotel and use the car for day trips. Drive to Cambridge only if you're feeling flush—you'll pay to park there, too. If you're not motoring and you decide to take a day trip (see chapter 11), you'll probably want to rent a car. Here's the scoop.

RENTALS

The major car-rental firms have offices at Logan Airport and in Boston, and some have other area branches. Seriously consider waiting to pick up the car until you need it, to save yourself the hassle of driving and parking. Rentals that originate in Boston carry a **$10 convention center surcharge**—you can get around it by picking up your car in Cambridge, Brookline, or another suburb.

If you're traveling at a busy time, especially during foliage season, reserve a car well in advance. Most companies set aside cars for nonsmokers, but you have to ask. To rent f-- the major national chains, you must be at least 25 years old and have a valid driver's license and credit card.

Companies with offices at the airport include **Alamo** (© 800/327-9633), **Avis** (© 800/831-2847), **Budget** (© 800/527-0700), **Dollar** (© 800/800-4000), **Hertz** (© 800/654-3131), and **National** (© 800/227-7368). **Enterprise** (© 800/325-8007) and **Thrifty** (© 800/367-2277) are nearby but not on the grounds, so leave time for the shuttle bus ride.

INSURANCE

If you hold a private auto insurance policy, you probably are covered in the U.S. for loss or damage to the car, and for liability in case a passenger is injured. The credit card you use to rent the car also may provide some coverage, but don't assume—check before you leave home.

Car-rental insurance typically does not cover liability if you caused the accident. Check your own auto insurance policy, the rental company policy, and your credit card coverage for the extent of coverage: Is your destination covered? Are other drivers covered? How much liability is covered if a passenger is injured? If you rely on your credit card for coverage, you may want to bring a second credit card with you, because damages may be charged to your card and you may find yourself stranded with no money.

Car rental insurance costs about $20 a day.

PACKAGE DEALS

Many packages include airfare, accommodations, and a rental car with unlimited mileage. Compare these prices with the cost of booking airline tickets and renting a car separately. Don't saddle yourself with a car for a long period if you won't be using it, though. And don't forget to add the price of parking.

BOOKING ONLINE

See the "Surfing for Rental Cars" section in chapter 2 for pointers on online booking.

PARKING

It's difficult to find your way around Boston and practically impossible to find parking in some areas. Most spaces on the street are metered (and patrolled until 6pm on the dot Mon–Sat) and are open to nonresidents for 2 hours or less

---

---

between 8am and 6pm. The penalty is a $25 to $40 ticket. Read the sign or meter carefully. In some areas parking is allowed only at certain hours. Rates vary in different sections of the city (usually $1 an hr. downtown); bring plenty of quarters. Time limits range from 15 minutes to 2 hours.

If you blunder into a tow-away zone, retrieving the car will cost you at least $100 and a lot of running around. The city tow lot (© **617/635-3900**) is at 200 Frontage Rd. in South Boston. Take a taxi, or ride the Red Line to Andrew and flag a cab.

It's best to leave the car in a garage or lot and walk, but be aware that Boston's parking is the second most expensive in the country (after Manhattan's). A full day at most garages costs no more than $25, but some downtown facilities charge as much as $35, and hourly rates can be exorbitant. Many lots charge a lower flat rate if you enter and exit before certain times or if you park in the evening. Some restaurants offer reduced rates at nearby garages; ask when you call for reservations.

The city-run garage under **Boston Common** (© 617/954-2096) accepts vehicles less than 6 feet, 3 inches tall. Enter from Charles Street between Boylston and Beacon streets. The **Prudential Center** garage (© 617/267-1002) has entrances on Boylston Street, Huntington Avenue, and Exeter Street, and at the Sheraton Boston Hotel. Parking is discounted if you buy something at the Shops at Prudential Center and have your ticket validated. The garage at **Copley Place** (© 617/375-4488), off Huntington Avenue, offers a similar deal. Many businesses in Faneuil Hall Marketplace validate parking at the **75 State St. Garage** (© 617/742-7275).

Good-size garages downtown are at **Government Center** off Congress Street (© 617/227-0385), at **Sudbury Street** off Congress Street (© 617/973-6954), at the **New England Aquarium** (© 617/723-1731), and at **Zero Post Office Square** in the Financial District (© 617/423-1430). In the Back Bay, there's a large facility near the Hynes Convention Center on **Dalton Street** (© 617/247-8006).

DRIVING RULES

When traffic permits, drivers may turn right at a red light after stopping, unless a sign is posted saying otherwise (as it often is downtown). Seat belts are mandatory for adults and children, children under 12 may not ride in the front seat, and infants and children under 5 must be strapped into car seats in the back seat. You can't be stopped just for having an unbelted adult in the car, but a youngster on the loose is reason enough to pull you over.

Be aware of two state laws, if only because drivers break them so frequently it'll take your breath away: Pedestrians in the crosswalk have the right of way (most suburbs actually enforce this one), and vehicles already in a rotary (traffic circle or roundabout) have the right of way.

BY BICYCLE

This is not a good option unless you're a real pro or plan to visit Cambridge, which has bike lanes. The streets of Boston proper, with their bloodthirsty drivers and oblivious pedestrians, are notoriously inhospitable to two-wheelers.

For information about renting a bike and about recreational biking, see "Biking" on p. 188 in chapter 7. If you bring or rent a bike, be sure to lock it securely when leaving it unattended, even for a short time.

 FAST FACTS: Boston

American Express The main office is at 1 State St. (© **617/723-8400**), opposite the Old State House. It's open weekdays from 8:30am to 5:30pm. The Back Bay office, 222 Berkeley St. (© **617/236-1334**), is open weekdays from 9am to 5:30pm. The Cambridge office, 39 John F. Kennedy St., Harvard Square (© **617/868-2600**), is open weekdays from 8:30am to 7:30pm, Saturday from 11am to 5:30pm, and Sunday from noon to 5pm.

Area Codes Eastern Massachusetts has eight area codes: Boston proper, **617** and **857**; immediate suburbs, **781** and **339**; northern and western suburbs, **978** and **351**; southern suburbs, **508** and **774**.

Note: To make a local call, you must dial all 10 digits.

ATM Networks Cirrus (© **800/424-7787**; www.mastercard.com), **PLUS** (© **800/843-7587**; www.visa.com), and **NYCE** (www.nycenet.com) cover most Boston-area banks.

Babysitters Many hotels maintain lists of reliable sitters; check at the front desk or with the concierge. Local agencies aren't a cost-effective option; most charge a steep annual fee on top of the daily referral charge and the sitter's hourly wage. If you're in town on business, ask whether the company you're visiting has a corporate membership in an agency.

Tip: If you already know that your visit will include a child-free evening out, make arrangements when you reserve your room.

Car Rentals See "Getting Around" earlier in this chapter.

Convention Centers **Hynes Convention Center**, 900 Boylston St. (© **617/954-2000** or 617/424-8585 for show info; www.jbhynes.com); **World Trade Center**, 164 Northern Ave. (© **800/367-9822** or 617/385-5000, or 617/385-5044 for show info; www.wtcb.com); **Bayside Expo Center**, 200 Mt. Vernon St., Dorchester (© **617/474-6000**; www.baysideexpo.com). The **Boston Convention & Exhibition Center**, 348 D St., South Boston (© **617/269-4924**; www.mccahome.com), is scheduled to open in the summer of 2004.

Dentists The desk staff or concierge at your hotel might be able to suggest a dentist. The **Massachusetts Dental Society** (© **800/342-8747** or 508/651-7511; www.massdental.org) can point you toward a member.

Doctors The desk staff or concierge at your hotel should be able to direct you to a doctor, but you can also try the physician referral service at one of the area's many hospitals. Among them are Beth Israel Deaconess (© **800/667-5356**), Brigham and Women's (© **800/294-9999**), Massachusetts General (© **800/711-4MGH**), and Tufts–New England Medical Center (© **617/636-9700**). An affiliate of Mass. General, **MGH Back Bay,** 388 Commonwealth Ave. (© **617/267-7171**), offers walk-in service and honors most insurance plans.

Driving Rules See "Getting Around" earlier in this chapter

Drugstores Downtown Boston has no 24-hour pharmacy. The pharmacy at the **CVS** at 155–157 Charles St. in Boston (© **617/523-1028**), next to the Charles T stop, is open until midnight. The pharmacy at the **CVS** in the Porter Square Shopping Center, off Mass. Ave. in Cambridge (© **617/876-5519**), is open 24 hours, 7 days a week. Some emergency rooms can fill your prescription at the hospital's pharmacy.

Embassies & Consulates See "Fast Facts: For the International Traveler" in chapter 3.

Emergencies Call © **911** for fire, ambulance, or the Boston, Brookline, or Cambridge police. This is a free call from pay phones. For the state police, call © **617/523-1212**.

Holidays See "Fast Facts: For the International Traveler" in chapter 3.

Hospitals **Massachusetts General Hospital,** 55 Fruit St. (© **617/726-2000**), and **Tufts–New England Medical Center,** 750 Washington St. (© **617/636-5000**), are closest to downtown. At the Harvard Medical Area on the Boston-Brookline border are **Beth Israel Deaconess Medical Center,** 330 Brookline Ave. (© **617/667-7000**); **Brigham and Women's Hospital,** 75 Francis St. (© **617/732-5500**); and **Children's Hospital,** 300 Longwood Ave. (© **617/355-6000**). In Cambridge are **Mount Auburn Hospital,** 330 Mount Auburn St. (© **617/492-3500**), and **Cambridge Hospital,** 1493 Cambridge St. (© **617/498-1000**).

Hot Lines **AIDS Hotline** (© **800/590-2437** or 617/451-5155), **Poison Control Center** (© **800/682-9211**), **Rape Crisis** (© **617/492-7273**), **Samaritans Suicide Prevention** (© **617/247-0220**), **Samariteens** (© **800/252-8336** or 617/247-8050).

Information See the "Orientation" section earlier in this chapter.

Internet Access For a tech-happy area, Boston has few cybercafes. Your hotel might have a terminal for guests' use. The ubiquitous **Kinko's** charges 10¢ to 20¢ a minute. Locations include 2 Center Plaza, Government Center (© **617/973-9000**); 10 Post Office Sq., Financial District (© **617/482-4400**); 187 Dartmouth St., Back Bay (© **617/262-6188**); and 1 Mifflin Place, off Mount Auburn Street near Eliot Street, Harvard Square (© **617/497-0125**). **Tech Superpowers,** 252 Newbury St., third floor (© **617/267-9716**; www.newburyopen.net), also offers access by the hour.

Liquor Laws The legal drinking age is 21. In many bars, particularly near college campuses, you might be asked to show identification if you appear to be under 30 or so. At sporting events, everyone buying alcohol must show ID. Liquor stores and a few supermarkets and convenience stores sell alcohol. Liquor stores (and the liquor sections of other stores) are closed on Sunday, but restaurants and bars may serve alcohol. Most restaurants have full liquor licenses; some serve only beer, wine, and cordials. Last call typically is 30 minutes before closing time (1am in bars, 2am in clubs). Some suburban towns, notably Rockport, are "dry."

Lost or Stolen Wallet Be sure to tell all of your credit card companies the minute you discover your wallet has been lost or stolen and file a report at the nearest police precinct. Your credit card company or insurer may require a police report number or record of the loss. Most credit card companies have an emergency toll-free number to call if your card is lost or stolen; they may be able to wire you a cash advance immediately or deliver an emergency credit card in a day or two. Visa's U.S. emergency number is ✆ **800/847-2911** or 410/581-9994. American Express cardholders and traveler's check holders should call ✆ **800/221-7282.** MasterCard holders should call ✆ **800/307-7309** or 636/722-7111. For other credit cards, call the toll-free directory at ✆ **800/555-1212.**

Identity theft or fraud are potential complications of losing your wallet, especially if you've lost your driver's license along with your cash and credit cards. Notify the major credit-reporting bureaus immediately; placing a fraud alert on your records may protect you against liability for criminal activity. The three major U.S. credit-reporting agencies are **Equifax** (✆ **800/766-0008;** www.equifax.com), **Experian** (✆ **888/397-3742;** www.experian.com), and **TransUnion** (✆ **800/680-7289;** www.transunion.com). Finally, if you've lost all forms of photo ID, call your airline and explain the situation; they might allow you to board the plane if you have a copy of your passport or birth certificate and a copy of the police report you've filed.

Luggage Storage & Lockers The desk staff or concierge at your hotel may be able to arrange storage. Lockers at the airport are unavailable indefinitely. Ticketed Amtrak passengers can check bags (during the day only) at South Station; Back Bay Station has no luggage facilities.

Maps See "Orientation" earlier in this chapter.

Newspapers & Magazines The *Boston Globe* and *Boston Herald* are published daily. See "Orientation" earlier in this chapter, for more information.

Pharmacies See "Drugstores" above.

Police Call ✆ **911** for emergencies.

Post Office The main post office at 25 Dorchester Ave. (✆ **617/654-5326**), behind South Station, is open 24 hours, 7 days a week.

Radio AM stations include **680** (WRKO: talk, sports, Celtics games), **850** (WEEI: sports, Red Sox games), **1030** (WBZ: news, Bruins games), **1090** (WILD: urban contemporary, soul), and **1510** (WWZN: sports talk). You can catch regular traffic updates on WBZ (every 10 min.) and WRKO (every 15 min.).

FM stations include **89.7** (WGBH: public radio, classical, jazz), **90.9** (WBUR: public radio, classical), **92.9** (WBOS: album rock), **93.7** (WQSX: dance hits), **94.5** (WJMN: dance, rap, hip-hop), **96.9** (WTKK: talk), **98.5** (WBMX: adult contemporary), **99.5** (WKLB: country), **100.7** (WZLX: classic rock), **101.7** (WFNX: progressive rock), **102.5** (WCRB: classical), **103.3** (WODS: oldies), **104.1** (WBCN: rock, Patriots games), **105.7** (WROR: '60s and '70s), and **106.7** (WMJX: pop, adult contemporary).

Restrooms The visitor center at 15 State St. has a public restroom, as do most tourist attractions, hotels, department stores, coffee bars, and public buildings. The CambridgeSide Galleria, Copley Place, Prudential Center, and Quincy Market shopping areas and most branches of Starbucks outlets have clean restrooms.

You'll find eight free-standing, self-cleaning **pay toilets** (25¢) around downtown. Locations include City Hall Plaza, up the steps from Congress Street, and Commercial Street at Snowhill Street, just off the Freedom Trail. Check these facilities carefully before using them; despite regular patrols, IV-drug users have been known to take advantage of the generous time limits.

Safety See "Staying Safe" in chapter 2.

Smoking Massachusetts is an anti-tobacco stronghold. In 2003, Boston banned smoking in all workplaces, including restaurants, bars, and clubs. Cambridge's laws are less strict, but a growing campaign to extend Boston's ban to the rest of the state may have succeeded by the time you visit. Always ask before lighting up.

Taxes The 5% sales tax does not apply to food, prescription drugs, newspapers, or clothing that costs less than $175; the tax on meals and takeout food is 5%. The lodging tax is 12.45% in Boston and Cambridge.

Taxis See "Getting Around" earlier in this chapter.

Television Stations include channels **2** (WGBH), public television; **4** (WBZ), CBS; **5** (WCVB), ABC; **7** (WHDH), NBC; **25** (WFXT), Fox; **38** (WSBK), UPN; and **56** (WLVI), WB. Cable TV is available throughout Boston and the suburbs.

Time Zone Boston is in the Eastern time zone, 5 hours behind Britain, 6 hours behind western Europe, and 3 hours ahead of Los Angeles. Daylight savings time begins on the first Sunday in April and ends on the last Sunday in October.

Transit Info Call ✆ **617/222-3200** for the MBTA (subways, local buses, commuter rail) and ✆ **800/23-LOGAN** for the Massachusetts Port Authority (airport transportation).

Weather Call ✆ **617/936-1234.**

5

Where to Stay

Boston has long had one of the busiest hotel markets, and some of the highest prices, in the country. Demand was softening even before the travel turmoil of late 2001, however, and although business has picked up somewhat, uncertainty continues to plague the market.

To innkeepers, the circumstances are more troublesome for being relatively unfamiliar: In the late 1990s, occupancy rates were so high that the factor determining the choice of hotel often wasn't price, location, or amenities, but room availability. A slew of new properties went into the pipeline back then; they started opening after the bubble had burst, putting the law of supply and demand back into play. These days, travelers may find that prices have held steady or even (particularly at slow times) dropped.

As you go through this chapter, keep Boston's relatively small size in mind, and check a map before you rule out a certain location. These listings match the neighborhood descriptions in chapter 4, "Getting to Know Boston." Especially downtown, the neighborhoods are so small and close together that the borders are somewhat arbitrary. The division to consider is **downtown versus the Back Bay or Cambridge,** and not, say, the Waterfront **versus** the Financial District.

With enough flexibility, you probably won't have much difficulty finding a suitable place to stay in or near the city, but it's always a good idea to make a reservation. Try to book ahead

if you plan on visiting between April and November, when conventions, college graduations, and vacations increase demand. Foliage season typically is the busiest and priciest time of year.

The scarcest lodging option in the immediate Boston area is the moderately priced chain motel. Land is so valuable and occupancy rates (usually) so high that developers build up, not out, and high-rises rather than family-oriented motor courts dominate the market. Brands that are bargains elsewhere may be pricey here—again, especially at busy times.

Every hotel in this area must accommodate both business travelers and families. That's not to say you'll trip over a hopscotch game in the elevator at the Ritz or a corporate takeover in the HoJo lobby, just that flexibility is the rule.

Most of the major hotel chains have a presence in the Boston area. There's a certain sameness to many of the larger establishments, but even that comes with a potential bonus: Hotels that share a corporate parent may offer flexibility. For instance, if one Starwood (Sheraton, Westin) property is overbooked, management can whisk you off to an affiliate and save you the trouble of calling around.

Besides Starwood, other chains operating in and around Boston include leisure-oriented Best Western, Holiday Inn, Howard Johnson, Ramada, and Radisson; luxury operators Fairmont, Four Seasons, Ritz-Carlton, and Sonesta; and

---

Tips **Last-Minute Pointers**

You waited until the last minute and you can't find a room. What to do?

- Call the **Hotel Hot Line** (*©* **800/777-6001**). A service of the **Greater Boston Convention & Visitors Bureau** (*©* **888/SEE-BOSTON** or **617/536-4100**; www.bostonusa.com), it can help make reservations even during the busiest times. It's staffed weekdays until 8pm, weekends until 4pm.
- If you're driving from the west, stop at the **Massachusetts Turnpike's Natick rest area** and try the reservation service at the visitor information center. If you arrive at Logan Airport without a room reservation (you daredevil), ask the staff at the **Visitor Service Center** in Terminal C for help.

---

business-traveler magnets Hilton, Hyatt, Marriott, and Wyndham (and Sheraton and Westin).

Rates in this chapter are for a double room; if you're traveling alone, single rates are almost always lower. The rates given here do not include the 5.7% state hotel tax. Boston and Cambridge add a 2.75% convention center tax on top of the 4% city tax, making the total tax 12.45%. Not all suburbs impose a local tax, so some towns charge only the state tax. These listings cover Boston, Cambridge, Brookline, and a few other convenient suburbs. (If you plan to visit a suburban town and want to stay overnight, see chapter 11 for suggestions.)

SAVING ON YOUR HOTEL ROOM

The **rack rate** is the maximum rate that a hotel charges for a room. Hardly anybody pays this price, however. To lower the cost of your room:

- **Ask about special rates or other discounts.** Always ask whether a price lower than the first one quoted is available, or whether any special rates apply to you. You may qualify for corporate, student, military, senior, or other discounts. Mention membership in AAA, AARP, frequent-flier programs, or trade unions, which may entitle you to special deals. Find out the hotel policy on children—do kids stay free in the room or is there a special rate?
- **Dial direct.** When booking a room in a chain hotel, you'll often get a better deal from the individual hotel's reservation desk than from the chain's main number.
- **Book online.** Many hotels offer Internet-only discounts, or supply rooms to Priceline, Hotwire, or Expedia at rates much lower than the ones you can get through the hotel itself. For pointers, turn to "Surfing for Hotels" on p. 25.
- **Remember the law of supply and demand.** Business-oriented hotels are busiest during the week, so you can expect discounts over the weekend, especially in Cambridge. Leisure hotels are most crowded and therefore most expensive on weekends, so discounts are usually available midweek.
- **Visit in the winter.** Boston-bound bargain hunters who don't mind cold and snow (sometimes *lots* of snow) aim for January through March, when you can find great deals, especially on weekends. The Convention & Visitors Bureau's "Boston Overnight! Just for the Fun of It" winter-weekend program targets suburbanites, but out-of-towners benefit, too.

- **Look into group or long-stay discounts.** If you come as part of a large group, you should be able to negotiate a bargain rate, because the hotel can then guarantee occupancy in a number of rooms. Likewise, if you're planning a long stay (at least 5 days), you might qualify for a discount. As a rule, expect 1 night free after a 7-night stay.
- **Avoid excess charges and hidden costs.** When you book a room, ask what the hotel charges for parking—almost every hotel in Boston and Cambridge charges a fee. Use your own cellphone, pay phones, or prepaid phone cards instead of dialing direct from hotel phones, which usually have exorbitant rates. If you know you'll be online a lot, seek out a hotel that offers free high-speed access. And don't be tempted by the minibar: Most hotels charge through the nose for water, soda, and snacks. Finally, ask about local taxes and service charges, which can increase the cost of a room by 15% or more.
- **Book an efficiency.** A room with a kitchenette allows you to shop for groceries and cook your own meals. This is a big money saver, especially for families on long stays.

LANDING THE BEST ROOM

Somebody has to get the best room in the house. It might as well be you. You can start by joining the hotel's frequent-guest program, which may make you eligible for upgrades. A hotel-branded credit card usually gives it owner free "silver" or "gold" status in frequent-guest programs. Always ask about a corner room. They're often larger and quieter, with more windows and light, and they often cost the same as standard rooms. When you make your reservation, ask if the hotel is renovating; if it is, request a room away from the construction. Ask about nonsmoking rooms (see box, "Where There's Smoke . . ." below), rooms with views, rooms with twin-, queen-, or king-size beds. If you're a light sleeper, request a quiet room away from vending machines, elevators, restaurants, bars, and discos. Ask for one of the rooms that have been most recently renovated or redecorated.

If you aren't happy with your room when you arrive, say so. If another room is available, most lodgings will be willing to accommodate you.

BED-AND-BREAKFASTS

Whether you're uncomfortable with chain hotels or just can't afford them, a B&B can be a good option. Home accommodations are usually less expensive than hotels and often more comfortable; most are near public transportation. As hotel prices soar, so does the popularity of B&Bs. Because most are small, they fill quickly; using an agency can save you a lot of calling around. An agency can match you with a lodging that accommodates your likes and dislikes, allergies,

---

Tips Where There's Smoke . . .

Accommodations reserved for nonsmokers have become the rule rather than the exception. However, nonsmokers should not assume that they'll get a smoke-free room without specifically requesting one. As hotels squeeze smokers into fewer and fewer rooms, the ones they use become saturated with the smell of smoke, even in lodgings that are otherwise antiseptic. To avoid this disagreeable situation, be sure that everyone who handles your reservation knows that you need a smoke-free room.

tolerance for noise and morning chitchat, and anything else you consider important. Reserve as soon as you start planning, especially if you hope to visit during fall foliage season.

At a B&B, expect to pay at least $75 a night for a double in the summer and fall, and more during special events. The room rate usually includes breakfast and often includes parking. Many lodgings require a minimum stay of at least 2 nights, and most offer winter specials—discounts or third-night-free deals.

The following organizations can help match you with a B&B in Boston, Cambridge, or the greater Boston area:

- **Bed and Breakfast Agency of Boston,** 47 Commercial Wharf, Boston, MA 02110 (© **800/248-9262,** 0800/89-5128 from the U.K., or 617/ 720-3540; fax 617/523-5761; www.boston-bnbagency.com)
- **Host Homes of Boston,** P.O. Box 117, Waban Branch, Boston, MA 02468 (© **800/600-1308** or 617/244-1308; fax 617/244-5156; www.hosthomesofboston.com)
- **Bed & Breakfast Reservations North Shore/Greater Boston/Cape Cod** (© **800/832-2632** outside Mass., 617/964-1606, or 978/281-9505; fax 978/281-9426; www.bbreserve.com)
- **Bed and Breakfast Associates Bay Colony,** P.O. Box 57166, Boston, MA 02457 (© **800/347-5088** or 617/720-0522; fax 781/647-7437; www. bnbboston.com)

1 Downtown

The downtown area includes most of the **Freedom Trail** and the neighborhoods defined in chapter 4 as the **Waterfront, Faneuil Hall Marketplace,** the **Financial District,** and **Downtown Crossing.** (The North End and Government Center are in the downtown area, too, but they don't have hotels.) Accommodations in the moderate and inexpensive price categories are mostly bed-and-breakfasts. For B&Bs, consult the agencies listed in the previous section.

THE WATERFRONT & FANEUIL HALL MARKETPLACE
At all hotels in these neighborhoods, **ask for a room on a high floor**—you'll want to be as far as possible from the noise and disarray of the Big Dig.

VERY EXPENSIVE
Boston Harbor Hotel 🟊🟊🟊   The Boston Harbor Hotel is one of the finest choices in town—and certainly the prettiest, whether you approach its landmark arch from land or sea (the Airport Water Shuttle stops here). The 16-story brick building is within walking distance of downtown and the waterfront attractions, and it prides itself on offering top-notch service to travelers pursuing both business and pleasure.

The plush guest rooms look out on the harbor or the skyline. Each standard unit is a luxurious bedroom/living-room combination, with mahogany furnishings that include an armoire, a desk, and comfortable chairs. Rooms with city views are less expensive, but just now I'd opt for the savings and an up-close look at the Big Dig (the water will always be there; the construction won't). If you don't share my fascination with the project, the best units are suites with private terraces and dazzling water vistas. *Tip:* The grand public spaces include a museum-quality collection of paintings, drawings, prints, and nautical charts.

Rowes Wharf (entrance on Atlantic Ave.), Boston, MA 02110. © 800/752-7077 or 617/439-7000. Fax 617/ 330-9450. www.bhh.com. 230 units. $375–$565 double; from $455 suite. Extra person $50. Children under

18 stay free in parent's room. Weekend packages available. AE, DC, DISC, MC, V. Valet parking $34 weekdays, $22 weekends; self-parking $30 weekdays, $17 weekends. T: Red Line to South Station or Blue Line to Aquarium. Pets accepted. **Amenities:** Excellent restaurant (New England); cafe; bar (p. 113); 60-ft. indoor lap pool; well-appointed health club and spa; concierge; courtesy car; state-of-the-art business center with professional staff; 24-hr. room service; in-room massage; babysitting; laundry service; dry cleaning; video rentals. Rooms for travelers with disabilities are available. *In room:* A/C, TV, dataport, minibar, hair dryer, robes.

Boston Marriott Long Wharf ⋆

The chief appeal of this standard-issue Marriott is its location, a stone's throw from the New England Aquarium. It attracts business travelers with its proximity to the Financial District and woos families with its easy access to downtown and waterfront attractions. The terraced brick exterior of the seven-story hotel is one of the most recognizable sights on the harbor.

Rooms and bathrooms underwent renovation in 2002; each large unit has either one king-size or two double beds, and a table and chairs in front of the window. Big Dig construction is directly under the windows of the rooms near the street. Ask to be as close to the water as possible and you'll have good views of the wharves and the waterfront without the attendant noise.

296 State St. (at Atlantic Ave.), Boston, MA 02109. ℂ 800/228-9290 or 617/227-0800. Fax 617/227-2867. www.marriott.com. 400 units. Apr–Nov $249–$450 double; Dec–Mar $159–$279 double; $450–$490 suite year-round. Weekend packages available. AE, DC, DISC, MC, V. Parking $32. T: Blue Line to Aquarium. **Amenities:** Restaurant (seafood); cafe and lounge; bar and grill; indoor pool; exercise room; Jacuzzi; sauna; game room; concierge; business center; room service until 1am; laundry service; dry cleaning; executive-level rooms. Rooms for travelers with disabilities are available. *In room:* A/C, TV, dataport, coffeemaker, hair dryer, iron, umbrella.

Millennium Bostonian Hotel ⋆⋆

The relatively small Bostonian offers excellent service and features that make it competitive with larger hotels. Although it doesn't provide wall-to-wall business features, it's popular with travelers who want a break from more convention-oriented rivals, as well as vacationers who appreciate the boutique atmosphere.

The traditionally appointed guest rooms vary in size. All boast top-of-the-line furnishings and amenities, with thoughtful extras such as heat lamps in the bathrooms. Half of the units have French doors that open onto small private balconies; the plushest rooms are good-size suites with working fireplaces or Jacuzzis. Soundproofing throughout allows views of Faneuil Hall Marketplace, Haymarket, or the Big Dig, without the accompanying noise. Three brick 19th-century buildings make up the hotel; the 38 units in the newest wing, added in 1999, include a suite and four rooms on the glass-enclosed top floor.

At Faneuil Hall Marketplace, 40 North St., Boston, MA 02109. ℂ 800/343-0922 or 617/523-3600. Fax 617/523-2454. www.millenniumhotels.com. 201 units. $149–$299 double; $265–$450 deluxe double; $439–$775 suite. Extra person $20. Children under 18 stay free in parent's room. Weekend and other packages available. AE, DC, DISC, MC, V. Valet parking $33 weekdays, $35 weekends. T: Green or Blue Line to Government Center, or Orange Line to Haymarket. **Amenities:** Restaurant (contemporary American); lobby lounge (The Atrium, p. 243); small fitness room; free access to nearby health club with swimming pool; in-room exercise equipment delivery on request; concierge; car-rental desk; business center; 24-hr. room service; in-room massage; babysitting; laundry service; same-day dry cleaning; executive-level rooms. Rooms for travelers with disabilities are available. *In room:* A/C, TV w/pay movies, dataport, minibar, hair dryer, iron, safe, umbrella, robes.

MODERATE

Harborside Inn ⋆⋆ *Value*

Under the same management as the Newbury Guest House in the Back Bay, the Harborside Inn offers a similar combination of location and (for this neighborhood) value. The renovated 1858 warehouse is across the street from Faneuil Hall Marketplace and the harbor, a short walk from the Financial District, and near the heart of the Big Dig. The nicely

Boston Accommodations

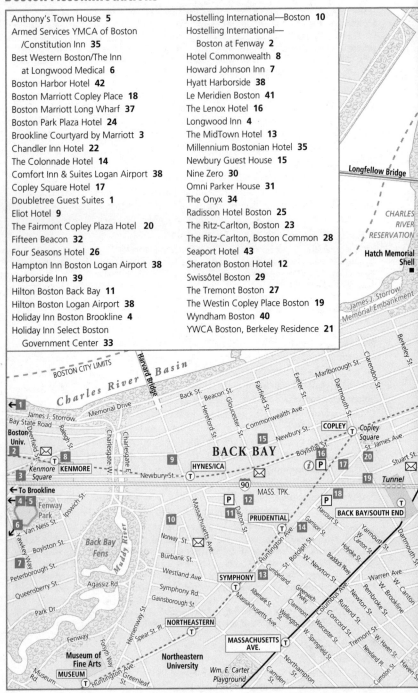

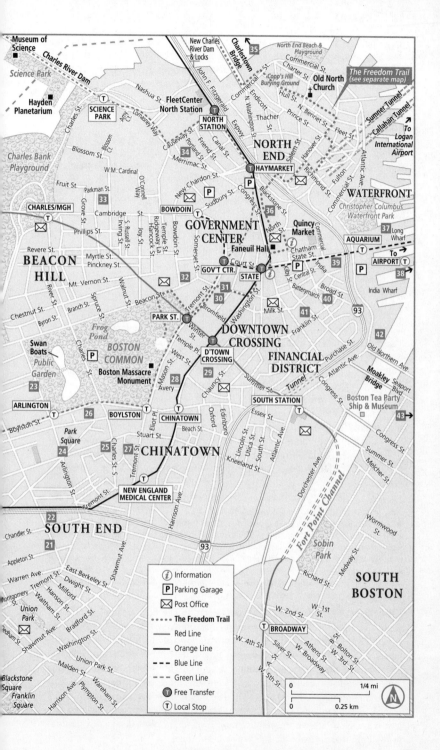

appointed guest rooms have queen-size beds, hardwood floors, Oriental rugs, and Victorian-style furniture. The rooms surround a sky-lit atrium; those with city views are more expensive but can be noisier. Still, they're preferable to the interior rooms, whose windows open only to the atrium. Rooms on the top floors of the eight-story building have lower ceilings but better views. The hotel has some features you'd expect at pricier lodgings, including free local phone calls and voice mail.

185 State St. (between I-93 and the Custom House Tower), Boston, MA 02109. © 800/437-7668 or 617/723-7500. Fax 617/670-2010. www.hagopianhotels.com. 54 units. $120–$210 double; $235–$310 suite. Extra person $15. Packages and long-term rates available. Rates may be higher during special events. AE, DC, DISC, MC, V. No parking available. T: Blue Line to Aquarium or Orange Line to State. **Amenities:** Restaurant (international bistro); access to nearby health club ($15); room service (lunch Mon–Fri, dinner Mon–Sat); laundry service; dry cleaning. Rooms for travelers with disabilities are available. *In room:* A/C, TV, dataport, hair dryer.

FINANCIAL DISTRICT & DOWNTOWN CROSSING

Besides being great for corporate travelers, the hotels in this area are closer than their Waterfront competitors to the major shopping areas and the start of the Freedom Trail. Especially in the winter, all offer sensational weekend packages.

VERY EXPENSIVE

Le Meridien Boston ★★   This is one of the best business hotels in the city, with the most central location if your destination is in the Financial District. Vacationing visitors, who seek out the excellent weekend rates, are near the waterfront and downtown attractions but not all that close to public transit. The multilingual staff and French style attract many international patrons.

Elegantly decorated and large enough to hold a good-size work area, the guest rooms have 153 configurations, including loft suites with two bathrooms. The glass mansard roof surrounds the top three stories, where a number of rooms have large sloped windows and excellent views. Buildings surround the hotel on three sides; the most desirable rooms are on the side that faces the park in Post Office Square. The imposing nine-story building, designed by R. Clipston Sturgis in 1922 in the style of a 16th-century Roman palace, originally housed the Federal Reserve Bank.

250 Franklin St. (at Post Office Sq.), Boston, MA 02110. © 800/543-4300 or 617/451-1900. Fax 617/423-2844. www.lemeridienboston.com. 326 units. $295–$515 double; $485–$1,330 suite. Extra person $30. Weekend rates from $159 per night. AE, DC, DISC, MC, V. Valet parking $39 Sun–Thurs, $25 Fri–Sat; self-parking $28 Sun–Thurs, $8 Fri–Sat. T: Red Line to Downtown Crossing or South Station, or Blue or Orange Line to State. Pets accepted. **Amenities:** Restaurant (French); cafe with Sun jazz brunch and Sat "Chocolate Bar Buffet" (Sept–May); bar with live piano most nights; 40-ft. indoor pool; well-equipped health club; concierge; weekend courtesy car to Newbury St.; staffed business center with library; 24-hr. room service; in-room massage; laundry service; same-day dry cleaning. Rooms for travelers with disabilities are available. *In room:* A/C, TV, fax, dataport, minibar, coffeemaker, hair dryer, iron, safe, robes.

Nine Zero ★   This is anything but a traditional Boston hotel. Sleek and sophisticated, it feels almost like a transplant from New York or L.A.—and that's a good thing. The decent-size guest rooms and oversize bathrooms contain opulent appointments, including luxurious linens, down comforters, cordless two-line phones, and extensive business features. The contemporary boutique atmosphere distinguishes Nine Zero from the more old-fashioned establishments that dominate this market. The 19-story hotel—new construction, not a rehab—opened in 2002. This neighborhood is convenient for both business and leisure travelers: It's within easy walking distance of most downtown destinations, and 2 blocks from the subway to Cambridge.

90 Tremont St. (near Bromfield St.), Boston, MA 02108. © **866/NINE-ZERO** or 617/772-5800. Fax 617/772-5810. www.ninezerohotel.com. 190 units. $289–$500 double; $500–$1,800 suite. Packages available. AE, DC, DISC, MC, V. Valet parking $32. T: Red or Green Line to Park St. Pets accepted. **Amenities:** Restaurant (modern French); bar; exercise room; access to nearby health club ($10); concierge; business center; 24-hr. room service; massage; babysitting; laundry service; same-day dry cleaning. Rooms for travelers with disabilities are available. *In room:* A/C, TV w/pay movies, high-speed Internet access, dataport, minibar, coffeemaker, hair dryer, iron, safe, umbrella, robes.

Swissôtel Boston ★ *Value* This centrally located 22-story hotel lives two lives. It's a busy convention and business destination during the week, and its excellent weekend packages make it a magnet for sightseers. The plain exterior contrasts with the elegant European style and luxurious appointments that take over in the second-floor lobby. Guest rooms cluster around four atriums with semiprivate lobbies, creating the effect of several small hotels in one. Rooms are large enough to hold sitting areas, a desk, and a settee; they have king-size or European twin-size beds. Ask for a room on a high floor; this neighborhood was ugly even before construction began all along nearby Washington Street.

1 Ave. de Lafayette (off Washington St.), Boston, MA 02111. © **888/73-SWISS** or 617/451-2600. Fax 617/451-0054. www.swissotel.com. 500 units. $250–$395 double; $280–$465 deluxe double; from $500 suite or Swiss Executive floor. Extra person $25. Children under 12 stay free in parent's room. Weekend packages from $139 per night. AE, DC, DISC, MC, V. Valet parking $30; self-parking $26. T: Red Line to Downtown Crossing, or Green Line to Boylston. Small pets accepted. **Amenities:** Restaurant (international); lounge; 52-ft. indoor pool; health club; sauna; concierge; high-tech business center; 24-hr. room service; laundry service; dry cleaning; executive-level rooms. Rooms for travelers with disabilities are available. *In room:* A/C, TV, dataport, minibar, coffeemaker, hair dryer, iron.

Wyndham Boston ★★ This luxury hotel is contemporary yet conservative—21st-century technology in an Art Deco package. The meticulously designed hotel (a complete rehab of the 1928 Batterymarch Building) opened in 1999. Like other downtown lodgings, it draws business travelers during the week and leisure travelers on weekends. The 14-story building is near Faneuil Hall Marketplace and the Waterfront, but not all that close (by downtown standards) to the T. The spacious guest rooms have 9½-foot ceilings and triple-glazed windows. The best units, on the upper floors, afford great views of the harbor and downtown. Soundproofing throughout makes the whole building—even the halls—exceptionally quiet. The Wyndham's closest competitor, literally and figuratively, is Le Meridien, which is less convenient to public transit but has a swimming pool.

89 Broad St., Boston, MA 02110. © **800/WYNDHAM** or 617/556-0006. Fax 617/556-0053. www.wyndham.com. 362 units. $215–$399 double weekdays, $169–$279 double weekends; $290–$474 suite weekdays, $244–$354 suite weekends. Children under 13 stay free in parent's room. Weekend, holiday, family, and other packages available. AE, DC, DISC, MC, V. Valet parking $32. T: Blue or Orange Line to State, or Red Line to South Station. **Amenities:** Restaurant (California-Italian); bar; 24-hr. exercise room; sauna; concierge; business center (staffed 7am–7pm); 24-hr. room service; laundry service; same-day dry cleaning; executive-level rooms. Rooms for travelers with disabilities are available. *In room:* A/C, TV w/pay movies, fax, dataport, minibar, coffeemaker, hair dryer, iron, safe, umbrella, robes.

EXPENSIVE

Omni Parker House ★★ The Parker House offers a great combination of nearly 150 years of history and extensive renovations. It has operated continuously longer than any other hotel in America (since 1855). A massive overhaul (completed in 2001) began when the detail-oriented Omni chain took over the hotel. The hotel underwent a complete upgrade and gained a business center and exercise facility. Guest rooms, a patchwork of more than 50 configurations,

---

Fun Fact **Food for Thought**

Yes, this is the Parker House of Parker House roll fame. The rolls were invented (if food is "invented") here, as was Boston cream pie.

That's not the hotel's only claim to fame. Malcolm X and Ho Chi Minh both worked there, and the room that's now Parker's Bar hosted the best-known group of guests: Henry Wadsworth Longfellow, Oliver Wendell Holmes, Ralph Waldo Emerson, Nathaniel Hawthorne, and sometimes Charles Dickens, who made up a literary salon called the Saturday Club.

---

aren't huge, but they are thoughtfully laid out and nicely appointed. Many overlook Old City Hall or Government Center. The range of features makes the hotel popular with business travelers, who can book a room with an expanded work area, as well as sightseers, who can economize by booking a small, less expensive unit—some are really tiny—or taking advantage of a weekend deal, especially in the winter. The pattern on the bedspreads, so gaudy that it's elegant, is a reproduction of the original, and the lobby of the 14-story hotel boasts its original American oak paneling.

60 School St., Boston, MA 02108. © **800/THE-OMNI** or 617/227-8600. Fax 617/742-5729. www.omni hotels.com. 551 units (some w/shower only). $179–$309 double; $249–$385 superior double; $209–$369 suite. Children under 18 stay free in parent's room. Weekend packages and AARP discount available. AE, DC, DISC, MC, V. Valet parking $35. T: Green or Blue Line to Government Center, or Red Line to Park St. Pets under 25 lb. accepted; $50 fee. **Amenities:** Restaurant (New England); 2 bars; 24-hr. exercise room; children's programs; concierge; business center; 24-hr. room service; laundry service; same-day dry cleaning; executive-level rooms. Rooms for travelers with disabilities are available. *In room:* A/C, TV w/pay movies and Nintendo, dataport, minibar, coffeemaker, hair dryer, iron, robes.

2 Beacon Hill

Less expensive lodgings in this neighborhood are mostly B&Bs. Save time by checking with the agencies listed in the introduction to this chapter.

VERY EXPENSIVE

Fifteen Beacon ★★ Nonstop pampering, high-tech appointments, and outrageously luxurious rooms make this boutique hotel *the* name to drop with the expense-be-hanged set. The 10-story hotel has attracted demanding travelers, especially businesspeople, since it opened in 2000. Management bends over backward to keep them returning, with attentive service and lavish perks—for instance, at check-in, guests receive business cards listing the personal phone and fax numbers they'll have during their stay. The individually decorated rooms contain queen-size canopy beds with Italian linens (300 thread count, of course), surround-sound stereo systems, gas fireplaces, and 4-inch TVs in the bathroom. "Studio" units have a sitting area. The lobby restaurant, though overpriced and a bit cramped, is one of the best places in the city to see (or be) movers and shakers, especially at breakfast.

15 Beacon St., Boston, MA 02108. © **877/XV-BEACON** or 617/670-1500. Fax 617/670-2525. www. xvbeacon.com. 61 units (some w/shower only). From $395 double; from $1,200 suite. Valet parking $30. T: Red or Green Line to Park, or Blue Line to Government Center. Pets under 20 lb. accepted. **Amenities:** Restaurant (French); bar; fitness room; free access to nearby health club; concierge; in-town courtesy car; 24-hr. room service; in-room massage; laundry service; same-day dry cleaning. Rooms for travelers with disabilities are available. *In room:* A/C, TV w/pay movies, fax/copier/printer, high-speed Internet access, dataport, minibar, hair dryer, iron, safe, umbrella, robes.

EXPENSIVE

The 10-story, 112-unit **Onyx,** 155 Portland St., near North Station (© **800/ KIMPTON;** www.onyxhotel.com), was under construction at press time and scheduled to open in late 2003. A Kimpton property (like Hotel Marlowe; see "Cambridge" later in this chapter), it's the closest full-service hotel to the FleetCenter.

Holiday Inn Select Boston Government Center ✦ At the base of Beacon

Hill, near Massachusetts General Hospital, this 15-story hotel was one of the chain's leaders in its battle for the business traveler. It also attracts guests with business at the hospital. The location is convenient to downtown, within walking distance of the Back Bay, and not far from East Cambridge. The recently renovated guest rooms are good-size and well appointed, with contemporary furnishings. Each has a picture-window view of the city or the State House (or the parking lot—ask to be as high up as possible). The building is part of a small retail complex with a supermarket and shops.

5 Blossom St., Boston, MA 02114. © **800/HOLIDAY** or 617/742-7630. Fax 617/742-4192. www.holiday-inn. com. 303 units. From $150 double. Extra person $20. Rollaway $20. Children under 19 stay free in parent's room. Weekend and corporate packages and 10% AARP discount available. AE, DC, DISC, MC, V. Parking $35. T: Red Line to Charles/MGH. **Amenities:** Restaurant (American); lounge; outdoor heated pool; small exercise room; concierge; tour desk; car-rental desk; room service until 11pm; coin laundry; same-day dry cleaning; executive-level rooms. Rooms for travelers with disabilities are available. *In room:* A/C, TV w/pay movies, dataport, coffeemaker, hair dryer, iron.

3 Charlestown

INEXPENSIVE

Armed Services YMCA of Boston/Constitution Inn In a corner of the

Charlestown Navy Yard, the Constitution Inn offers basic but comfortable accommodations and access to excellent fitness facilities at a great price. Room arrangements vary; most units have twin beds, and some have a queen or king. About half have kitchenettes, making this a good choice if you plan to eat some meals in. The rooms aren't fancy, but they're good-size and tastefully furnished. They occupy five floors of a six-story building about 5 blocks from the USS *Constitution* ("Old Ironsides"), the next-to-last stop on the Freedom Trail. Ask for a room that faces Second Avenue; the view from the back of the building (facing Chelsea St.) is grim.

Most guests are budget-conscious tourists; a few long-term lodgings are set aside for recovering members of substance-abuse groups. Guests have the use of the Partners/MGH shuttle bus, which runs to and from the east end of this building to North Station and Massachusetts General Hospital.

150 Second Ave., Charlestown Navy Yard, Charlestown, MA 02129. © **800/495-9622** or 617/241-8400. Fax 617/241-2856. www.constitutioninn.com. 147 units. $99 double. Discounts for active-duty, reserve, and retired military available. AE, MC, V. Parking $6 with hotel validation at garage 1 block away. T: Green or Orange Line to North Station, then shuttle bus, or ferry from Lovejoy Wharf to Navy Yard. Or Blue Line to Aquarium and ferry from Long Wharf to Navy Yard. **Amenities:** Access to fully equipped YMCA health club with Olympic-size indoor pool; shuttle bus; coin laundry. Rooms for travelers with disabilities are available. *In room:* A/C, TV, coffeemaker, hair dryer, iron.

4 South Boston Waterfront (Seaport District)

EXPENSIVE

Seaport Hotel ✦✦ (Kids) The independent Seaport Hotel rises out of the Big

Dig like the Emerald City, and it has an air of fantasy about it. The hotel was designed and built (by Fidelity Investments) with every feature the pampered, techno-savvy business traveler might dream of. It's across the street from the World Trade Center and about 10 minutes by cab from the airport or the Financial District. If you plan to take public transit, leave time for the hotel shuttle from South Station or for a long walk through and around heavy construction.

The decent-size rooms are exceptionally well appointed, with all the usual perks plus extras such as Logan Airport flight information on the TV and fog-free mirrors in the well-appointed bathrooms. The views (of the city, including the Big Dig, or the harbor) are excellent, especially from the higher floors. The kid-conscious staff, pool, and proximity to the Children's Museum make this a good choice for families, too. T-1 lines throughout the building (among other appealing features) and great weekend packages are some of the reasons the hotel has been busy since it opened in 1998.

1 Seaport Lane, Boston, MA 02210. ℂ 877/SEAPORT or 617/385-4000. Fax 617/385-5090. www.seaport hotel.com. 426 units. $189–$299 double; $450–$1,700 suite. Service charge $3 per room per night. Children under 17 stay free in parent's room. Weekend packages available. AE, DC, DISC, MC, V. Valet parking $30; self-parking $23. T: Red Line to South Station, then take free shuttle bus (or walk 20 min.). Or ferry from Lovejoy Wharf (behind North Station) to World Trade Center. Pets accepted. **Amenities:** Well-regarded restaurant (contemporary American); cafe; lounge; 50-ft. indoor pool; newly expanded health club; sauna; bike rental; concierge; car-rental desk; courtesy car; shuttle to South Station; 24-hr. business center with professional staff (7am–8pm); 24-hr. room service; massage; same-day dry cleaning; executive suites. In room: A/C, TV w/pay movies and Nintendo, minibar, coffeemaker, hair dryer, iron, safe, robes.

5 Chinatown/Theater District

VERY EXPENSIVE

The Ritz-Carlton, Boston Common ⚑   This plush, ultramodern hotel is at the heart of an enormous complex that incorporates offices, condos, a 19-screen movie theater, and the state-of-the-art Sports Club/LA. Challenging the Four Seasons's claim to the starriest visiting celebrities, the "new Ritz" opened in 2001. It boasts the cachet and top-notch service of the original, traditional Ritz (see "The Back Bay" below), without a ruffle in sight. The good-size guest rooms contain the latest in indulgent amenities, including luxury linens and feather duvets, and the large bathrooms have phones and a separate tub and shower enclosure. Guest rooms contain Bose radio/CD players; suites have Bang + Olufsen CD stereos. Rooms occupy the top four floors of the 12-story building, with the public spaces at street level. You'll pay more for a room with a view of the Common. This neighborhood is the urban-planning equivalent of a self-fulfilling prophesy: The area is not the greatest, but the presence of the hotel automatically improves it—and as the other phases of the development open, it's sure to get even better.

10 Avery St. (between Tremont and Washington sts.), Boston, MA 02111. ℂ 800/241-3333 or 617/574-7100. Fax 617/574-7200. www.ritzcarlton.com. 193 units. From $495 double; from $595 Club Level; from $695 suite. Weekend and other packages available. AE, DC, DISC, MC, V. Valet parking $34; self-parking $28. T: Green Line to Boylston. Pets accepted; $35 charge. **Amenities:** Restaurant (contemporary American); bar; lounge; free access to adjoining Sports Club/LA, 100,000-sq.-ft. facility with lap pool, complete spa services, salon, regulation basketball court, 10,000-sq.-ft. weight room, steam rooms, saunas, 5 exercise studios, 4 squash courts; concierge; business center; 24-hr. room service; in-room massage; babysitting; laundry service; same-day dry cleaning; club-level rooms. Rooms for travelers with disabilities are available. In room: A/C, TV w/pay movies, high-speed Internet access, minibar, hair dryer, iron, safe, umbrella, robes.

EXPENSIVE

Radisson Hotel Boston ⚑⚑   The chain is fairly new to the Northeast and the location isn't the most attractive, so this Radisson can be a pleasant surprise.

It's popular with business travelers, tour groups, and vacationers alike. Though less than scenic, the Theater District is convenient to both the Back Bay and downtown, and this would be a prime property anywhere. For starters, its guest rooms are among the largest in the city. Each has a private balcony (with great views from the higher floors), a sitting area, and a king or two queen beds. It underwent a complete renovation in 1997 and has another upgrade scheduled for late 2003; ask for a room away from the work area. The best units are the executive-level rooms on the top five floors of the 24-story building. The **Stuart Street Playhouse** (© **617/426-4499**), a small theater in the hotel, often stages one-person shows. The hotel also has an **indoor golf school** and practice facility (© **617/457-2699**).

200 Stuart St. (at Charles St. S.), Boston, MA 02116. © **800/333-3333** or 617/482-1800. Fax 617/451-2750. www.radisson.com/bostonma. 356 units (some w/shower only). $159–$359 double. Extra person $20. Cot $20. Cribs free. Children under 18 stay free in parent's room. Weekend, theater, and other packages available. AE, DC, DISC, MC, V. Valet parking $21; self-parking $19. T: Green Line to Boylston, or Orange Line to New England Medical Center. **Amenities:** Restaurant (steakhouse); cafe; indoor pool; exercise room; concierge; staffed business center; room service until 11pm; babysitting; laundry service; same-day dry cleaning; executive-level rooms. Rooms for travelers with disabilities are available. *In room:* A/C, TV w/pay movies, dataport, coffeemaker, hair dryer, iron.

MODERATE

The Tremont Boston   The Tremont, a Wyndham Historic Hotel, is as close to Boston's theaters as you can get without actually attending a show. The improving neighborhood is also convenient to downtown and the Back Bay. Wyndham announced its arrival by spending some $15 million on a renovation (completed in 2000) that expanded some units and spruced up all of them, but standard lodgings are still rather small and can be a bit dingy—if you're not happy with your room, ask to be moved to one that suits you better. The hotel books vacationers and tour groups, plus some business travelers. The public areas of the 15-story building capture the style that prevailed when the hotel was built in 1924. The original gold-leaf decorations and crafted ceilings in the huge lobby and ballrooms have been restored, and the original marble walls and columns have been refurbished.

275 Tremont St., Boston, MA 02116. © **800/331-9998** or 617/426-1400. Fax 617/482-6730. www.wyndham. com. 322 units (some w/shower only). $179–$349 double, winter $129–$309 double; $399–$599 suite. Extra person $20. Children under 17 stay free in parent's room. Weekend packages and 10% AAA discount available. AE, DC, DISC, MC, V. Valet parking $27. T: Orange Line to New England Medical Center or Green Line to Boylston. **Amenities:** Restaurant (American/Italian); cabaret bar; dance club (the Roxy, p. 236); exercise room; concierge; tour desk; airport shuttle; business center; room service until 11pm; dry cleaning. Rooms for travelers with disabilities are available. *In room:* A/C, TV w/pay movies, dataport, coffeemaker, hair dryer, iron.

6 The South End

Berkeley Street runs from the Back Bay across the Mass. Pike to the most convenient corner of the sprawling South End, where you'll find these two lodgings.

MODERATE

Chandler Inn Hotel 🎯 *Value*   The Chandler Inn is a bargain for its location, just 2 blocks from the Back Bay. It underwent $1 million in renovations in 2000, and even with the accompanying price hike, the comfortable, unpretentious hotel is still a deal. The revamped guest rooms have individual climate control and tasteful contemporary-style furniture, including desks, small wardrobes, and TV armoires. Each holds either a queen or double bed or two twin beds, without enough room to squeeze in a cot. Bathrooms are tiny, and the one elevator in the eight-story inn can be slow, but the staff is welcoming and help-ful. This is a gay-friendly hotel (Fritz, the bar next to the lobby, is a neighbor-hood hangout) and often books up early. Plan ahead.

26 Chandler St. (at Berkeley St.), Boston, MA 02116. (② 800/842-3450 or 617/482-3450. Fax 617/542-3428. www.chandlerinn.com. 56 units. Apr–Dec $139–$169 double; Jan–Mar $129–$139 double. Children under 12 stay free in parent's room. AE, DC, DISC, MC, V. No parking available. T: Orange Line to Back Bay. Pets under 25 lb. accepted with prior approval. **Amenities:** Lounge; access to nearby health club ($10); airport shuttle. *In room:* A/C, TV, dataport, hair dryer.

INEXPENSIVE

YWCA Boston, Berkeley Residence   This pleasant, convenient women-only hotel and residence offers a dining room, patio garden, piano, and library. The well-kept public areas also include a TV lounge. The dorm-style guest rooms are basic, containing little more than beds, but they're well maintained and comfortable—not plush, but not cells, either. That description might not seem to justify the prices, but check around a little before you turn up your nose.

40 Berkeley St., Boston, MA 02116. (② 617/375-2524. Fax 617/375-2525. www.ywcaboston.org. 200 units, none with bathroom. $56 single; $86 double; $99 triple. Rates include full breakfast. Long-term rates avail-able (3-week minimum). MC, V. No parking available. T: Orange Line to Back Bay or Green Line to Arlington. **Amenities:** Coin-op laundry; computer with Internet access. *In room:* No phone.

7 The Back Bay

BOSTON COMMON/PUBLIC GARDEN
VERY EXPENSIVE

Four Seasons Hotel ★★★   Many hotels offer exquisite service, a beautiful location, elegant guest rooms and public areas, a terrific health club, and won-derful restaurants. But no other hotel in Boston—indeed, in New England—combines every element of a luxury hotel as seamlessly as the Four Seasons. If I were traveling with someone else's credit cards, I'd head straight here.

Overlooking the Public Garden, the 16-story brick-and-glass building (the hotel occupies 8 floors) incorporates the traditional and the contemporary. Each spacious room is elegantly appointed and has a striking view. The best accom-modations overlook the Public Garden; city views from the back of the hotel aren't as desirable but can be engaging, especially from the higher floors. Chil-dren are catered to with bedtime snacks and toys, and you can ask at the concierge desk for duck food to take to the Public Garden. Small pets even enjoy a special menu and amenities. Larger accommodations range from executive suites with parlor areas for meetings or entertaining, to luxurious deluxe suites with sweeping views.

200 Boylston St., Boston, MA 02116. (② 800/332-3442 or 617/338-4400. Fax 617/423-0154. www.four seasons.com. 274 units. $425–$815 double; from $1,600 1-bedroom suite; from $2,200 2-bedroom suite. Weekend and family packages available. AE, DC, DISC, MC, V. Valet parking $36. T: Green Line to Arlington. Pets under 15 lb. accepted. **Amenities:** Restaurant (Aujourd'hui, p. 123); bar (Bristol Lounge, p. 243); heated 51-ft. pool and whirlpool overlooking the Public Garden; health club and spa; concierge; tour desk; car-rental desk; limo to downtown; airport shuttle; business center; 24-hr. room service; in-room massage; babysitting; laundry service; same-day dry cleaning. Rooms for travelers with disabilities are available. *In room:* A/C, TV w/pay movies, dataport, minibar, coffeemaker, hair dryer, iron, safe, umbrella, robes.

The Ritz-Carlton, Boston ★   This legendary hotel overlooking the Public Garden has attracted both the "proper Bostonian" and the celebrated visitor since 1927. A top-to-bottom $50 million restoration completed in 2002 upgraded the building throughout. One of the most traditional lodgings in town, it offers fewer amenities than its sister property in the Theater District and

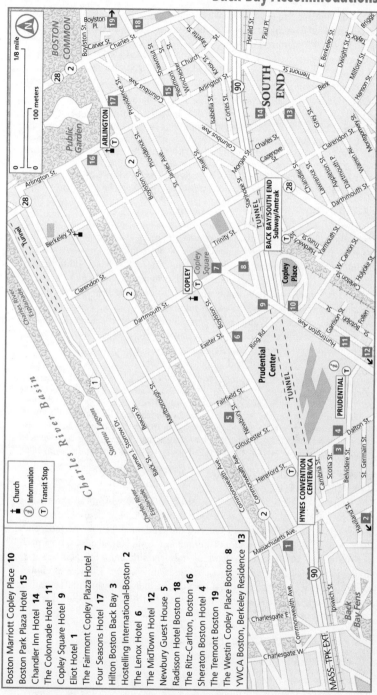

Boston Marriott Copley Place **10**
Boston Park Plaza Hotel **15**
Chandler Inn Hotel **14**
The Colonnade Hotel **11**
Copley Square Hotel **9**
Eliot Hotel **1**
The Fairmont Copley Plaza Hotel **7**
Four Seasons Hotel **17**
Hilton Boston Back Bay **3**
Hostelling International-Boston **2**
The Lenox Hotel **6**
The MidTown Hotel **12**
Newbury Guest House **5**
Radisson Hotel Boston **18**
The Ritz-Carlton, Boston **16**
Sheraton Boston Hotel **4**
The Tremont Boston **19**
The Westin Copley Place Boston **8**
YWCA Boston, Berkeley Residence **13**

the archrival Four Seasons (both have an on-premises health clubs with pools), but the original Ritz maintains the cachet accumulated during nearly 8 decades of doing everything in style.

The elegantly appointed guest rooms have plush linens, feather duvets, crystal chandeliers, three phones (1 in the bathroom), and windows that open. You'll pay more for a room with a view. The best units are the suites, which have wood-burning fireplaces; the "fireplace butler" can help you choose the right wood.

15 Arlington St., Boston, MA 02117. ⓒ **800/241-3333** or 617/536-5700. Fax 617/536-1335. www.ritz carlton.com. 273 units. $395–$525 double; from $600 suite. Extra person $20. Weekend packages available. AE, DC, DISC, MC, V. Valet parking $34. T: Green Line to Arlington. Small pets accepted; $35 charge. **Amenities:** 2 restaurants; bar; lounge; exercise room; access to Sports Club/LA ($20; see Ritz-Carlton, Boston Common listing, above); concierge; business center; 24-hr. room service; in-room massage; babysitting; laundry service; same-day dry cleaning; club-level rooms. Rooms for travelers with disabilities are available. *In room:* A/C, TV w/pay movies, high-speed Internet access, minibar, hair dryer, iron, safe, umbrella, robes.

EXPENSIVE

Boston Park Plaza Hotel 🖈   A Boston mainstay—it was built as the Statler Hilton in 1927—the Park Plaza Hotel does a hopping convention and function business. It's the antithesis of generic, with an old-fashioned atmosphere and a cavernous, ornate lobby, yet it offers modern comforts. A $60 million renovation completed in 2001 updated the hotel throughout, with new furniture, accessories, carpets, and bathtubs in the guest rooms. The least expensive units are quite small; if you're not a crash-and-dash traveler, the extra space might be worth the extra money. Don't expect personalized service in a hotel this large— the typical guest is busy with convention activities or meetings. The lobby of the 15-story building is a little commercial hub, with a travel agency, pharmacy, currency exchange, and Amtrak and airline ticket offices.

64 Arlington St., Boston, MA 02116. ⓒ **800/225-2008** or 617/426-2000. Fax 617/423-1708. www.boston parkplaza.com. 950 units. $139–$299 double; $375–$2,000 suite. Extra person $20. Children under 18 stay free in parent's room. Senior discount and weekend and family packages available. AE, DC, DISC, MC, V. Parking $27. T: Green Line to Arlington. Pets under 20 lb. accepted. **Amenities:** 2 restaurants; pub; bar (Whiskey Park, p. 242); exercise room; access to nearby health club ($20); concierge; airport shuttle; business center; salon; room service until midnight; laundry service; same-day dry cleaning; executive-level rooms. Rooms for travelers with disabilities are available. *In room:* A/C, TV w/pay movies, dataport, coffeemaker, hair dryer, iron.

COPLEY SQUARE/HYNES CONVENTION CENTER
VERY EXPENSIVE

The Colonnade Hotel 🖈🖈 *Kids*   The seasonal "rooftop resort" and swimming pool are probably this hotel's best-known features, with excellent service a close runner-up. Adjacent to Copley Place and the Prudential Center, the independently owned Colonnade is a slice of Europe in the all-American shopping paradise of the Back Bay. It caters to working travelers with a new business center, to fitness-conscious guests with a new exercise facility, and to children of all ages with the "VIKids" program and a rubber duckie in every bathroom. You might hear a dozen languages spoken by the guests and friendly, professional staff of the 11-story concrete-and-glass hotel.

⌒*Tips* **Planning Pointer**

If your trip involves a cultural event—for example, a big museum show or *The Nutcracker*—look into a hotel package that includes tickets. Usually offered on weekends, these deals always save time and can save money.

The elegance of the quiet, high-ceilinged public spaces carries over to the large guest rooms, which were spruced up in 2000. All have contemporary oak or mahogany furnishings and marble bathrooms (each with its own phone). Units on the Huntington Avenue side overlook the bustling Prudential Center complex, while rooms at the back survey the pleasant patchwork of the South End. Suites have dining rooms and sitting areas, and the "author's suite" contains autographed copies of the work of celebrated (or at least published) literary guests.

120 Huntington Ave., Boston, MA 02116. © **800/962-3030** or 617/424-7000. Fax 617/424-1717. www. colonnadehotel.com. 285 units. $199–$450 double; $575–$1,600 suite. Children under 12 stay free in parent's room. Weekend, family, and other packages available. AE, DC, DISC, MC, V. Parking $29. T: Green Line E to Prudential. Pets accepted. **Amenities:** Restaurant (Brasserie Jo, p. 129); bar; heated outdoor rooftop pool; fitness center; concierge; business center; 24-hr. room service; laundry service; same-day dry cleaning. Rooms for travelers with disabilities are available. *In room:* A/C, TV w/pay movies, fax, high-speed Internet access, dataport, minibar, hair dryer, iron, safe, umbrella, robes, CD player.

Eliot Hotel ★★

This exquisite hotel combines the flavor of Yankee Boston with European-style service and abundant amenities. On tree-lined Commonwealth Avenue, it feels more like a classy apartment building than a hotel, with a romantic atmosphere that belies the top-notch business features. Every unit is a spacious suite with antique furnishings, traditional English-style chintz fabrics, down comforters, and authentic botanical prints. French doors separate the living rooms and bedrooms, and bathrooms are outfitted in Italian marble. Many suites have a pantry with a microwave. The hotel is near Boston University and MIT (across the river), and the location contrasts pleasantly with the bustle of Newbury Street, a block away.

370 Commonwealth Ave. (at Mass. Ave.), Boston, MA 02215. © **800/44-ELIOT** or 617/267-1607. Fax 617/ 536-9114. www.eliothotel.com. 95 units. $255–$435 1-bedroom suite for 2; $510–$750 2-bedroom suite. Extra person $20. Children under 18 stay free in parent's room. Packages available. AE, DC, MC, V. Valet parking $28. T: Green Line B, C, or D to Hynes/ICA. Pets accepted. **Amenities:** Restaurant (Clio, p. 123); concierge; business center; 24-hr. room service; in-room massage; babysitting; laundry service; dry cleaning. Rooms for travelers with disabilities are available. *In room:* A/C, TV/VCR, fax/copier/printer, high-speed Internet access, dataport, minibar, hair dryer, iron, robes.

The Fairmont Copley Plaza Hotel ★★

The "grande dame of Boston" is a true grand hotel, an old-fashioned lodging that recalls the days when an out-of-town trip (by train, of course) was an event, not an ordeal. Built in 1912, the six-story Renaissance-revival building faces Copley Square, with Trinity Church and the Boston Public Library on either side. Already known for superb service, the Copley Plaza has enjoyed a renaissance of its own since becoming a Fairmont property in 1996. In late 2002 it launched a $29 million renovation and redecoration of the spacious guest rooms, which should be complete by early 2004; the project is being done floor by floor, but ask for a room away from the work area just in case. The traditional furnishings, which include oversize desks, reflect the elegance of the opulent public spaces. Rooms that face the lovely square or Clarendon Street afford better views than those that overlook busy Dartmouth Street.

138 St. James Ave., Boston, MA 02116. © **800/441-1414** or 617/267-5300. Fax 617/247-6681. www. fairmont.com/copleyplaza. 390 units. From $249 double; from $429 suite. Extra person $30. Weekend and other packages available. AE, DC, MC, V. Valet parking $32. T: Green Line to Copley, or Orange Line to Back Bay. Pets under 20 lb. accepted; $25 fee. **Amenities:** 2 restaurants (steakhouse, New England); bar; lounge (Oak Bar, p. 243); exercise room; concierge; well-equipped business center; 24-hr. room service; babysitting; laundry service; dry cleaning. Rooms for travelers with disabilities are available. *In room:* A/C, TV w/pay movies, high-speed Internet access (when renovations are complete), dataport, minibar, hair dryer, iron, safe, umbrella, robes.

Kids Family-Friendly Hotels

Almost every hotel in the Boston area regularly plays host to children, and many offer special family packages. Moderately priced chains have the most experience with youngsters—you can't go wrong at a **Howard Johnson** or **Holiday Inn**—but their higher-end competitors put on a good show.

Units at the **Doubletree Guest Suites** (p. 92) are a great deal—they have two rooms in which to spread out, and they cost far less than adjoining rooms at any other hotel this nice. You can use the in-room coffeemaker and refrigerator to prepare breakfast, then splurge on lunch and dinner.

In the Back Bay, the **Colonnade Hotel** (p. 86) offers a family weekend package that includes parking, breakfast for two adults, up to four passes (2 adult, 2 children) to an attraction of your choice, and a fanny pack for younger guests that holds sunglasses, a pad and pen, a yo-yo, and a toy duck.

The **Seaport Hotel** (p. 81), near Museum Wharf, offers excellent weekend deals, splendid views of the Big Dig and the airport, underwater music piped into the swimming pool, and even a grandparent-grandchild package.

In Cambridge, the **Royal Sonesta Hotel** (p. 98) is around the corner from the Museum of Science and has a large indoor/outdoor pool. It fills the vacation months with Summerfest, which includes free use of bicycles, ice cream, and boat rides along the Charles River. On off-season weekends, the Family Fun package includes four passes to the Museum of Science or the Aquarium.

Another riverfront hotel, the **Hyatt Regency Cambridge** (p. 95), courts families with its pool, bicycle rentals, easy access to the banks of the Charles, and discounted rates (subject to availability) on a separate room for the kids.

Just across the street, **Hotel Marlowe** (p. 98) boasts an excellent location, the welcoming atmosphere that family travelers have come to expect from the Kimpton chain, and special weekend packages.

The Lenox Hotel ★★   The Lenox was the latest thing when it opened in 1900, and in its second century, it echoes that fin de siècle splendor everywhere, from the ornate lobby to the spacious, luxurious rooms. Because of its central location, the hotel is popular with business travelers, and its relatively small size and accommodating staff make it a welcome alternative to the huge convention hotels that dominate this neighborhood. The high-ceilinged guest rooms are large enough to contain sitting areas; custom-designed wood furnishings and marble bathrooms add to the anything-but-generic vibe. The best accommodations are the 12 corner units with wood-burning fireplaces; rooms on the top two floors of the 11-story hotel have excellent views.

61 Exeter St. (at Boylston St.), Boston, MA 02116. (℃ **800/225-7676** or 617/536-5300. Fax 617/236-0351. www.lenoxhotel.com. 212 units (some w/shower only). $250–$498 double; $695 fireplace suite. Extra person $20. Cots $20. Cribs free. Children under 18 stay free in parent's room. Corporate, weekend, and family

packages available. AE, DC, DISC, MC, V. Valet parking $32. T: Green Line to Copley. Pets accepted. **Amenities:** Well-regarded restaurant (contemporary American); bar; pub; small exercise room; bike rental; concierge; tour desk; car-rental desk; airport shuttle; business center; room service until 11:30pm; babysitting; laundry service; same-day dry cleaning. Rooms for travelers with disabilities and wheelchair lift to the lobby are available. *In room:* A/C, TV w/pay movies, dataport, hair dryer, iron, umbrella, robes.

EXPENSIVE

Boston Marriott Copley Place ☆   Yes, 1,147 units. This 38-story tower feels generic, but it does offer something for everyone—namely, complete business facilities, a good-size pool, and easy access to Boston's shopping wonderland. The guest rooms have Queen Anne–style mahogany furniture and are large enough to hold a desk and a table and either two armchairs or an armchair and an ottoman. As with the Back Bay's other high-rise lodgings, ask for the highest possible floor and you'll enjoy excellent views. This is New England's biggest convention hotel (the Sheraton Boston is larger but attracts more vacationers), so if you're not part of a group, you might feel out of place—but if you're planning at the last minute, a hotel this large offers pretty good odds of finding a room.

110 Huntington Ave., Boston, MA 02116. ℭ **800/228-9290** or 617/236-5800. Fax 617/236-5885. www. marriott.com. 1,147 units. $159–$329 double; $500–$1,200 suite. Children stay free in parent's room. Weekend and other packages available. AE, DC, DISC, MC, V. Valet parking $32; self-parking $28. T: Orange Line to Back Bay, Green Line to Copley, or Green Line E to Prudential. **Amenities:** 2 restaurants (Italian, American); sushi bar; sports bar; lounge; heated indoor pool; well-equipped health club; whirlpool; sauna; game room; concierge; tour desk; car-rental desk; airport shuttle; full-service business center; 24-hr. room service; massage; laundry service; dry cleaning; concierge-level rooms. Rooms for travelers with disabilities are available. *In room:* A/C, TV w/pay movies, dataport, coffeemaker, hair dryer, iron, safe.

Copley Square Hotel   The Copley Square Hotel offers a great location along with the pluses and minuses of its relatively small size. Built in 1891, the seven-story hotel extends attentive service that's hard to find at the nearby megahotels, without those giants' abundant amenities. If you don't need to engineer a corporate takeover from your room, it's a fine choice, but larger competitors generally offer more features for comparable prices. Each attractively decorated unit has a queen- or king-size bed or two double beds; some rooms are on the small side.

47 Huntington Ave., Boston, MA 02116. ℭ **800/225-7062** or 617/536-9000. Fax 617/236-0351. www. copleysquarehotel.com. 143 units (some w/shower only). $189–$295 double; $405 suite. Rates include afternoon tea. Children under 17 stay free in parent's room. Packages and senior discounts available. AE, DC, DISC, MC, V. Parking in adjacent garage $30. T: Green Line to Copley, or Orange Line to Back Bay. **Amenities:** 2 restaurants (barbecue, American); nightclub; exercise room; bike rental; concierge; tour desk; car-rental desk; airport shuttle; business center; room service until 11pm; babysitting; laundry service; same-day dry cleaning. Rooms for travelers with disabilities are available. *In room:* A/C, TV w/pay movies, dataport, coffeemaker, hair dryer, iron.

Hilton Boston Back Bay ☆   Across the street from the Prudential Center complex, the Hilton is primarily a business hotel, but vacationing families also find it convenient and comfortable. Guest rooms are large, soundproofed, and furnished in modern style, with oversize work desks. Units on higher floors of the 26-story tower enjoy excellent views. The weekend packages, especially during the winter, can be a great deal. Across the street is its closest competitor, the Sheraton, which is three times the Hilton's size (which generally means less personalized service), has a better pool, and books more vacation and function business.

40 Dalton St., Boston, MA 02115. ℭ **800/874-0663,** 800/HILTONS, or 617/236-1100. Fax 617/867-6104. www.hilton.com. 385 units (some w/shower only). $179–$295 double; from $450 suite. Packages and AAA discount available. Extra person $20. Rollaway $20. Children under 18 stay free in parent's room. AE, DC, DISC, MC, V. Valet parking $24; self-parking $17. T: Green Line B, C, or D to Hynes/ICA. Small pets accepted. **Amenities:** Restaurant (steakhouse); bar; heated indoor pool; well-equipped fitness center; concierge; 24-hr.

business center; room service until 1am; laundry service; dry cleaning; currency exchange. Rooms for travelers with disabilities are available. *In room:* A/C, TV w/pay movies, high-speed Internet access, dataport, fridge, coffeemaker, hair dryer, iron.

Sheraton Boston Hotel ★★   Its central location, range of accommodations, lavish convention and function facilities, and huge pool make this recently refurbished 29-story hotel one of the most popular in the city. It attracts both business and leisure travelers with direct access to the Hynes Convention Center and the Prudential Center complex. Because it's so big, it often has available rooms when smaller properties are full. A $100 million overhaul completed in 2001 upgraded the entire property, including the lobby and meeting facilities. The fairly large guest rooms are decorated in sleek contemporary style and contain the chain's signature sleigh beds. Units on the highest floors are suites and executive-level rooms, but even standard accommodations on higher floors afford gorgeous views.

39 Dalton St., Boston, MA 02199. © **800/325-3535** or 617/236-2000. Fax 617/236-1702. www.sheraton. com/boston. 1,215 units. $149–$369 double; suites from $400. Children under 17 stay free in parent's room. Weekend packages available. 25% discount for students, faculty, and retired persons with ID, depending on availability. AE, DC, DISC, MC, V. Valet parking $33; self-parking $32. T: Green Line E to Prudential, or B, C, or D to Hynes/ICA. Pets accepted. **Amenities:** Restaurant (New England); lounge; heated indoor/outdoor pool; well-equipped health club; Jacuzzi; sauna; concierge; car-rental desk; courtesy car; business center; 24-hr. room service; laundry service; same-day dry cleaning; executive-level rooms. Rooms for travelers with disabilities are available. *In room:* A/C, TV, coffeemaker, hair dryer, iron, safe.

The Westin Copley Place Boston ★★   Towering 36 stories above Copley Square, the Westin attracts business travelers, convention-goers, sightseers, and dedicated shoppers. Sky bridges link the hotel to Copley Place and the Prudential Center complex, and Copley Square is across the street from the pedestrian entrance. The spacious guest rooms—all on the eighth floor or higher—have traditional oak and mahogany furniture, including Westin's beloved pillow-top mattresses. All underwent refurbishment in 2000 and 2001. You might not notice any of that at first because you'll be captivated by the best views in town. Qualms that you might have had about choosing a huge chain hotel will fade as you survey downtown Boston, the airport and harbor, or the Charles River and Cambridge.

10 Huntington Ave., Boston, MA 02116. © **800/WESTIN-1** or 617/262-9600. Fax 617/424-7483. www. westin.com/copleyplace. 803 units. $239–$599 double; $289–$2,200 suite. Extra person $25–$50. Weekend packages available. AE, DC, DISC, MC, V. Valet parking $32. T: Green Line to Copley, or Orange Line to Back Bay. **Amenities:** 2 restaurants (a branch of New York's famous Palm steakhouse, and Turner Fisheries, a good choice for seafood); bar (Bar 10, p. 243); indoor pool; health club and spa; concierge; car-rental desk; airport shuttle; well-equipped business center; 24-hr. room service; in-room massage; laundry service; executive-level rooms. 48 guest units for travelers with disabilities adjoin standard units. *In room:* A/C, TV/VCR, high-speed Internet access, dataport, minibar, coffeemaker, hair dryer, iron, safe, robes.

MODERATE

The MidTown Hotel ★ *Value*   Even without free parking and an outdoor pool, this centrally located two-story hotel would be a good deal for families and budget-conscious businesspeople. It also books a lot of tour groups. It's on a busy street within easy walking distance of Symphony Hall and the Museum of Fine Arts. The well-maintained rooms are large, bright, and attractively outfitted, although bathrooms are on the small side. Some units have connecting doors that allow families to spread out. The best rooms are at the back of the building, away from Huntington Avenue. For business travelers: Many rooms have two-line phones, and photocopying and fax services are available at the front desk.

220 Huntington Ave., Boston, MA 02115. ℂ **800/343-1177** or 617/262-1000. Fax 617/262-8739. www.
midtownhotel.com. 159 units. $89–$209 double. Extra person $15. Children under 18 stay free in parent's
room. Packages and AAA, AARP, and government employees' discounts available, subject to availability. AE,
DC, DISC, MC, V. Free parking (1 car per room). T: Green Line E to Prudential, or Orange Line to Mass. Ave.
Amenities: Restaurant (breakfast only); heated outdoor pool; concierge; airport shuttle. *In room:* A/C, TV
w/pay movies, dataport, coffeemaker, hair dryer, iron.

Newbury Guest House ★★ *Value* After just a little shopping in the Back
Bay, you'll appreciate what a find this cozy inn is: a bargain on Newbury Street.
It's a pair of brick town houses built in the 1880s and combined into a refined
guesthouse. It offers comfortable furnishings, a pleasant staff, nifty architectural
details, and a buffet breakfast served in the ground-level dining room, which
adjoins a brick patio. Rooms are modest in size but nicely appointed and well
maintained. The largest and most expensive are the bay-window units, which
overlook the lively street. The Hagopian family opened the B&B in 1991, and
it operates near capacity year-round, drawing business travelers during weekdays
and sightseers on weekends. At these prices in this location, there's only one
caveat: Reserve early.

261 Newbury St. (between Fairfield and Gloucester sts.), Boston, MA 02116. ℂ **617/437-7666.** Fax 617/
670-6100. www.newburyguesthouse.com. 32 units (some w/shower only). $140–$195 double. Winter
discounts available. Extra person $15. Rates include continental breakfast. Rates might be higher during spe-
cial events. Minimum 2 nights on weekends. AE, DC, DISC, MC, V. Parking $15 (reservation required). T: Green
Line B, C, or D to Hynes/ICA. **Amenities:** Rooms for travelers with disabilities are available. *In room:* A/C, TV,
hair dryer.

INEXPENSIVE

Hostelling International–Boston This hostel near the Berklee College of
Music and Symphony Hall caters to students, youth groups, and other travelers in
search of comfortable, no-frills lodging. Accommodations are dorm-style, with six
beds per room. There are also a couple of private rooms. The hostel has two full
dine-in kitchens, 19 bathrooms, a large common room, and meeting and work-
shop space. It provides linens, or you can bring your own; sleeping bags are not
permitted. The enthusiastic staff organizes free and inexpensive cultural, educational, and recreational programs on the premises and throughout the Boston area.

Note: To get a bed during the summer, you must be a member of Hostelling
International–American Youth Hostels. For information and an application,
contact HI–AYH, P.O. Box 37613, Washington, DC 20013 (ℂ **202/783-
6161;** www.hiayh.org). If you are not a U.S. citizen, apply to your home country's hostelling association.

12 Hemenway St., Boston, MA 02115. ℂ **800/909-4776** or 617/536-9455. Fax 617/424-6558. www.boston
hostel.org. 205 beds. Members $32 per bed; nonmembers $35 per bed. Members $87 per private unit; non-
members $93 per private unit. Children 3–12 half-price; children under 3 free. MC, V. T: Green Line B, C, or D
to Hynes/ICA. **Amenities:** Airport shuttle; coin laundry; Internet access (for a fee). 1st-floor units and bathrooms are wheelchair-accessible; wheelchair lift at building entrance. *In room:* No phone; lockers.

Impressions

*I have just returned from Boston. It is the only thing to do if you find
yourself up there.*

　　　　　　　　　　　　　—Fred Allen, letter to Groucho Marx, 1953

*Never go to Boston. Boston is a singularly horrific city, full of surly
weirdos with scraggly beards and terrible manners.*

　　　　　　　　　　　　　—Cynthia Heimel, Sex Tips for Girls, 1983

8 Outskirts & Brookline

What Bostonians consider "outskirts" would be centrally located in many larger cities. Brookline starts about 3 blocks beyond Boston's Kenmore Square. Staying in this area means essentially becoming a commuter to downtown Boston (unless you're in town only to visit Fenway Park or the Longwood Medical Area). It's not a great choice if your destination is Cambridge because of the unwieldy public transit connections.

VERY EXPENSIVE

Scheduled to open in mid–2003, the **Hotel Commonwealth,** 650 Beacon St. (© **800/784-4000** or 617/927-4445; www.hotelcommonwealth.com), is a six-story, 150-unit luxury lodging in the heart of Kenmore Square.

EXPENSIVE

The 188-room **Brookline Courtyard by Marriott,** 40 Webster St., Brookline (© **800/321-2211** or 617/734-1393; fax 617/734-1392; www.brookline courtyard.com), opened in 2003 near the busy Coolidge Corner neighborhood. The eight-story hotel has a breakfast cafe, an indoor pool, an exercise room, and shuttle service to the nearby Longwood Medical Area.

Doubletree Guest Suites ★★ *Kids* *Value*   This hotel is one of the best deals in town—every unit is a two-room suite with a living room, bedroom, and bathroom. Business travelers can entertain in their rooms, and families can spread out, making this a good choice for both (see "Family-Friendly Hotels" on p. 88). Overlooking the Charles River at the Allston/Cambridge exit of the Mass. Pike, the hotel is near Cambridge and the riverfront bike-and-jogging path, but not in an actual neighborhood. Room rates include scheduled van service to and from attractions and business areas in Boston and Cambridge, making the somewhat inconvenient location easier to handle.

The suites, which were renovated in 2002, surround a 15-story atrium. Rooms are large and attractively furnished, and most bedrooms have a king-size bed (some have 2 oversize twins) and a writing desk. Each living room contains a full-size sofa bed, a dining table, and a good-size refrigerator. The Hyatt Regency Cambridge, the hotel's nearest rival, is more convenient but generally more expensive.

400 Soldiers Field Rd., Boston, MA 02134. © **800/222-TREE** or 617/783-0090. Fax 617/783-0897. www. doubletree.com. 308 units. $129–$309 double. Extra person $20. Children under 18 stay free in parent's room. Weekend packages $154–$264. AARP and AAA discounts available. AE, DC, DISC, MC, V. Parking $20. **Amenities:** Restaurant (American); lounge; excellent Scullers Jazz Club (p. 238); indoor pool; exercise room; free access to nearby health club; whirlpool; sauna; concierge; car-rental desk; shuttle service; 24-hr. business center; 24-hr. room service; babysitting; coin laundry; laundry service; same-day dry cleaning. Suites for travelers with disabilities on each floor. *In room:* A/C, TV w/pay movies, dataport, minibar, fridge, coffeemaker, hair dryer, iron.

MODERATE

Best Western Boston/The Inn at Longwood Medical ★   Next to Children's Hospital in the Longwood Medical Area, this eight-story hotel is a good base for those with business at the hospitals. Beth Israel Deaconess and Brigham and Women's hospitals, the Dana-Farber Cancer Institute, and the Joslin Diabetes Center are within walking distance. Near museums, colleges, and Fenway Park, the hotel is about 20 minutes from downtown Boston by T.

Guest rooms are quite large and furnished in contemporary style, and rates include free local phone calls. Try to stay on the highest floor possible, not just

Accommodations from Mass. Ave. to Brookline

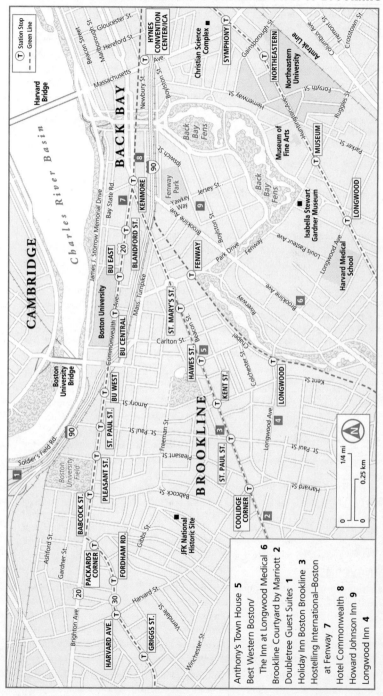

Anthony's Town House 5
Best Western Boston/
The Inn at Longwood Medical 6
Brookline Courtyard by Marriott 2
Doubletree Guest Suites 1
Holiday Inn Boston Brookline 3
Hostelling International–Boston
at Fenway 7
Hotel Commonwealth 8
Howard Johnson Inn 9
Longwood Inn 4

(T) Station Stop
- - - Green Line

CAMBRIDGE

Charles River Basin

Harvard Bridge

Boston University Bridge

BACK BAY

BROOKLINE

HYNES CONVENTION CENTER/ICA

Christian Science Complex ■

SYMPHONY

NORTHEASTERN

Northeastern University

Amtrak Line

Museum of Fine Arts

MUSEUM

Isabella Stewart Gardner Museum ■

Harvard Medical School

LONGWOOD

Back Bay Fens

Fenway Park

KENMORE

BU EAST

BLANDFORD ST.

FENWAY

ST. MARY'S ST.

HAWES ST.

KENT ST.

LONGWOOD

Boston University

BU CENTRAL

BU WEST

ST. PAUL ST.

PLEASANT ST.

BABCOCK ST.

PACKARDS CORNER

FORDHAM RD.

HARVARD AVE.

GRIGGS ST.

ST. PAUL ST.

COOLIDGE CORNER

JFK National Historic Site ■

Boston University Field

93

because the views are better but because the busy intersection of Longwood and Brookline avenues is less than scenic. Suites have kitchen facilities that make them a good choice for long-term guests. The hotel adjoins the Longwood Galleria business complex, which has a food court and shops, including a drugstore.

342 Longwood Ave., Boston, MA 02115. ℂ 800/468-2378 or 617/731-4700. TDD 617/731-9088. Fax 617/731-6273. www.innatlongwood.com. 161 units (18 w/kitchenette). $139–$209 double; $219–$259 suite. Extra person $15. Long-term discounts available. Children under 18 stay free in parent's room. AE, DC, DISC, MC, V. Parking $16. T: Green Line D or E to Longwood. **Amenities:** Restaurant (international); lounge; exercise room; access to nearby health club ($8–$10 per day); concierge; tour desk; airport shuttle; room service until 11pm; coin laundry; laundry service; same-day dry cleaning. Rooms for travelers with disabilities are available. *In room:* A/C, TV w/pay movies, dataport, coffeemaker, hair dryer, iron.

Holiday Inn Boston Brookline ★★
Just 15 minutes from downtown on the subway, this six-story hotel is more than just another Holiday Inn. In a mostly residential area not far from the Longwood Medical Area, it offers up-to-date accommodations at lower prices than more centrally located hotels. Many guests are visiting the nearby hospitals and Boston University. The recently redecorated rooms are large and well appointed, with oversize work desks. Units at the front of the building have more interesting views but overlook Beacon Street, where there's a busy trolley route. The bustling Coolidge Corner neighborhood is a 10-minute walk away.

1200 Beacon St., Brookline, MA 02446. ℂ 800/HOLIDAY or 617/277-1200. Fax 617/734-6991. www.holidayinnbrookline.com. 225 units (some w/shower only). $139–$239 double; $209–$309 suite. Extra person $10. Children under 18 stay free in parent's room. AE, MC, V. Parking $12. T: Green Line C to St. Paul St. Pets accepted; $15 charge. **Amenities:** Restaurant (American); lounge; coffee shop; small indoor pool; exercise room; whirlpool; shuttle to hospitals; laundry service; same-day dry cleaning. Rooms for travelers with disabilities are available. *In room:* A/C, TV, dataport, coffeemaker, hair dryer, iron.

Howard Johnson Inn
This motel is as close to Fenway Park as you can get without buying a ticket. The outdoor pool and free parking make it particularly attractive to vacationing families. The rooms are of a decent size; some have microwaves and refrigerators (convenient if you plan to eat some meals in). The busy street in a commercial-residential neighborhood is convenient to the Back Bay, the Museum of Fine Arts, and the Isabella Stewart Gardner Museum, but not all that close to public transit—a consideration when you're hauling kids through the summer heat. During baseball season, guests contend with crowded sidewalks and raucous Red Sox fans who flood the area.

1271 Boylston St., Boston, MA 02215. ℂ 800/446-4656 or 617/267-8300. Fax 617/267-2763. www.hojo.com. 94 units. $125–$195 double. Extra person $10. Children under 18 stay free in parent's room. Family packages and senior and AAA discounts available. AE, DC, DISC, MC, V. Free parking. T: Green Line B, C, or D to Kenmore; 10-min. walk. Pets accepted. **Amenities:** Restaurant (steakhouse); lounge; outdoor pool; babysitting; laundry service; dry cleaning. *In room:* A/C, TV, dataport, coffeemaker.

INEXPENSIVE

A summer-only hostel occupies a former Howard Johnson hotel just outside Kenmore Square: **Hostelling International—Boston at Fenway,** 575 Commonwealth Ave. (ℂ **617/267-8599;** fax 617/424-6558; www.bostonhostel.org; T: Green Line B, C, or D to Kenmore). The 485-bed hostel charges $35 per person for well-equipped accommodations in a building that doubles as a Boston University dorm during the school year.

Anthony's Town House
The Anthony family has operated this four-story brownstone guesthouse since 1944, and a stay here is very much like tagging along with a friend who's spending the night at Grandma's. Many patrons are Europeans accustomed to guesthouse accommodations with shared bathrooms,

but budget-minded Americans won't be disappointed. Each floor has three high-ceilinged rooms furnished in rather ornate Queen Anne or Victorian style, and a bathroom with enclosed shower. Smaller rooms (1 per floor) have twin beds; the large front rooms have bay windows. Guests have the use of two refrigerators. The guesthouse is 1 mile from Boston's Kenmore Square, about 15 minutes from downtown by T, and 2 blocks from a busy commercial strip. The late-19th-century building is listed on the National Register of Historic Places.

1085 Beacon St., Brookline, MA 02446. ℂ **617/566-3972.** Fax 617/232-1085. www.anthonystownhouse. com. 12 units, none with private bathroom. $68–$98 double. Extra person $10. Weekly rates and winter discounts available. No credit cards. Limited free parking. T: Green Line C to Hawes St. *In room:* A/C, TV, no phone.

Longwood Inn In a residential area 3 blocks from the Boston-Brookline border, this well-maintained three-story Victorian guesthouse offers comfortable accommodations at modest rates. Guests have the use of a fully equipped kitchen, common dining room, and TV lounge. There's one apartment with a private bathroom, kitchen, and balcony. Tennis courts, a running track, and a playground at the school next door are open to the public. Public transportation is easily accessible, and the Longwood Medical Area and busy Coolidge Corner neighborhood are within walking distance.

123 Longwood Ave., Brookline, MA 02446. ℂ **617/566-8615.** Fax 617/738-1070. go.boston.com/long woodinn. 22 units, 17 with private bathroom (4 w/shower only). Apr–Nov $89–$109 double; Dec–Mar $69–$89 double. 1-bedroom apt. (sleeps 4-plus) $99–$119. Weekly rates available. No credit cards. Free parking. T: Green Line D to Longwood, or C to Coolidge Corner. **Amenities:** Coin laundry. *In room:* A/C.

9 Cambridge

A city so close to Boston that they're usually thought of as one, Cambridge has its own attractions and excellent hotels. Graduation season (May and early June) is especially busy, but campus events can cause high demand at unexpected times, so plan ahead.

VERY EXPENSIVE

The Charles Hotel ⭐⭐⭐ This nine-story brick hotel a block from Harvard Square has been *the* place for business and leisure travelers to Cambridge since it opened in 1985. Much of its fame derives from its excellent restaurants, jazz bar, and day spa; the service is equally impeccable. In the newly refurbished guest rooms, the style is contemporary country, with custom adaptations of early American Shaker furniture. The austere design contrasts with the indulgent amenities, which include down quilts and state-of-the-art Bose Wave radios; bathrooms contain telephones and TVs. And it wouldn't be Cambridge if your intellectual needs went unfulfilled—there's a library in the lobby.

1 Bennett St., Cambridge, MA 02138. ℂ **800/882-1818** outside Mass. or 617/864-1200. Fax 617/864-5715. www.charleshotel.com. 293 units. $229–$599 double; $279–$4,000 suite. Extra person $20. Weekend packages available. AE, DC, MC, V. Valet parking $28; self-parking $20. T: Red Line to Harvard. Pets under 25 lb. accepted; $50 fee. **Amenities:** 2 restaurants (Rialto, one of Boston's best [p. 134], and Henrietta's Table, with a lavish Sun brunch); bar; Regattabar jazz club (p. 238); free access to adjacent health club with glass-enclosed pool, Jacuzzi, and exercise room; adjacent spa and salon; concierge; car-rental desk; business center; 24-hr. room service; in-room massage; babysitting; same-day dry cleaning. Rooms for travelers with disabilities are available. *In room:* A/C, TV/DVD w/pay movies, high-speed Internet access, minibar, hair dryer, iron, safe, umbrella, robes.

The Hyatt Regency Cambridge ⭐⭐ *Kids* The location is the Hyatt Regency's main drawback but also part of its appeal. Across the street from the

Cambridge Accommodations

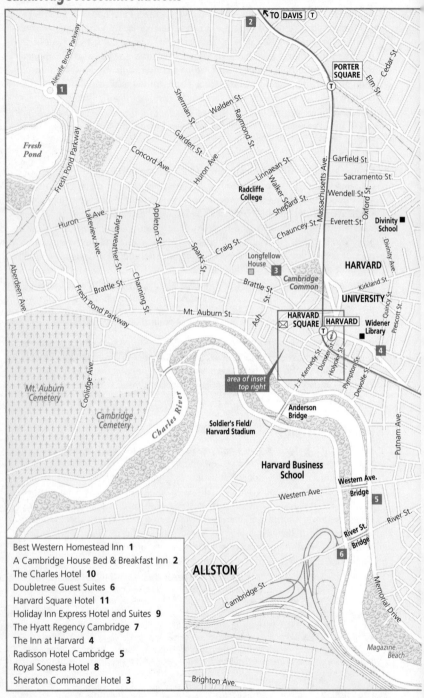

Best Western Homestead Inn **1**
A Cambridge House Bed & Breakfast Inn **2**
The Charles Hotel **10**
Doubletree Guest Suites **6**
Harvard Square Hotel **11**
Holiday Inn Express Hotel and Suites **9**
The Hyatt Regency Cambridge **7**
The Inn at Harvard **4**
Radisson Hotel Cambridge **5**
Royal Sonesta Hotel **8**
Sheraton Commander Hotel **3**

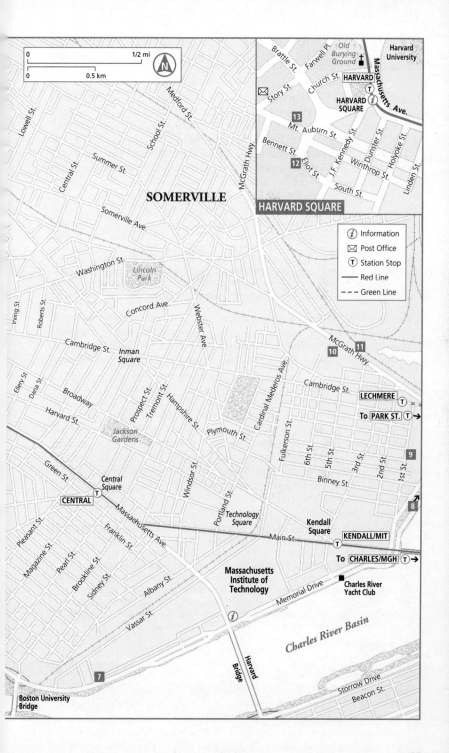

Charles River and not far from the Allston/Brighton exit of the turnpike, it's a self-contained destination that's convenient to Kendall and Harvard squares and Boston University. Scheduled shuttle service and luxurious appointments help make up for the not-exactly taxing distance from downtown Boston (about 10 min. by car). The dramatic brick building encloses a 16-story atrium with glass elevators, fountains, trees, and balconies. The best of the spacious guest rooms, which were last renovated in 1997, afford breathtaking views of Boston and the river. A business destination during the week, the hotel also courts families (see "Family-Friendly Hotels" on p. 88) with special two-room rates, subject to availability. If you plan to rely on public transit, allow plenty of time for bus rides, and acquaint yourself with the hotel shuttle schedule. The closest competitor is the Doubletree, which is even less centrally located but consists of all suites.

575 Memorial Dr., Cambridge, MA 02139. ☎ **800/233-1234** or 617/492-1234. Fax 617/491-6906. www.cambridge.hyatt.com. 469 units (some w/shower only). $245–$465 double weekday; $129–$309 double weekend; $450–$750 suite. Extra person $25. Children under 18 stay free in parent's room. Weekend packages available. AE, DC, DISC, MC, V. Valet parking $22; self-parking $20. **Amenities:** Revolving rooftop restaurant and lounge (Italian); lobby restaurant and lounge (international); 75-ft. indoor lap pool; health club; Jacuzzi; sauna; bike rental; concierge; shuttle to Cambridge and Boston destinations; business center; room service until late evening; laundry service; dry cleaning; ATM and currency exchange. Rooms for travelers with disabilities are available. In room: A/C, TV, fax, coffeemaker, hair dryer.

Royal Sonesta Hotel 🛊🛊 (Kids)   This luxurious hotel is in a curious location—it's close to only a few things but convenient to everything, making it a good choice for both business travelers and families (see "Family-Friendly Hotels" on p. 88). The CambridgeSide Galleria mall is across the street, and the Museum of Science is around the corner on the bridge to Boston, which is closer than Harvard Square. In the other direction, MIT and the techno hotbed of Kendall Square are 10 minutes away on foot. Even in the midst of all this activity, the hotel achieves a serene atmosphere, thanks in part to the ever-helpful staff. Most of the spacious rooms in the 10-story building have lovely views of the river or the city (higher prices are for better views). Everything is custom-designed in modern yet comfortable style, and regularly refurbished. Original contemporary artwork, including pieces by Andy Warhol and Frank Stella, hangs throughout the public spaces and guest rooms. The closest competition is the new Hotel Marlowe, across the street, which offers less extensive fitness options (there's no pool) and fewer river views.

5 Cambridge Pkwy., Cambridge, MA 02142. ☎ **800/SONESTA** or 617/806-4200. Fax 617/806-4232. www.sonesta.com/boston. 400 units (some w/shower only). $239–$279 standard double; $259–$299 superior double; $279–$319 deluxe double; $339–$1,000 suite. Extra person $25. Children under 18 stay free in parent's room. Weekend, family, and other packages available. AE, DC, DISC, MC, V. Valet or self-parking $19. T: Green Line to Lechmere; 10-min. walk. Pets accepted with prior approval. **Amenities:** Restaurant (a branch of Davio's, p. 127); cafe; heated indoor/outdoor pool with retractable roof; well-equipped health club and spa; bike rental (seasonal); concierge; courtesy van; business center; room service until 1am; massage; dry cleaning. Rooms for travelers with disabilities are available; staff is trained in disability awareness. In room: A/C, TV w/pay movies and Sony PlayStation, dataport, minibar, coffeemaker, hair dryer, iron, safe, umbrella.

EXPENSIVE

Hotel Marlowe 🛊🛊 (Kids)   Hotel Marlowe is the first venture into the Northeast by detail-oriented Kimpton Boutique Hotels, best known for the beloved Hotel Monaco brand. It opened in March 2003 in a new eight-story building adjacent to the CambridgeSide Galleria mall and across the street from the Museum of Science. It's chic yet comfortable, with abundant amenities for both businesspeople and leisure travelers. The elegantly decorated guest rooms are good-size, with enough room to hold a work desk and armchair. They have down comforters and three phones (1 in the bathroom), plus funky-boutique-hotel touches like leopard-print carpeting and a faux-fur throw across the foot of the bed. They overlook the river (across the busy boulevard), a small canal, or the landscaped courtyard/driveway that shields the lobby from the street. The Marlowe's closest competition is the Royal Sonesta Hotel, across the street, which is more expensive but has a pool and health club.

25 Edwin H. Land Blvd., Cambridge, MA 02141. (*) **800/825-7040**, 800/KIMPTON, or 617/868-8000. Fax 617/868-8001. www.hotelmarlowe.com. 236 units (some w/shower only). $189–$349 double; $389–$449 suite. Extra person $25. Rates include evening cocktail reception. Children under 18 stay free in parent's room. Weekend, family, and other packages available. AARP and AAA discounts available. AE, DC, DISC, MC, V. Valet parking $28, self-parking $20. T: Green Line to Lechmere or Red Line to Kendall. Pets accepted. **Amenities:** Restaurant (regional American); bar; exercise room; access to nearby health club (for a fee); bike rental; concierge; morning shuttle to local businesses; business center; 24-hr. room service; laundry service; same-day dry cleaning. Rooms for travelers with disabilities are available. *In room:* A/C, TV w/pay movies and Nintendo, high-speed Internet access, dataport, minibar, coffeemaker, hair dryer, iron, safe, umbrella, robes.

The Inn at Harvard 🏵🏵   At first glance, the redbrick Inn at Harvard looks almost like a college dorm—it's adjacent to Harvard Yard, and its Georgian-style architecture would fit nicely on campus. Inside, there's no mistaking it for anything other than an elegant hotel, popular with business travelers and university visitors. The elegant guest rooms, which were redecorated in 2002, contain either a lounge chair or two armchairs around a table, a work area, and an original painting from the Fogg Art Museum. Some units have dormer windows and window seats. The four-story sky-lit atrium holds the "living room," a huge, well-appointed guest lounge that's suitable for meeting with a visitor if you don't want to conduct business in your room.

1201 Massachusetts Ave. (at Quincy St.), Cambridge, MA 02138. (*) **800/458-5886** or 617/491-2222. Fax 617/491-6520. www.theinnatharvard.com. 109 units (some w/shower only). $199–$359 double; $650 presidential suite. AAA and AARP discounts available. AE, DC, DISC, MC, V. Valet parking $30. T: Red Line to Harvard. **Amenities:** Restaurant (New England); dining privileges at the nearby Harvard Faculty Club; free access to nearby health club; concierge; room service until 10:30pm; laundry service; dry cleaning. 6 rooms for travelers with disabilities are available. *In room:* A/C, TV, dataport, hair dryer, iron.

Sheraton Commander Hotel 🏵   This six-story hotel in the heart of Cambridge's historic district opened in 1927, and it's exactly what you'd expect of a traditional hostelry within sight of the Harvard campus. The colonial-style decor begins in the elegant lobby and extends to the decent-size guest rooms, which are attractively furnished and well maintained. Ask the pleasant front-desk staff for a room facing Cambridge Common; even if you aren't on a (relatively) high floor, you'll have a decent view. Suites have two TVs, and some have wet bars, refrigerators, and whirlpools. The Sheraton Commander doesn't have the Charles Hotel's cachet and amenities, but it doesn't have the Charles's prices, either. Plan far ahead if you're visiting during a Harvard event.

16 Garden St., Cambridge, MA 02138. (*) **800/325-3535** or 617/547-4800. Fax 617/868-8322. www.sheratoncommander.com. 175 units (some w/shower only). $109–$385 double; $295–$750 suite. Extra person $20. Children under 18 stay free in parent's room. Weekend packages and AAA and AARP discounts available. AE, DC, DISC, MC, V. Valet parking $18. T: Red Line to Harvard. **Amenities:** Restaurant (American) and lounge; exercise room; concierge; business center; room service until 11pm; dry cleaning; executive-level rooms. Rooms for travelers with disabilities are available. *In room:* A/C, TV w/pay movies, coffeemaker, hair dryer, iron, umbrella.

MODERATE

The **Hampton Inn Boston/Cambridge,** 191 Msgr. O'Brien Hwy., Cambridge ((*) **800/426-7866** or 617/494-5300; www.hamptoninn.com), is a 5-minute walk from the Green Line Lechmere stop. Rates at the 114-room hotel start at

$129 for a double and include continental breakfast. The Hampton Inn is 1 block closer to the T than the Holiday Inn Express (see listing below), but on the opposite side of the very busy street from the station.

Best Western Hotel Tria ⚡ This four-story establishment (formerly the Best Western Homestead Inn) underwent a $3 million renovation in 2003. It's now a sophisticated blend of chain-motel convenience and boutique-hotel features— such as homemade soap sliced to order at check-in. Guest rooms are spacious, with sleek but comfy contemporary furnishings, and are at least one floor up from the busy street. Room rates include 30 free minutes of local phone calls. The commercial neighborhood is nothing to write home about, but the pool and free parking and breakfast help make up for the less-than-scenic location. A 2½-mile jogging trail circles Fresh Pond, across the street. There's a restaurant next door and a shopping center with a 10-screen movie theater nearby. Boston is about a 15-minute drive or a 30-minute T ride away; Lexington and Concord are less than a half-hour away by car.

220 Alewife Brook Pkwy., Cambridge, MA 02138. ② **866/333-8742** or 617/491-8000. Fax 617/491-4932. www.hoteltria.com. 69 units. Mid-Mar to Oct $129–$299 double; Nov to mid-Mar $109–$159 double. Extra person $10. Rates include continental breakfast. Rates may be higher during special events. Children under 16 stay free in parent's room. AE, DC, MC, V. Free parking. T: Red Line to Alewife, 10-min. walk. **Amenities:** Indoor pool; exercise room; Jacuzzi; shuttle service; laundry service; same-day dry cleaning. *In room:* A/C, TV, high-speed Internet access, dataport, coffeemaker, hair dryer, iron, robes.

A Cambridge House Bed & Breakfast Inn ⚡⚡ A Cambridge House feels almost like a country inn but is on a busy stretch of Cambridge's main street (Mass Ave.), set back from the sidewalk by a lawn. The three-story building is a beautifully restored 1892 Victorian that's listed on the National Register of Historic Places. The well-maintained rooms vary widely in size; they're warmly decorated with Waverly-Schumacher fabrics and period antiques. Most contain fireplaces and four-poster canopy beds with down comforters. The best rooms face away from the street, which is a bus route. The inn serves a generous breakfast and afternoon refreshments.

2218 Massachusetts Ave., Cambridge, MA 02140. ② **800/232-9989** or 617/491-6300; 800/96-2079 in the U.K. Fax 617/868-2848. www.acambridgehouse.com. 15 units (some w/shower only). $139–$350 double. Extra person $35. Rates include buffet breakfast. AE, DISC, MC, V. Free parking. T: Red Line to Porter. **Amenities:** Concierge. 1 room for travelers with disabilities is available. *In room:* A/C, TV, fax, dataport, hair dryer.

Harvard Square Hotel Smack in the middle of "the Square," this six-story brick hotel is a favorite with visiting parents and budget-conscious business travelers. The lobby and the unpretentious guest rooms were renovated in 2003. They're relatively small but comfortable and neatly decorated in contemporary style; some overlook Harvard Square. The front desk handles faxing and copying.

110 Mount Auburn St., Cambridge, MA 02138. ② **800/458-5886** or 617/864-5200. Fax 617/864-2409. www.harvardsquarehotel.com. 73 units (some w/shower only). $129–$209 double. Extra person $10. Children under 17 stay free in parent's room. Corporate rates and AAA and AARP discounts available. AE, DC, DISC, MC, V. Parking $25. T: Red Line to Harvard. **Amenities:** Dining privileges at the Harvard Faculty Club; free access to nearby health club; car-rental desk; laundry service; dry cleaning. Rooms for travelers with disabilities are available. *In room:* A/C, TV, fridge, coffeemaker, hair dryer, iron.

Holiday Inn Express Hotel & Suites *Value* A limited-services lodging on a busy street, the Holiday Inn Express is a great deal. It's comfortable and convenient—just a 5-minute walk from the Green Line—for businesspeople on tight budgets as well as vacationers. Each decent-size room has a fridge and microwave, making this a good choice for families who plan to eat some meals in. The eight-story building sits slightly back from the street, but you'll still want to be as high up as possible to get away from the street. If you're willing to do without a restaurant, business center, or exercise facility, you'll probably find that the reasonable rates, which include parking—a big plus in Cambridge—more than make up for them.

250 Msgr. O'Brien Hwy., Cambridge, MA 02141. © 888/887-7690 or 617/577-7600. Fax 617/354-1313. www.hiexpress.com/boscambridgema. 112 units. From $99 double; from $119 suite. Rates include continental breakfast. Discounts for hospital patients and families available, subject to availability. AE, DC, DISC, MC, V. Free parking. T: Green Line to Lechmere. **Amenities:** Laundry service. Rooms for travelers with disabilities are available; some units adjoin standard units. *In room:* A/C, TV w/pay movies, dataport, fridge, coffeemaker, hair dryer, iron, microwave.

Radisson Hotel Cambridge 🗡 This former Howard Johnson hotel is an attractive, modern 16-story tower across the street from the Charles River. It has an indoor swimming pool, and Radisson replaced all the furniture when it took over in 2000. Each room has a picture window, and some have private balconies. Prices vary with the size of the room, the floor, and the view; the panorama of the Boston skyline from higher floors on the river side of the building is worth the extra money. The hotel is near the major college campuses and the Mass. Pike. It's 10 minutes by car from downtown Boston but not near public transit— leave time for the hotel shuttle.

777 Memorial Dr., Cambridge, MA 02139. © 800/333-3333 or 617/492-7777. Fax 617/492-6038. www.radisson.com/cambridgema. 205 units. $119–$235 double. Extra person $10. Rollaway $20. Cribs free. Children under 18 stay free in parent's room. AARP and AAA discounts available. AE, DC, DISC, MC, V. Free parking. Pets accepted. **Amenities:** 2 restaurants (Japanese, Greek); indoor pool; exercise room; shuttle to Harvard, Central, and Kendall squares and Massachusetts General Hospital; business center; room service until 11pm; laundry service; dry cleaning. Rooms for travelers with disabilities are available. *In room:* A/C, TV, dataport, coffeemaker, hair dryer, iron.

10 At & Near the Airport

EXPENSIVE

Hilton Boston Logan Airport 🗡🗡 This relatively new (1999) hotel smack in the middle of the airport draws most of its guests from meetings, conventions, and recently canceled flights. It's convenient and well equipped for business travelers, and it's an excellent fallback for vacationers in search of a deal who don't mind a short commute to downtown. Guest rooms are large and tastefully furnished, with plenty of business features, including two-line speakerphones. The best units, on the higher floors of the 10-story building, afford sensational views of the airport and harbor. The big concern with a hotel this close to the runways is noise, but the picture-window views of approaching aircraft look like TV with the sound off. A shuttle bus connects the hotel to all airport locations; walkways also link the building to Terminals E (a long walk) and A (which is closed for construction). The Hyatt Harborside (discussed below) is the closest competition; it's at the edge of the airport, on the water, which means less commotion outside but less convenient access to the T.

85 Terminal Rd., Logan International Airport, Boston, MA 02128. © 800/HILTONS or 617/568-6700. Fax 617/568-6800. www.hilton.com. 599 units. $99–$299 double; from $500 suite. Children under 18 stay free in parent's room. Weekend and other packages available. AE, DC, DISC, MC, V. Valet parking $25; self-parking $22. T: Blue Line to Airport, then take shuttle bus. **Amenities:** Restaurant (American); Irish pub; coffee counter; indoor lap pool; health club and spa; concierge; 24-hr. shuttle bus service to airport destinations, including car-rental offices and ferry dock, with on-bus electronic check-in; shuttle to downtown Boston; wellequipped business center; 24-hr. room service; laundry service; dry cleaning; executive-level rooms. *In room:* A/C, TV w/pay movies, high-speed Internet access, dataport, minibar, coffeemaker, hair dryer, iron.

Hyatt Harborside ⭐ This striking 14-story waterfront hotel offers unobstructed views of the harbor and city skyline. It caters to the convention and business trade; sightseers whose budget for transportation doesn't include a fair amount of time (on the shuttle bus and subway) or money (on ferries, parking, or cabs) will be better off closer to downtown. The Airport Water Shuttle leaves from the ferry dock behind the hotel.

The good-size guest rooms, which were renovated in 2000, afford dramatic views from the higher floors. They have all the features you'd expect at a deluxe hotel; the surprises here are in the public areas. The lobby is a work of art, with a map inlaid in the floor and the "sky" on the rotunda ceiling. And the building's tower is a lighthouse—the airport control tower manages the beacon so that it doesn't interfere with runway lights.

101 Harborside Dr., Boston, MA 02128. ⓒ 800/233-1234 or 617/568-1234. Fax 617/568-6080. www. harborside.hyatt.com. 270 units (some w/shower only). From $169 double. Children under 12 stay free in parent's room. AE, DC, DISC, MC, V. Parking $20. T: Blue Line to Airport, then take shuttle bus. By car, follow signs to Logan Airport and take Harborside Dr. past car-rental area and tunnel entrance. **Amenities:** Restaurant (New England); lounge; 40-ft. indoor pool; exercise room; whirlpool; sauna; concierge; 24-hr. airport shuttle service; business center; room service until midnight; laundry service; same-day dry cleaning; executive-level rooms. Ferries to Rowes Wharf and Long Wharf dock outside. Rooms for travelers with disabilities are available. *In room:* A/C, TV w/pay movies, hair dryer, iron.

MODERATE

The **Hampton Inn Boston Logan Airport,** 2300 Lee Burbank Hwy., Revere (ⓒ **800/426-7866** or 781/286-5665; www.hamptoninn.com), is on an ugly commercial-industrial strip about 3 miles north of the airport. A free shuttle bus serves the 227-room hotel, which has a pool; rates start at about $129 for a double and include continental breakfast.

Comfort Inn & Suites Logan Airport *Value* Although it loses points for the misleading name—the airport is about 3½ miles south—the well-equipped Comfort Inn ranks high in other areas. The eight-story hotel, which opened in 2001, sits on a hill set back from the street near a busy traffic circle. It offers a good range of amenities for business and leisure travelers, including free local phone calls, continental breakfast, and an indoor pool. Suites are oversize rooms that contain sofa beds, and king suites have refrigerators as well. The staff offers the attentive service you'd expect from a property in the Saunders Hotel Group (which also owns the luxurious Lenox Hotel). The somewhat inconvenient location translates to reasonable rates, and the North Shore is easily accessible if you plan to take a day trip. Revere Beach is about 2 minutes away by car.

85 American Legion Hwy. (Route 60), Revere, MA 02151. ⓒ 800/228-5150, or (local toll-free) 888/283-9300, or 781/485-3600. Fax 781/485-3601. www.comfortinnboston.com. 208 units. $99–$199 double; $119–$229 suite. Rates include continental breakfast. Senior and AAA discounts available. AE, DC, DISC, MC, V. Free parking. T: Blue Line to Airport, then take shuttle bus. Pets accepted; $10 charge. **Amenities:** Restaurant (Italian/American); lounge; indoor pool; exercise room; shuttle to subway and airport; business center; room service (noon–8pm); coin-op laundry; laundry service; same-day dry cleaning. Rooms for travelers with disabilities are available. *In room:* A/C, TV w/pay movies and WebTV, dataport, coffeemaker, hair dryer, iron.

6

Where to Dine

Friends tell me I'm too tough, that a couple of subpar meals at a particular restaurant shouldn't automatically exclude it from this chapter.

I think I'm not tough enough, and here's why: I live here. I can return to the place that disappointed me and try it again. You're here for just a few days, and you probably don't have the time—or the inclination or the budget—for a second chance.

That's not to say that every restaurant in this chapter gets high marks for every aspect of every meal. If the space isn't the loveliest, the service isn't the greatest, or (rarely) the food is less impressive than some other element of the experience, I'll point that out.

The guiding thought for this chapter, without regard to price, was, "If this were your only meal in Boston, would you be delighted with it?" At all of the restaurants we list, the answer, for one reason or another, is yes.

THE FOOD

The days when restaurant snobs sniffed that they had to go to New York to get a decent meal are long gone. Especially in warm weather, when excellent local produce appears on menus in every price range, the Boston area holds its own with any other market in the country. Celebrity chefs and rising stars spice up a dynamic restaurant scene, and traditional favorites occupy an important niche. The huge student population seeks out value, which it often finds at ethnic restaurants.

Seafood is a specialty in Boston, and you'll find it on the menu at almost every restaurant—trendy or classic, expensive or cheap, American (whatever that is) or ethnic. Some pointers: **Scrod** or **schrod** is a generic term for fresh white-fleshed fish, usually served in filets. **Local shellfish** includes Ipswich and Essex clams, Atlantic lobsters, Wellfleet oysters, scallops, mussels, and shrimp.

Lobster was once so abundant that the Indians showed the Pilgrims how to use the ugly crustaceans as fertilizer, and prisoners rioted when it turned up on the menu too often. Order lobster boiled or steamed and you'll get a plastic bib, a nutcracker (for the claws and tail), a pick (for the legs), and drawn butter (for dipping). Restaurants price lobsters by the pound; the ones in this chapter typically charge at least $15 to $20 for a "chicken" (1- to 1¼-lb.) lobster, and more for the bigger specimens. If you want someone else to do the work, lobster is available in a "pie" (casserole), in a "roll" (sandwich), stuffed and baked or broiled, in or over pasta, in salad, and in bisque.

Well-made **New England clam chowder** is a white soup studded with fresh clams and thickened with cream. Recipes vary, but they never, ever include tomatoes. (Tomatoes go in Manhattan clam chowder.) If you want clams but not soup, many places serve **steamers,** or soft-shell clams cooked in the shell, as an appetizer or main dish. More common are hard-shell clams—**littlenecks** (small) or **cherrystones** (medium-size)—served raw, like oysters.

Tips **Time Is Money**

Lunch is an excellent, economical way to check out a fancy restaurant without breaking the bank. At restaurants that take reservations, it's always a good idea to make them, particularly for dinner. Boston-area restaurants are far less busy early in the week than they are Friday through Sunday. If you're flexible about when you indulge in fine cuisine and when you go for pizza and a movie, choose the low-budget option on the weekend and pamper yourself on a weeknight.

Note: The axiom that you should order **oysters** only in months with an "R" in them originates in biology. Summer is breeding season, when the energy that usually goes into bulking up (and making lots of juicy meat) gets diverted to reproduction. To experience the best the oyster has to offer, wait till the weather turns colder.

Traditional **Boston baked beans,** which date from colonial days, when cooking on the Sabbath was forbidden, earned Boston the nickname "Beantown." House-made baked beans can be hard to find (Durgin-Park does an excellent rendition), but when you do, you'll probably also find good cornbread and **brown bread**—more like a steamed pudding, of whole wheat and rye flour, cornmeal, molasses, buttermilk, and, usually, raisins.

Finally, **Boston cream pie** is golden layer cake sandwiched around custard and topped with chocolate glaze—no cream, no pie.

1 Restaurants by Cuisine

AFGHAN

The Helmand ✯ (Cambridge, $$, p. 139)

AMERICAN

Aujourd'hui ✯✯✯ (Back Bay, $$$$, p. 123)

Grill 23 & Bar ✯✯ (Back Bay, $$$$, p. 124)

Jacob Wirth Company (Theater District, $$, p. 121)

Johnny's Luncheonette ✯ (Cambridge, $, p. 136)

Milk Street Café kiosk (Financial District, $, p. 129)

Mr. Bartley's Burger Cottage ✯✯ (Cambridge, $, p. 136)

Troquet ✯✯ (Theater District, $$$$, p. 119)

Zaftigs Delicatessen (Kenmore Square to Brookline, $, p. 130)

ASIAN

Billy Tse Restaurant (North End, $$, p. 110)

Jae's Café ✯ (South End, $$$, p. 122)

BARBECUE

East Coast Grill & Raw Bar ✯✯ (Cambridge, $$$, p. 137)

Redbones ✯ (Somerville, $$, p. 140)

BRAZILIAN

Midwest Grill ✯ (Cambridge, $$, p. 139)

CAJUN

Bob the Chef's Jazz Cafe ✯ (South End, $$, p. 122)

Border Café (Cambridge, $$, p. 135)

CAMBODIAN

The Elephant Walk ✦✦ (Kenmore Square to Brookline, $$$, p. 130)

CANTONESE

East Ocean City ✦ (Chinatown, $$, p. 120)

Grand Chau Chow (Chinatown, $$, p. 121)

CARIBBEAN

Green Street Grill ✦ (Cambridge, $$, p. 138)

CHINESE

Billy Tse Restaurant (North End, $$, p. 110)

East Ocean City ✦ (Chinatown, $$, p. 120)

Grand Chau Chow (Chinatown, $$, p. 121)

CONTINENTAL

Locke-Ober ✦ (Downtown Crossing, $$$$, p. 116)

CUBAN

Chez Henri ✦ (Cambridge, $$$$, p. 131)

DELI

S&S Restaurant ✦✦ (Cambridge, $, p. 140)

Zaftigs Delicatessen (Kenmore Square to Brookline, $, p. 130)

ECLECTIC

The Bay Tower ✦ (Faneuil Hall, $$$$, p. 114)

The Blue Room ✦✦✦ (Cambridge, $$$, p. 137)

Clio ✦✦ (Back Bay, $$$$, p. 123)

Hamersley's Bistro ✦✦ (South End, $$$$, p. 121)

Icarus ✦✦ (South End, $$$$, p. 122)

Olives ✦✦ (Charlestown, $$$$, p. 118)

Upstairs on the Square ✦ (Cambridge, $$$$, p. 134)

FRENCH

Brasserie Jo ✦ (Back Bay, $$, p. 129)

Chez Henri ✦ (Cambridge, $$$$, p. 131)

The Elephant Walk ✦✦ (Kenmore Square to Brookline, $$$, p. 130)

Garden of Eden (South End, $$, p. 123)

L'Espalier ✦✦✦ (Back Bay, $$$$, p. 124)

Les Zygomates ✦✦ (Financial District, $$$, p. 114)

No. 9 Park ✦✦ (Beacon Hill, $$$$, p. 117)

Sel de la Terre ✦✦ (Waterfront, $$$, p. 107)

GERMAN

Jacob Wirth Company (Theater District, $$, p. 121)

INDIAN

Bombay Club ✦ (Cambridge, $$, p. 135)

ITALIAN

Artú (North End, $$, p. 110)

Cosí Sandwich Bar ✦ (Financial District, $, p. 116)

Daily Catch ✦ (North End, $$, p. 111)

Davio's ✦✦ (Back Bay, $$$, p. 127)

Galleria Umberto (North End, $, p. 113)

Giacomo's Ristorante ✦ (North End, $$, p. 112)

La Groceria Ristorante Italiano (Cambridge, $$, p. 139)

La Summa ✦ (North End, $$, p. 112)

Mamma Maria ✦✦ (North End, $$$$, p. 110)

No. 9 Park ✦✦ (Beacon Hill, $$$$, p. 117)

Piccola Venezia (North End, $$, p. 112)

JAPANESE
Ginza Japanese Restaurant ★★
(Chinatown, $$$, p. 119)

MEDITERRANEAN
Casablanca ★ (Cambridge, $$$,
p. 135)
Oleana ★★ (Cambridge, $$$,
p. 138)
Rialto ★★★ (Cambridge, $$$$,
p. 134)

MEXICAN
Casa Romero ★ (Back Bay, $$$,
p. 127)
Tu y Yo Mexican Fonda
(Cambridge, $$, p. 140)

MIDDLE EASTERN
Café Jaffa (Back Bay, $, p. 130)

NEW ENGLAND
Durgin-Park ★★ (Faneuil Hall,
$$, p. 115)
L'Espalier ★★★ (Back Bay, $$$$,
p. 124)
Ye Olde Union Oyster House ★
(Faneuil Hall, $$$, p. 115)

PIZZA
Pizzeria Regina ★★ (North End,
$, p. 114)

SANDWICHES
Cosí Sandwich Bar ★ (Financial
District, $, p. 116)
Garden of Eden (South End, $$,
p. 123)
Nashoba Brook Bakery ★ (South
End, $, p. 123)

SEAFOOD
Daily Catch ★ (North End, $$,
p. 111)
East Coast Grill & Raw Bar ★★
(Cambridge, $$$, p. 137)
East Ocean City ★ (Chinatown,
$$, p. 120)
Giacomo's Ristorante ★ (North
End, $$, p. 112)
Green Street Grill ★ (Cambridge,
$$, p. 138)
Jasper White's Summer Shack ★
(Cambridge, $$$, p. 138)
Jimbo's Fish Shanty (South Boston
Waterfront, $, p. 107)
Jimmy's Harborside Restaurant ★
(South Boston Waterfront, $$$,
p. 107)
Legal Sea Foods ★★★ (Back Bay,
$$$, p. 128)
Ye Olde Union Oyster House ★
(Faneuil Hall, $$$, p. 115)

SOUTHERN
Bob the Chef's Jazz Cafe ★ (South
End, $$, p. 122)

SPANISH
Dalí ★★ (Cambridge, $$$,
p. 137)
Tapéo (Back Bay, $$$, p. 126)

SUSHI
Billy Tse Restaurant (North End,
$$, p. 110)
Ginza Japanese Restaurant ★★
(Chinatown, $$$, p. 119)
Jae's Café ★ (South End, $$$,
p. 122)

TEX-MEX
Border Café (Cambridge, $$,
p. 135)
Fajitas & 'Ritas (Downtown
Crossing, $, p. 117)

THAI
Bangkok Cuisine ★ (Back Bay, $$,
p. 128)

TURKISH
Istanbul Café (Beacon Hill, $$,
p. 118)

WINE BARS
Les Zygomates ★★ (Financial
District, $$$, p. 114)
Troquet ★★ (Theater District,
$$$$, p. 119)

2 The Waterfront

EXPENSIVE

Legal Sea Foods (p. 128) has a branch at 255 State St. (© **617/227-3115;** www.legalseafoods.com), opposite the Aquarium.

Jimmy's Harborside Restaurant ✿ SEAFOOD   This Boston landmark—the sign out front reads HOME OF THE CHOWDER KING—offers tasty seafood and fine views of the harbor to businesspeople at lunch and tourists at dinner. In the summer, seating extends outside onto the harbor-front deck. You might start with the "King's" fish chowder, with generous chunks of whitefish, or excellent Maine crab cakes. Entrees include simple but flavorful seafood preparations (grilled, broiled, blackened, or fried) and more ambitious specialties—for instance, bouillabaisse and Jimmy's famous "finnan haddie" (smoked haddock in cream sauce), which is famous for good reason. If you don't like fish, wait until Friday or Saturday night and come for prime rib.

Meter parking is available on Northern Avenue. Getting a cab is usually not difficult, but the walk from South Station is tough because of Big Dig construction.

In the same building, **Jimbo's Fish Shanty** is a casual, less expensive sibling with equally fresh food. Main dishes run $11 to $18. It's a child-friendly place with great desserts.

242 Northern Ave. © **617/423-1000.** www.jimmysharborside.com. Reservations recommended at dinner. Main courses $9–$34 at lunch, $16–$34 at dinner. AE, DC, DISC, MC, V. Mon–Thurs noon–9:30pm; Fri–Sat noon–10pm (lunch until 4pm); Sun 4–9pm. Closed Dec 25. Valet parking available. T: Red Line to South Station; 25-min. walk.

Sel de la Terre ✿✿ PROVENÇAL   Side by side with the Big Dig, Sel de la Terre is a peaceful taste of southern France. Executive chef Geoff Gardner (a partner with L'Espalier owners Frank and Catherine McClelland) uses fresh local ingredients in his subtly flavorful food: scallops handled so gently that they're still sweet, roasted chicken almost as juicy as a good peach, haddock infused with rosemary. Banquettes, earth tones, and professional service add up to a relaxing atmosphere that belies the mayhem outside as well as the go-go business-lunch crowd (dinner is calmer). The unusual pricing structure—the same amount for every dish—feels like a deal when you're tucking into a generous portion of steak frites with Black Angus rib-eye, and less of a bargain if you're eating gnocchi. The sly sense of humor that's apparent in the name ("salt of the earth") crops up on the children's menu, which includes *tartine au fromage fondu* ("grilled-cheese sandwich" to non-Francophones). Whatever your age, try a side of sublime *pommes frites* (french fries). The *boulangerie* (bakery) at the entrance sells the out-of-this-world breads to go.

255 State St. © **617/720-1300.** www.seldelaterre.com. Reservations recommended. Main courses $14 at lunch, $23 at dinner; sandwiches (lunch only) $8.50. Children's menu $7. AE, DC, DISC, MC, V. Mon–Fri 11:30am–2:30pm and 5:30–10pm; Sat–Sun 11am–3:30pm and 5–10pm. Valet and validated parking available at dinner. T: Blue Line to Aquarium.

3 The North End

Boston's Italian-American enclave has dozens of restaurants; many are tiny and don't serve dessert and coffee. Hit the *caffès* for coffee and fresh pastry in an atmosphere where lingering is welcome. Now that Boston's smoking ban is in

Boston Dining

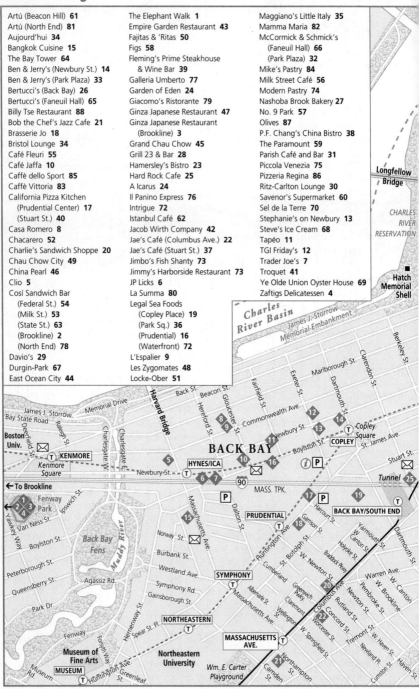

Charles River Basin

James J. Storrow Memorial Embankment

Longfellow Bridge

CHARLES RIVER RESERVATION

■ Hatch Memorial Shell

James J. Storrow Memorial Drive

Bay State Road

Boston Univ.

Deerfield St.

Raleigh St.

Charlesgate W.

Charlesgate E.

Back St.

Harvard Bridge

Hereford St.

Gloucester St.

Fairfield St.

Exeter St.

Beacon St.

Commonwealth Ave.

Marlborough St.

Dartmouth St.

Clarendon St.

Berkeley St.

Newbury St.

Boylston St.

Copley Square

St. James Ave.

Stuart St.

Tunnel

BACK BAY

KENMORE

Kenmore Square

← To Brookline

HYNES/ICA

COPLEY

Newbury St.

MASS. TPK.

90

Fenway Park

Ipswich St.

Van Ness St.

Yawkey Way

Boylston St.

Peterborough St.

Queensberry St.

Park Dr.

Fenway

Back Bay Fens

Muddy River

Agassiz Rd.

Norway St.

Burbank St.

Westland Ave.

Symphony Rd.

Gainsborough St.

Hemenway St.

Massachusetts Ave.

Dalton St.

PRUDENTIAL

Huntington Ave.

Cumberland

St. Botolph St.

Garrison St.

Harcourt St.

W. Newton St.

Greenwich

Albemarle St.

Wellington

SYMPHONY

NORTHEASTERN

Museum of Fine Arts

MUSEUM

Museum Rd.

Forsyth Way

Spear Pl.

Greenleaf St.

Northeastern University

Wm. E. Carter Playground

MASSACHUSETTS AVE.

Columbus Ave.

Rutland St.

Concord St.

W. Springfield St.

Worcester St.

Tremont St.

W. Newton St.

Pembroke St.

W. Canton St.

Warren Ave.

W. Brookline St.

Newton St.

Haven St.

Newland Pl.

Northampton St.

Camden St.

Cumston St.

Dartmouth St.

Yarmouth St.

Canton St.

Braddock Pkwy.

Hoyoke St.

BACK BAY/SOUTH END

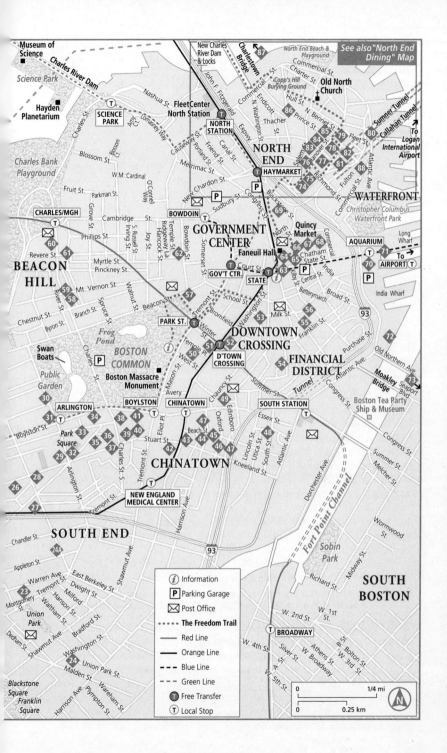

See also"North End Dining" Map

Museum of Science

Science Park

Charles River Dam

Hayden Planetarium

SCIENCE PARK

Charles Bank Playground

New Charles River Dam & Locks

Charlestown Bridge

87

North End Beach & Playground

Commercial St.
Charter St.

Copp's Hill Burying Ground

Old North Church

Sumner Tunnel
Callahan Tunnel

To Logan International Airport

FleetCenter North Station

NORTH STATION

NORTH END

86

85
84
83
82
79
80
81
78
77
76
88

HAYMARKET

74
75

WATERFRONT

Christopher Columbus Waterfront Park

CHARLES/MGH

60
61

BOWDOIN

GOVERNMENT CENTER

Faneuil Hall

Quincy Market

62
67
65
68
64
63
66

AQUARIUM

71

To AIRPORT

70

Long Wharf

India Wharf

BEACON HILL

59
58

57

PARK ST.

53

Milk St.

56
55

72

GOV'T CTR.

STATE

DOWNTOWN CROSSING

51
52
50

FINANCIAL DISTRICT

54

93

Swan Boats

Public Garden

BOSTON COMMON

Boston Massacre Monument

Frog Pond

Moakley Bridge

13

ARLINGTON

30
31
34

BOYLSTON

CHINATOWN

47

SOUTH STATION

Boston Tea Party Ship & Museum

Park Square

33
32
29
37
35
36
39
40
38
41
42
43
44
45
46
47

48
49

CHINATOWN

26
28
27

NEW ENGLAND MEDICAL CENTER

Fort Point Channel

SOUTH END

24A
23

Union Park

24

Sobin Park

SOUTH BOSTON

Blackstone Square Franklin Square

BROADWAY

Legend

(i) Information
P Parking Garage
✉ Post Office
···· The Freedom Trail
— Red Line
— Orange Line
-- Blue Line
-- Green Line
(T) Free Transfer
(T) Local Stop

0   1/4 mi
0   0.25 km

N

place, this is an even more enjoyable experience. My favorite destinations are **Caffè dello Sport,** 308 Hanover St. (© **617/523-5063**), and **Caffè Vittoria,** 296 Hanover St. (© **617/227-7606**). There's also table service at **Mike's Pastry,** 300 Hanover St. (© **617/742-3050**), a bakery that's famous for its bustling takeout business and its cannoli. If you plan to eat in, find what you want in the cases first, then take a seat and order from the server.

VERY EXPENSIVE

Mamma Maria ⭐⭐ NORTHERN ITALIAN   In a town house overlooking North Square and the Paul Revere House, this traditional-looking restaurant offers innovative cuisine and a level of sophistication far removed from the North End's familiar "hello, dear" service. The menu changes seasonally. Start with excellent soup, risotto, or a pasta special; I'd go for any of those over the less exciting cured-meat sampler. The superb entrees are unlike anything else in this neighborhood, except in size—portions are more than generous. Fork-tender osso buco, a limited-quantity nightly special, is almost enough for two, but you'll want it all for yourself. You can't go wrong with main-course pastas, either, and the fresh seafood specials (say, succulent grilled tuna over squid-ink linguine with tomatoes, olives, capers, and anchovies) are uniformly marvelous. The pasta, bread, and desserts are homemade, and the shadowy, whitewashed rooms make this a popular spot for popping the question.

3 North Sq. © **617/523-0077.** www.mammamaria.com. Reservations recommended. Main courses $19–$35. AE, DC, DISC, MC, V. Sun–Thurs 5–9:30pm; Fri–Sat 5–10:30pm. Closed 1 week in Jan. Valet parking available. T: Green or Orange Line to Haymarket.

MODERATE

Artú ITALIAN   Plates of roasted vegetables draw your eye to the front window, and the accompanying aromas will reel in the rest of you. Don't resist—this is a neighborhood favorite for a reason, and a good stop for Freedom Trail walkers. The best appetizer consists of those gorgeous veggies. Trust the chef to choose, or ask to have something included (excellent carrots) or left out (licorice-tasting fennel isn't for everyone). The helpful staff can offer advice. Move on to superb roasted meats or bounteous home-style pasta dishes. Roast lamb, ziti with sausage and broccoli rabe, and chicken stuffed with ham and cheese are all terrific. *Panini* (sandwiches) are big in size and flavor—prosciutto, mozzarella, and tomato is sublime, and chicken parmigiana is tender and filling. This isn't a great place for quiet conversation, especially during dinner in the noisy main room, but do you really want to talk with your mouth full?

There's another Artú on **Beacon Hill** at 89 Charles St. (© 617/227-9023). It keeps the same hours, except that it opens at 4pm on Sunday and Monday.

6 Prince St. © **617/742-4336.** Reservations recommended at dinner, not accepted Sat. Main courses $9.50–$18; sandwiches $4.75–$7. AE, MC, V. Daily 11am–11pm. T: Green or Orange Line to Haymarket.

Billy Tse Restaurant CHINESE/PAN-ASIAN/SUSHI   A Pan-Asian restaurant on the edge of the Italian North End might seem incongruous, but this casual spot is no ordinary Chinese restaurant. It serves excellent renditions of the usual dishes, and the kitchen also has a flair for fresh seafood. The Pan-Asian selections and sushi are just as enjoyable as the Chinese classics. Start with wonderful soup, sinfully good crab Rangoon, or fried calamari with garlic and pepper. Main dishes range from seven kinds of fried rice to scallops with garlic sauce to the house special: fried noodles, topped with shrimp, calamari, and scallops in a scrumptious sauce.

La Familia 112 Salem

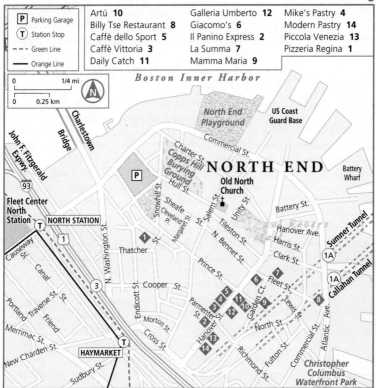

P Parking Garage	Artú **10**	Galleria Umberto **12**	Mike's Pastry **4**
T Station Stop	Billy Tse Restaurant **8**	Giacomo's **6**	Modern Pastry **14**
- - - Green Line	Caffè dello Sport **5**	Il Panino Express **2**	Piccola Venezia **13**
—— Orange Line	Caffè Vittoria **3**	La Summa **7**	Pizzeria Regina **1**
	Daily Catch **11**	Mamma Maria **9**	

Be sure to ask about the daily specials—bitter Chinese broccoli, when it's available, is deftly prepared. Lunch specials, served until 4pm, include vegetable fried rice or vegetable lo mein. You can eat in the comfortable main dining room or near the bar, which has French doors that open to the street. Although it's opposite a trolley stop, Billy Tse doesn't have an especially touristy clientele—the neighborhood patrons obviously welcome a break from pizza and pasta.

240 Commercial St. ☎ 617/227-9990. Reservations recommended at dinner on weekends. Main courses $5–$20; lunch specials $6–$8. AE, DC, DISC, MC, V. Mon–Thurs 11:30am–11:30pm; Fri–Sat 11:30am–midnight; Sun 11:30am–11pm. Closed 1 week in Feb. T: Green or Orange Line to Haymarket, or Blue Line to Aquarium.

Daily Catch ★ SOUTHERN ITALIAN/SEAFOOD   This storefront restaurant is about the size of a large kitchen (it seats just 20), but it packs a wallop—of garlic. It's a North End classic, with excellent food, chummy service, and very little elbow room. The surprisingly varied menu includes Sicilian-style calamari (squid stuffed with bread crumbs, raisins, pine nuts, parsley, and garlic), fresh clams, squid-ink pasta puttanesca, and a variety of broiled, fried, and sautéed fish and shellfish. Calamari comes any number of ways—even the garlic-and-oil pasta sauce has ground squid in it. Fried calamari makes an excellent appetizer. All food is prepared to order, and some dishes arrive at the table still in the frying pan.

This is the original Daily Catch. The **Brookline** location, at 441 Harvard St. (☎ 617/734-5696), opens at 5pm nightly and accepts credit cards (AE, MC, V).

323 Hanover St. ☎ 617/523-8567. www.dailycatch.com. Reservations not accepted. Main courses $12–$19. No credit cards. Sun–Thurs 11:30am–10pm; Fri–Sat 11:30am–11pm. T: Green or Orange Line to Haymarket.

Giacomo's Ristorante ☆ ITALIAN/SEAFOOD   Fans of Giacomo's seem to have adopted the U.S. Postal Service's motto: They brave snow, sleet, rain, and gloom of night. The line forms early and grows long, especially on weekends. No reservations, cash only, a tiny dining room with an open kitchen—what's the attraction? Well, the food is terrific, there's plenty of it, and the we're-all-in-this-together atmosphere certainly helps. My dad is a New York–ethnic-dining snob, and this is his favorite Boston restaurant.

The fried calamari appetizer, served with marinara sauce, is ultralight and crisp. You can take the chef's advice or put together your own main dish from the list of ingredients on a board on the wall. The best suggestion is salmon and sun-dried tomatoes in tomato cream sauce over fettuccine; any dish with shrimp is delectable, too. Nonseafood offerings such as butternut squash ravioli in mascarpone cheese sauce are equally memorable. Service is friendly but incredibly swift, and lingering is not encouraged—but unless you have a heart of stone, you won't want to take up a table when people are standing outside in (no kidding) 90° heat or an ice storm waiting for your seat.

355 Hanover St. ☎ 617/523-9026. Reservations not accepted. Main courses $11–$18. No credit cards. Mon–Thurs 5–10pm; Fri–Sat 5–10:30pm; Sun 4–10pm. T: Green or Orange Line to Haymarket.

La Summa ☆ SOUTHERN ITALIAN   Because La Summa isn't on the restaurant rows of Hanover and Salem streets, it maintains a cozy neighborhood atmosphere. Unlike some neighborhood places, it's friendly to outsiders—you'll feel welcome even if your server doesn't greet you by name. La Summa is worth seeking out just for the wonderful homemade pasta and desserts, and the more elaborate entrees are scrumptious, too. You might start with ravioli or a superb soup (our waitress one night didn't know exactly what was in the butternut-squash soup because, and I quote, "My mother made it"). Or stick to the salad that comes with each meal, and save room for sweets.

Try any seafood special, lobster ravioli, *pappardelle e melanzane* (strips of eggplant tossed with ethereal fresh pasta in light marinara sauce), or the house special—veal, chicken, sausage, shrimp, artichokes, pepperoncini (pickled hot peppers), olives, and mushrooms in white-wine sauce. Desserts, especially tiramisu, are terrific.

30 Fleet St. ☎ 617/523-9503. Reservations recommended on weekends. Main courses $11–$24. AE, DC, DISC, MC, V. Sun–Fri 4:30–10:30pm; Sat 4:30–11pm. T: Green or Orange Line to Haymarket.

Piccola Venezia ITALIAN   The glass front wall of Piccola Venezia ("little Venice") shows off the exposed-brick dining room, decorated with prints and photos and filled with happy locals and out-of-towners. Portions are large, and the homey food tends to be heavy on red sauce, although more sophisticated

---

⸙ Finds Go Straight to the Source

The tiramisu at many North End restaurants comes from **Modern Pastry,** 257 Hanover St. (☎ 617/523-3783). The surreally good concoction ($3.50 a slice at the shop) makes an excellent picnic dessert in the summer—head 4 blocks down Richmond Street to eat in Waterfront Park.

Breakfast & Sunday Brunch

Several top hotels serve Sunday brunch buffets of monstrous proportions—outrageous spreads that are outrageously expensive. They're worth the investment for a special occasion, but you can have a less incapacitating experience for considerably less money.

Good options in Cambridge include the **S&S Restaurant** (p. 140) and **Johnny's Luncheonette** (p. 136). Across the river, **Charlie's Sandwich Shoppe,** 429 Columbus Ave. (© 617/536-7669), is a longtime South End favorite not far from the Back Bay—just the right distance to walk off some blueberry-waffle calories. **The Paramount,** 44 Charles St., Beacon Hill (© 617/720-1152), is a classic destination for eggs and a glimpse of the real community behind the neighborhood's redbrick facade. In Jamaica Plain, locals tough out long weekend waits for the delicious specials and strong coffee at the **Centre Street Café,** 669 Centre St. (© 617/524-9217).

If you have your heart set on a fancy brunch at a hotel, make reservations (especially on holidays) but do *not* make elaborate dinner plans. **Aujourd'hui** (p. 123), in the Four Seasons Hotel, 200 Boylston St. (© 617/451-2071) charges $58 for adults, $28 children; at **Café Fleuri,** in Le Meridien Boston, 250 Franklin St. (© 617/451-1900), adults pay $39 to $49, children $17.

A good alternative is the brunch buffet at the Boston Harbor Hotel's ground-floor cafe, **Intrigue** (© 617/856-7744), which is less extravagant and more casual than the usual hotel spread, but still scrumptious. It serves brunch on Saturday and Sunday from 7 to 11:30am ($18 adults, $11 children); reservations aren't necessary.

dishes are available. The delicious sautéed mushroom appetizer is solidly in the latter category; a more traditional starter is tasty *pasta e fagioli* (bean-and-pasta soup). Then dig into spaghetti and meatballs, chicken parmigiana, eggplant rolatini, or pasta puttanesca. This is a good place to try traditional Italian-American favorites such as polenta (home-style, not the yuppie croutons available at so many other places), *baccala* (reconstituted salt cod), or the house specialty, tripe.

263 Hanover St. © 617/523-3888. Reservations recommended at dinner. Main courses $11–$21; lunch specialties $5–$10. AE, DISC, MC, V. Daily 11am–10pm (lunch Mon–Fri until 4pm). Validated parking available. T: Green or Orange Line to Haymarket.

INEXPENSIVE

Galleria Umberto *Value* ITALIAN   The long, fast-moving line of business-people and tourists tips you off to the fact that this cafeteria-style spot just off the Freedom Trail is a bargain. The food is good, too. You can fill up on a couple of slices of pizza, but if you're feeling adventurous, try *arancini* (a rice ball filled with ground beef, peas, and cheese). Calzones—ham and cheese, spinach, spinach and cheese, or spinach and sausage—and potato croquettes are also tasty. Study the cases while you wait and be ready to order at once when you reach the head of the line. Have a quick lunch and get on with your sightseeing.

289 Hanover St. ℂ **617/227-5709**. All items less than $3. No credit cards. Mon–Sat 11am–2pm. Closed July. T: Green or Orange Line to Haymarket.

Pizzeria Regina ⭐⭐ PIZZA   Regina's looks almost like a movie set, but look a little closer—this local legend is the place the movie sets are trying to re-create. Busy waitresses who might call you "dear" weave through the boisterous dining room delivering peerless pizza steaming hot from the brick oven. (You can also drop in for a slice, weekdays at lunch only.) Let it cool a little before you dig in. Nouveau ingredients such as sun-dried tomatoes appear on the list of toppings, but that's not authentic. House-made sausage, maybe some pepperoni, and a couple of beers—now, *that's* authentic.

11½ Thacher St. ℂ **617/227-0765**. www.pizzeriaregina.com. Reservations not accepted. Pizza $9–$16. No credit cards. Mon–Thurs 11am–11:30pm; Fri–Sat 11am–midnight; Sun noon–11pm. T: Green or Orange Line to Haymarket.

4 Faneuil Hall Marketplace & the Financial District

VERY EXPENSIVE

The Bay Tower ⭐ ECLECTIC   Let's cut to the chase: Would you pay this much at a restaurant with a view of a brick wall or a street corner? No. Is it worth it? If you're out to make a statement, absolutely. The beautiful 33rd-floor dining room has glass walls facing a panorama of Faneuil Hall Marketplace, the harbor, and the airport. The terraced seating ensures that every table in the romantic, candlelit room has a view.

The seasonal menu incorporates traditional and contemporary options. You might start with lobster bisque, shrimp cocktail, or beef carpaccio. Entrees include the usual meat, chicken, and seafood, often with a twist. Yellow- and red-pepper emulsions accent salmon steak over ginger basmati rice; for more traditional palates, Long Island duck breast with cranberry-orange sauce comes with parsnip purée. There's always at least one vegetarian entree. Many people come just for sweets, drinks, and dancing in the lounge, so desserts are wonderful, with an emphasis on chocolate.

60 State St. ℂ **617/723-1666**. www.baytower.com. Reservations recommended. Main courses $29–$38. AE, DC, MC, V. Mon–Thurs 5:30–10pm; Fri 5:30–11pm; Sat 5–11pm. Validated parking available. T: Blue or Orange Line to State, or Green Line to Government Center.

EXPENSIVE

The national chain **McCormick & Schmick's Seafood Restaurant** has a branch at Faneuil Hall Marketplace in the North Market Building (ℂ **617/720-5522**).

Les Zygomates ⭐⭐ FRENCH/WINE BAR   You might have to brave the construction near South Station to reach this delightful bistro and wine bar, but it's worth the trip. The bar in the high-ceilinged, brick-walled space serves a great selection of wine, available by the bottle, the glass, and the 2-ounce "taste." The efficient staff will guide you to a good accompaniment for chef-owner Ian

---

Impressions

Their hotels are bad. Their pumpkin pies are delicious. Their poetry is not so good.

—Edgar Allan Poe, *Broadway Journal*, 1845

(*Tips*   **It's Nothing Personal**

State law requires the scary disclaimer that appears on menus to alert you to the potential danger of eating raw or undercooked meat (such as rare burgers), seafood (raw oysters, for instance), poultry, or eggs.

Just's delicious food. Salads are excellent, lightly dressed and garden-fresh, and main courses are hearty and filling but not heavy. The roasted salmon with arugula, shaved fennel, pear tomatoes, and roasted almonds is toothsome, and meat-lovers will savor the grilled smoked pork chop with sweet potato–plantain hash. For dessert, try not to fight over warm chocolate cake. A popular business-lunch destination, Les Zygomates has a chic, romantic atmosphere at night, when live jazz (in its own dining room) helps set the mood.

129 South St. ① 617/542-5108. www.winebar.com. Reservations recommended. Main courses $17–$26; prix-fixe $15 at lunch, $29 at dinner. AE, DC, DISC, MC, V. Mon–Fri 11:30am–1am (lunch until 2pm, dinner until 10:30pm); Sat 6pm–1am (dinner until 11:30pm). Valet parking available at dinner. T: Red Line to South Station.

Ye Olde Union Oyster House ✸ NEW ENGLAND/SEAFOOD   America's oldest restaurant in continuous service, the Union Oyster House opened in 1826, and the booths and oyster bar haven't moved since. The food is tasty, traditional New England fare, popular with tourists on the adjacent Freedom Trail and savvy locals. They're not looking for anything fancy, and you shouldn't, either—the best bets are simple, classic preparations. At the crescent-shaped bar on the lower level of the cramped, low-ceilinged building, "where Daniel Webster drank many a toddy in his day," try oyster stew or the cold seafood sampler of oysters, clams, and shrimp to start. Follow with a broiled or grilled dish such as scrod or salmon, or perhaps fried seafood or grilled pork loin. A "shore dinner" of chowder, steamers or mussels, lobster, corn, potatoes, and dessert is an excellent introduction to local favorites. For dessert, try gingerbread with whipped cream. *Tip:* A plaque marks John F. Kennedy's favorite booth (no. 18), where he often sat to read the Sunday papers.

41 Union St. (between North and Hanover sts.). ① 617/227-2750. www.unionoysterhouse.com. Reservations recommended. Main courses $9–$21 at lunch, $16–$30 at dinner. Children's menu $5–$11. AE, DC, DISC, MC, V. Sun–Thurs 11am–9:30pm (lunch menu until 5pm); Fri–Sat 11am–10pm (lunch until 6pm). Union Bar daily 11am–midnight (lunch until 3pm, late supper until 11pm). Valet parking available. T: Green or Orange Line to Haymarket.

MODERATE

Durgin-Park ✸✸ *Kids* NEW ENGLAND   For huge portions of delicious food, a rowdy atmosphere where CEOs share tables with students, and run-ins with the famously cranky waitresses, people have poured into Durgin-Park since 1827. It's everything it's cracked up to be—a tourist magnet that attracts many locals, where everyone's disappointed when the waitresses are nice, as they often are. Approximately 2,000 people a day join the line that stretches down a flight of stairs to the first floor of Faneuil Hall Marketplace's North Market building. The queue moves quickly, and you'll probably wind up seated at a long table with other people (smaller tables are available).

The food is wonderful, and there's plenty of it—prime rib the size of a hubcap, lamb chops, fried seafood, and roast turkey are sure bets. The cooks broil steaks and chops on an open fire over wood charcoal. Fresh seafood arrives twice daily, and fish dinners are broiled to order. Vegetables come a la carte; Boston baked beans are a signature dish, and this is the best place to try them. For dessert, strawberry shortcake is justly celebrated, and Indian pudding (molasses and cornmeal baked for hours and served with ice cream) is a New England classic.

340 Faneuil Hall Marketplace. © 617/227-2038. www.durgin-park.com. Reservations accepted only for parties of 15 or more. Main courses $5–$9 at lunch, $7–$25 at dinner; specials $19–$40. AE, DC, DISC, MC, V. Daily 11:30am–2:30pm; Mon–Sat 2:30–10pm; Sun 2:30–9pm. Validated parking available. T: Green or Blue Line to Government Center, or Orange Line to Haymarket.

INEXPENSIVE

Cosí Sandwich Bar 🗯 SANDWICHES/ITALIAN   Flavorful fillings on delectable bread make Cosí a downtown lunch hot spot. This location, right on the Freedom Trail, makes a delicious refueling stop. Italian flatbread baked fresh all day—so tasty that it's even good plain—gets split open and filled with your choice of meat, fish, vegetables, cheese, and spreads. The more fillings you choose, the more you pay; the total can really climb, so don't go too wild if you're on a budget. Tandoori chicken with caramelized onions is sensational, as is smoked salmon with spinach-artichoke spread.

Other branches are at 14 Milk St. (© 617/426-7565), near Downtown Crossing, and 133 Federal St. (© 617/292-2674), which has patio seating in warm weather.

53 State St. (at Congress St.). © 617/723-4447. Sandwiches $6–$9; soups and salads $3–$7. AE, DC, MC, V. Mon–Thurs 7am–6pm; Fri 7am–5pm. T: Orange or Blue Line to State.

5 Downtown Crossing

VERY EXPENSIVE

Locke-Ober 🗯 CONTINENTAL   "Locke's" is *the* traditional Boston restaurant, a power-broker favorite since 1875. It changed hands and underwent a refurbishment in 2001, but that was just cosmetic—even with some physical upgrades and a female owner (famed Boston restaurateur Lydia Shire), it feels like a time machine. In an alley off the Winter Street pedestrian mall, the wood-paneled restaurant entertainingly evokes a Waspy men's club. The long, mirrored downstairs bar dates from 1880, and the service can feel equally antique (as it did when a 20-something waiter called our party of 30-something women "my ladies" throughout lunch).

The food is unapologetically old-fashioned, though chef Jacky Robert injects a contemporary French touch. Traditional fish cakes come with new-fangled jasmine rice; salmon is tea-smoked; delectable scalloped potatoes accompany the signature roast beef hash. Other traditions, including excellent steaks and chops, Wiener schnitzel a la Holstein, and broiled scrod with brown bread, endure. So does Locke-Ober, an "only in Boston" experience if ever there was one.

⌐Tips Boston Restaurant Week

The third week of August is the annual Boston Restaurant Week, when dozens of terrific spots serve a three-course prix-fixe lunch for the decimal equivalent of the year—in 2004, $20.04. The Convention & Visitors Bureau (© 888/SEE-BOSTON; www.bostonusa.com) lists names of participating restaurants and individual numbers to call for reservations. Popular places book up quickly, so plan accordingly.

Finds **The Lunch Line**

Every weekday without fail, a queue forms in front of a takeout window on the Franklin Street side of Filene's. Downtown diners can't get enough of the scrumptious Chilean sandwiches at **Chacarero,** 426 Washington St. (© **617/542-0392**). At the first window, order chicken, beef, or vegetarian "with everything"—tomatoes, cheese, avocado, hot sauce, and (unexpected but delicious) green beans. Take your receipt to the end of the fast-moving line at the pickup window, seek out a seat, and pat yourself on the back. For less than $7, you're a savvy Bostonian.

3–4 Winter Place. © **617/542-1340.** Reservations recommended. Jacket suggested for men; no shorts or sneakers. Main courses $8–$32 at lunch; $26–$48 at dinner. AE, DISC, MC, V. Mon–Fri 11:30am–2:30pm; Mon–Thurs 5:30–10pm; Fri–Sat 5:30–11pm. Closed 1st 2 weeks of July. Valet parking available after 5:30pm. T: Red or Orange Line to Downtown Crossing or Green Line to Park St.

INEXPENSIVE

There's a **Cosí Sandwich Bar** (see the listing in the previous section "Faneuil Hall Marketplace & the Financial District") at 14 Milk St. (© **617/426-7565**).

Fajitas & 'Ritas TEX-MEX   This entertaining restaurant isn't the most authentic in town, but it's one of the most fun. It serves nachos, quesadillas, burritos, and, oh, yeah, fajitas. There's nothing exotic, just the usual beef, chicken, shrimp, beans, and so forth. You can also try barbecue items, such as smoked brisket or pulled pork, and (a recent addition) fish tacos. Mark your selections on a checklist, and a member of the somewhat harried staff quickly returns with big portions of fresh food—this place is too busy for anything to be sitting around for very long. As the name indicates, 'ritas (margaritas) are a house specialty. Primarily a casual business destination at lunch, it's livelier at dinner—probably thanks to all those margaritas.

25 West St. (between Washington and Tremont sts.). © **617/426-1222.** www.fajitasandritas.com. Reservations accepted only for parties of 8 or more. Main dishes $5–$8 at lunch, $5–$12 at dinner. AE, DC, DISC, MC, V. Mon–Tues 11:30am–9pm; Wed–Thurs 11:30am–10pm; Fri–Sat 11:30am–11pm; Sun noon–7pm. T: Red or Green Line to Park St., or Orange Line to Downtown Crossing.

6 Beacon Hill

VERY EXPENSIVE

No. 9 Park 🏵🏵 FRENCH COUNTRY/ITALIAN   One of Boston's most acclaimed restaurants sits in the shadow of the State House, an area better known for politicians' pubs than for fine dining. The legislators must make room for foodies here, thanks to chef-owner Barbara Lynch's flair for strong flavors and superb pasta. To start, try beet salad—an upright cylinder of shredded vegetables atop blue cheese, surrounded by greens—or oysters on the half shell with unusually tasty mignonette sauce. Move on to braised short ribs of beef served with marrow custard, striped bass with mushroom fricassee, or a sampler of those famous pastas. For dessert, profiteroles (a chocolate version served with coconut ice cream) are worth every calorie. *One caveat:* The austere but comfortable space can get quite loud.

9 Park St. © **617/742-9991.** www.no9park.com. Reservations recommended. Main courses $15–$23 at lunch, $27–$40 at dinner. Chef's tasting menu $85 for 7 courses, $110 for 9 courses. AE, DC, MC, V. Mon–Fri 11:30am–2:30pm; Mon–Sat 5:30–10:30pm. Valet parking available at dinner. T: Green or Red Line to Park St.

MODERATE

Artú (p. 110) has a branch at 89 Charles St. (© **617/227-9023**). It's open Sunday and Monday from 4 to 11pm, Tuesday through Saturday from 11am to 11pm.

Istanbul Café TURKISH   Tucked away behind the State House, this small, crowded place is worth seeking out. Four steps down from the street, it attracts neighborhood residents, politicians, and staffers from nearby Mass. General Hospital. It's not a great place to go if you're in a rush, because the always-helpful service sometimes grinds to a halt. That's not a complaint—I go there to catch up with friends and linger over the food, which ranges from familiar and unusually good to just unusual (and good). The appetizer sampler makes a great introduction to the cuisine. *Adana kebab* (elongated meatballs of spiced ground lamb, threaded onto skewers and grilled) appears several times in main dishes; it's a must if you like lamb. Cheese lovers will monopolize the plainest version of Turkish pizza, an odd but delicious dish. But unless you can't get enough okra, steer clear of *etli bamya*, which is more vegetable than meat. The baklava is a lovely rendition of the traditional dessert, crunchy and not too sweet, perfect with a Turkish coffee.

37 Bowdoin St. © 617/227-3434. Main courses $7–$17; sandwiches $5–$7. MC, V. Mon–Wed 11am–10pm; Thurs–Sat 11am–11pm; Sun noon–10pm. T: Red or Green Line to Park St., or Blue Line to Bowdoin.

7 Charlestown

VERY EXPENSIVE

Olives ★★ ECLECTIC   This informal bistro near the Charlestown Navy Yard is so popular that a line often forms shortly after 5pm—befriending five strangers and making a reservation won't sound farfetched after a daunting wait for a table. If you don't arrive by 5:45pm, expect the charm-free front-desk staff to banish you for at least 2 hours; camp at the bar, if there's room. Once you're seated in the glass-walled dining room, perhaps on a cushy banquette, you'll find the noise level high (thanks partly to the open kitchen), the service uneven, and the ravenous customers festive.

Happily, the food is worth the ordeal. Celebrity chef Todd English, though not a hands-on owner, is a culinary genius—as he demonstrates at branches around the country. Classics on the regularly changing menu include the delicious Olives tart (olives, caramelized onions, and anchovies), and juicy spit-roasted chicken flavored with herbs and garlic. The seafood specials are always

---

Overrated **Celebrity-Chef Alert**

You won't get far in Boston's culinary circles without hearing about Todd English, the photogenic face of a four-state empire that started with a little place in Charlestown and now extends as far as Las Vegas. My favorite parts of his realm are the originals, **Figs** and **Olives**. You'll also find his signature style—fresh, original, uncomplicated yet sophisticated—in Faneuil Hall Marketplace at **KingFish Hall**, a seafood restaurant in the South Market Building, and at **Bonfire**, a steakhouse in the Boston Park Plaza Hotel, 50 Park Plaza (© **617/262-3473**). Two constants across English's kingdom: noisy dining rooms and high prices.

worth investigating—perhaps crisp-skin black sea bass with cauliflower purée, rock shrimp, and saffron butter. When you order your entree, the server will ask if you want falling chocolate cake for dessert. Say yes.

10 City Sq. ② 617/242-1999. www.toddenglish.com/Restaurants/Olives.html. Reservations accepted only for parties of 6 or more. Main courses $18–$32. AE, DC, MC, V. Mon–Fri 5:30–10pm; Sat 5–10:30pm. Valet parking available. T: Orange or Green Line to North Station; 10-min. walk.

8 Chinatown/Theater District

The most entertaining and delicious introduction to Chinatown's cuisine is **dim sum** (see "Yum, Yum, Dim Sum," below). If you're eating dinner, many restaurants have a second menu for Chinese patrons (often written in Chinese). You can ask for it or tell your waiter that you want your meal Chinese-style.

The area around Park Square (Columbus Ave. and South Charles St., between the Theater District and the Public Garden) is a hotbed of upscale national chain restaurants. None of these places offers a unique or even unusual experience, but they're all reliable destinations if you're feeling homesick or unadventurous. They include **Fleming's Prime Steakhouse & Wine Bar,** 217 Stuart St. (② 617/292-0808); **Maggiano's Little Italy,** 4 Columbus Ave. (② 617/542-3456); **McCormick & Schmick's Seafood Restaurant,** 34 Columbus Ave., in the Boston Park Plaza Hotel (② 617/482-3999); and **P. F. Chang's China Bistro,** 8 Park Plaza (② 617/573-0821).

VERY EXPENSIVE

Troquet ✦✦ NEW AMERICAN/WINE BAR Troquet's menu consists of three columns, with starters and main courses along either side and wines down the middle—a good arrangement, because wine is the centerpiece here. Troquet (French slang for "small wine cafe") offers 40-plus wines by the 2- or 4-ounce glass and hundreds more by the bottle. Because the restaurant's markup is lower than usual, sampling several selections is surprisingly affordable. The menu recommends pairings, and you'll want just the right thing to complement the exceptional cuisine, which emphasizes seasonal ingredients and never overwhelms the wine. The word that keeps coming back to me is *subtle*—a salad with hazelnut chèvre tempura and marinated beets was flavorful but not overpowering; wild-mushroom pithivier was rich and earthy; panko-crusted cod seemed perfumed rather than punched up with red curry and kaffir lime. Best of all, whether you're a novice or a pro, the staff offers as much wine advice as you need. I'll offer some dessert advice: chocolate fondant cake. The restaurant is a family affair—wine director Chris Campbell is co-owner with his wife, Diane, and chef Scott Hebert is married to pastry chef Natalia Andalo.

140 Boylston St. ② 617/695-9463. Reservations recommended. Main courses $21–$36. AE, DC, DISC, MC, V. Tues–Sun 5–11pm. T: Green Line to Boylston.

EXPENSIVE

There's a branch of **Legal Sea Foods** (p. 128) at 36 Park Sq., between Columbus Avenue and Stuart Street (② 617/426-4444; www.legalseafoods.com). **Jae's Café** (p. 122) has a location at 212 Stuart St. (② 617/451-5237).

Ginza Japanese Restaurant ✦✦ JAPANESE/SUSHI On a side street in Chinatown, you'll find one of the city's best Japanese restaurants. Track down the nondescript entrance, settle into one of the two rooms (in a booth, if you're lucky), and watch as kimono-clad waitresses glide past, bearing sushi boats the size of small children. Ginza is a magnet for Japanese expatriates, sushi-lovers,

Yum, Yum, Dim Sum

Many Chinatown restaurants offer dim sum, the traditional midday meal featuring appetizer-style dishes. You'll see steamed buns *(bao)* filled with pork or bean paste; meat, shrimp, and vegetable dumplings; spareribs; shrimp-stuffed eggplant; sticky rice dotted with sausage and vegetables; spring rolls; sweets such as sesame balls and coconut gelatin, and more. Waitresses wheel carts laden with tempting dishes to your table, and you order by pointing (unless you know Chinese). The waitress then stamps your check with the symbol of the dish, adding about $1 to $3 to your tab. Unless you're ravenous or you order a la carte items from the regular menu, the total usually won't be more than about $10 to $12 per person.

Dim sum varies from restaurant to restaurant, chef to chef, and even day to day; if something looks familiar, don't be surprised if it's different from what you're accustomed to, and equally good. This is a great group activity, especially on weekends. The selection is wider than on weekdays, and you'll see three generations of families sharing large tables. Even picky children can usually find something they enjoy. If you don't eat pork and shrimp, be aware that many, but not all, dishes include one or the other; calorie counters should know that many dishes (again, not all) are fried.

Empire Garden Restaurant *₭₭*, 690–698 Washington St., 2nd floor (② **617/482-8898**), serves a dazzling variety of dishes in a cavernous, ornate former theater balcony. Also known as Emperor's Garden, it opened in 1998 and instantly challenged the dim sum supremacy of **China Pearl** *₭*, 9 Tyler St., 2nd floor (② **617/426-4338**), and **Chau Chow City**, 83 Essex St. (② **617/338-8158**). All three are excellent.

and, in the wee hours, club-hoppers. It's not the only place in town where expert chefs work wonders with ocean-fresh ingredients, but it serves the most creative creations (including "spider maki," a soft-shelled crab fried and tucked into a seaweed wrapper with avocado, cucumber, and flying-fish roe). An excellent starter is *edamame*—addictive boiled and salted soybeans served in the pod (you pull the beans out with your teeth). Then let your imagination run wild, or trust the chefs to assemble something dazzling. Green-tea ice cream makes an unusually satisfying dessert, but nobody will blame you for finishing with a second (or 3rd) round of California maki.

There's another Ginza in **Brookline,** at 1002 Beacon St. (② **617/566-9688**). It serves a similar menu, but not to night-crawlers (the late nights are Fri and Sat, when closing time is 10:30pm).

14 Hudson St. ② **617/338-2261.** Reservations accepted only for parties of 6 or more. Sushi from $3.50; main courses $11–$20. AE, DC, MC, V. Mon–Fri 11:30am–2:30pm; Sat–Sun 11:30am–4pm; Sun–Mon 5pm–2am; Tues–Sat 5pm–4am. T: Orange Line to New England Medical Center.

MODERATE

East Ocean City *₭* CANTONESE/SEAFOOD   Don't get too attached to the inhabitants of the fish tanks here—they might turn up on your plate. Tanks make up one wall of the high-ceilinged space, decorated with lots of glass and

Booked aisle seat.

Reserved room with a view.

With a queen – no, make that a king-size bed.

other hard surfaces that make it rather noisy. The encyclopedic menu offers a huge range of dishes, but, as the name indicates, seafood is the focus. It's fresh, delicious, and carefully prepared. One specialty is clams in black-bean sauce, a spicy rendering of a messy, delectable dish. Just about anything that swims can be ordered steamed with ginger and scallions; for variety, check out the tasty noodle dishes.

25–29 Beach St. ✆ 617/542-2504. Reservations accepted only for parties of 6 or more. Main courses $5–$26; lunch specials (Mon–Fri until 3pm) $5. AE, MC, V. Sun–Thurs 11am–3am; Fri–Sat 11am–4am. Validated parking available weeknights and weekends. T: Orange Line to Chinatown.

Grand Chau Chow CANTONESE   This is one of the best and busiest restaurants in Chinatown, with niceties that the smaller restaurants don't offer, such as tablecloths and tuxedoed waiters. If you have the heart, you can watch your dinner swimming around in the large fish tanks, both salt- and freshwater. Clams with black-bean sauce is a signature dish, as is gray sole with fried fins and bones. Stick to seafood and you can't go wrong. Lunch specials are a great deal, but skip the chow fun, which quickly turns gelatinous. If you're in town during Chinese New Year celebrations, phone ahead and request a banquet for your group. For about $25 a person, you'll get so many courses that you'll lose track.

45 Beach St. ✆ 617/292-5166. Reservations accepted only for parties of 10 or more. Main courses $6–$24. AE, DC, DISC, MC, V. Sun–Thurs 10am–3am; Fri–Sat 10am–4am. T: Orange Line to Chinatown.

Jacob Wirth Company GERMAN/AMERICAN   In the heart of the Theater District, "Jake's" has been serving Bostonians since 1868—even before there were theaters here. The wood floor and brass accents give the room the feeling of a saloon, or perhaps a beer garden. The hearty German specialties include Wiener schnitzel, mixed grills, bratwurst, and knockwurst. Daily specials, a large selection of sandwiches and brews on tap, and more contemporary American fare—often including excellent prime rib—round out the menu. Service at lunchtime is snappy, but if you want to be on time for the theater, the suspense might be greater in the restaurant than at the show.

33–37 Stuart St. ✆ 617/338-8586. www.jacobwirth.com. Reservations recommended at dinner. Main courses $7–$23. AE, DC, DISC, MC, V. Mon 11:30am–8pm; Tues–Thurs 11:30am–11pm; Fri–Sat 11:30am–midnight; Sun noon–8pm. Validated parking available. T: Green Line to Boylston, or Orange Line to New England Medical Center.

9 The South End

VERY EXPENSIVE

Hamersley's Bistro ⭐⭐ ECLECTIC   This is the place that put the South End on Boston's culinary map, a pioneering restaurant that's both classic and contemporary. One of its many claims to fame is its status as a Julia Child favorite. The husband-and-wife team of Gordon and Fiona Hamersley presides over a long dining room with lots of soft surfaces that absorb sound, so you can see but not quite hear what's going on at the tables around you. That means you'll have to quiz one of the courteous servers about the dish that just passed by—perhaps the signature appetizer of grilled mushrooms and garlic on country bread.

The menu changes seasonally and offers about a dozen carefully considered entrees noted for their emphasis on local ingredients and classic preparations. I find the famed roast chicken with garlic a bit tame, but cassoulet with pork, duck confit, and garlic sausage is a gorgeously executed combination of flavors and textures. This kitchen also has a way with seafood—perhaps sea scallops served with spring vegetables and lemon sauce. The wine list is excellent.

553 Tremont St. © **617/423-2700**. www.hamersleysbistro.com. Reservations recommended. Main courses $24–$39; tasting menu varies. AE, DISC, MC, V. Mon–Fri 6–10pm; Sat 5:30–10:30pm; Sun 5:30–9:30pm. Closed 1 week in Jan. Valet parking available. T: Orange Line to Back Bay.

Icarus ✦✦ ECLECTIC   This shamelessly romantic subterranean restaurant is perfect for everything from helping a friend heal a broken heart to celebrating a milestone anniversary. Marble accents and dark-wood trim lend an elegant air to the two-level dining room, and the service is efficient but not formal. Chef and co-owner Chris Douglass uses choice local seafood, poultry, meats, and produce to create his imaginative dishes. The menu changes regularly. You might start with braised exotic mushrooms atop polenta, succulent lobster salad, or the daily "pasta whim" (but make sure the server quotes the price, which can be extravagant). Move on to pine-nut-and-lemon–crusted lamb chops served with lamb osso buco or a scrumptious seafood special like seared tuna Provençal with Meyer lemon confit, tomatoes, and risotto cakes. Finally, save room for dessert: The trio of seasonal fruit sorbets is one of the best nonchocolate desserts I've ever tasted.

3 Appleton St. © **617/426-1790**. www.icarusrestaurant.com. Reservations recommended. Main courses $24–$33. AE, DC, DISC, MC, V. Mon–Thurs 6–10pm; Fri 6–10:30pm; Sat 5:30–10:30pm; Sun 5:30–10pm. Valet parking available. T: Green Line to Arlington, or Orange Line to Back Bay.

EXPENSIVE

Jae's Café ✦ PAN-ASIAN/SUSHI   The original Jae's is a busy neighborhood favorite with the motto "Eat at Jae's, live forever." (Well, you can't prove it *isn't* true.) Locals and fans of flavorful food pack the sleek two-level space; seating extends onto a small patio in warm weather. The wide-ranging menu includes excellent traditional and "designer" sushi, unusual salads and soups, and a variety of Asian specialties. A fragrant Vietnamese-style spring roll makes a good starter. Traditional dishes such as Korean *bibim bop* (spicy beef cooked in a stone pot) and pad Thai are excellent renditions; mix-and-match noodle dishes let you put together your own favorites, or take your server's advice.

Call before heading over here—the Jae's in Cambridge closed recently, and I don't want you to be disappointed. At press time, there was another Jae's in the **Theater District** at 212 Stuart St. (© 617/451-5237).

520 Columbus Ave. © **617/421-9405**. www.jaescafe.com. Reservations recommended at dinner. Main courses $9–$25; sushi from $3.50. AE, DC, MC, V. Mon–Sat 11:30am–4pm; Mon–Wed 5–10:30pm; Thurs–Sat 5–11pm; Sun noon–10pm. T: Green Line E to Prudential, or Orange Line to Mass. Ave.

MODERATE

Bob the Chef's Jazz Cafe ✦ SOUTHERN/CAJUN   Bob the Chef's resembles a yuppie fern bar, but it serves generous portions of Southern specialties against a backdrop of jazz. The music is live Thursday through Saturday nights and at Sunday brunch. You'll find dishes such as fried chicken, served alone or with barbecued ribs; meatloaf; "soul fish" (in cornmeal batter); and Creole specialties such as jambalaya and shrimp étouffée. Dinners come with a corn muffin and your choice of two side dishes—including black-eyed peas, macaroni and cheese, collard greens, and candied yams. Frying is done in vegetable oil, not the customary lard, and everywhere you'd expect bacon for flavoring, the kitchen uses smoked turkey. For dessert, try the amazing sweet-potato pie, which makes pumpkin pie taste like vanilla pudding.

604 Columbus Ave. © **617/536-6204**. www.bobthechefs.com. Main courses $9–$15; sandwiches $5–$8. AE, DISC, MC, V. Tues–Wed 11:30am–10pm; Thurs–Sat 11:30am–midnight; Sun 11am–9pm (brunch until 3pm). T: Orange Line to Mass. Ave.

Garden of Eden SANDWICHES/FRENCH   Almost as well known for its people-watching as for its cuisine, Garden of Eden sits on a busy corner on the South End's main drag. It's a good place to go for neighborhood gossip as well as tasty food served at communal tables (and on the patio in good weather). You can order everything from breakfast to cappuccino with a delectable pastry to a full meal. The unusual sandwiches on fresh-baked bread are especially popular—chicken breast and Swiss cheese with cucumbers and Dijon vinaigrette on whole-wheat raisin-pecan sounds like too much, but it's just right; the namesake sandwich of mesclun, red onion, blue cheese, and (of course) apples on a baguette is equally satisfying. Dinner entrees are French country comfort food—coq au vin, yummy macaroni and cheese, and a chicken pot pie whose entire description reads "Wow is this good." True all around.

571 Tremont St. © **617/247-8377**. www.goeboston.com. Sandwiches and salads $5–$9.50; main courses $5.50–$15. AE, DC, DISC, MC, V. Mon–Fri 7am–11pm; Sat–Sun 7:30am–11pm. T: Orange Line to Back Bay.

INEXPENSIVE

Nashoba Brook Bakery ✫ SANDWICHES   This little neighborhood cafe serves baked goods so scrumptious you'll wish the South End were your neighborhood. The soups, salads, breads, and pastries make a reverse commute every day from the original location in suburban Concord. Everything is fresh and delicious, especially the sandwiches—like ham and cheese with the tasty addition of apple slices—on incredible artisan breads. You can sit toward the front, where you'll have a view of the street, or closer to the counter, where you can ponder what to order for a snack to eat later.

288 Columbus Ave. © **617/236-0777**. www.slowrise.com. Most items less than $6. MC, V. Mon–Fri 7am–6pm; Sat 8am–5pm; Sun 8am–4pm. T: Orange Line to Back Bay.

10 The Back Bay

VERY EXPENSIVE

Aujourd'hui ✫✫✫ CONTEMPORARY AMERICAN   On the second floor of the city's premier luxury hotel, the most beautiful restaurant in town has floor-to-ceiling windows overlooking the Public Garden. But even if it were under a pup tent, the incredible service and food would make Aujourd'hui a hit with its special-occasion and expense-account clientele. Yes, the cost is astronomical, but how often is it true that you get what you pay for? Here, you do.

The regularly changing menu encompasses basic hotel-restaurant offerings and the creations that characterize an inventive kitchen. Executive chef Edward Gannon uses regional products and the freshest ingredients available, and the wine list is excellent. To start, try a perfectly balanced seasonal soup or a huge salad. Entrees might include pepper-crusted tuna with balsamic vinegar sauce, or grilled beef tenderloin with parsnip purée, oxtail ravioli, and grilled oyster mushrooms; there's always a lobster option, too. The dessert menu also changes; it includes picture-perfect soufflés and homemade sorbets.

In the Four Seasons Hotel, 200 Boylston St. © **617/351-2037**. Reservations recommended (required on holidays). Main courses $19–$24 at lunch, $35–$45 at dinner; tasting menus vary; Sun buffet brunch $58 adults, $28 children. AE, DC, DISC, MC, V. Mon–Fri 6:30–11am; Sat 7–11am; Mon–Fri 11:30am–2:30pm; Sun brunch 11:30am–2pm; Mon–Sat 5:30–10:30pm; Sun 6–10pm. Valet parking available. T: Green Line to Arlington.

Clio ✫✫ ECLECTIC   Clio is a trip. Chef Ken Oringer operates a kitchen that's part chemistry lab and a dining room that's part game-show set. It sounds like an episode of "Jeopardy!": Does the maple make the white-asparagus soup too sweet? Does the suckling pig still have its head? What are the emerald green drops alongside the chocolate cake? (The answers: No, no, and basil syrup.) Popular with businesspeople and couples, Clio is a plush room with funky accents—check out the leopard-print rug—that match the mood of food. The menu changes daily, according to what Oringer can find fresh or fly in. More than at any other restaurant in town, rely on the good-natured servers' expert advice. You'll bond quickly as you sort out various ingredients ("forgotten" vegetables? bee pollen? pistachio broth? argan oil? grains of paradise? brandade broth?).

A common complaint is that portions are too small for the price, but this chowhound disagrees. They're not so skimpy, and you wouldn't want too much of food this rich and complicated, anyway. You won't be stuffed, but you will be satisfied—and you'll have room for dessert, which Oringer, a former pastry chef, takes as seriously as anything else.

In the Eliot Hotel, 370A Commonwealth Ave. ℂ 617/536-7200. www.cliorestaurant.com. Reservations recommended. Main courses $29–$45. AE, DC, DISC, MC, V. Sun and Tues–Thurs 5:30–10pm; Fri–Sat 5:30–10:30pm. Valet parking available. T: Green Line B, C, or D to Hynes/ICA.

Grill 23 & Bar ★★ AMERICAN   The best steakhouse in town, a wood-paneled, glass-walled place with a businesslike air, is more than just a steakhouse. A briefcase-toting crowd fills its two levels in search of traditional slabs of beef and chops as well as more-creative options. Steak au poivre and lamb chops are perfectly grilled, crusty, juicy, and tender. The inventively updated meatloaf incorporates sirloin and chorizo, and pork shank comes with toasted pasta and dandelion and onion greens. Fish dishes aren't quite as memorable as the meat offerings, but hey, it's a steakhouse. The bountiful a la carte side dishes include creamed spinach and out-of-this-world garlic mashed potatoes. Desserts are toothsome but (this is *not* your father's steakhouse) don't always include cheesecake. The service is exactly right for the setting, helpful but not familiar.

A couple of caveats: The excellent wine list is quite pricey, and the noise level rises as the evening progresses. Still, you probably won't realize that you're shouting until you're outside yelling about what a good meal you had.

161 Berkeley St. ℂ 617/542-2255. www.grill23.com. Reservations recommended. Main courses $23–$40. AE, DC, DISC, MC, V. Mon–Thurs 5:30–10:30pm; Fri–Sat 5:30–11pm; Sun 5:30–10pm. Valet parking available. T: Green Line to Arlington.

L'Espalier ★★★ NEW ENGLAND/FRENCH   Dinner at L'Espalier is a unique experience, very much like spending the evening at the home of a dear friend who has only your pleasure in mind—and a dozen helpers in the kitchen. Owners Catherine and Frank McClelland (he's the chef) preside over three dining rooms on the second floor of an 1886 town house. The space is formal yet inviting, and the service is excellent. The food, an exploration of the freshest and most interesting ingredients available, is magnificent.

A first course of flambéed Maine lobster arrives with baby zucchini and creamed spiced pumpkin, and perfectly balanced fresh cabernet grape vinaigrette dresses a salad of greens with wild rice, herbed polenta, and white asparagus. Main courses are equally imaginative: perhaps arctic char in a parsley-citrus crust with red-pepper relish and lemony rosemary broth, or beef filet and prawn with a sauce of cabernet sauvignon, black truffle, and marrow. The breads, sorbets, ice creams, and alarmingly good desserts (many adapted from the family's heirloom cookbooks) are made in-house. Even if you order one of the superb soufflés, ask to see the beautiful desserts. Or finish with the celebrated cheese tray, which always includes two local selections.

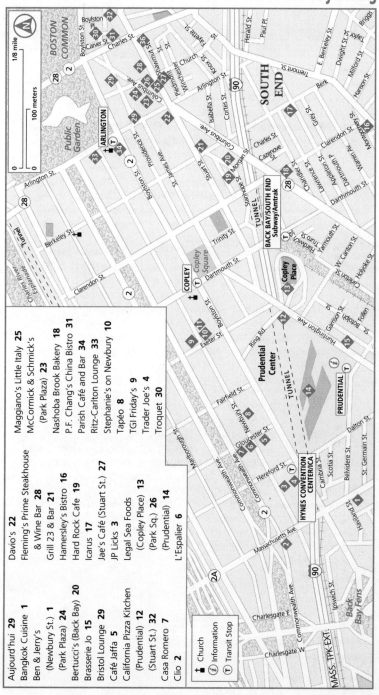

Aujourd'hui **29**
Bangkok Cuisine **1**
Ben & Jerry's
(Newbury St.) **1**
(Park Plaza) **24**
Bertucci's (Back Bay) **20**
Brasserie Jo **15**
Bristol Lounge **29**
Café Jaffa **5**
California Pizza Kitchen
(Prudential) **12**
(Stuart St.) **32**
Casa Romero **7**
Clio **2**

Davio's **22**
Fleming's Prime Steakhouse
& Wine Bar **28**
Grill 23 & Bar **21**
Hamersley's Bistro **16**
Hard Rock Cafe **19**
Icarus **17**
Jae's Café (Stuart St.) **27**
JP Licks **3**
Legal Sea Foods
(Copley Place) **13**
(Park Sq.) **26**
(Prudential) **14**
L'Espalier **6**

Maggiano's Little Italy **25**
McCormick & Schmick's
(Park Plaza) **23**
Nashoba Brook Bakery **18**
P.F. Chang's China Bistro **31**
Parish Café and Bar **34**
Ritz-Carlton Lounge **33**
Stephanie's on Newbury **10**
Tapéo **8**
TGI Friday's **9**
Trader Joe's **4**
Troquet **30**

+ Church
(i) Information
(T) Transit Stop

⌒Kids Family-Friendly Restaurants

Like chocolate and champagne, well-behaved children are welcome almost everywhere. Most Boston-area restaurants can accommodate families, and many youngsters can be stunned into tranquillity if a place is fancy enough. If your kids can't or won't sign a good-conduct pledge, here are some suggestions.

The **Bertucci's** chain of pizzerias appeals to children and adults equally, with wood-fired brick ovens that are visible from many tables, great rolls made from pizza dough, and pizzas and pastas that range from basic to sophisticated. There are convenient branches at Faneuil Hall Marketplace (② **617/227-7889**), on Merchants Row off State Street; in the Back Bay at 43 Stanhope St. (② **617/247-6161**), around the corner from the Hard Rock Cafe; and in Cambridge at 21 Brattle St., Harvard Square (② **617/864-4748**), and 799 Main St. (② **617/661-8356**), a short walk from Central Square.

The **Hard Rock Cafe,** 131 Clarendon St., Back Bay (② **617/424-ROCK**), and **House of Blues,** 96 Winthrop St., Cambridge (② **617/491-2583**), serve music with their food—and your kids will think you're *so* cool.

Another chain, **TGI Friday's,** 26 Exeter St., at Newbury Street, Back Bay (② **617/266-9040**), made its reputation by catering to singles, and all that pairing off apparently led to children. Young eaters receive a kids' package with balloons, crayons, a coloring book, peanut butter and crackers, and surprises wrapped in the chain's signature red-and-white stripes.

The **California Pizza Kitchen** chain has two Boston locations, 137 Stuart St., in the Theater District (② **617/720-0999**), and the Prudential Center, near the Huntington Avenue entrance (② **617/247-0888**), and a branch at the CambridgeSide Galleria mall (② **617/225-2772**).

The nonstop activity and smart-mouthed service at **Durgin-Park** (p. 115) will entrance any child, and parents of picky eaters appreciate the straightforward New England fare. Three good nonchain choices for kids are **Johnny's Luncheonette** (p. 136), **Jasper White's Summer Shack** (p. 138), and **La Groceria Ristorante Italiano** (p. 139).

The **Bristol Lounge,** in the Four Seasons Hotel, 200 Boylston St., Back Bay (② **617/351-2053**), looks almost too nice to have a kids' menu (with appetizers, plain main courses, desserts, and beverages). The unflappable staff is accommodating, and high chairs and sticker fun books are available.

---

30 Gloucester St. ② 617/262-3023. www.lespalier.com. Reservations required. Prix-fixe (3 courses) $68; degustation menu (7 courses; whole tables only) $85. AE, DC, DISC, MC, V. Mon–Sat 5:30–10pm. Valet parking available. T: Green Line B, C, or D to Hynes/ICA.

EXPENSIVE

Tapéo, 266 Newbury St. (② **617/267-4799**), has the same owners and menu as **Dalí** (p. 137).

Casa Romero ⭐ *Finds* MEXICAN   There's something about restaurants in alleys. They feel like secret clubs, and stumbling upon one can make a hungry diner feel like a daring explorer. Casa Romero is just such a place. The tiled floor, wood furnishings, dim lighting, and clay pots lend an authentic feel—you're definitely not at the local Tex-Mex counter. The food is excellent, with generous portions of spicy-hot and milder dishes; the friendly staff will help you negotiate the menu. If the soup of the day is garlic, don't miss it. Main-dish specialties include several kinds of enchiladas, excellent stuffed squid in tomato-and-chipotle sauce, chicken breast in mole poblano sauce (a spicy concoction with a hint of chocolate), and terrific pork tenderloin marinated with oranges and chipotle peppers. The walled garden is the "find" here; on a summer evening, it's a peaceful retreat.

30 Gloucester St., side entrance. ℭ 617/536-4341. www.casaromero.com. Reservations recommended. Main courses $14–$27. DISC, MC, V. Sun–Thurs 5–10pm; Fri–Sat 5–11pm. T: Green Line B, C, or D to Hynes/ICA.

Davio's ⭐⭐ CREATIVE NORTHERN ITALIAN   Davio's moved here from its longtime home in a cozy Newbury Street brownstone in late 2002. Fans (including this one) worried that the relocation to a chic, cavernous space would destroy the restaurant's comfortable vibe, but Davio's is, if anything, even more enjoyable. Owner-chef Steve DiFillippo built the restaurant's excellent reputation on its top-notch kitchen and dedicated staff; here, they're the same, only bigger. The flavors are big, too: homemade sausage, savory soups, out-of-this-world pasta and risotto. A la carte grilled meats are a terrific addition to the menu, but I prefer main courses such as pan-roasted salmon with crab risotto and wild rice, or pork chop alla Milanese with creamy potatoes, fried onions, and lemon-caper sauce. The excellent breads and desserts are made in-house. Davio's also has a well-edited wine list, including some rare and expensive Italian vintages. Despite the open kitchen, the bar in the middle of the room, and the lively lounge area, the noise level allows for conversation, even at busy times.

There's another Davio's in **Cambridge**, at the Royal Sonesta Hotel, 5 Cambridge Pkwy. (ℭ **617/661-4810**). Dinner service ends at 10pm nightly, and there's outdoor seating in good weather.

Finds Boston Tea Party, Part 2

In Boston, the only city that has a tea party named after it, the tradition of afternoon tea at a posh hotel is alive and well. The best afternoon tea in town is at the **Bristol Lounge** in the Four Seasons Hotel, 200 Boylston St. (ℭ **617/351-2037**). The gorgeous room, lovely view, and courtly ritual elevate scones, pastries, tea sandwiches, and nut bread from delicious to unforgettable. The Bristol serves tea ($23, or $30 with a kir royale) every day from 3 to 4:30pm; reservations are essential. The **Ritz-Carlton, Boston,** 15 Arlington St. (ℭ **617/536-5700**), serves tea in the celebrated **Lounge** Wednesday through Sunday at 2:30 and 4pm. Prices range from $16 for the children's tea to $38 for a luxurious spread of pastries and sandwiches with a glass of champagne. You'll need reservations. Less formal but still delicious is the a la carte service at **Intrigue** (ℭ **617/856-7744**), in the Boston Harbor Hotel, Rowes Wharf, which serves tea daily.

75 Arlington St. ℂ **617/357-4810**. www.davios.com. Reservations recommended. Main courses $17–$36. AE, DC, DISC, MC, V. Mon–Sat 11:30am–3pm; Sun brunch 11am–3pm; daily 5–11pm. Lounge menu Sun–Thurs 3–11pm; Fri–Sat 3pm–midnight. Validated parking available. T: Green Line to Arlington.

Legal Sea Foods ✦✦✦ SEAFOOD   The food at Legal Sea Foods isn't the fanciest, cheapest, or trendiest. It's the freshest, and management's commitment to that policy has produced a thriving chain. Out-of-towners sometimes react suspiciously when I recommend Legal's—they're expecting an insider tip, and I'm suggesting a place they've already heard of. Just remember that this family-owned business enjoys an international reputation for serving only top-quality fish and shellfish. The menu includes regular selections (scrod, haddock, blue-fish, salmon, shrimp, calamari, and lobster, among others) plus whatever was at market that morning, prepared in every imaginable way, and it's all splendid. The clam chowder is great, the fish chowder lighter but equally good. Entrees run the gamut from grilled fish served plain or with Cajun spices (try the arctic char) to seafood fra'diavolo on fresh linguine to salmon baked in parchment with vegetables and white wine. Or go the luxurious route and order a mammoth lob-ster. The classic dessert is ice cream bonbons, but the Boston cream pie is so good that you might come back just for that.

I suggest the Prudential Center branch because it takes reservations (at lunch only), a deviation from a long tradition. Another tradition that's mercifully fad-ing is the policy of serving each dish when it's ready—these days, you'll proba-bly get your food at the same time as the rest of your party.

Legal's has other locations at 255 State St., on the waterfront (ℂ **617/227-3115;** T: Blue Line to Aquarium); at 36 Park Sq., between Columbus Avenue and Stuart Street (ℂ **617/426-4444;** T: Green Line to Arlington); and at Cop-ley Place, 2nd level (ℂ **617/266-7775;** T: Orange Line to Back Bay or Green Line to Copley). In Cambridge, branches are in the courtyard of the Charles Hotel, 1 Bennett St. (ℂ **617/491-9400;** T: Red Line to Harvard), and at 5 Cambridge Center (ℂ **617/864-3400;** T: Red Line to Kendall/MIT).

In the Prudential Center, 800 Boylston St. ℂ 617/266-6800. www.legalseafoods.com. Reservations recom-mended at lunch, not accepted at dinner. Main courses $8–$17 at lunch, $11–$35 at dinner. AE, DC, DISC, MC, V. Mon–Thurs 11am–10:30pm; Fri–Sat 11am–11:30pm; Sun noon–10pm. T: Green Line B, C, or D to Hynes/ICA or E to Prudential.

MODERATE

Bangkok Cuisine ✦ THAI   Extremely popular with patrons of nearby Sym-phony Hall and the students who dominate this neighborhood, Bangkok Cui-sine is a classic. The first Thai restaurant in Boston, it opened in 1979 and set (and has maintained) a high standard for the many others that followed. For the unadventurous, it serves fantastic pad Thai. The rest of the menu runs the gamut from excellent basil chicken to all sorts of curry offerings, pan-fried or deep-fried

---

⟮*Tips* **Beat the Rush**

If you plan to dine in a neighborhood that's near a performing arts or sports venue, try to arrive after the performance or game begins so you don't get caught in the frenzy. This is especially true in the Symphony Hall area and the Theater District, as well as Harvard Square, the North End (when there's an event at the FleetCenter), and Kenmore Square (during baseball season).

Quick Bites & Picnic Provisions

Takeout food particularly appeals to two kinds of out-of-towners: eat-and-run sightseers, and picnickers looking to take advantage of the acres of waterfront property in Boston and Cambridge. Some suggestions:

If you're walking the Freedom Trail, pick up food at **Faneuil Hall Marketplace** and cross the street under the Expressway, or buy a tasty sandwich in the North End at **Il Panino Express,** 266 Hanover St. ((℗ 617/720-5720), and stroll down Richmond Street toward the harbor. From either place, walk past the Marriott to the end of Long Wharf and eat on the plaza as you watch the boats and planes, or stay to the left of the hotel and eat in Christopher Columbus Waterfront Park, overlooking the marina.

In the **Financial District,** the **Milk Street Café** operates a kiosk ((℗ 617/350-7275) in the park at Zero Post Office Square. Its kosher offerings include salads, sandwiches (on bread and rolled up in a pita), fish dishes, fruit, and pastries. Eat in the park or head to the harbor.

Two neighborhoods abut the Charles River Esplanade, a great destination for a picnic, concert, or movie. In the **Back Bay,** stop at **Trader Joe's,** 899 Boylston St. ((℗ 617/262-6505), for prepared food. At the foot of **Beacon Hill,** pick up all you need for a do-it-yourself feast at **Savenor's Supermarket,** 160 Charles St. ((℗ 617/723-6328). Or call ahead to **Figs,** 42 Charles St. ((℗ 617/742-3447), a minuscule pizzeria that's an offshoot of the celebrated Olives. The upscale fare isn't cheap, but avoiding that long line is worth the price—as is the delectable pizza.

On the Cambridge side of the river, **Harvard Square** is close enough to the water to allow a riverside repast. **Formaggio's,** in the Garage mall, 81 Mount Auburn St. ((℗ 617/547-4795), serves excellent gourmet sandwiches and salads. Take yours to John F. Kennedy Park, on Memorial Drive and Kennedy Street, or right to the riverbank.

whole fish, noodle soups, and hot-and-sour salads. Green curry in coconut milk and vegetables prepared with strong green Thai chile pepper are the most incendiary dishes. In this long, narrow room, there are no secrets—if the person at the next table is eating something appealing, ask what it is.

177A Mass. Ave. (℗ 617/262-5377. Reservations not accepted. Main courses $5–$8 at lunch; $8–$15 at dinner. AE, DISC, MC, V. Daily 11:30am–10:30pm. T: Green Line B, C, or D to Hynes/ICA.

Brasserie Jo ⟨ REGIONAL FRENCH   One of the most discriminating diners I know lit up like a marquee upon hearing that Boston has a branch of this Chicago favorite. The food is classic—house-made patés, fresh baguettes, superb shellfish, salade Niçoise, Alsatian onion tart, choucroute, coq au vin—but never boring. The house beer, an Alsace-style draft, is a good accompaniment. The casual, all-day French brasserie and bar fits well in this neighborhood, where shoppers can always use a break but might not want a full meal. It's also a good bet before or after the symphony, and it's popular for business lunches. The only drawbacks are the noise level, which can be high when the spacious room is full, and the uneven service, which ranges from solicitous to forgetful.

120 Huntington Ave. © **617/425-3240**. Reservations recommended at dinner. Main courses $6–$15 at lunch, $15–$27 at dinner; *plats du jour* $18–$32. AE, DC, DISC, MC, V. Mon–Fri 6:30am–11pm; Sat 7am–11pm; Sun 7am–10pm; late-night menu daily until 1am. Valet parking available. T: Green Line E to Prudential.

INEXPENSIVE

Café Jaffa MIDDLE EASTERN   A long, narrow brick room with a glass front, Café Jaffa looks more like a snazzy pizza place than the excellent Middle Eastern restaurant it is. The reasonable prices, high quality, and large portions draw hordes of students and other young people for traditional Middle Eastern offerings such as falafel, baba ghanouj, and hummus, as well as burgers and steak tips. Lamb, beef, and chicken kabobs come with Greek salad, rice pilaf, and pita bread. For dessert, try the baklava if it's fresh (give it a pass if not). There is a short list of beer and wine, and many fancy coffee offerings.

48 Gloucester St. © **617/536-0230**. Main courses $5–$16. AE, DC, DISC, MC, V. Mon–Thurs 11am–10:30pm; Fri–Sat 11am–11pm; Sun noon–10pm. T: Green Line B, C, or D to Hynes/ICA.

11 Kenmore Square to Brookline

EXPENSIVE

Ginza Japanese Restaurant (p. 119) has a second location at 1002 Beacon St., Brookline (© **617/566-9688**). Unlike the Boston location, the Brookline branch doesn't cater to an after-hours crowd; its late nights are Friday and Saturday, when closing time is 10:30pm.

The Elephant Walk ★★ FRENCH/CAMBODIAN   France meets Cambodia on the menu at this madly popular spot, 4 blocks from Kenmore Square and decorated with lots of pachyderms. The menu is French on one side and Cambodian on the other, but the boundary is quite porous. Many Cambodian dishes have part-French names, such as *poulet dhomrei* (chicken with Asian basil, bamboo shoots, fresh pineapple, and kaffir lime leaves) and *curry de crevettes* (shrimp curry with picture-perfect vegetables). My mouth is still burning from *loc lac,* fork-tender beef cubes in addictively spicy sauce. On the French side, you'll find pan-seared filet mignon with *pommes frites* (french fries), and pan-seared tuna with three-peppercorn crust. Many dishes are available with tofu substituted for animal protein. The pleasant staff members will help if you need guidance. Ask to be seated in the plant-filled front room, which is less noisy than the main dining room and has a view of the street.

900 Beacon St., Boston. © **617/247-1500**. www.elephantwalk.com. Reservations recommended at dinner Sun–Thurs, not accepted Fri–Sat. Main courses $7–$19 at lunch; $11–$27 at dinner. AE, DC, DISC, MC, V. Mon–Sat 11:30am–2:30pm; Mon–Thurs 5–10pm; Fri 5–11pm; Sat 4:30–11pm; Sun 4:30–10pm. Valet parking available at dinner. T: Green Line C to St. Mary's St.

MODERATE

There's a branch of the **Daily Catch** (p. 111) at 441 Harvard St., Brookline (© **617/734-5696;** www.dailycatch.com).

INEXPENSIVE

Zaftigs Delicatessen DELI/AMERICAN   The magical phrase "breakfast served all day" might be enough to lure you to this bustling restaurant, but even breakfast haters (yes, there is such an animal) will be happy at Zaftigs. The name, Yiddish for "pleasingly plump," is no joke—everything is good, and

The Great Outdoors: Alfresco Dining

Cambridge is a better destination for outdoor dining than Boston, but both cities offer agreeable spots to lounge under the sun or stars.

Across the street from the Charles River near Kendall Square, the **Sail Loft,** 1 Memorial Dr. (✆ **617/225-2222**), opens onto a leafy plaza that usually picks up a breeze from the water. Both restaurant patios at the **Royal Sonesta Hotel,** 5 Cambridge Pkwy. (✆ **617/491-3600**), have great views. The hotel's **Gallery Café** is casual; its **Davio's** (p. 127) is a bit fancier. On one of Harvard Square's main drags, **Shay's Pub & Wine Bar,** 58 John F. Kennedy St. (✆ **617/864-9161**), has a small, lively seating area. More peaceful are the patios at the **Blue Room** (p. 137) and **Oleana** (p. 138).

On the other side of the river, try the airy terrace at **Intrigue** (✆ **617/856-7744**), in the Boston Harbor Hotel, Rowes Wharf, which overlooks the harbor and the airport. Most bars and restaurants in **Faneuil Hall Marketplace** offer outdoor seating and great people-watching. In the Back Bay, Newbury Street is similarly diverting; a good vantage point is **Stephanie's on Newbury,** 190 Newbury St. (✆ **617/236-0990**). A popular shopping stop and after-work hangout is the **Parish Café and Bar,** 361 Boylston St. (✆ **617/247-4777**), where the sandwich menu is a "greatest hits" roster of top local chefs' creations. A laid-back alternative in this area is the hideaway garden at **Casa Romero** (p. 127).

portions are more than generous. Try fluffy pancakes, challah French toast, or a terrific omelet. They share the menu with wonderful deli sandwiches as well as entrees that seem basic but demonstrate a certain flair. Roasted chicken is juicy and flavorful, meatloaf and gravy equally enjoyable. The knock on Boston-area deli food is that it's not New York (well, duh), but the hard-core deli items here are more than acceptable. The gefilte fish is light, blintzes have a tang of citrus in the filling, and the chicken soup is excellent.

335 Harvard St., Brookline. ✆ 617/975-0075. www.zaftigs.com. Reservations recommended. Main courses $8–$17; breakfast items $3–$9. AE, DC, DISC, MC, V. Daily 8am–10pm. T: Green Line C to Coolidge Corner.

12 Cambridge

The dining scene in Cambridge, as in Boston, offers something for everyone, from penny-pinching students to the tycoons many of them aspire to become. The Red Line runs from Boston to Harvard Square, and many of the restaurants listed here are within walking distance; others (including a couple of real finds over the Somerville border) are under the heading "Outside Harvard Square."

To locate the restaurants reviewed in this section, see the "Cambridge Dining" map on p. 132.

HARVARD SQUARE & VICINITY
VERY EXPENSIVE

Chez Henri ✿ FRENCH/CUBAN   In a dark, elegant space off Mass. Ave. near Harvard Law School, Chez Henri is an example of how good fusion cuisine can be. Academic types and foodies flock here for French bistro–style food

Cambridge Dining

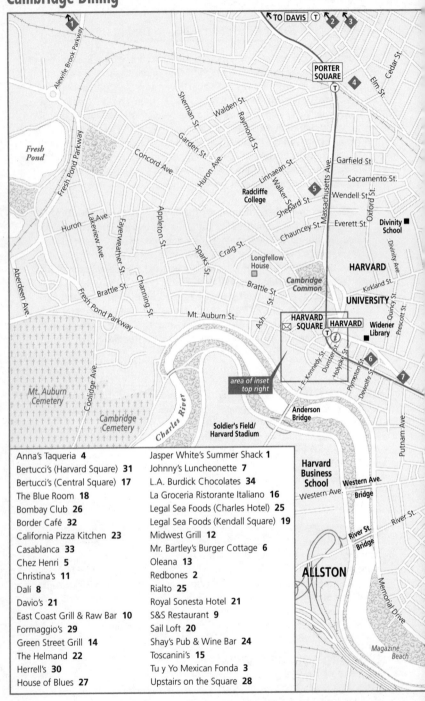

Anna's Taqueria **4**
Bertucci's (Harvard Square) **31**
Bertucci's (Central Square) **17**
The Blue Room **18**
Bombay Club **26**
Border Café **32**
California Pizza Kitchen **23**
Casablanca **33**
Chez Henri **5**
Christina's **11**
Dalí **8**
Davio's **21**
East Coast Grill & Raw Bar **10**
Formaggio's **29**
Green Street Grill **14**
The Helmand **22**
Herrell's **30**
House of Blues **27**

Jasper White's Summer Shack **1**
Johnny's Luncheonette **7**
L.A. Burdick Chocolates **34**
La Groceria Ristorante Italiano **16**
Legal Sea Foods (Charles Hotel) **25**
Legal Sea Foods (Kendall Square) **19**
Midwest Grill **12**
Mr. Bartley's Burger Cottage **6**
Oleana **13**
Redbones **2**
Rialto **25**
Royal Sonesta Hotel **21**
S&S Restaurant **9**
Sail Loft **20**
Shay's Pub & Wine Bar **24**
Toscanini's **15**
Tu y Yo Mexican Fonda **3**
Upstairs on the Square **28**

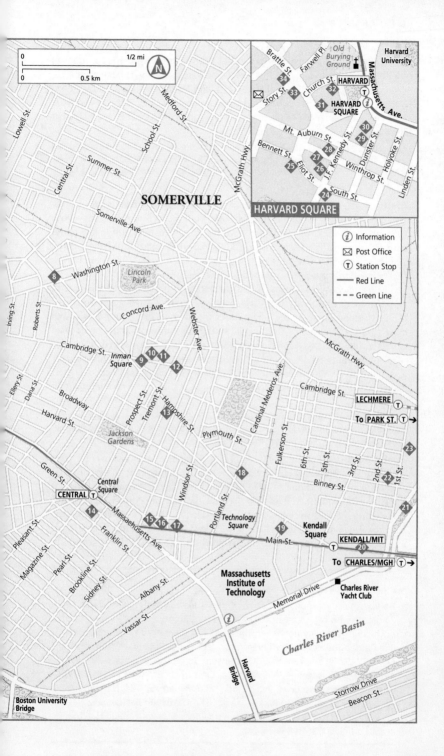

with Cuban accents. The menu changes regularly; to start, try house-made paté or veal sweetbreads served with garlic flan. Entrees include generous portions of meat, seafood, and vegetables. You might find a creative interpretation of steak frites (with Worcestershire demiglace), cod with lobster bordelaise and whipped potatoes, or a toothsome cassoulet. The dessert menu can be short on chocolate options, but creative use of seasonal fruit takes up the slack. The food at the bar is Cuban, as are the strong specialty drinks.

1 Shepard St. (at Mass. Ave.). © 617/354-8980. Reservations accepted only for parties of 6 or more. Main courses $23–$28; 3-course prix-fixe $36; bar food $6–$12. AE, MC, V. Mon–Thurs 6–10pm; Fri–Sat 5:30–10:30pm; Sun 5:30–9pm. Bar menu Mon–Thurs until 11pm, Fri–Sat until midnight, Sun until 10pm. T: Red Line to Harvard.

Rialto ★★★ MEDITERRANEAN This is my favorite Boston-area restaurant. Every element is carefully thought out, from the architecture to the service to chef Jody Adams's extraordinary food. It's a dramatic but comfortable room, with floor-to-ceiling windows overlooking Harvard Square, cushy banquettes, and standing lamps that cast a golden glow. It attracts a chic crowd, but it's not such a scene that out-of-towners will feel left behind.

The menu changes regularly. You might start with grilled Wellfleet clams with garlic bread, or Provençal fisherman's soup with rouille, Gruyère, and basil oil—the very essence of seafood. Main courses are so good that you might as well close your eyes and point. Tuscan-style steak with portobella-and-arugula salad is wonderful, and any seafood is a guaranteed winner—say, seared skate with sugar-pumpkin purée. A plate of creamy potato slices and mushrooms is so rich and juicy that it's almost like eating meat. For dessert, seasonal sorbets are a great choice, alone or in a combination such as lemon pound cake with Meyer lemon sorbet.

In the Charles Hotel, 1 Bennett St. © 617/661-5050. www.rialto-restaurant.com. Reservations recommended. Main courses $22–$36. AE, DC, MC, V. Sun–Thurs 5:30–10pm; Fri–Sat 5:30–11pm. Bar Sun–Thurs 4:30pm–midnight, Fri–Sat 5pm–1am. Valet and validated parking available. T: Red Line to Harvard.

Upstairs on the Square ★ ECLECTIC Upstairs on the Square is the reincarnation of a longtime Harvard Square favorite, Upstairs at the Pudding. It opened in its new location in late 2002 and immediately reestablished itself as the kind of restaurant that puts the "special" in "special occasion." The Soiree Room, atop the four-story building, is the place for that big anniversary dinner: It's a jewel box of pinks and golds under a low, mirrored ceiling. The menu is enjoyably old-fashioned, with straightforward main courses (a slab of swordfish,

---

(Kids The Scoop on Ice Cream

No less an expert than Ben Cohen of Ben & Jerry's has described Boston as "a great place for ice cream." That goes for Cambridge, too—residents of both cities famously defy even the most frigid weather to get their fix. I like Cambridge better: Try **Christina's,** 1255 Cambridge St., Inman Square (© 617/492-7021); **Herrell's,** 15 Dunster St., Harvard Square (© 617/497-2179); or **Toscanini's,** 899 Main St., Central Square (© 617/491-5877). Favorite Boston destinations include **Ben & Jerry's,** 174 Newbury St. (© 617/536-5456) and 20 Park Plaza (© 617/426-0890); **JP Licks,** 352 Newbury St. (© 617/236-1666); and **Steve's,** Quincy Market, Faneuil Hall Marketplace (© 617/367-0569).

a generous rack of lamb) that contrast with bolder starters (luscious Jerusalem artichoke or watercress soup, a simple but superb *haricots verts* [green beans] salad). Downstairs, the second-floor Monday Club Bar dining room is a casual yet romantic space where firelight flickers on jewel-toned walls. The food—salads, sandwiches (including a daily grilled-cheese option), fried chicken, steak with baked potato and onion rings—is homey and satisfying. In both rooms, you'll find outstanding wine selections and desserts.

91 Winthrop St. ✆ 617/864-1933. www.upstairsonthesquare.com. Reservations recommended. Main courses $19–$32 upstairs, $7–$26 downstairs. AE, DC, DISC, MC, V. Upstairs Mon–Sat 5:30–10pm; Sun brunch 11am–2pm. Downstairs Mon–Fri 11:30am–2:30pm; daily 5:30–11:30pm. Valet parking available. T: Red Line to Harvard.

EXPENSIVE

There's a **Legal Sea Foods** (p. 128) in the Charles Hotel courtyard, 1 Bennett St. (✆ **617/491-9400**).

Casablanca ✦ MEDITERRANEAN This old-time Harvard Square favorite has long been better known for its hopping bar scene than for its food, but these days the dining room is the place where you're sure to get lucky. Service is erratic (it's better at lunch than at dinner), and there's plenty to look at while you wait. The walls of the long, sky-lit dining room and crowded, noisy bar sport murals of scenes from the movie. Humphrey Bogart looks as though he might lean down to ask for a taste of mushroom risotto cake with fontina, braised greens, and mushroom broth, or juicy grilled lamb steak with cannellini beans and escarole. The appetizers are so good that you might want to assemble them into a meal. Just be sure to leave room for dessert. The plate of cookies is a good choice, as is gingerbread.

40 Brattle St. ✆ 617/876-0999. www.casablanca-restaurant.com. Reservations recommended at dinner. Main courses $7–$12 at lunch, $17–$24 at dinner. AE, DC, MC, V. Mon–Sat 11:30am–2:30pm; Sun–Thurs 5:30–10pm; Fri–Sat 5:30–11pm. Validated parking available. T: Red Line to Harvard.

MODERATE

Bombay Club ✦ *Value* INDIAN This third-floor spot overlooking Harvard Square gained fame through its lunch buffet, a generous assortment of some of the best items on the menu. The buffet's reasonable price and the lively scene make midday the best time to dine here. At all times, the food—a selection of typical dishes from across the subcontinent—is flavorful and fresh (with yogurt and cheese made in-house daily). The breads, baked to perfection in a traditional charcoal-fired clay oven, and the lamb offerings are especially tasty. The "chef's recommendations" platters of assorted meat or vegetarian dishes make good samplers if you're new to the cuisine or can't make up your mind. If grazing isn't your thing, tandoori kebabs, *rogan josh* (lamb in garlicky tomato sauce), and fiery chicken vindaloo merit ordering full portions.

57 John F. Kennedy St. ✆ 617/661-8100. www.bombayclub.com. Lunch buffet $8 Mon–Fri, $9–$12 Sat–Sun; main courses $5–$9 at lunch, $11–$18 at dinner. AE, DC, MC, V. Daily 11:30am–11pm (lunch until 3pm). Discounted parking available. T: Red Line to Harvard.

Border Café TEX-MEX/CAJUN When you see this restaurant, your thoughts might turn to, of all people, baseball Hall of Famer Yogi Berra. He supposedly said, "Nobody goes there anymore; it's too crowded." He was talking about a New York club, but people have been saying it about this Harvard Square hangout for nearly 20 years. Patrons loiter at the bar for hours, enhancing the festival atmosphere. Many are waiting to be seated for generous portions

---

Tips   Sweet-Tooth Alert

As a rule, nonfranchise businesses that carve out a niche in Harvard Square do one thing and do it extremely well. Case in point: **L.A. Burdick Chocolates,** 52 Brattle St., Cambridge (② **617/491-4340;** T: Red Line to Harvard). The amazing confections include sublime hot chocolate to stay or go.

---

of tasty (if not completely authentic) food. The menu features Tex-Mex, Cajun, and some Caribbean specialties, and the beleaguered staff keeps the chips and salsa coming. When you shout your order over the roar of the crowd, try the excellent chorizo appetizer, enchiladas (seafood is particularly delectable), any kind of tacos, or popcorn shrimp. Fajitas for one or two, sizzling noisily, are also a popular choice. Set aside a couple of hours, get yourself into a party mood, and ask to be seated downstairs if you want to be able to hear your companions.

32 Church St. ② **617/864-6100.** Reservations not accepted. Main courses $7–$15. AE, MC, V. Mon–Thurs 11am–1am; Fri–Sat 11am–2am; Sun noon–11pm. T: Red Line to Harvard.

INEXPENSIVE

Johnny's Luncheonette ✹ *Kids* AMERICAN   Johnny's is a madly popular breakfast and brunch place that also serves terrific "real" food in a neighborhood that embraces its no-frills approach. On the lowest (below street) level of an apartment-retail complex, it's a refreshingly retro place with booths along the back wall and a jukebox. Huge portions of breakfast food (served all day) include tasty omelets, fluffy flapjacks, entertainingly named egg dishes, and even fantastic porridge. Later in the day, choose from chargrilled burgers, nearly a dozen salads, excellent sandwiches, and diner-style entrees like meatloaf, macaroni and cheese, and roast turkey with all the trimmings. It gets noisy, but not as noisy as it could—my favorite menu note anywhere nicely asks that "crying or misbehaving children be removed from our dining area."

1105 Mass. Ave. ② **617/495-0055.** Reservations not accepted. Main courses $7–$11; breakfast items from $1.95. MC, V. Daily 7am–10pm. T: Red Line to Harvard.

Mr. Bartley's Burger Cottage ✹✹ AMERICAN   Great burgers and the best onion rings in the world make Bartley's a perennial favorite with a cross section of Cambridge, from Harvard students to regular folks. The 40-plus-year-old family business isn't a cottage, but a high-ceilinged, crowded room plastered with signs and posters (there's also a small outdoor seating area). Burgers bear the names of local and national celebrities, notably political figures; the names change, but the ingredients stay the same.

Anything you can think of to put on ground beef is available, from American cheese to béarnaise sauce. Good dishes that don't involve meat include veggie burgers and creamy, garlicky hummus. And Bartley's is one of the only places in the area where you can still get a real raspberry lime rickey (raspberry syrup, lime juice, lime wedges, and club soda—the taste of summer even in the winter).

1246 Mass. Ave. ② **617/354-6559.** www.mrbartleys.com. Most items less than $9. No credit cards. Mon–Sat 11am–9pm. Closed Dec 25–Jan 1. T: Red Line to Harvard.

OUTSIDE HARVARD SQUARE
EXPENSIVE

There's a **Legal Sea Foods** (p. 128) at 5 Cambridge Center, Kendall Square (② **617/864-3400**). **Davio's** (p. 127) has a branch at the Royal Sonesta Hotel,

5 Cambridge Pkwy (℃ **617/661-4810**), that's open daily from 11:30am to 10pm.

The Blue Room ★★★ ECLECTIC   The Blue Room sits below plaza level in an office-retail complex, a slice of foodie paradise in high-tech heaven. Its out-of-the-way location means that it doesn't get as much publicity as it deserves, but it's one of the best restaurants in the Boston area. The cuisine is a rousing combination of top-notch ingredients and layers of aggressive flavors, the service is excellent, and the crowded dining room is not as noisy as you might fear when you first spy it through the glass front wall. Upholstery and carpeting help soften the din, but this is still not a place for cooing lovers—it's a place for food lovers, who savor co-owner Steve Johnson's regularly changing menu.

Appetizers range from imaginative salads to seared scallops with hoisin and sesame to delectable pizza. Entrees tend to be roasted, grilled, or braised, with at least one well-conceived vegetarian choice. The roast chicken, served with garlic mashed potatoes, is world-class. Seafood is always a wise choice (braised cod with littlenecks—yum!), and grilled pork chop with apples, cider, and celery root will make you think twice the next time you skip over pork on a menu to get to the steak. In warm weather, there's seating on the brick patio.

1 Kendall Sq. ℃ 617/494-9034. Reservations recommended. Main courses $17–$24. AE, DC, DISC, MC, V. Sun–Thurs 5:30–10pm; Fri–Sat 5:30–11pm; Sun brunch 11am–2:30pm. Validated parking available. T: Red Line to Kendall/MIT; 10-min. walk.

Dalí ★★ SPANISH   This festive restaurant casts an irresistible spell—it doesn't take reservations, it's noisy and inconvenient, and it still fills with people cheerfully waiting an hour or more for a table. The bar offers plenty to look at while you wait, including a clothesline festooned with lingerie. The payoff is authentic Spanish food, notably tapas, little plates of hot or cold creations that burst with flavor.

Entrees include excellent paella, but most people come with friends and explore the 3 dozen or more tapas offerings, all perfect for sharing. They include *patatas ali-oli* (garlic potatoes), *albóndigas de salmón* (salmon balls with not-too-salty caper sauce), *setas al ajillo* (sautéed mushrooms), and *lomito al cabrales* (pork tenderloin with blue goat cheese and mushrooms). The helpful staff sometimes seems rushed but never fails to supply bread for sopping up juices and sangria for washing it all down. Finish with excellent flan, or try the luscious *tarta de chocolates.*

The owners of Dalí also run **Tapéo** at 266 Newbury St. (℃ **617/267-4799**), between Fairfield and Dartmouth streets in Boston's **Back Bay.** It offers the same menu and similarly wacky decor in a more sedate two-level setting.

415 Washington St., Somerville. ℃ 617/661-3254. www.dalirestaurant.com. Reservations not accepted. Tapas $4–$8; main courses $19–$24. AE, DC, MC, V. Daily summer 6–11pm; winter 5:30–11pm. T: Red Line to Harvard; follow Kirkland St. to intersection of Washington and Beacon sts. (20 min. or $5 cab ride).

East Coast Grill & Raw Bar ★★ SEAFOOD/BARBECUE   Huge portions, a dizzying menu, and funky decor make the East Coast Grill madly popular. The kitchen handles fresh seafood (an encyclopedic variety), barbecue, and grilled fish and meats with equal authority. The influence of founder Chris Schlesinger, a national expert on grilling and spicy food, is apparent in the exuberant menu descriptions ("super fresh catch o' the moment," "grilled jerk pork cutlet from hell!"). To start, check out the raw-bar offerings, or try sublime fried oysters. The seafood entrees are exceptional—always check the specials board, and you may luck into something like plantain-crusted cod, my new favorite. Barbecue comes on abundant platters in three styles: Texas beef, Memphis spareribs, and North Carolina pork. Desserts are just decent, but there's a great ice-cream store (Christina's) up the street. *A note to parents:* Because there's no children's menu, I don't feel comfortable adding a "Kids" icon, but the menu includes plenty of options for less adventuresome palates, and during a recent meal (anonymous, as always) with two well-behaved but active little boys, the staff couldn't have been nicer.

1271 Cambridge St., Inman Sq. ℰ 617/491-6568. www.eastcoastgrill.net. Reservations accepted only for parties of 5 or more, Sun–Thurs. Main courses $14–$30; sandwich plates $8–$9. AE, DISC, MC, V. Sun–Thurs 5:30–10pm; Fri–Sat 5:30–10:30pm; Sun brunch 11am–2:30pm. T: Red Line to Harvard, then no. 69 (Harvard-Lechmere) bus to Inman Sq. Or Red Line to Central, 10-min. walk on Prospect St.

Jasper White's Summer Shack ⭐ *Kids* SEAFOOD   An enormous space with a lobster tank in the middle of the floor, the Summer Shack feels like an overgrown seaside clam shack—but one that's been to cooking school. All the basics are here: raw bar, excellent french fries, and even a clambake, which consists of a lobster, clams, mussels, potatoes, sausage, and corn on the cob. But check the restaurant's name again—Jasper White is famous for seafood, and his pan-roasted lobster, on the aptly named "big bucks lobster" section of the menu, has been a local foodie favorite for well over a decade (since his days at the fine-dining restaurant Jasper's). Yes, the contrast is incongruous, but it works. You might find yourself sitting at a picnic table between a kid chowing down on a corn dog and a suburban couple savoring wok-seared lobster with ginger and scallions or steamed mussels in wine-and-herb broth—and they'll all be equally happy. You'll be able to hear them exclaiming, too: When it's full, this is one of the loudest restaurants in the Boston area. Arrive early, ask to sit on the second level (just a few steps up, but much quieter), and you might be able to have a conversation.

149 Alewife Brook Pkwy. ℰ 617/576-2433. www.summershackrestaurant.com. Reservations accepted only for parties of 8 or more. Main courses $15–$22; sandwiches $4–$12; specials market price. AE, DISC, MC, V. Mon–Fri 11:30am–2:30pm; Sun–Thurs 5–10pm; Fri–Sat 5pm–11pm. Free parking. T: Red Line to Alewife.

Oleana ⭐⭐ MEDITERRANEAN   Both casual neighborhood place and culinary travelogue, Oleana occupies a cozy, welcoming space outside Inman Square. It opened in 2001 and quickly cemented the rising-star status of chef and co-owner Ana (short for Oleana) Sortun. The seasonal menu, which features cuisine typical of and inspired by the Mediterranean, relies on fresh ingredients and Sortun's signature unusual flavors. Clams cataplana, a traditional Portuguese dish with sausage and tomatoey broth, arrives in a domed copper dish that releases a cloud of tempting aromas. Fava-bean moussaka accompanies juicy grilled lamb steak with Turkish spices. Even better is spicy tuna, in a peppery sauce that trades intense heat for intense flavor, a perfect match for the meaty fish. Service is polished, portions are generous, and the dessert menu is heavy on house-made ice cream. In warm weather, there's seating on the peaceful patio.

134 Hampshire St., Inman Sq. ℰ 617/661-0505. Reservations recommended. Main courses $17–$24. AE, MC, V. Sun–Thurs 5:30–10pm; Fri–Sat 5:30–11pm. Free parking. T: Red Line to Central; 10-min. walk.

MODERATE
Green Street Grill ⭐ CARIBBEAN/SEAFOOD   Out-of-towners ask conspiratorially, "Where do people who live here *really* go?" This is one good answer. The Green Street Grill is a splash of the tropics on a colorless side street. Formerly a divey bar, the sleek two-level space attracts a local crowd with generous portions of exotic, flavorful cuisine. Start with crunchy conch-and-cod

fritters, served with spicy rémoulade. Entrees please the eye and the palate—a special of spice-dusted tilapia, smoky from the grill, arrives buried in colorful fruits and vegetables. Pumpkin, spinach, and roasted garlic ravioli (half egg pasta, half spinach) swims in a sauce of wild mushrooms, asparagus, pumpkin chunks, roasted red peppers, and plum tomatoes. It sounds like too much, but the waitress who recommended it was right on. Disappointingly, there's no dessert menu, but several dishes incorporate tropical fruit (think mango and papaya), and there's a menu of sweet rum and vodka drinks.

280 Green St., Central Sq. ℂ 617/876-1655. www.greenstreetgrill.com. Reservations accepted only for parties of 6 or more. Main courses $5–$8 at lunch, $13–$20 at dinner. AE, DC, MC, V. Mon–Fri 11:30am–2pm; Mon–Wed 6–10pm; Thurs–Sat 6–11pm; Sun 5:30–9:30pm. (Bar closes at 1am Sun–Wed, 2am Thurs–Sat.) T: Red Line to Central Sq.

The Helmand ⭐ AFGHAN   Never exactly a secret, the Helmand enjoyed a burst of publicity when the manager's brother took over the provisional government of Afghanistan, and it's hardly had a slow night since. The elegant setting belies the reasonable prices at this spacious spot near the CambridgeSide Galleria mall. The unusual cuisine evokes Middle Eastern, Indian, and Pakistani food, with its own delectable flavors and textures. Many dishes are vegetarian, and meat is often one element of a dish rather than the centerpiece. Every meal comes with delectable bread made fresh in a wood-fired brick oven near the entrance.

To start, you might try slightly sweet baked pumpkin topped with a spicy ground meat sauce—a great contrast of flavors and textures—or *aushak,* pasta pockets filled with leeks or potatoes and buried under a sauce of split peas and carrots. *Aushak,* also available as a main course, can be prepared with meat sauce as well. In several dishes, grilling brings out the flavor of lamb and chicken. Other entrees include several versions of what Americans would call stew, including *deygee kabob,* an excellent mélange of lamb, yellow split peas, onion, and red peppers. For dessert, don't miss the Afghan version of baklava.

143 First St. ℂ 617/492-4646. Reservations recommended. Main courses $10–$18. AE, MC, V. Sun–Thurs 5–10pm; Fri–Sat 5–11pm. T: Green Line to Lechmere.

La Groceria Ristorante Italiano (Kids) ITALIAN   The Mastromauro family has dished up large portions of delicious Italian food at this colorful, welcoming restaurant since 1972. You'll see business meetings at lunch, family outings at dinner, and students and bargain-hunters at all times. Cheery voices bounce off the stucco walls and tile floors, but it seldom gets terribly noisy, probably because everyone's mouth is full. You might start with the house garlic bread, lavished with chopped tomato, red onion, fennel seed, and olive oil. The antipasto platter overflows with the chef's choice of meats, cheeses, and roasted vegetables. Main dishes include homemade pasta from the machine you see as you enter—the daily specials are always good bets. Lasagna (a vegetarian version) is an excellent choice, as are lobster ravioli, roasted chicken, and savory chicken Marsala.

853 Main St., Central Sq. ℂ 617/497-4214. www.lagroceriarestaurant.com. Reservations accepted only for parties of 6 or more. Main courses $7–$16 at lunch, $11–$19 at dinner. Children's menu $7. AE, DC, DISC, MC, V. Mon–Fri 11:30am–10pm (lunch until 4pm); Sat–Sun 2:30–10pm. Free parking. T: Red Line to Central Sq.

Midwest Grill ⭐ (Value) BRAZILIAN   As soon as you open the door of the Midwest Grill, the aroma of garlic and meat starts your mouth watering. Distractions abound: personable waiters, lively music, the salad bar–like selection of side dishes (superb potatoes, black-bean stew, salads, olives, and rice). But you can't ignore the scent of meat juices dripping onto an open fire. Finally, here come the waiters, bearing the long, swordlike skewers of meat that make up *rodizio,* or Brazilian barbecue. They slice off portions of perfectly grilled pork, lamb, or beef, as you help with salad tongs. They return with linguiça sausage, chicken, and even chicken hearts. Take a break and check out the gregarious families, voracious students, and other carnivores around you, then flag down a circulating waiter and dig in again.

1124 Cambridge St., Inman Sq. ℭ 617/354-7536. www.midwestgrill.com. Reservations recommended Mon–Thurs; accepted only for parties of 8 or more Fri–Sun. *Rodizio* $19; main courses $12–$15. AE, DISC, MC, V. Daily 11:30am–11:30pm. T: Red Line to Harvard, then no. 69 (Harvard-Lechmere) bus just past Inman Sq. Or Red Line to Central, 10-min. walk on Prospect St.

Redbones ℛ BARBECUE   Geographically, this raucous restaurant is in Somerville, but in spirit it's on a Southern back road—where the sun is hot, the beer is cold, and a slab of meat is done to a turn. Barbecued ribs (Memphis-, Texas-, and Arkansas-style), smoked beef brisket, fried Louisiana catfish, and grilled chicken come with appropriate side dishes alone or in combinations. The chummy staff can help you choose sweet, hot, mild, or vinegar sauce. The best nonbarbecue dish is a starter or dinner of succulent buffalo shrimp, swimming in hot sauce. Portions are large, so pace yourself. You'll want to try the appetizers and sides—catfish "catfingers," succotash, corn pudding—and desserts, especially pecan pie. The only less-than-tasty dish I've had here was watery broccoli (cosmic payback for ordering a vegetable other than coleslaw, no doubt). There's a huge selection of beers, and valet parking for your bike in warm weather. Given a choice, sit upstairs—Underbones, downstairs, is a noisy bar.

55 Chester St. (off Elm St.), Somerville. ℭ 617/628-2200. www.redbones.com. Reservations not accepted. Main courses $6–$19. No credit cards. Mon–Sat 11:30am–10:30pm; Sun noon–10:30pm; daily lunch until 4pm, late-night menu until 12:30am. T: Red Line to Davis.

Tu y Yo Mexican Fonda REGIONAL MEXICAN   A large, colorful storefront near the Tufts University campus, Tu y Yo specializes in authentic Mexican food in a style that dates to the 16th century. Settlers lived and ate at *fondas,* or boarding houses, that served home-style cooking. They ate well, too—I've never had a disappointing meal here. The menu looks short, but many dishes are available with a choice of beef, chicken, pork, sausage, shrimp, or fish, and in vegetarian versions. To start, try *sopes* (fried disks of *masa,* or corn flour) topped with beans, cheese, and onions, or stuffed tortillas known as *gringas.* Many maincourse descriptions include the dish's date and place of origin (owner Epi Guzman's family figures prominently), but even the options that have no pedigree are delicious. I especially like sausage or shrimp *Alambre* (with shredded cheese, onions, and peppers), which the diner scoops into a tortilla, and spinach a la Carlos (with potatoes in a garlic sauce). For the full experience, try one of the three versions of sangria, and finish with cinnamon-infused coffee and unbelievable flan.

885 Broadway, Powderhouse Sq., Somerville. ℭ 617/623-5411. www.tuyyomexicanfonda.com. Main courses $10–$14. MC, V. Mon–Thurs 5–10pm; Fri–Sat 4–11pm; Sun 2–9pm. T: Red Line to Davis, 10-min. walk (follow College Ave. to the traffic circle and take sharp left).

INEXPENSIVE

S&S Restaurant ℛℛ DELI   *Es* is Yiddish for "eat," and this Cambridge classic is as straightforward as its name ("eat and eat"). Founded in 1919 by the great-grandmother of the current owners, the wildly popular brunch spot draws what seems to be half of Cambridge at busy times on weekends. It's northeast of

---

Finds **Worth the Trip**

Anna's Taqueria, 822 Somerville Ave., Cambridge (② **617/661-8500;** T: Red
Line to Porter), a branch of a small local chain, serves fresh, delicious Mexican food. It was already a Boston-area favorite when it received national
attention in 2002. I can't promise you'll be as devoted as the *New York
Times* writer who made the trip from Manhattan and back in a single day
just for a burrito . . . but I can't promise you won't.

Harvard Square and west of MIT, and worth a visit during the week, too. With
huge windows and lots of light wood and plants, it looks contemporary, but
the brunch offerings are traditional dishes such as pancakes, waffles, fruit salad,
and fantastic omelets. The bagels are among the best in the area; you'll also find
traditional deli items (corned beef, pastrami, tongue, potato pancakes, and
blintzes), and breakfast anytime. Be early for brunch, or plan to spend a good
chunk of your Saturday or Sunday standing around people-watching and getting hungry. Or dine on a weekday and soak up the neighborhood atmosphere.

1334 Cambridge St., Inman Sq. ② **617/354-0777.** www.sandsrestaurant.com. Main courses $4–$12. AE,
MC, V. Mon–Wed 7am–11pm; Thurs–Fri 7am–midnight; Sat 8am–midnight; Sun 8am–10pm; brunch Sat–Sun
until 4pm. T: Red Line to Harvard, then no. 69 (Harvard-Lechmere) bus to Inman Sq. Or Red Line to Central,
10-min. walk on Prospect St.

What to See & Do in Boston

Whether you want to immerse your-self in the colonial era or just cruise around the harbor, Boston offers something for everyone, and plenty of it. Throw out your preconceptions of the city as some sort of open-air history museum—although that's certainly one of the guises it can assume—and allow your interests to dictate where you go.

It's possible but not advisable to take in most major attractions in 2 or 3 days if you don't linger anywhere too long. For a more enjoyable, less rushed visit, plan fewer activities and spend more time on them.

Budget cuts have slashed state con-tributions to many cultural organiza-tions. Admissions fees in this chapter are current at press time, but establish-ments that rely heavily on state aid

may cost a bit more by the time you visit. If you're on a tight budget, call ahead.

Increased security has led some attractions to require that adult patrons show ID before entering. Double-check that you have your license or passport before you leave the hotel.

The **Boston Tea Party Ship & Museum** (© 617/338-1773; www. bostonteapartyship.com) closed indef-initely after a fire in 2001; if you hope to visit, call ahead to see whether it's open.

Two other attractions reopened in 2002 after extensive renovations: The **Longfellow National Historic Site** (p. 171) and the **Mapparium,** which is now part of the new Mary Baker Eddy Library (p. 167).

SUGGESTED ITINERARIES

If You Have 1 Day

Sample some experiences unique to Boston—you won't have time to do much, but you can touch on several singular attractions. Follow part of the **Freedom Trail** on your own from Boston Common to **Faneuil Hall Marketplace.** Alternatively, National Park Service rangers lead free 90-minute tours from the visi-tor center at 15 State St. (© 617/ 242-5642; www.nps.gov/bost). The tours start as often as four times a day during busy periods and once daily in the winter. They cover the "heart" of the trail, from the Old South Meeting House to the Old North Church. You don't need a

reservation, but call for schedules. **Boston By Foot** (© 617/367-2345; www.bostonbyfoot.com) offers a "Heart of the Freedom Trail" tour at 10am Tuesday through Saturday in warm weather. It starts at the Samuel Adams statue on Congress Street at Faneuil Hall. Tickets are $9, and you don't need reservations.

After your tour, launch a picnic with takeout food from Faneuil Hall Marketplace or the North End. Head to the plaza at the end of Long Wharf (pass the Marriott and keep going) or to Christopher Columbus Waterfront Park (across Atlantic Avenue from the market-place). If you'd rather eat indoors, stay at the marketplace and have lunch at Durgin-Park, or go across the street to Ye Olde Union Oyster House (see chapter 6). In the afternoon, complete your independent Freedom Trail foray in the North End and take a sightseeing cruise from Long Wharf or Rowes Wharf. Or cruise and then explore the New England Aquarium or the Children's Museum. Or skip the afternoon sightseeing altogether and go shopping at Downtown Crossing, home to Filene's Basement, or on Newbury Street. See the accompanying box "Suggested Evening Itineraries" for more ideas.

If You Have 2 Days

On the first day, follow the suggestions for 1 day or pick and choose—you can spend more time along the Freedom Trail, on a longer harbor cruise, or at another destination. On the second day, branch out a little, again letting your preferences be your guide. Spend the morning at the **Museum of Fine Arts,** and have lunch there or at the **Isabella Stewart Gardner Museum.** Start the afternoon at the Gardner Museum or, if it's a Friday during the season, at the **Boston Symphony Orchestra** (see chapter 10). If art isn't your passion, start the day at the **Museum of Science** or the **John F. Kennedy Library and Museum,** followed by lunch at the Prudential Center and a **Duck Tour.**

Then take a leisurely trek around the **Back Bay** (see "Walking Tour 1" in chapter 8) or a high-intensity shopping trip to **Newbury Street** (see chapter 9). In warm weather, leave time for a **swan boat** ride. If you had a light lunch (or skipped it so you could start shopping earlier), have **afternoon tea** at the Four Seasons or Ritz-Carlton (see box, "Boston Tea Party, Part 2" in chapter 6). On summer weekdays, **Boston By Foot** (© 617/367-2345; www.bostonbyfoot.com) conducts a tour of **Beacon Hill** ($9) that starts at the State House at 5:30pm.

If You Have 3 Days

The options seem to expand to fill the time you have. The suggestions for the first 2 days can easily fill another day, but you'll probably want to branch out. A visit to **Cambridge** is the logical next step. Ride the MBTA Red Line from downtown or the no. 1 bus from the Back Bay to Harvard Square. Take a walking tour (see chapter 8), squeeze in some shopping, or head straight to one of the university's museum complexes. Have lunch in Harvard Square and continue exploring, or visit **Mount Auburn Cemetery** (see the "Celebrity Cemetery" box later in this chapter). You can also venture farther from the city. You might start in Cambridge and have lunch in **Concord** or **Lexington** (see chapter 11). Spend the afternoon exploring the area, or communing with nature at **Walden Pond.** Without a car, you can use public transportation to reach Lexington or Concord but not to travel between them; forced

---

Tips One Singular Sensation

On a 1-day visit, consider concentrating on just **one or two things** you're most excited about (plus a good meal or two). If what really gets you going is the Museum of Fine Arts, the Museum of Science, the Newbury Street art galleries, or even a day trip (see chapter 11), you have a built-in excuse for not doing more—and for a return trip to Boston!

Boston Attractions

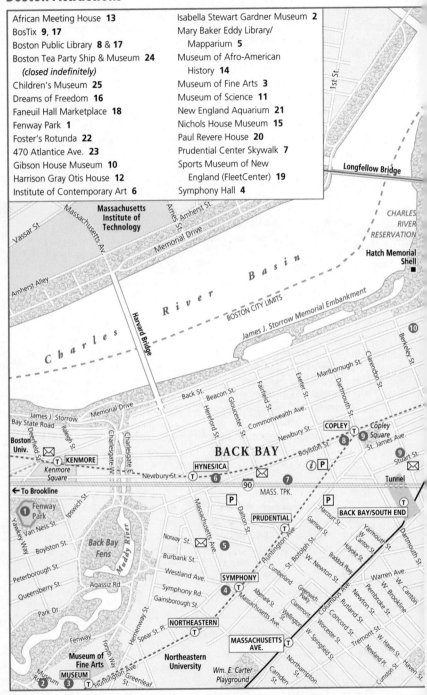

144

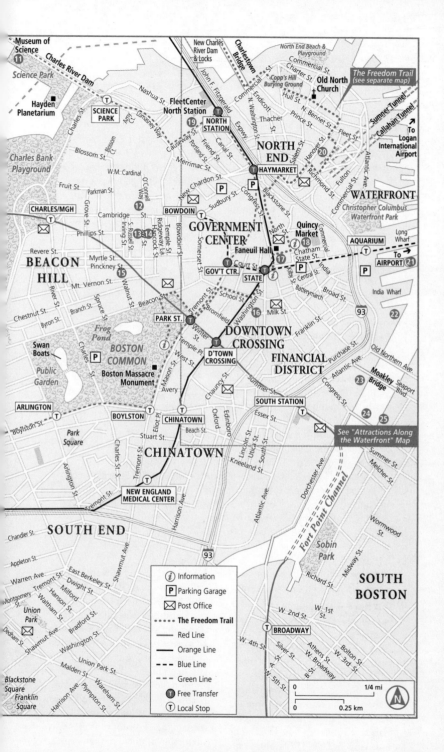

> *Tips* **Suggested Evening Itineraries**
>
> If you're traveling as a family, you might be getting your evening itin-
> eraries out of the TV listings. If not—or if you had the foresight to
> book a sitter—here are some suggestions. See chapter 6 for restaurant
> reviews and chapter 10 for nightlife listings.
>
> - Dinner in the North End, and coffee and dessert at a *caffè*. After-
>   ward, a show at the Comedy Connection at Faneuil Hall or the
>   Improv Asylum, and a drink at the *Cheers* bar in Quincy Market.
> - Dinner at the Legal Sea Foods in the Prudential Center, followed by
>   a visit to the 50th-floor Prudential Center Skywalk or a drink in the
>   lounge at Top of the Hub, on the 52nd floor.
> - Summer only: Assemble a picnic and head to the Hatch Shell for
>   music or a movie, or to Boston Common for a play or concert.
> - Winter only: A Boston Symphony Orchestra or Boston Ballet per-
>   formance, then late supper at Brasserie Jo or dessert at Finale.
> - Dinner at the Sel de la Terre or the State Street Legal Sea Foods,
>   then a stroll to the plaza at the end of Long Wharf, followed by
>   dessert and dancing in the lounge at the Bay Tower, on the 33rd
>   floor of 60 State St.
> - Dinner at Bob the Chef's Jazz Café and music at Wally's Café.
> - Dinner at L'Espalier, Aujourd'hui, or Clio, and a nightcap at the Bris-
>   tol Lounge.
> - Shopping at the Coop, the Harvard Book Store, or WordsWorth,
>   then dinner at Mr. Bartley's Burger Cottage. Contemplate Harvard
>   Yard from the Widener Library steps, and finish up with ice cream at
>   Herrell's.
> - Dinner at Rialto and music at the Regattabar or the House of Blues.
> - Dinner at the Green Street Grill, ice cream at Toscanini's, and music
>   at the Middle East, T.T. the Bear's, or Scullers Jazz Club.
> - A movie at the Kendall Square Cinema, dinner at the Blue Room or
>   Oleana, then music at the Kendall Café.
> - Dinner at Redbones or Tu y Yo Mexican Fonda, and a show at
>   Johnny D's or the Somerville Theater.

to choose, history buffs opt for Lexington, literary types for Concord.

If You Have 4 Days or More

Now you're cooking. Having
scratched the surface in the first 3
days, you'll have a better sense of
what you want to explore more
extensively. Check out other Boston
attractions that catch your fancy,
perhaps including one or more of
the historic **house museums,** and
plan a full day trip—to Lexington
and Concord, to **Plymouth,** to

Marblehead and **Salem,** or to
Gloucester and **Rockport.** Visit
Museum Wharf, where you'll find
the **Children's Museum** and (if it's
open) the **Boston Tea Party Ship
& Museum.** Go on a **whale watch**
or make an unstructured visit to a
city **neighborhood** (see the section
"Boston Neighborhoods to Explore"
later in this chapter). If you haven't
taken a sightseeing cruise or completed the Freedom Trail, visit
Charlestown, where you can explore

the **USS** *Constitution* and **Bunker Hill.** Take in a large-format film at the Museum of Science or the New England Aquarium, or evaluate Boston's reputation as a great sports town by attending a pro or college event. Then hit one of the restaurants or nightspots that you couldn't fit in earlier, and start planning your next visit to Boston.

1 The Top Attractions

The establishments in this section are easily accessible by **public transportation;** given the difficulty and expense of parking, it's preferable to take the T everywhere. Even the Kennedy Library, which has a large free parking lot, operates a free shuttle bus that connects it to the Red Line. To maximize your enjoyment, try to visit these attractions during relatively slow times. If possible, especially in the summer, sightsee on weekdays; if you're traveling without children, aim for times when school is in session. And if you're in town on a July or August weekend, relax and try to convince yourself that you love crowds.

Dreams of Freedom ⭐ *Kids*   The Freedom Trail isn't just about colonial Boston. If you need proof, detour from the trail to the city's museum of immigration. Boston native Ben Franklin is the "host" of a multimedia show about the changing face of the population. It's an interactive experience unlike the city's typically low-tech attractions—a big plus if you're traveling with wired (in both senses) kids. You'll have your passport stamped as you make your way through the exhibits. They include a gallery of bags and suitcases that offers a look at what people brought on their journeys to the New World, gangplanks that move, walls that "talk," and the interiors of two important modes of transportation: an early-20th-century ship and a jet liner. Temporary exhibits on immigration-related topics change every 3 months. Allow at least an hour.

1 Milk St., off Washington St. ℂ **617/338-6022.** www.dreamsoffreedom.org. Admission $7.50 adults, $6.50 seniors and students, $3.50 children ages 6–17, free for children under 6. Daily 10am–6pm. T: Orange or Blue Line to State, or Red Line to Downtown Crossing.

Faneuil Hall Marketplace ⭐⭐ *Kids*   Since Boston's most popular attraction opened in 1976, cities all over the country have imitated the "festival market" concept. Each new complex of shops, food counters, restaurants, bars, and public spaces in urban centers reflects its city. Faneuil Hall Marketplace, brimming with Boston flavor (and national chain outlets), is no exception. Its success with tourists and suburbanites is so great, in fact, that you could be forgiven for thinking that the only Bostonians in the crowd are employees.

   The marketplace includes five buildings—the central three-building complex is on the National Register of Historic Places—set on brick and stone plazas that teem with crowds shopping, eating, performing, watching performers, and just people-watching. In warm weather, it's busy from just after dawn until well past

---

(Tips   A Note on Online Ticketing

Many museums and other attractions sell tickets online, subject to a service charge, through their websites or by linking to an agency. This can be handy, but it can also cost you some flexibility and perhaps some money. If there's even a small chance that your plans will change, make sure you understand the refund policy before you enter your credit card info—you may not be able to return or exchange prepaid tickets.

dark. **Quincy Market** (you'll also hear the whole complex called by that name) is the central three-level Greek revival–style building. It reopened after extensive renovations on August 26, 1976, 150 years of hard use after Mayor Josiah Quincy opened the original market. The **South Market building** reopened on August 26, 1977, the **North Market building** on August 26, 1978.

The central corridor of Quincy Market is the food court, where you can find anything from a bagel to a full Greek dinner, a fruit smoothie to an ice cream sundae. On either side, under the glass canopies, there are full-service restaurants as well as pushcarts that hold everything from crafts created by New England artisans to hokey souvenirs. Here you'll also see a new bar that exactly replicates the set of the TV show *Cheers.* In the plaza between the **South Canopy** and the South Market building is an **information kiosk,** and throughout the complex you'll find an enticing mix of chain stores and unique shops (see chapter 9). On warm evenings, the tables that spill outdoors from the restaurants and bars fill with people. One constant since the year after the market—the *original* market—opened is **Durgin-Park** ✿✿ (p. 115), a traditional New England restaurant with traditionally crabby waitresses.

Faneuil Hall ✿ itself sometimes gets overlooked, but it's well worth a visit. Known as the "Cradle of Liberty" for its role as a center of inspirational (some might say inflammatory) speech in the years leading to the Revolutionary War, the building opened in 1742 and was expanded using a Charles Bulfinch design in 1805. National Park Service rangers give **free 20-minute talks** every half-hour from 9am to 5pm in the second-floor auditorium.

Between North, Congress, and State sts. and I-93. ✆ 617/523-1300. www.faneuilhallmarketplace.com. Marketplace Mon–Sat 10am–9pm, Sun noon–6pm. Food court opens earlier; some restaurants close later. T: Green Line to Government Center, Orange Line to Haymarket or State, or Blue Line to Aquarium.

Isabella Stewart Gardner Museum ✿✿ Isabella Stewart Gardner (1840–1924) was an incorrigible individualist long before strong-willed behavior was acceptable for women in polite Boston society, and her iconoclasm paid off for art lovers. "Mrs. Jack" designed her exquisite home in the style of a 15th-century Venetian palace and filled it with European, American, and Asian painting and sculpture, much chosen with the help of her friend and protégé Bernard Berenson. You'll see works by Titian, Botticelli, Raphael, Rembrandt, Matisse, and Mrs. Gardner's friends James McNeill Whistler and John Singer Sargent.

Kids **On Top of the World**

The **Prudential Center Skywalk** ✿, 800 Boylston St. ((✆ **617/859-0648**), offers a 360° view of Boston and far beyond. From the enclosed observation deck on the 50th floor of the Prudential Tower, you can see for miles, even (when it's clear) as far as the mountains of southern New Hampshire to the north and the beaches of Cape Cod to the south. The accompanying exhibits sketch out the city's history through photos and newspaper headlines. Call before visiting, because the space sometimes closes for private events. Hours are 10am to 10pm daily. Admission is $7 for adults, $4 for seniors and children 2 to 10, and adults must show a photo ID to enter the Prudential Tower. T: Green Line E to Prudential, or B, C, or D to Hynes/ICA.

Attractions Along the Waterfront

North End Beach & Playground
Commercial St.
Battery Wharf
Charlestown Bridge
Copp's Hill Burying Ground
Old North Church
Salem St.
Paul Revere Mall
Union Wharf
North Station
Prince St.
Hanover St.
Fleet St.
Paul Revere House
Lewis Wharf
NORTH STATION
Causeway St.
Richmond St.
Commercial St.
Commercial Wharf
Merrimac St.
HAYMARKET
Fitzgerald Expressway
Waterfront Park
BOWDOIN
Cambridge St.
Boston City Hall
North St.
Quincy Market
7
New England Aquarium
8
Long Wharf
GOVERNMENT CENTER
Faneuil Hall
Central Wharf
AQUARIUM
1
Museum of African-American History
Court House
Old State House
State St.
Custom House
India Wharf
Tremont St.
Court St.
STATE
Milk St.
Rowes Wharf
State House
Beacon St.
Congress St.
Atlantic Ave.
2
3
Washington St.
Post Office Square
9
Franklin St.
High St.
Purchase St.
DOWNTOWN CROSSING
4
Moakley Bridge
Summer St.
6
Essex St.
Atlantic Ave.
SOUTH STATION
Congress
5
South Station (Amtrak)
Summer St.

T Station Stop

0 — 1/4 mi
0 — 0.25 km

Boston Tea Party Ship & Museum **6**
  (closed indefinitely)
Children's Museum **5**
Faneuil Hall **7**
Foster's Rotunda **2**
470 Atlantic Ave. **4**
Long Wharf **8**
  (sightseeing cruises)
New England Aquarium **1**
Rowes Wharf **3**
  (sightseeing cruises)

Titian's magnificent *Europa*, which many scholars consider his finest work, is one of the most important Renaissance paintings in the United States. If you enjoy representational art and ornate architecture, run right over; if not, you'll probably be happier at the nearby Museum of Fine Arts.

The building, which opened to the public after Mrs. Gardner's death, holds a glorious hodgepodge of furniture and architectural details imported from European churches and palaces. The pièce de résistance is the magnificent sky-lit courtyard, filled year-round with fresh flowers from the museum green-house. Although the terms of Mrs. Gardner's will forbid changing the arrangement of the museum's content, there has been some evolution: A special exhibition gallery, which opened in 1992, features two or three changing shows a year, often by contemporary artists in residence.

See chapter 10 for a description of the **concert series** ✦ (© **617/734-1359**). The cafe serves lunch and desserts, and there's an excellent gift shop.

280 The Fenway. ⓒ 617/566-1401. www.gardnermuseum.org. Admission $11 adults weekends, $10 adults weekdays, $7 seniors, $5 college students with ID, free for children under 18. Tues–Sun, some Mon holidays 11am–5pm. Closed Thanksgiving, Dec 25, Dec 31. T: Green Line E to Museum.

John F. Kennedy Library and Museum ★★ Kids
The Kennedy era springs to life at this dramatic library, museum, and educational research complex overlooking Dorchester Bay. It captures the 35th president's accomplishments and legacy in video and sound recordings and fascinating displays of memorabilia and photos. Far from being a static experience, it changes regularly, with temporary shows and reinterpreted displays that highlight and complement the permanent exhibits.

> **More JFK**
>
> For details about visiting President Kennedy's birthplace in suburban Brookline, see the "Historic Houses" section beginning on p. 168.

Your visit begins with a 17-minute film narrated by John F. Kennedy—a detail that seems eerie for a moment, then perfectly natural. Through skillfully edited audio clips, he discusses his childhood, education, war experience, and early political career. Then you enter the museum to spend as much time as you like on each exhibit. Starting with the 1960 presidential campaign, the displays immerse you in the era. The connected galleries hold campaign souvenirs, a film of Kennedy debating Richard Nixon and delivering his inaugural address, a replica of the Oval Office, gifts from foreign dignitaries, letters, documents, and keepsakes. There's a film about the Cuban Missile Crisis and displays on Attorney General Robert F. Kennedy, First Lady Jacqueline Bouvier Kennedy, the civil rights movement, the Peace Corps, the space program, and the Kennedy family. As the tour winds down, you pass through a darkened chamber where news reports of John Kennedy's assassination and funeral play. From the final room, the soaring glass-enclosed pavilion that is the heart of the I. M. Pei design, there's a glorious view of the water and the Boston skyline.

Columbia Point. ⓒ 877/616-4599 or 617/514-1600. www.jfklibrary.org. Admission $8 adults, $6 seniors and students with ID, $4 youths 13–17, free for children under 13. Surcharges may apply for special exhibitions. Daily 9am–5pm (last film begins at 3:55pm). Closed Jan 1, Thanksgiving, Dec 25. T: Red Line to JFK/UMass, then take free shuttle bus, which runs every 20 min. By car, take Southeast Expressway (I-93/Rte. 3) south to Exit 15 (Morrissey Blvd./JFK Library), turn left onto Columbia Rd., and follow signs to free parking lot.

Museum of Fine Arts ★★★ Kids
One of the world's great art museums, the MFA works nonstop to become even more accessible and interesting. It's also expanding; construction of the new East Wing, designed by Norman Foster, should begin in early 2004. Meanwhile, the museum is rearranging some collections and closing some exhibition space. Check ahead before visiting if you have your heart set on seeing one particular piece of art—or just show up and see what catches your eye.

You're sure to find something entrancing in these magnificent collections. Every installation reflects a curatorial attitude that makes even those who go in with a feeling of obligation leave with a sense of discovery and wonder. That includes children, who can launch a scavenger hunt, admire the mummies, or participate in family-friendly programs scheduled year-round and the extra offerings presented during school vacations. The MFA is especially noted for its **Impressionist** ★★★ paintings (including 43 Monets—the largest collection outside of Paris), Asian and Old Kingdom Egyptian collections, classical art, Buddhist temple, and medieval sculpture and tapestries. It's also expanding its

> **Tips** **MFA FYI**
>
> The Huntington Avenue entrance to the Museum of Fine Arts is usually much less busy than the West Wing lobby. Walk back along Huntington Avenue when you leave the T, enter from the curved driveway, and stop to take in the recently restored John Singer Sargent murals.

modern and contemporary art collections and rearranging some galleries to display paintings and sculpture along with related decorative objects and even furniture.

The works that you might find most familiar are paintings and sculpture by Americans and Europeans. Some favorites: Renoir's *Dance at Bougival,* van Gogh's *Postman Joseph Roulin,* Childe Hassam's *Boston Common at Twilight,* Gilbert Stuart's 1796 portrait of George Washington, John Singleton Copley's 1768 portrait of Paul Revere, a bronze casting of Edgar Degas's sculpture *Little Dancer,* John Singer Sargent's *The Daughters of Edward Darley Boit,* and Fitz Hugh Lane's Luminist masterpieces. There are also magnificent holdings of prints, photographs, furnishings, and decorative arts, including the finest collection of Paul Revere silver in the world.

None of this comes cheap: The MFA's adult admission fees (which covers 2 visits within 30 days) are among the highest in the country. A Boston CityPass (see the "Let's Make a Deal" box on p. 155) is a great deal if you plan to visit enough of the other included attractions.

To begin, pick up a floor plan at the information desk, or take a free guided tour (weekdays except Mon holidays at 10:30am and 1:30pm, Wed at 6:15pm, Sat at 10:30am and 1pm). To date, the latest addition to the original 1909 structure was I. M. Pei's West Wing (1981). It contains the main entrance, an auditorium, and an atrium with a tree-lined "sidewalk" cafe. There are also a restaurant and a cafeteria. The excellent Museum Shop carries abundant souvenirs and a huge book selection.

Special exhibitions during the lifespan of this book include **Thomas Gainsborough, 1727–1788** (June 15–Sept 14, 2003), **Rembrandt's Journey: Painter, Draftsman, Etcher** (Oct 26, 2003–Jan 18, 2004), and **The Maker's Hand: American Studio Furniture** (Nov 11, 2003–Feb 8, 2004).

465 Huntington Ave. © 617/267-9300. www.mfa.org. Adults $15, students and seniors $13 when entire museum is open, or $13 and $11, respectively, when only West Wing is open. Children 7–17 $6.50 on school days before 3pm, otherwise free. Admission good for 2 visits within 30 days. Voluntary contribution ($15 suggested) Wed 4–9:45pm. Surcharges may apply for special exhibitions. No admission fee for Museum Shop, library, restaurants, or auditoriums. Entire museum Mon–Tues 10am–4:45pm, Wed 10am–9:45pm, Thurs–Fri 10am–5pm, Sat–Sun 10am–5:45pm; West Wing only, Thurs–Fri 5–9:45pm. Closed Jan 1, Patriots Day, July 4, Thanksgiving, Dec 25. T: Green Line E to Museum, or Orange Line to Ruggles.

Museum of Science ★★★ *Kids*   For the ultimate pain-free educational experience, head to the Museum of Science. The demonstrations, experiments, and interactive displays introduce facts and concepts so effortlessly that everyone winds up learning something. Take a couple of hours or a whole day to explore the permanent and temporary exhibits, most of them hands-on and all of them great fun.

Among the 500-plus exhibits, you might meet an iguana or a dinosaur, find out how much you'd weigh on the moon, or climb into a space module. Activity centers and exhibits focus on fields of interest—natural history (with live

(Kids) Scavenger Hunt: Freedom Trail Menagerie

Considering that humans thought of it, the Freedom Trail is home to a surprising number of animals. Kids might enjoy searching for them as they make their way across downtown—and they might even learn something. For you to complete this hunt, most of the attractions don't have to be open, but you do need daylight. You also need a bit of trivia that's only available from the "Old Ironsides" tour guides—and from the answers on p. 195.

- **Boston Common:** There's a huge horse in the middle of the memorial to Colonel Shaw and the 54th Massachusetts Colored Regiment. What are the two birds on either side of the bas-relief?
- **Massachusetts State House:** A bird tops the column behind the building that shows the hill's original height. What is it?
- En route to **Park Street Church:** The church, a typical Protestant edifice, is unadorned, but as you walk down Park Street, you'll see a bird on the wall of the Catholic Paulist Center. (Hint: It symbolizes peace.)
- **Old Granary Burying Ground:** A number of gravestones bear a traditional symbol that incorporates a bird and a helmeted soldier, but that's no fun. Seek out **John Hancock's grave** (on the left, about halfway back) and study the symbols on his memorial. A mythical creature sits above the coat of arms, which incorporates the name of the family. (Hint: Another word for rooster is "cock.")
- **King's Chapel Burying Ground:** The church is another simple building, but the graveyard is full of decorations such as flying skulls and dancing skeletons. The animals are on Governor Winthrop's family vault, to the left not far from the fence. Here the mythical creature is in the coat of arms, beneath a familiar woodland animal.
- **First Public School:** The sidewalk mosaic is a little zoo. I counted 12 animals; how many can you find?
- **Benjamin Franklin Statue:** Across the courtyard from Ben are symbols of the two major political parties, one full-size, one underfoot. What are they? Extra credit: What parties do they represent?

animals), computers, the human body—as well as interdisciplinary approaches. **Investigate!** teaches visitors to think like scientists, formulating questions, finding evidence, and drawing conclusions through activities such as strapping on a skin sensor to measure reactions to stimuli or sifting through an archaeological dig. In the **Seeing Is Deceiving** section, auditory and visual illusions challenge your belief in what is "real." The **Science in the Park** exhibit introduces the concepts of Newtonian physics—through familiar recreational tools such as playground equipment and skateboards. Visitors between October 11, 2003, and March 7, 2004 can see an exhibit called **"Magic: The Science of Illusion,"** which looks at entertainment magic through four illusions, including levitation.

The separate-admission **theaters** are worth planning for. Even if you're skipping the exhibits, try to see a show. If you're making a day of it, buy all

- **En route to Old South Meeting House:** The meetinghouse is an unadorned colonial structure; before you reach it, you'll see a matching pair of heads at the entrance to 13–15 School Street. What are they?
- **Old State House:** Two of the most famous animals in Boston history, the lion and the unicorn, adorn the east end of this building. What's at the west end? *Bonus:* The office building at the southeast corner of State and Congress streets, Exchange Place, has a row of animal heads across its second floor.
- **Faneuil Hall:** Another famous creature is the grasshopper on the weather vane. At ground level, stop in front of the Samuel Adams statue and look down at the engravings that show the shoreline in 1630. What might you expect to see along the shore?
- **Paul Revere House:** This house would have had plenty of animals around it, but it's a workingman's home, plain and functional. The small playground across the way honors Paul's second wife, Rachel, with a plaque. What bird is on the plaque?
- **Old North Church:** At the front of the gift shop alongside the church entrance is a small flight of stairs. What animals guard it?
- **Copp's Hill Burying Ground:** Seek out Prince Hall's monument and look across the path to the grave of John James. The poem engraved on it mentions small animals that you might expect to find in a graveyard.
- **Charlestown Navy Yard:** The abundant maritime symbols around the navy yard include even more eagles, but nothing terribly exciting. Here's a bonus question: The small boys who worked in the rigging of the ship, bringing supplies to the sailors, went by what animal nickname?
- **En route to the Bunker Hill Monument:** At the entrance to City Square Park, at Rutherford Avenue and Chelsea Street, is a large fountain. What are in and around it, and what's on the weather vane?

your tickets at once—shows sometimes sell out. Tickets are for sale in person and, subject to a service charge, over the phone and on the Web (www.tickets. mos.org).

The **Mugar Omni Theater** ★★★, which shows IMAX movies, is an intense experience. It bombards you with images on a five-story domed screen and sound from a new digital system. The engulfing sensations and steep pitch of the seating area will have you hanging on for dear life, whether the film is about Mount Everest, bears, or wild chimpanzees. Features change every 4 to 6 months. The **Charles Hayden Planetarium** ★★ takes visitors into space with daily star shows and shows on special topics that change several times a year. On weekends, rock-music laser shows take over. At the entrance is a hands-on astronomy exhibit called **Welcome to the Universe.**

The museum has a terrific gift shop, where toys and games promote learning without lecturing. The ground-floor Galaxy Cafés have spectacular views of the skyline and river. There's a parking garage on the premises, but it's on a busy street, and entering and exiting can be harrowing.

Science Park, off O'Brien Hwy. on bridge between Boston and Cambridge. ⓒ 617/723-2500. www.mos.org. Admission to exhibit halls $12 adults, $10 seniors, $9 children 3–11, free for children under 3. To Mugar Omni Theater, Hayden Planetarium, or laser shows $8 adults, $7 seniors, $6 children 3–11, free for children under 3. July 5 to Labor Day Sat–Thurs 9am–7pm, Fri 9am–9pm; day after Labor Day to July 4 Sat–Thurs 9am–5pm, Fri 9am–9pm. Closed Thanksgiving, Dec 25. T: Green Line to Science Park.

New England Aquarium ⭐ *Kids*   This entertaining complex is home to more than 7,000 fish and aquatic mammals. At busy times, it seems to contain at least that many people—in July and August, try to make this your first stop of the morning, especially on weekends. You'll want to spend at least half a day, and huge afternoon crowds can make merely getting around painfully slow. Also consider investing in a Boston CityPass (see the "Let's Make a Deal" box on p. 155); it allows you to skip the ticket line, which can be uncomfortably long, and may represent a savings on the steep admission charge. The **Simons IMAX Theatre** ⭐⭐⭐, which has its own building, hours, and admission fees, is worth planning ahead for, too. Its 85-foot-by-65-foot screen shows 3D films with digital sound that concentrate on the natural world. It's a dizzying experience.

The focal point of the main building is the four-story, 200,000-gallon **Giant Ocean Tank.** A four-story spiral ramp encircles the tank, which contains a replica of a Caribbean coral reef and an assortment of sea creatures that seem to coexist amazingly well. Part of the reason for the peace might be that scuba divers feed the sharks five times a day. Other exhibits show off freshwater and tropical specimens, denizens of the Amazon, sea otters, and the ecology of Boston Harbor. The floating marine mammal pavilion, **Discovery,** is home to performing sea lions. At the **Edge of the Sea** exhibit, visitors can touch the sea stars, sea urchins, and horseshoe crabs in the tide pool. The **Aquarium Medical Center** is especially involving—it's a working veterinary hospital.

Naturalist-led **harbor tours** that teach "Science at Sea" run daily in the spring, summer, and fall. Discounts are available when you combine a visit to the aquarium with an IMAX film, harbor tour, or whale watch (see the "Organized Tours" section beginning on p. 181).

Central Wharf. ⓒ 617/973-5200. www.neaq.org. Admission $16 adults, $14 seniors, $8.50 children 3–11. Harbor tour $13 adults, $10 seniors and college students with ID, $9 youths 12–18, $9 children 3–11. Free for children under 3 and for those visiting only the outdoor exhibits, cafe, and gift shop. July to Labor Day Mon–Tues and Fri 9am–6pm, Wed–Thurs 9am–8pm, Sat–Sun and holidays 9am–7pm; day after Labor Day to June Mon–Fri 9am–5pm, Sat–Sun and holidays 9am–6pm. Simons IMAX Theatre: ⓒ 866/815-4629. Tickets $8.50 adults, $6.50 seniors and children 3–11. Daily 10am–9pm. T: Blue Line to Aquarium.

⟨ *Finds* ⟩ Gone Fishing

Many fascinating interactive exhibits from the defunct Computer Museum now delight patrons of the Museum of Science. The most popular is the **Virtual FishTank** ⭐⭐⭐, which uses 3-D computer graphics and character-animation software to allow visitors to program their own virtual fish. You can even "build" fish on your home computer (through www.virtualfish tank.com) and launch them at the museum.

Value Let's Make a Deal

As you plan your sightseeing, consider these money-saving offers.

If you'll be in town for more than a day or so, pick up an **Arts/ Boston coupon book.** It offers discounts on admission to many museums and attractions, including (among others) the Museum of Fine Arts, the New England Aquarium, the Kennedy Library, Massachusetts Bay Lines cruises, and Beantown and Old Town trolleys. It's not worth the money ($9) for single travelers because many of the deals are two-for-one, but couples and families can take good advantage. They're on sale at **BosTix** booths (✆ **617/482-2849;** www.artsboston.org) at Faneuil Hall Marketplace (on the south side of Faneuil Hall) and in Copley Square (at the corner of Boylston and Dartmouth sts.), and by phone, Web, and mail.

If you concentrate on the included attractions, a **CityPass** offers great savings. It's a booklet of tickets (so you can go straight to the entrance) to the Harvard Museum of Natural History, the Kennedy Library, the New England Aquarium, the Museum of Fine Arts, the Museum of Science, and the Prudential Center Skywalk. If you visit all five, the price gives adults a 50% savings. At press time, the cost was $34 for adults, $20 for youths 3 to 17; subject to change as admission prices rise, but still a great savings. It feels like an even better deal on a steamy day when the line at the aquarium is long. The passes, good for 9 days from the date of purchase, are on sale at participating attractions, at the Boston Common and Prudential Center visitor information centers, through the Greater Boston Convention & Visitors Bureau (✆ **800/SEE-BOSTON;** www.bostonusa.com), through some hotel concierge desks and travel agents, and from www.citypass.com.

Even if you're visiting for only 1 day, the MBTA's **Boston Visitor Pass** (✆ **877/927-7277** or 617/222-5218; www.mbta.com) can be a good deal. See p. 62.

2 The Freedom Trail

A line of red paint or red brick on the sidewalk, the 3-mile **Freedom Trail** ★★★ links 16 historic sights, many of them associated with the Revolution and the early days of the United States. The route cuts across downtown, passing through the busy shopping area around Downtown Crossing, the Financial District, and the North End on the way to Charlestown. Markers identify the stops, and plaques point the way from one to the next.

The nonprofit **Freedom Trail Foundation** (✆ **617/227-8800;** www.the freedomtrail.org) is an excellent resource as you plan your visit. Call for a guide or, even better, check out the interactive website. If you're interested, it's the only way to rub gravestones legally.

This section lists the stops on the trail in order, from Boston Common to the Bunker Hill Monument. Note that this is the *suggested* route, and nobody's checking up on you. You don't have to visit every stop or even go in order—you

---

(*Moments*   A Pep Talk: Get Lost!

Almost nothing is as stereotypical or as distressing as sightseers shuffling along in lockstep, looking only at what's described in their travel guides and going only where the Freedom Trail takes them. This is a *guide*book, not the boot-camp curriculum, and getting really lost in downtown Boston is nearly impossible—it's just too small. If time allows, wander away from the line and look around on your own. I promise you won't be sorry.

---

can skip around, start in Charlestown and work backward, visit different sights on different days, or even (horrors!) omit some sights. Here's a suggestion: If you find yourself sighing and saying "should" a lot, take a break.

A hard-core history fiend who peers at every artifact and reads every plaque can easily spend 4 hours along the trail. A family with restless children will probably appreciate the enforced efficiency of a free 90-minute ranger-led tour. The excursions, from the **Boston National Historic Park Visitor Center,** 15 State St. (© **617/242-5642;** www.nps.gov/bost), cover the "heart" of the trail, from the Old South Meeting House to the Old North Church. At press time, tours were offered daily from mid-April to November. You don't need a reservation, but call for schedules and to check whether off-season tours are available.

The best time to start on the trail is in the morning. During the summer and fall, aim for a weekday if possible. Try not to set out later than midafternoon, because attractions will be closing and you'll run into the evening rush hour.

Boston Common   In 1634, when their settlement was just 4 years old, the town fathers paid the Rev. William Blackstone £30 for this property. In 1640 it was set aside as common land. The 45 or so acres of the country's oldest public park have served as a cow pasture, a military camp, and the site of hangings, protest marches, and visits by dignitaries. Today the Common is a bit run-down, especially compared with the adjacent Public Garden, but it buzzes with activity all day. You might see a demonstration, a musical performance, a picnic lunch, or a game of tag—almost everything but a cow. Cows have been banned since 1830, which seems to be one of the few events related to the Common that isn't commemorated with a plaque.

One of the loveliest markers is on this route; head up the hill from the train station inside the fence. At Beacon Street is a **memorial** *★★★* designed by Augustus Saint-Gaudens to celebrate the deeds (indeed, the very existence) of Col. Robert Gould Shaw and the Union Army's **54th Massachusetts Colored Regiment,** who fought in the Civil War. You might remember the story of the first American army unit made up of free black soldiers from the movie *Glory.*

To continue on the Freedom Trail: Cross Beacon Street.

Between Beacon, Park, Tremont, Boylston, and Charles sts. Visitor information center: 146 Tremont St. © **888/SEE-BOSTON** or 617/536-4100. www.bostonusa.com. Mon–Sat 8:30am–5pm; Sun 9am–5pm. T: Green or Red Line to Park St.

Massachusetts State House   Boston is one of the only American cities where a building whose cornerstone was laid in 1795 (by Governor Samuel Adams) would be called the "new" anything. Nevertheless, this is the new State House, as opposed to the Old State House (discussed below). The great Federal-era architect Charles Bulfinch designed the central building of the state capitol,

The Freedom Trail

1 Boston Common
2 Massachusetts State House
3 Park Street Church
4 Old Granary Burying Ground
5 King's Chapel and Burying Ground
6 First Public School/ Benjamin Franklin Statue
7 Old Corner Bookstore Building
8 Old South Meeting House
9 Old State House
10 Boston Massacre Site
11 Faneuil Hall
12 The New England Holocaust Memorial
13 Paul Revere House
14 James Rego Square (Paul Revere Mall)
15 Old North Church
16 Copp's Hill Burying Ground
17 USS Constitution
18 USS Constitution Museum
19 Bunker Hill Monument

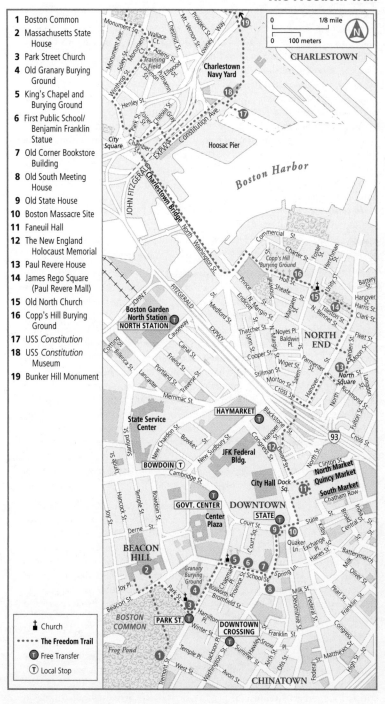

✝ Church
••••• The Freedom Trail
Ⓣ Free Transfer
Ⓣ Local Stop

and in 1802 copper sheathing manufactured by Paul Revere replaced shingles on the landmark dome. Gold leaf now covers the dome; during World War II blackouts, it was painted black. The state legislature, or Massachusetts General Court, meets here. The House of Representatives congregates under a wooden fish, the **Sacred Cod.** John Rowe, known as "Merchant" Rowe (Rowes Wharf bears his name), donated the carving in 1784 as a reminder of fishing's importance to the local economy. Tours (guided and self-guided) leave from the second floor; call ahead to see whether weekend hours have been reinstated.

Whether or not you go inside, be sure to study some of the many statues outside. Subjects range from **Mary Dyer,** a Quaker hanged on the Common in 1660 for refusing to abandon her religious beliefs, to President **John F. Kennedy.** The 60-foot monument at the rear (off Bowdoin St.) illustrates Beacon Hill's original height, before the top was shorn off to use in 19th-century landfill projects.

To continue on the Freedom Trail: Walk down Park Street (which Bulfinch laid out in 1804) to Tremont Street.

Beacon St. at Park St. ☎ 617/727-3676. Mon–Fri 9am–5pm. Free tours Mon–Fri 10am–3:30pm. T: Green or Red Line to Park St., or Blue Line to Bowdoin.

Park Street Church Henry James described this 1809 structure with a 217-foot steeple as "the most interesting mass of bricks and mortar in America." The church has accumulated an impressive number of firsts: The first missionaries to Hawaii left from here in 1819; the prominent abolitionist William Lloyd Garrison gave his first antislavery speech here on July 4, 1829; and "America" (commonly known as "My Country 'Tis of Thee") was first sung here on July 4, 1831. You're standing on **"Brimstone Corner,"** named either for the passion of the Congregational ministers who have declaimed from the pulpit or for the fact that, during the War of 1812, gunpowder (made from brimstone) was stored in the basement. This was part of the site of a huge granary that became a public building after the Revolutionary War. In the 1790s, the sails for the USS *Constitution* (Old Ironsides) were manufactured in that building.

To continue on the Freedom Trail: Walk away from the Common on Tremont Street.

1 Park St. ☎ 617/523-3383. www.parkstreet.org. Tours July–Aug Tues–Sat 9:30am–3:30pm. Sun services year-round 8:30 and 11am, 4 and 6pm. T: Green or Red Line to Park St.

Old Granary Burying Ground 🕇 This cemetery, established in 1660, was once part of Boston Common. You'll see the graves of patriots **Samuel Adams, Paul Revere, John Hancock,** and **James Otis;** merchant **Peter Faneuil** (spelled "Funal"); and Benjamin Franklin's parents. Also buried here are the victims of the **Boston Massacre** (discussed below) and the wife of Isaac Vergoose, who is believed to be **"Mother Goose"** of nursery rhyme fame. Note that gravestone rubbing, however tempting, is illegal in Boston's historic cemeteries.

To continue on the Freedom Trail: Turn left as you leave the cemetery and continue 1½ blocks on Tremont Street.

Tremont St. at Bromfield St. Daily 9am–5pm (until 3pm in winter). T: Green or Red Line to Park St.

King's Chapel and Burying Ground Architect Peter Harrison sent the plans for this Georgian-style building from Newport, Rhode Island, in 1749. Rather than replacing the existing wooden chapel, the granite edifice was constructed around it. Completed in 1754, it was the first Anglican church in Boston. George III sent gifts, as did Queen Anne and William and Mary, who presented the communion table and chancel tablets (still in use today) before the church was even built. The Puritan colonists had little use for the royal religion; after the Revolution, this became the first Unitarian church in the new nation. It conducts Unitarian Universalist services, using the Anglican Book of Common Prayer.

The **burying ground** ⟨★★, on Tremont Street, is the oldest in the city; it dates to 1630. Among the scary colonial headstones (winged skulls are a popular decoration) are the graves of **John Winthrop,** the first governor of the Massachusetts Bay Colony; **William Dawes,** who rode with Paul Revere; **Elizabeth Pain,** the model for Hester Prynne in Nathaniel Hawthorne's novel *The Scarlet Letter;* and **Mary Chilton,** the first female colonist to step ashore on Plymouth Rock.

To continue on the Freedom Trail: Follow the trail back along Tremont Street and turn left onto School Street.

58 Tremont St. ⓒ 617/523-1749. Chapel: Summer daily 9:30am–1pm, winter Sat 10am–2pm; check at entrance for up-to-date hours. Donation requested from adults. Services Wed 12:15pm, Sun 11am. Burying ground daily 8am–5:30pm (until 3pm in winter). T: Green or Blue Line to Government Center.

First Public School/Benjamin Franklin Statue

A colorful folk-art mosaic in the sidewalk marks the site of the first public school in the country. It was founded in 1634, 2 years before Harvard College. Samuel Adams, Benjamin Franklin, John Hancock, and Cotton Mather studied there. The original building (1645) was demolished to make way for the expansion of King's Chapel, and the school moved across the street. Now called Boston Latin School, the prestigious institution is in the Fenway neighborhood. Other alumni include Charles Bulfinch, Ralph Waldo Emerson, George Santayana, Arthur Fiedler, and Leonard Bernstein.

Behind the fence in the courtyard to your left is the **Benjamin Franklin statue,** the first portrait statue erected in Boston (1856). Franklin was born in Boston in 1706 and was apprenticed to his half-brother James, a printer, but they got along so poorly that in 1723 Benjamin ran away to Philadelphia. Plaques on the base describe his numerous accomplishments. The lovely granite building behind the statue is **Old City Hall** (1865), designed in Second Empire style by Arthur Gilman (who laid out the Back Bay) and Gridley J. F. Bryant, and opened in 1865. The administration moved to Government Center in 1969, and the building now houses commercial tenants.

To continue on the Freedom Trail: Follow School Street to Washington Street.

School St. at City Hall Ave. T: Blue or Orange Line to State.

Old Corner Bookstore Building

Built in 1718, it's on a plot of land that was once home to the religious reformer Anne Hutchinson, who was excommunicated and expelled from Boston in 1638 for heresy. In the middle of the 19th century, the little brick building held the publishing house of Ticknor & Fields, which effectively made this the literary center of America. Publisher James Fields, known as "Jamie," counted among his friends Henry Wadsworth Longfellow, James Russell Lowell, Henry David Thoreau, Ralph Waldo Emerson, Nathaniel Hawthorne, and Harriet Beecher Stowe. For many years this was the Globe Corner Bookstore, which is now in Harvard Square (see chapter 9). Today the building houses the **Boston Globe Store** (ⓒ 617/367-4000), which sells souvenirs and newspaper-related merchandise.

To continue on the Freedom Trail: Turn right and walk 1 block.

3 School St. T: Blue or Orange Line to State.

Old South Meeting House ⭐ Look for the clock tower that tops this religious and political gathering place, best known as the site of an important event leading to the Revolution. On December 16, 1773, a restive crowd of several thousand, too big to fit into Faneuil Hall, gathered here. They were waiting for word from the governor about whether three ships full of tea—priced to undercut the cost of smuggled tea and force the colonists to trade with merchants approved by the Crown—would be sent back to England from Boston. The ships were not, and revolutionaries poorly disguised as Mohawks cast the tea into the harbor. The meetinghouse commemorates that uprising, the **Boston Tea Party.** You can even see a vial of the tea.

Originally built in 1670 and replaced by the current structure in 1729, the building underwent extensive renovations in the 1990s. In 1872 the devastating fire that destroyed most of downtown stopped at Old South, a phenomenon considered evidence of the building's power. An interactive multimedia exhibit, *Voices of Protest,* tells its story. The meetinghouse frequently schedules speeches, readings, panel discussions, and children's activities, often with a colonial theme. Each December, it stages a reenactment of the debate that led to the tea party. Call ahead or check the website for schedules.

Exit through the gift shop and look across Milk Street at **Benjamin Franklin's birthplace.** In a little house at 17 Milk St., Franklin was born in 1706, the 15th child of Josiah Franklin. The house is long gone, but step to the curb and look across at the second floor of what's now 1 Milk St. (home of the Dreams of Freedom center; p. 147). When the building went up after the fire of 1872, the architect guaranteed that the Founding Father wouldn't be forgotten: A bust and the words BIRTHPLACE OF FRANKLIN adorn the facade.

To continue on the Freedom Trail: Backtrack on Washington Street (passing Spring Lane, one of the first streets in Boston and originally the site of a real spring) to State Street.

310 Washington St. ✆ 617/482-6439. www.oldsouthmeetinghouse.org. Admission $5 adults, $4 seniors and students, $1 children 6–18, free for children under 6. Daily Apr–Oct 9:30am–5pm; Nov–Mar 10am–4pm. T: Blue or Orange Line to State St.

Old State House Built in 1713, this brick structure served as the seat of colonial government before the Revolution and as the state capitol until 1797. From its balcony, the Declaration of Independence was first read to Bostonians on July 18, 1776. In 1789, President George Washington reviewed a parade from here. The exterior decorations are particularly interesting—the clock was installed in place of a sundial, and the gilded lion and unicorn are reproductions of the original symbols of British rule that were ripped from the facade and burned the day the Declaration of Independence was read.

Impressions

I do not speak with any fondness, but the language of coolest history, when I say that Boston commands attention as the town which was appointed in the destiny of nations to lead the civilization of North America.
—Ralph Waldo Emerson, *The Natural History of Intellect,* 1893

From John Adams to George Apley, Bostonians are smugly apt to like their own town best.
—Esther Forbes, *Paul Revere and the World He Lived In,* 1942

(Moments Trail Mix

Faneuil Hall Marketplace is a great spot for a break. Time your walk right, and it can be the starting point of a picnic lunch. Visit the **Quincy Market** food court for takeout, and head toward the water. Two good places to picnic lie nearby, across Atlantic Avenue on the other side of the Big Dig. At the foot of State Street is **Long Wharf,** Boston's principal wharf since 1710 and a busy sightseeing-cruise dock. Pass the Marriott to reach the brick plaza at the end of the wharf. The granite building dates to 1846, and the plaza affords a great view of the harbor and the airport. Or stay at **Christopher Columbus Waterfront Park,** on the other side of the hotel, watch the action at the marina, and play in the playground.

As you walk from Faneuil Hall to the Paul Revere House, you'll find yourself in the midst of **Haymarket.** On Friday and Saturday, the bustling open-air market on Hanover and Blackstone streets consists of stalls piled high with fruit, vegetables, and flowers. Shoppers aren't allowed to touch anything they haven't bought, a rule you might learn from a hollering vendor or a cutthroat customer. It's a great scene and a favorite with photographers.

Inside is the **Bostonian Society's museum** ✸ of the city's history. The society was founded in 1881 to save this building, which was badly deteriorated and, incredibly, about to be sold and shipped to Chicago. Exhibits include an introductory video on the history of the building and regularly changing displays that draw on the society's extensive collections of artifacts and documents.

To continue on the Freedom Trail: Leave the building, turn left, and walk half a block.

206 Washington St. ⓒ 617/720-1713. www.bostonhistory.org. Admission $5 adults, $4 seniors and students, $1 children 6–18, free for children under 6. Daily 9am–5pm. T: Blue or Orange Line to State.

Boston Massacre Site   A ring of cobblestones on a traffic island marks the location of the skirmish that helped consolidate the spirit of rebellion in the colonies. On March 5, 1770, angered at the presence of royal troops in Boston, colonists threw snowballs, garbage, rocks, and other debris at a group of redcoats. The soldiers panicked and fired into the crowd, killing five men. Their graves, including that of Crispus Attucks, the first black man to die in the Revolution, are in the Old Granary Burying Ground.

To continue on the Freedom Trail: Turn left onto Congress Street and walk down the hill.

State St. at Devonshire St. T: Blue or Orange Line to State.

Faneuil Hall ✸   Built in 1742 (and enlarged using a Charles Bulfinch design in 1805), this building was a gift to the town from prosperous merchant Peter Faneuil. The "Cradle of Liberty" rang with speeches by orators such as Samuel Adams—whose statue stands outside the Congress Street entrance—in the years leading to the Revolution. Abolitionists, temperance advocates, and suffragists used it as a pulpit in the years afterward. The upstairs is still a public meeting and concert hall, and downstairs holds retail space, all according to Faneuil's will. The grasshopper **weather vane,** the sole remaining detail from the original building, is modeled after the weather vane on London's Royal Exchange.

National Park Service rangers give **free 20-minute talks** every half-hour from 9am to 5pm in the second-floor auditorium and operate a visitor center on the first floor. On the top floor is a small museum that houses the weapons collection and historical exhibits of the Ancient and Honorable Artillery Company of Massachusetts. Admission is free.

To continue on the Freedom Trail: Leave Faneuil Hall, cross North Street, and follow the trail through the "Blackstone Block." These buildings, among the oldest in the city, give a sense of the scale of 18th- and 19th-century Boston. Pause on Union Street.

Dock Sq. (Congress St. and North St.). ℂ 617/242-5675. Daily 9am–5pm. T: Green or Blue Line to Government Center, or Orange Line to Haymarket.

The New England Holocaust Memorial 🎭🎭 Erected in 1995, these six glass towers spring up in the midst of attractions that celebrate freedom, reminding visitors of the consequences of a world without it. The pattern on the glass, which at first appears merely decorative, is actually 6 million random numbers, one for each Jew who died during the Holocaust. As you pass through, pause to read the inscriptions.

To continue on the Freedom Trail: The trail passes under the expressway through widespread Big Dig construction (you might not be able to find the trail—ask the police officer at the corner of Hanover and Blackstone sts. for help if you get lost) and emerges in the North End. Follow Cross Street to Hanover Street, turn left, and follow Hanover to Richmond Street. Turn right, go 1 block, and turn left.

Union St. between North and Hanover sts. ℂ 617/457-8755. www.nehm.org. T: Orange or Green Line to Haymarket.

Paul Revere House 🎭🎭🎭 One of the most pleasant stops on the Freedom Trail, this 2½-story wood structure presents history on a human scale. Revere was living here when he set out for Lexington on April 18, 1775, a feat immortalized in Henry Wadsworth Longfellow's poem "Paul Revere's Ride" ("Listen, my children, and you shall hear, / Of the midnight ride of Paul Revere"). The oldest house in downtown Boston, it was built around 1680, bought by Revere in 1770, and put to a number of uses before being turned into a museum in the early 20th century. It holds neatly arranged and identified 17th- and 18th-century furnishings and artifacts, including the famous Revere silver, considered some of the finest anywhere.

The thought-provoking tour is self-guided, with staff members around in case you have questions. The format allows you to linger on the artifacts that hold your interest. Revere had 16 children (he called them "my lambs")—eight with each of his two wives—and supported the family with his thriving silversmith's trade. At his home, you'll get a good sense of the risks he took with his role in the events that led to the Revolutionary War.

Across the courtyard is the home of Revere's Hichborn cousins, the **Pierce/Hichborn House** 🎭. The 1711 Georgian-style home is a rare example of 18th-century middle-class architecture. It's suitably furnished and shown only by guided tour (usually twice a day at busy times). Call the Paul Revere House for schedules.

Before you leave North Square, look across the cobblestone plaza at **Sacred Heart Church.** It was established in 1833 as the Seamen's Bethel, a church devoted to the needs of the mariners who frequented the area. Today it's Roman Catholic, and one Mass every Sunday is said in Italian. Wharves ran up

Welcome to the North End

The Paul Revere House and the Old North Church are the best-known buildings in the **North End** 🌟🌟, Boston's "Little Italy" (although it's *never* called that). Home to natives of Italy and their assimilated children, numerous Italian restaurants and private social clubs, and many historic sights, this is one of the oldest neighborhoods in the city. It was home in the 17th century to the **Mather family** of Puritan ministers, who certainly would be shocked to see the merry goings-on at the festivals and street fairs that take over different areas of the North End on weekends in July and August.

The Italians (and their yuppie neighbors who have made inroads since the 1980s) are only the latest immigrant group to dominate the North End. In the mid–19th century, this was an eastern European Jewish enclave and later an Irish stronghold. In 1894, Rose Fitzgerald, mother of President John F. Kennedy, was born on Garden Court Street and baptized at St. Stephen's Church.

Modern visitors might be more interested in a Hanover Street *caffè*, the perfect place to have coffee or a soft drink and feast on sweets. **Mike's Pastry** 🌟🌟🌟, 300 Hanover St. (📞 **617/742-3050**), is a bakery that does a frantic takeout business and has tables where you can sit down and order one of the confections on display in the cases. Mike's claim to fame is its cannoli (tubes of crisp-fried pastry filled with sweetened ricotta cheese); the cookies, cakes, and other pastries are excellent, too. You can also sit and relax at **Caffè dello Sport** or **Caffè Vittoria,** on either side of Mike's.

almost this far in colonial days; in the 19th century, this was a notorious red-light district.

To continue on the Freedom Trail: The trail leaves the square on Prince Street and runs along Hanover Street past Clark Street. Before turning onto Prince Street, take a few steps down Garden Court Street and look for no. 4, on the right. The private residence was the birthplace of Rose Fitzgerald (later Kennedy).

19 North Sq. 📞 617/523-2338. www.paulreverehouse.org. Admission $3 adults, $2.50 seniors and students, $1 children 5–17, free for children under 5. Daily Apr 15–Oct 9:30am–5:15pm; daily Apr 1–14 and Nov–Dec 9:30am–4:15pm; Jan–Mar Tues–Sun 9:30am–4:15pm. Closed Jan 1, Thanksgiving, and Dec 25. T: Green or Orange Line to Haymarket, or Blue Line to Aquarium.

James Rego Square (Paul Revere Mall) A pleasant little brick-paved park known as the Prado, the mall holds a famous equestrian statue of Paul Revere. Take time to read some of the **tablets** 🌟 on the left-hand wall that describe famous people and places in the history of the North End.

To continue on the Freedom Trail: Walk around the fountain and continue to Salem Street.

Hanover St. at Clark St. T: Green or Orange Line to Haymarket.

Old North Church 🌟 Officially named Christ Church, this is the oldest church building in Boston (1723). The building is in the style of Sir Christopher Wren. In the original steeple, sexton Robert Newman hung two lanterns on the night of April 18, 1775, to signal Paul Revere that British troops were setting out for Lexington and Concord in boats across the Charles River, not on foot ("One if by land, and two if by sea"). The steeple fell in hurricanes in 1804 and 1954; the current version is an exact copy of the original. The 190-foot spire, long a reference point for sailors, appears on navigational charts to this day. And how's this for a coincidence: Newman was a great-grandson of George Burroughs, one of the victims of the Salem witch trials of 1692.

Members of the Revere family attended this church (their plaque is on pew 54); famous visitors have included Presidents James Monroe, Theodore Roosevelt, Franklin D. Roosevelt, and Gerald R. Ford, and Queen Elizabeth II. There are markers and plaques throughout; note the bust of George Washington, reputedly the first memorial to the first president. The **gardens** on the north side of the church (dotted with more plaques) are open to the public. On the south side of the church, volunteers maintain an 18th-century garden. Proceeds from the quirky gift shop and museum go to support the church.

Free tours of the church begin every 15 minutes. The 50-minute behind-the-scenes tour ($8 adults, $5 children) starts on the hour from June through August, and the rest of the year by appointment. Reservations are recommended.

To continue on the Freedom Trail: Cross Salem Street onto Hull Street, and walk uphill toward Copp's Hill Burying Ground. On the left you'll pass 44 Hull St., a private residence that's the narrowest (10 ft. wide) house in Boston.

193 Salem St. ✆ 617/523-6676. www.oldnorth.com. Donations appreciated. Daily 9am–5pm. Sun services (Episcopal) 9 and 11am. T: Orange or Green Line to Haymarket.

Copp's Hill Burying Ground ★

The second-oldest cemetery (1659) in the city is the burial place of Cotton Mather and his family, Robert Newman, and Prince Hall. Hall, a prominent member of the free black community that occupied the north slope of the hill in colonial times, fought at Bunker Hill and established the first black Masonic lodge. The highest point in the North End, Copp's Hill was the site of a windmill and of the British batteries that destroyed the village of Charlestown during the Battle of Bunker Hill on June 17, 1775. Charlestown is clearly visible (look for the masts of the USS *Constitution*) across the Inner Harbor. No gravestone rubbing is allowed.

To continue on the Freedom Trail: Follow Hull Street down the hill to Commercial Street (note that there's no crosswalk on Commercial at the dangerous intersection with Hull) and follow the trail to North Washington Street and across the bridge. Follow signs and the trail to the Charlestown Navy Yard.

Off Hull St. near Snowhill St. Daily 9am–5pm (until 3pm in winter). T: Green or Orange Line to North Station.

USS *Constitution* ★★ *Kids*

"**Old Ironsides**," one of the U.S. Navy's six original frigates, never lost a battle. The ship was constructed in the North End from 1794 to 1797 at a cost of $302,718, using bolts, spikes, and other fittings from Paul Revere's foundry. As the new nation made its naval and military reputation, the *Constitution* played a key role, battling French privateers and Barbary pirates, repelling the British fleet during the War of 1812, participating in 40 engagements, and capturing 20 vessels. The frigate earned its nickname during an engagement on August 19, 1812, when shots from the French warship *Guerriere* bounced off its thick oak hull as if it were iron. Today, the active-duty sailors who lead tours wear 1812 dress uniforms.

Retired from combat in 1815, the *Constitution* was rescued from destruction when Oliver Wendell Holmes's poem *Old Ironsides* launched a preservation movement in 1830. The frigate was completely overhauled for its bicentennial in 1997, when it sailed under its own power for the first time since 1881, drawing international attention. Tugs tow the *Constitution* into the harbor every **Fourth of July** and turn it to ensure that the ship weathers evenly.

To continue on the Freedom Trail: Walk straight ahead to the museum entrance.

Off First Ave., Charlestown Navy Yard. © 617/242-5670. Free tours daily 9:30am–3:50pm. T: Ferry from Long Wharf or Lovejoy Wharf, or Green or Orange Line to North Station.

USS *Constitution* Museum *(Kids)*   Just inland from the vessel, the museum features participatory exhibits that allow visitors to hoist a flag, fire a cannon, and learn more about the ship. The interactive computer displays and naval artifacts appeal to visitors of all ages. The museum's collections include more than 3,000 original items, arranged and interpreted in ways that put them in context.

Also at the navy yard, **National Park Service** rangers (© **617/242-5601**) staff an **information booth** and give free 1-hour guided tours of the base.

To continue on the Freedom Trail: Follow the trail up Constitution Road, crossing Chelsea Street, and continue to the Bunker Hill Monument. A more interesting, slightly longer route runs from Chelsea Street and Rutherford Avenue (back at the bridge) across City Square Park.

Off First Ave., Charlestown Navy Yard. © 617/426-1812. www.ussconstitutionmuseum.org. Free admission. Daily May–Oct 15 9am–6pm; Oct 16–Apr 10am–5pm. Closed Jan 1, Thanksgiving, Dec 25. T: Ferry from Long Wharf or Lovejoy Wharf, or Green or Orange Line to North Station.

Bunker Hill Monument   The 221-foot granite obelisk honors the memory of the colonists who died in the Battle of Bunker Hill on June 17, 1775. The rebels lost the battle, but nearly half the British troops were killed or wounded, a loss that contributed to the redcoats' decision to abandon Boston 9 months later. The Marquis de Lafayette, the celebrated hero of the American and French revolutions, helped lay the monument's cornerstone in 1825. He is buried in Paris under soil taken from the hill. A punishing flight of 294 stairs leads to the top. There's no elevator, and although the views of the harbor and the northern portion of the Big Dig are good, the windows are quite small. The ranger-staffed lodge at the base of the monument holds dioramas and exhibits.

Monument Sq., Charlestown. © 617/242-5641. www.nps.gov/bost. Free admission. Exhibits daily 9am–5pm; monument daily 9am–4:30pm. T: Ferry from Long Wharf or Lovejoy Wharf to Navy Yard, or Orange Line to Community College.

Tips **Inside Info**

One quick way to announce yourself as a tourist is to pause on Hanover Street between Prince and Fleet streets and proclaim that you see the Old North Church. The first house of worship you see is **St. Stephen's,** the only Charles Bulfinch–designed church still standing in Boston. It was Unitarian when it was dedicated in 1804. The next year, the congregation bought a bell from Paul Revere's foundry for $800. Architecture buffs get a kick out of the design, a paragon of Federal-style symmetry. St. Stephen's became Roman Catholic in 1862 and was moved when Hanover Street was widened in 1870. During refurbishment in 1965, it regained its original appearance, with clear glass windows, white walls, and gilded organ pipes. It's one of the plainest Catholic churches you'll ever see.

> ### *Tips* Trailing Off
>
> If you don't feel like retracing your steps at the end of the Freedom Trail, you have two public transit options. Return to the Charlestown Navy Yard for the **ferry** to Long Wharf, which leaves every half-hour from 6:45am to 8:15pm on weekdays (every 15 min. 6:45–9:15am and 3:45–6:45pm), and every half-hour on the quarter-hour from 10:15am to 6:15pm on weekends. The 10-minute trip costs $1.25, and the dock is an easy walk from Old Ironsides. Alternatively, walk to the foot of the hill; on Main Street, take **bus no. 92 or 93** to Haymarket (Green or Orange Line).

3 More Museums & Attractions

Boston Public Library   The central branch of the city's library system is an architectural and intellectual monument. The original 1895 building, a National Historic Landmark designed by Charles F. McKim, is an Italian Renaissance–style masterpiece that fairly drips with art. The **lobby doors** are the work of Daniel Chester French (who also designed the Abraham Lincoln statue in the memorial in Washington, the *Minute Man* statue in Concord, and the John Harvard statue in Cambridge). The recently restored **murals** are by John Singer Sargent and Pierre Puvis de Chavannes, among others. Visit the lovely **courtyard** ✿ or peek at it from a window on the stairs. The adjoining addition, of the same height and material (pink granite), was designed by Philip Johnson and opened in 1972. The lobby holds changing exhibits.

Free **Art & Architecture Tours** (www.bpl.org/guides/tours.htm) begin year-round Monday at 2:30pm, Tuesday and Thursday at 6pm, Friday and Saturday at 11am, and September through May on Sunday at 2pm. Call ✆ **617/536-5400,** ext. 216, to arrange group tours.

700 Boylston St., Copley Sq. ✆ **617/536-5400.** www.bpl.org. Free admission. Mon–Thurs 9am–9pm; Fri–Sat 9am–5pm; Sun (Oct–May only) 1–5pm. Closed Sun June–Sept and legal holidays. T: Green Line to Copley.

Commonwealth Museum/Massachusetts Archives   The nearby Kennedy Library explores the history of one of Boston's most famous families; here, you might find your own clan's history. Neither collection is worth a trip on its own, but this is a worthwhile detour on the way to or from the Kennedy Library.

The **Commonwealth Museum** has videos, slide shows, and other interactive exhibits on the state's people, places, and politics. Topics covered recently in the regularly changing exhibits include the archaeology of the Big Dig, the Civil War, and state history. In the same building, the state **archives** contain passenger lists for ships that arrived in Boston from 1848 to 1891; state census schedules that date to 1790; and documents, maps, and military and court records starting with the Massachusetts Bay Company (1628–29). Knowledgeable staff members are on hand to answer researchers' questions in person, by mail, or by phone.

220 Morrissey Blvd., Columbia Point. Museum ✆ **617/727-9268.** www.state.ma.us/sec/mus/. Archives ✆ **617/727-2816.** www.state.ma.us/sec/arc/. Free admission. Mon–Fri 9am–5pm; Sat 9am–3pm. Closed legal holidays. T: Red Line to JFK/UMass.

Institute of Contemporary Art   Across from the Hynes Convention Center, the ICA mounts rotating exhibits of 20th- and 21st-century art, including painting, sculpture, photography, and video and performance art. The institute also offers films, lectures, music, video, poetry, and educational programs for children and adults. The 1886 building, originally a police station, is a showpiece in its own right.

The ICA's profile is on the rise. It's in the process of building a new museum at Fan Pier, on the South Boston waterfront near the federal courthouse. A $37 million project designed by the pioneering New York firm Diller + Scofidio, it's scheduled to open in 2006. Check at this location for details and updates.

955 Boylston St. ℭ **617/266-5152.** www.icaboston.org. Admission $7 adults, $5 seniors and students, free for children under 12; free to all Thurs 5–9pm. Wed and Fri noon–5pm; Thurs noon–9pm; Sat–Sun 11am–5pm. Closed major holidays. T: Green Line B, C, or D to Hynes/ICA.

Larz Anderson Auto Museum   Formerly the Museum of Transportation, the Larz Anderson Auto Museum occupies an 1888 carriage house modeled after a French château. Beginning in 1899, Larz and Isabel Anderson acquired the cars that form the core of the collection, now the country's oldest private assemblage of antique autos. The cars boast what was then the latest equipment, from a two-cylinder engine (in a 1901 Winton race car) to a full lavatory (in a 1906 CGV). Autos and memorabilia from the collection and from other sources are on display.

The museum has a good gift shop and frequently schedules special events such as lectures and family programs. On most warm-weather Sundays, outdoor **lawn events** include displays of vehicles such as Corvettes, Cadillacs, Triumphs, European motorcycles, or Italian imports. Call to find out what's featured during your visit.

15 Newton St., Larz Anderson Park, Brookline. ℭ **617/522-6547.** www.mot.org. Admission $5 adults, $3 seniors, students, and children 6–18, free for children under 6. Tues–Sun and Mon holidays 10am–5pm. Closed Jan 1, Thanksgiving, Dec 25. T: Green Line D to Reservoir, then take bus no. 51 (Forest Hills); museum is 5 blocks from intersection of Newton and Clyde sts. Call for driving directions.

Mary Baker Eddy Library/Mapparium 𝘒𝘪𝘥𝘴   The Mary Baker Eddy Library, a research center with two floors of interactive and multimedia exhibits, opened in 2002. Its mission is to explore ideas through history, with a central role for Mary Baker Eddy, the founder of Christian Science. The library's most intriguing exhibit is the **Mapparium** 𝘨, a unique hollow globe 30 feet across. A work of both art and history, it consists of a bronze framework that connects 608 stained-glass panels. Because sound bounces off the nonporous surfaces, the acoustics are as unusual as the aesthetics. As you cross the glass bridge just south of the equator, you'll see the political divisions of the world from 1932 to 1935, when the globe was constructed.

⟮Moments⟯ Eyes in the Skies

For a smashing view of the airport, the harbor, and the South Boston waterfront, stroll along the harbor or Atlantic Avenue to Northern Avenue. On either side of this intersection are buildings with free observation areas. Be ready to show an ID to gain entrance. The first, on the 14th floor of 470 Atlantic Ave., is open daily from 11am to 5pm. The other, Foster's Rotunda, is on the ninth floor of 30 Rowes Wharf, in the Boston Harbor Hotel complex. Open Monday to Friday from 11am to 4pm.

World Headquarters of the First Church of Christ, Scientist, 200 Mass. Ave. © **888/222-3711**. www. marybakereddylibrary.org. Admission $5 adults, $3 seniors, students, and children 6–17. Tues–Fri 10am–9pm; Sat 10am–5pm; Sun 11am–5pm. Closed Jan 1, Thanksgiving, Dec 25. MBTA: Green Line E to Symphony, Green Line B, C, or D to Hynes/ICA, or Orange Line to Mass. Ave.

4 Historic Houses

The home in Boston imbued with the most history is the **Paul Revere House** (p. 162). A visit to his home brings the legendary revolutionary to life. For information on the **Longfellow National Historic Site**, see p. 171.

On **Beacon Hill,** you'll find houses that are as interesting for their architecture as for their occupants. The south slope, facing Boston Common, has been a fashionable address since the 1620s; excellent tours of two houses (one on the north slope) focus on the late 18th and early 19th centuries. The architect of the homes was Charles Bulfinch; he also designed the State House, which sits at the hill's summit.

The **Society for the Preservation of New England Antiquities (SPNEA)** owns and operates the Otis House (see below) and dozens of other historic properties throughout New England. The results of its restoration techniques can be seen at museums all over the region. Contact the society, 141 Cambridge St., Boston, MA 02114 (© **617/227-3956**; www.spnea.org), for brochures, visiting hours, and admission fees.

Gibson House Museum　In the Back Bay, the Gibson House is an 1859 brownstone that embodies the word "Victorian." You'll see decorations of all kinds, including family photos and portraits, petrified-wood hat racks, a sequined pink velvet pagoda for the cat, a Victrola, and an original icebox. Check ahead for the schedule of lectures and other special events.

137 Beacon St. © **617/267-6338**. www.thegibsonhouse.org. Admission $5. Tours on the hour Wed–Sun 1–3pm. T: Green Line to Arlington.

Harrison Gray Otis House ★★　Legendary architect Charles Bulfinch designed this gorgeous 1796 mansion for an up-and-coming young lawyer who later became mayor of Boston. The restoration was one of the first in the country to use computer analysis of paint, and the result was revolutionary: It revealed that the colors on the walls were drab because the paint was faded, not because they started out dingy. Furnished in the style to which a wealthy family in the young United States would have been accustomed, the Federal-style building is a colorful, elegant treasure. Guided tours (the only way to see the house) discuss its architecture and post-Revolutionary social, business, and family life, and touch on the history of the neighborhood.

141 Cambridge St. © **617/227-3956**. www.spnea.org. Guided tour $5 adults, $4 seniors, $2.50 students. Tours on the hour. Wed–Sun 11am–4pm. T: Blue Line to Bowdoin (closed weekends), Green or Blue Line to Government Center, or Red Line to Charles/MGH.

John F. Kennedy National Historic Site　A unit of the National Park Service, the 35th president's birthplace is restored to its appearance in 1917. The guided ranger tour discusses domestic life of the period and the roots of the Kennedy family. If you miss the last guided tour, ask about the self-guided option. One-hour walking tours of the neighborhood start at 12:45pm on weekends.

83 Beals St., Brookline. © **617/566-7937**. www.nps.gov/jofi. Tours $3 adults, free for children under 17. May–Oct Wed–Sun 10am–4:30pm. Tours every 30 min. 10am–3:30pm. Closed Nov–Apr. T: Green Line C to Coolidge Corner, then walk 4 blocks north on Harvard St.

Nichols House Museum   This 1804 Beacon Hill home is decorated with beautiful antique furnishings collected by several generations of the Nichols family. Its most prominent occupant, Rose Standish Nichols, was a suffragist and a pioneering landscape designer. Check ahead for events celebrating the house's 2004 bicentennial. Open days may vary, so call ahead.

55 Mount Vernon St. ℂ 617/227-6993. www.nicholshousemuseum.org. Admission $5. May–Oct, tours Tues–Sat; Nov–Apr, tours Thurs–Sat. Tours every 30 min. noon–4pm. Closed Jan. T: Red or Green Line to Park St.

5 African-American History

The **Black Heritage Trail** covers sites on Beacon Hill that are part of the history of 19th-century Boston. You can take a free 2-hour guided tour with a ranger from the National Park Service's **Boston African American National Historic Site,** which starts at the visitor center, 46 Joy St. (ℂ **617/742-5415;** www.nps.gov/boaf). They're available daily from Memorial Day to Labor Day, and by request at other times. Or go on your own, using a brochure that includes a map and descriptions of the buildings. The sites include stations of the Underground Railroad, homes of famous citizens, and the first integrated public school. Check ahead for special programs if you're visiting during February.

One of the most interesting sites on the Black Heritage Trail is the **African Meeting House,** 8 Smith Court. Opened in 1806, it's the oldest standing black church in the United States. William Lloyd Garrison founded the New England Anti-Slavery Society in this building, where Frederick Douglass made some of his great abolitionist speeches. Once known as the "Black Faneuil Hall," it offers an informative audiovisual presentation and schedules lectures, concerts, and church meetings.

The **Museum of Afro-American History** ⚓, 46 Joy St. (ℂ **617/725-0022;** www.afroammuseum.org), has the most comprehensive information on the history and contributions of blacks in Boston and Massachusetts. From Memorial Day to Labor Day, it's open daily from 10am to 4pm; the rest of the year, it's open Monday to Saturday from 10am to 4pm. Admission is free.

Focus on Women's History

The **Boston Women's Heritage Trail** (ℂ **617/522-2872;** www.bwht.org) creates walking tours with stops at the homes, churches, and social and political institutions where women lived, made great contributions to society, or both. Subjects include Julia Ward Howe, social reformer Dorothea Dix, the colonial religious leader Anne Hutchinson, and less famous Bostonians, such as Phillis Wheatley, a slave who became the first African-American published poet, and abolitionist and feminist Lucy Stone. You can buy a guidebook at the National Park Service Visitor Center at 15 State St., at local historic sites, by mail, or online.

March is Women's History Month; special events include lectures, walking tours, museum events, and workshops. Check with the Greater Boston Convention & Visitors Bureau (ℂ **800/SEE-BOSTON;** www.bostonusa.com) for details.

The Boston History Collaborative website **www.bostonfamilyhistory.org** lists resources for many ethnic groups, including African Americans.

Across the river, the **Cambridge African American Trail** focuses on significant sites in the history of the city's large black community. To buy the guide, send a check for $7.45 (includes shipping), payable to the Cambridge Historical Society, to the **Cambridge Historical Commission,** 831 Mass. Ave., Cambridge, MA 02139 (www.ci.cambridge.ma.us/~historic).

6 Parks & Gardens

Green space is an important part of Boston's appeal, and the public parks are hard to miss. The world-famous **Emerald Necklace,** Frederick Law Olmsted's vision for a loop of green spaces, runs through the city. (See p. 182 for information about seeing part or all of the Emerald Necklace with a Boston park ranger.)

The best-known park, for good reason, is the spectacular **Public Garden** ★★★, bordered by Arlington, Boylston, Charles, and Beacon streets. Something lovely is in bloom at the country's first botanical garden at least half the year. The spring flowers are particularly impressive, especially if your visit happens to coincide with the first really warm day of the year. It's hard not to enjoy yourself when everyone around you seems ecstatic just to be seeing the sun.

For many people, the official beginning of spring coincides with the return of the **swan boats** ★ (© 617/522-1966; www.swanboats.com). The pedal-powered vessels—the attendants pedal, not the passengers—plunge into the lagoon on the Saturday before Patriots Day (the 3rd Mon of Apr). Although they don't move fast, they'll transport you. They operate daily from 10am to 5pm in the summer, daily from 10am to 4pm in the spring, and weekdays noon to 4pm and weekends 10am to 4pm from Labor Day to mid-September. The cost for the 15-minute ride is $2 for adults, $1.50 for seniors, and $1 for children 2 to 15.

Across Charles Street is **Boston Common,** the country's first public park. The property was purchased in 1634 and officially set aside as public land in 1640, so if it seems a bit run-down (especially compared to the Public Garden), it's no wonder. The Frog Pond, where there really were frogs at one time, makes a pleasant spot to splash around in the summer and skate in the winter. At the Boylston Street side is the **Central Burying Ground,** where you can see the grave of famed portraitist Gilbert Stuart. There's also a bandstand where you might take in a free concert or play, and many beautiful shade trees.

The most spectacular garden is the **Arnold Arboretum** ★★, 125 Arborway, Jamaica Plain (© 617/524-1718; www.arboretum.harvard.edu). One of the oldest parks in the United States, founded in 1872, it is open daily from sunrise to sunset. Its 265 acres contain more than 15,000 ornamental trees, shrubs, and vines from all over the world. In the spring, the grounds are ablaze with blossoming dogwood, azaleas, and rhododendrons, and the air fills with the dizzying scent of hundreds of varieties of lilacs, for which the arboretum is especially famous. This is definitely a place to take a camera—but not food. Lilac Sunday, in May, is the only time the arboretum allows picnicking.

There is no admission fee for the National Historical Landmark, which Harvard University administers in cooperation with the Boston Department of Parks and Recreation. To get there, take the MBTA Orange Line to the Forest Hills stop and follow signs to the entrance. The visitor center is open weekdays from 9am to 4pm, and weekends from noon to 4pm. Call for information about educational programs.

7 Cambridge

Boston and Cambridge are so closely associated that many people believe they're the same—a notion that both cities' residents and politicians are happy to dispel. Cantabrigians are often considered more liberal and better educated than Bostonians, which is another idea that's sure to get you involved in a lively discussion. Take the Red Line across the river and see for yourself.

For a good overview, begin at the main Harvard T entrance. Follow the **walking tour** (p. 200), or set out on your own. At the **information booth** (© **800/862-5678** or 617/497-1630) in the middle of Harvard Square at the intersection of Mass. Ave., John F. Kennedy Street, and Brattle Street, trained volunteers dispense maps and brochures and answer questions Monday through Saturday from 9am to 5pm and Sunday from 1 to 5pm. From mid-June to Labor Day, there are guided tours that include the entire old Cambridge area. Check at the booth for rates, meeting places, and times, or call ahead. If you prefer to sightsee on your own, you can buy a *Revolutionary Cambridge* walking guide ($2) prepared by the Cambridge Historical Commission.

Whatever you do, spend some time in **Harvard Square.** It's a hodgepodge of college and high school students, professors and instructors, commuters, street performers, and sightseers. Near the information booth are two well-stocked newsstands, **Nini's Corner** and **Out of Town News,** and the **Harvard Coop** bookstore. There are restaurants and stores along all three streets that spread out from the center of the square and on the streets that intersect them. If you follow **Brattle Street** to the residential area just outside the square, you'll come to a part of town known before and during the American Revolution as **"Tory Row"** because the residents were loyal to King George.

The yellow mansion at 105 Brattle St. is the **Longfellow National Historic Site** ⋆ (© **617/876-4491;** www.nps.gov/long), where the books and furniture have remained intact since the poet Henry Wadsworth Longfellow died there in 1882. During the siege of Boston in 1775–76, the house served as the headquarters of General George Washington, with whom Longfellow was fascinated. The poet first lived there as a boarder in 1837. When he and Fanny Appleton married in 1843, her father made it a wedding present. On a tour—the only way to see the house—you'll learn about the history of the building and its famous occupants.

The recently refurbished site is open May through October Wednesday through Sunday from 10am to 4:30pm. Tours begin at 10:30 and 11:30am, and 1, 2, 3, and 4pm. Admission is $3 for adults, free for children under 17.

Farther west, near where Brattle Street and Mount Auburn Street intersect, is **Mount Auburn Cemetery** (see the box titled "Celebrity Cemetery"). It's a pleasant but long walk; you might prefer to drive or take the bus. Or you can return to the square and investigate Harvard.

HARVARD UNIVERSITY

The **walking tour** (p. 200) describes many of the buildings you'll see on the Harvard campus. Free student-led tours leave from the **Events & Information Center** in Holyoke Center, 1350 Mass. Ave. (© **617/495-1573**). They operate during the school year twice a day on weekdays and once on Saturday, except during vacations, and during the summer four times a day Monday through Saturday. Call for exact times; reservations aren't necessary. The Events & Information Center has maps, illustrated booklets, and self-guided walking-tour

Celebrity Cemetery

Three important colonial burying grounds—Old Granary, King's Chapel, and Copp's Hill—are in Boston on the Freedom Trail (see section 2, "The Freedom Trail"). The most famous cemetery in the area is in Cambridge.

Mount Auburn Cemetery ⍟, 580 Mount Auburn St. (© **617/547-7105**), the final resting place of many well-known people, is also famous simply for existing. Dedicated in 1831, it was the first of America's rural, or garden, cemeteries. The establishment of burying places removed from city centers reflected practical and philosophical concerns. Development was encroaching on urban graveyards, and the ideas associated with the Greek revival (the word *cemetery* derives from the Greek for "sleeping place") and Transcendentalism dictated that communing with nature take precedence over organized religion. Since the day it opened, Mount Auburn has been a popular place to retreat and reflect—in the 19th century, it was often the first place out-of-town visitors asked to go.

A modern visitor will find history and horticulture coexisting with celebrity. The graves of Henry Wadsworth Longfellow, Oliver Wendell Holmes, Julia Ward Howe, and Mary Baker Eddy are here, as are those of Charles Bulfinch, James Russell Lowell, Winslow Homer, Transcendentalist leader Margaret Fuller, and abolitionist Charles Sumner. In season you'll see gorgeous flowering trees and shrubs (the Massachusetts Horticultural Society had a hand in the design). Stop at the office or front gate to pick up brochures and a map. You can rent an audiotape tour ($5; a $15 deposit is required) and listen in your car or on a portable tape player; there's a 60-minute driving tour and two 75-minute walking tours. **The Friends of Mount Auburn Cemetery** conduct workshops and lectures and coordinate walking tours. Call the main number for topics, schedules, and fees.

The cemetery is open daily from 8am to 5pm October through April, 8am to 7pm May through September; admission is free. Animals and recreational activities such as jogging, biking, and picnicking are not allowed. MBTA bus nos. 71 and 73 start at Harvard station and stop near the cemetery gates; they run frequently on weekdays and less often on weekends. By car (5 min.) or on foot (30 min.), take Mount Auburn Street or Brattle Street west from Harvard Square; just after the streets intersect, the gate is on the left.

directions, as well as a bulletin board where campus activities are publicized. You might want to check out the university website (www.harvard.edu) before you visit.

The best-known part of the university is **Harvard Yard,** actually two large quadrangles. Daniel Chester French's **John Harvard statue,** a rendering of one of the school's original benefactors, is in the Old Yard, which dates to the college's founding in 1636. Most first-year students live in the dormitories here—even in the school's oldest building, **Massachusetts Hall** (1720). The other side

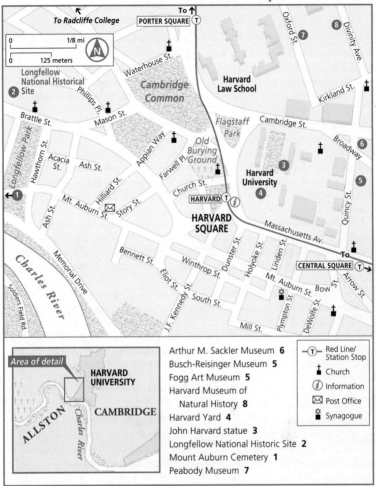

Arthur M. Sackler Museum **6**
Busch-Reisinger Museum **5**
Fogg Art Museum **5**
Harvard Museum of
    Natural History **8**
Harvard Yard **4**
John Harvard statue **3**
Longfellow National Historic Site **2**
Mount Auburn Cemetery **1**
Peabody Museum **7**

–Ⓣ– Red Line/
    Station Stop
🕇 Church
ⓘ Information
✉ Post Office
⚕ Synagogue

of the Yard (sometimes called Tercentenary Theater because the college's 300th-anniversary celebration was held there) is home to the imposing **Widener Library,** named after a Harvard graduate who perished when the *Titanic* sank.

Also on campus are two engaging museum complexes:

Harvard University Art Museums ⚛ The Harvard art museums house some 160,000 works in three collections: the Fogg Art Museum, the Busch-Reisinger Museum, and the Arthur M. Sackler Museum. The exhibit spaces also serve as teaching and research facilities. If you prefer not to explore on your own, take a guided tour of the Fogg daily at 11am, of the Busch-Reisinger daily at 1pm (both year-round), or of the Sackler at 2pm daily September through June, Wednesdays only in July and August.

The **Fogg Art Museum** (32 Quincy St., near Broadway) centers on an impressive 16th-century Italian stone courtyard, with two floors of galleries opening off it. Each of the 19 rooms shows something different—17th-century

---

Value **The Harvard Hot Ticket**

One ticket covers admission to Harvard's art museums and natural-history museums (and to the Semitic Museum, which is free anyway). You don't have to visit them all in a day, either—the pass is good for a year. It costs $10 for adults, $8 for seniors and students, and is available at the museums and at the Harvard Collections store in Holyoke Center, 1350 Mass. Ave., Harvard Square.

Dutch and Flemish landscapes, 19th-century British and American paintings and drawings, French paintings and drawings from the 18th century through the Impressionist period, and contemporary sculpture. Changing exhibits often draw on the museum's extensive collections of paintings, drawings, prints, and photos.

The **Busch-Reisinger Museum** in Werner Otto Hall (enter through the Fogg) is devoted to the painting, sculpture, and decorative art of northern and central Europe, specifically Germany. Particularly notable are the early-20th-century collections, including works by Klee, Feininger, Kandinsky, and artists and designers associated with the Bauhaus.

The **Arthur M. Sackler Museum** (485 Broadway, at Quincy St.) houses the university's collections of Asian, ancient, and Islamic art. They include internationally renowned Chinese jades and cave reliefs, superb Roman sculpture, Korean ceramics, Greek vases, and Persian miniature paintings and calligraphy.

32 Quincy St. and 485 Broadway. ⓒ 617/495-9400. www.artmuseums.harvard.edu. Admission to all 3 museums $6.50 adults, $5 seniors and students, free for children under 18; free to all until noon Sat. Harvard Hot Ticket (see box) $10 adults, $8 seniors and students. Mon–Sat 10am–5pm; Sun 1–5pm. Closed major holidays. T: Red Line to Harvard. Cross Harvard Yard diagonally from the T station and cross Quincy St., or turn your back on the Coop and follow Mass. Ave. to Quincy St., then turn left.

Harvard Museum of Natural History and Peabody Museum of Archaeology & Ethnology ⭐ *Kids*   These fascinating museums house the university's collections of items and artifacts related to the natural world. The world-famous academic resource offers interdisciplinary programs and exhibitions that tie in elements of all the associated fields. You'll certainly find something interesting here, be it a dinosaur skeleton, a hunk of meteorite, a Native American artifact, or the Glass Flowers.

The **Glass Flowers** ⭐⭐⭐ are 3,000 models of more than 840 plant species devised between 1887 and 1936 by the German father-and-son team of Leopold and Rudolph Blaschka. You might have heard about them, and you might be skeptical, but it's true: They look real. The flowers are the centerpiece of the **Botanical Museum.** Children love the **Museum of Comparative Zoology** ⭐⭐, where the dinosaurs share space with preserved and stuffed insects and animals that range in size from butterflies to giraffes. The **Mineralogical Museum** is the most specialized but can be just as interesting as the others, especially if gemstones hold your interest. The **Peabody Museum of Archaeology & Ethnology** ⭐ boasts the **Hall of the North American Indian,** where 500 artifacts representing 10 cultures are on display.

Museum of Natural History: 26 Oxford St. ⓒ 617/495-3045. www.hmnh.harvard.edu. Peabody Museum: 11 Divinity Ave. ⓒ 617/496-1027. www.peabody.harvard.edu. Admission to both $6.50 adults, $5 seniors and students, $4 children 3–18, free for children under 3; free to all until noon Sun year-round and Wed 3–5pm

Sept–May. Harvard Hot Ticket (see box, above) $10 adults, $8 seniors and students. Daily 9am–5pm. T: Red Line to Harvard. Cross Harvard Yard, keeping John Harvard statue on right, and turn right at Science Center. First left is Oxford St.

MASSACHUSETTS INSTITUTE OF TECHNOLOGY (MIT)

The public is welcome at the Massachusetts Institute of Technology campus, a mile or so from Harvard Square, across the Charles River from Beacon Hill and the Back Bay. Visit the **Information Office,** 77 Mass. Ave. (© **617/253-4795**), to take a free, guided tour (weekdays at 10am and 2pm), or pick up a copy of the *Walk Around MIT* map and brochure. At the same address, the **Hart Nautical Galleries** (open daily 9am–5pm) contain ship and engine models that trace the development of marine engineering.

MIT's campus is known for its art and architecture. The excellent **outdoor sculpture** collection includes works by Picasso and Alexander Calder, and notable modern buildings include designs by Eero Saarinen and I. M. Pei. Even more engaging are the holography displays at the **MIT Museum,** 265 Mass. Ave. (© **617/253-4444;** web.mit.edu/museum), where you'll also find works in more conventional media. The museum is open Tuesday through Friday from 10am to 5pm, and weekends from noon to 5pm; it's closed on major holidays. Admission is $5 for adults, $2 for seniors, and $1 for students and children under 18. The school's contemporary art repository, the **List Visual Arts Center,** 20 Ames St. (© **617/253-4680;** web.mit.edu/lvac), is open Tuesday through Sunday from noon to 6pm, until 8pm on Friday. Admission is free.

To get to MIT, take the MBTA Red Line to Kendall/MIT. The scenic walk from the Back Bay takes you along Mass. Ave. over the river straight to the campus. By car from Boston, cross the river at the Museum of Science, Cambridge Street, or Mass. Ave., and follow signs to Memorial Drive, where you can usually find parking during the day.

8 Boston Neighborhoods to Explore

This section attempts to answer briefly the second most-asked question visitors have for Boston residents: "Where do people who live here go?" (The most-asked question is "Why aren't there more public bathrooms?" We wish we knew.)

Boston is a city of neighborhoods, some of which I've described in talking about the Freedom Trail (see section 2 in this chapter) and in the walking tours in chapter 8. Here are several other areas that are fun to explore. Bear in mind that many of the buildings you will see are private homes, not tourist attractions. See chapter 6 for dining suggestions and chapter 9 for shopping tips.

BEACON HILL

The original Boston settlers, clustered around what are now the Old State House and the North End, considered Beacon Hill outlandishly distant. Today the distance is a matter of atmosphere; climbing "the Hill" is like traveling back in

---

Impressions

I should sooner live in a society governed by the first 2,000 names in the Boston telephone directory than in a society governed by the 2,000 faculty members of Harvard University.
   —Yale alumnus William F. Buckley Jr., *Rumbles Left and Right,* 1963

time. Lace up your walking shoes (the brick sidewalks gnaw at anything fancier, and driving is next to impossible), wander the narrow streets, and admire the brick and brownstone architecture.

At Beacon and Park streets is a figurative high point (literally, it's *the* high point): Charles Bulfinch's magnificent **State House.** The 60-foot **monument** at the rear illustrates the hill's original height, before the top was shorn off to use in the landfill projects of the 19th century. **Beacon and Mount Vernon streets** run downhill to commercially dense **Charles Street,** but if ever there was an area where there's no need to head in a straight line, it's this one. Your travels might take you past former homes of Louisa May Alcott (10 Louisburg Sq.), Henry Kissinger (1 Chestnut St.), Julia Ward Howe (13 Chestnut St.), Edwin Booth (29A Chestnut St.), or Robert Frost (88 Mount Vernon St.). One of the oldest black churches in the country, the **African Meeting House,** is at 8 Smith Court.

> ## Impressions
> For we must consider that we shall be as a city upon a hill. The eyes of all people are upon us . . .
> —John Winthrop, "A Model of Christian Charity" (sermon), 1630

These days, Alcott probably wouldn't be able to afford even the rent for a home on **Louisburg Square** (say "Lewis-burg"). Twenty-two homes where a struggling writer would more likely be an employee than a resident surround the lovely park. The iron-railed square is open only to tenants with keys.

Your wandering will probably lead you down to Charles Street. After you've had your fill of the shops and restaurants, you might want to investigate the architecture of the **"flats,"** between Charles Street and the Charles River. Built on landfill, the buildings are younger than those higher up, but many are just as eye-catching. This is the area where you can look for signs that MTV's **"The Real World"** passed through. You might recognize the converted firehouse where the cast of the 1997 show lived, and also a one-time *Spenser: For Hire* set, it's at Mount Vernon and River streets.

T: Red Line to Charles/MGH, Green Line to Park Street, or Blue Line to Bowdoin (weekdays only).

CHINATOWN

This close-knit residential and commercial community is constantly pushing its borders, expanding into the nearly defunct "Combat Zone" (the red-light district, now sometimes called the Ladder District) on Washington Street and crossing the Massachusetts Turnpike extension into the South End. It's also including more Vietnamese and Cambodian residents. The Expressway, the downtown shopping district, the Theater District, and the Tufts University medical complex border the heart of Chinatown.

Start your visit where Beach Street meets the Surface Artery, at the three-story **Chinatown Gateway.** The arched gate with four marble lions was a bicentennial gift from the government of Taiwan.

Beach Street is the closest thing Chinatown has to a main drag, and the streets that cross it and run parallel are nearly as congested and equally interesting. You'll see fish tanks full of entrees-to-be, produce stands, gift shops, and markets. The wares in the gift shops run from classic to cartoonish, and prices tend to be reasonable. After wandering around for a while and working up an appetite, stop at a restaurant for **dim sum** (see chapter 6 for pointers) or at a bakery—perhaps **Hing Shing Pastry,** 67 Beach St. (© **617/451-1162**), or **Ho Yuen Bakery,** 54 Beach St. (© **617/426-8320**)—for giant walnut cookies, pastries in the shape of animals, fried sesame balls, and moon cakes.

During the celebration of **Chinese New Year** (Jan or Feb, depending on the moon), masses of people turn out even in the harshest weather to watch the parade. Dragons dance in the streets, and firecrackers punctuate the musical accompaniment. In the summer, you'll see the **August Moon Festival,** a local street fair. Call the **Chinese Merchants Association,** 20 Hudson St. (© **617/482-3972**), for information on special events. The building's bronze bas-reliefs represent the eight immortals of Taoism, and there are mirrored plaques along Oxford Alley to ward off evil spirits.

Before you leave, you might want to stop at a food store for supplies to take home. One of the largest in size and selection, the **88 Supermarket,** 50 Herald St., at Washington Street (© **617/423-1688**), is across the Pike extension. It's not just Chinese—every ingredient of every Asian cuisine seems to be on the shelves somewhere, and the fresh produce ranges from lemons to lemon grass. In Chinatown proper, **See Sun Co.,** 25 Harrison Ave. (© **617/426-0954**), isn't as large, but the selection and prices are good.

T: Orange Line to Chinatown, or Green Line to Boylston.

THE SOUTH END

One of the city's most diverse neighborhoods is also one of its largest, but fans of Victorian architecture won't mind the sore feet they have after trekking around the South End.

The neighborhood was laid out in the mid–19th century, before the Back Bay. While the newer area's grid echoes the boulevards of Paris, the South End tips its hat to London. The main streets are broad, and pocket parks dot the side streets. The gentrification movement of the 1970s saw many South End brownstones reclaimed from squalor and converted into luxury condominiums. That trend accelerated in the late 1990s, driving out many longtime residents and making construction materials as widespread as falling leaves. Even on the few remaining run-down buildings, you'll see wonderful details.

With Back Bay Station to your left, walk down **Dartmouth Street,** crossing Columbus Avenue. Proceed on Dartmouth and explore some of the streets that extend to the left, including **Chandler, Lawrence, and Appleton streets.** This area is known as **Clarendon Park.** Turn left on any of these streets and walk to

---

Moments Written in Stone

As you explore Boston, you might notice that nearly every block in the central part of the city contains a plaque commemorating some long-gone person, event, or even place ("on this site stood . . ."). Each one tells a little story, not just in its text but also in its context. A marker describing the Molasses Flood of 1919 (on Commercial St. near Hull St.) recalls the days when manufacturing and industry dominated an area that's now the residential North End and scenic waterfront. A plaque honoring the first Catholic Mass in Boston (on School St. near Borders, across the street from the Freedom Trail) doesn't seem like a big deal now, but in a Puritan city, toleration of "popery" couldn't have come easily. Look around as you walk around—history is everywhere, just waiting for you to discover it.

Tips **A Different Voice**

Mytown multicultural youth walking tours (© 617/536-8696; www.
mytowninc.com) take visitors around the South End under the direction of
a local high school student. The Youth Guide program trains participants
in historical research and encourages them to put a personal spin on their
narration. The result is a uniquely fascinating take on a relatively unex-
plored area of the city. Tours ($10) operate from late April through Octo-
ber; call for meeting times and reservations.

Clarendon Street. Its intersection with Tremont Street is the part of the South
End you're most likely to see if you're not out exploring. This is the area where
businesses and restaurants surround the **Boston Center for the Arts** (© 617/
426-7700 for events; 617/426-0320 for box office). The BCA's **Cyclorama**
building (the interior is dome-shaped), at 539 Tremont St., is listed on the
National Register of Historic Places. Here you can see a show, have a meal, or
continue your expedition, perhaps to Shawmut Avenue or Washington Street.
This is not the greatest neighborhood to roam through at night, but in daylight
you can feel comfortable wandering and exploring all the way to Mass. Ave.
From there, you can take the no. 1 bus to the Back Bay or into Cambridge, or
the Orange Line downtown.

T: Orange Line to Back Bay, or Green Line to Copley.

JAMAICA PLAIN

You can combine a visit to the **Arnold Arboretum** (p. 170) with a stroll around
Jamaica Pond or along Centre Street. Culturally diverse Jamaica Plain abounds
with interesting architecture and open space. The pond is especially pleasant in
good weather, when people walk, run, skate, fish, picnic, and sunbathe. Many
of the 19th-century mansions overlooking the pond date to the days when families fled the oppressive heat downtown and moved to the "country" for the
summer.

After you've had your fill of nature (or before you set out), Centre Street
makes a good destination for wandering and snacking. The AIDS Action Committee's excellent resale shop, **Boomerangs,** 716 Centre St. (© 617/524-5120),
is worth a look for its upscale merchandise and reasonable prices. Another
favorite destination is **JP Licks Homemade Ice Cream,** 674 Centre St.
(© 617/524-6740). Across the street from the T stop is the **Dogwood Café,**
3712 Washington St. (© 617/522-7997), a family-friendly bar and restaurant
with plenty of beers on tap and tasty pizza.

T: Orange Line to Forest Hills.

9 Especially for Kids

What can the children do in Boston? A better question might be "What *can't*
the children do in Boston?" Just about every major destination in the city either
is specifically designed to appeal to youngsters or can easily be adapted to do so.

I wouldn't ordinarily make such an insulting suggestion, but experience tells
me that some parents need reminding: Allowing your kids some input while
you're planning your trip and incorporating suggestions (especially from
teenagers) cuts down on eye-rolling and sighing. And the college tour, whale

watch, or day trip that you might not have considered may turn out to be one of the highlights of your vacation.

The following attractions are covered extensively elsewhere in this chapter; here's the boiled-down version for busy parents.

Destinations with something for every member of the family include **Faneuil Hall Marketplace** (© 617/338-2323; p. 147) and the **Museum of Fine Arts** (© 617/267-9300; p. 150), which offers special weekend and after-school programs.

Hands-on exhibits and large-format films are the headliners at the **New England Aquarium** (© 617/973-5200; p. 154), where you'll find the Simons IMAX Theatre, and at the **Museum of Science** (© 617/723-2500; p. 151), home to the Mugar Omni Theater as well as the Hayden Planetarium.

You might get your hands on a baseball at a **Red Sox game** (p. 192) or the **Sports Museum of New England** (© 617/624-1234; p. 191).

The allure of seeing people the size of ants draws young visitors to the **Prudential Center Skywalk** (© 617/859-0648; p. 148). And they can see actual ants—although they might prefer the dinosaurs—at the **Harvard Museum of Natural History** (© 617/495-3045; p. 174).

Older children who have studied modern American history will enjoy a visit to the **John F. Kennedy Library and Museum** (© 617/929-4523; p. 150). And kids interested in cars will like the **Larz Anderson Auto Museum** (© 617/522-6547; p. 167).

Middle-schoolers who enjoyed Esther Forbes's *Johnny Tremain* might get a kick out of the **Paul Revere House** (© 617/523-2338; p. 162). Young visitors who have read Robert McCloskey's classic *Make Way for Ducklings* will relish a visit to the **Public Garden,** and fans of E. B. White's *The Trumpet of the Swan* certainly will want to ride on the **swan boats** (© 617/522-1966; p. 170).Considerably less tame (and much longer) are **whale watches** (p. 186).

Note: The **Boston Tea Party Ship & Museum** (© 617/338-1773; www.bostonteapartyship.com) closed indefinitely after a fire in late 2001. Its centerpiece, the brig *Beaver II,* is a full-size (110 ft.) replica of one of the three merchant ships that were raided during the colonial uprising in December 1773. Call ahead to see whether the ship and its accompanying museum have reopened; they make an entertaining stop on the way to or from the Children's Museum. The season runs from March through November.

Tips More Kid Stuff

For more suggestions, check (or let the kids check) elsewhere in this book. Chapter 10 lists nightlife destinations for all ages. Before night falls (and sometimes afterward), the whole family can have a great time at the **House of Blues** or the **Hard Rock Cafe** (food and music), **Jillian's Boston** (pool and all manner of arcade and virtual-reality games), *Shear Madness* (audience-participation theater), **Blue Man Group** (performance art), and the **Puppet Showplace Theater.**

Turn to chapter 9 for shopping recommendations—**Beadworks,** the **CambridgeSide Galleria** mall, **Curious George Goes to WordsWorth, Pearl Art & Craft Supplies,** and the various **college bookstores** can be as fun as toy stores.

Finally, check chapter 11 for information about day trips. Fun destinations include **Salem, Plymouth,** and (for *Little Women* fans) **Concord.**

WALKING TOURS

Boston By Foot ((✆ **617/367-2345,** or 617/367-3766 for recorded information; www.bostonbyfoot.com) has a special program, **"Boston By Little Feet,"** that's geared to children 6 to 12 years old. The 60-minute walk gives a child's-eye view of the architecture along the Freedom Trail and of Boston's role in the American Revolution. Children must be accompanied by an adult, and a map is provided. Tours run from May through October and meet at the statue of Samuel Adams on the Congress Street side of Faneuil Hall, Saturday at 10am, Sunday at 2pm, and Monday at 10am, rain or shine. The cost is $6 per person.

The **Historic Neighborhoods Foundation** ((✆ **617/426-1885;** www.historic-neighborhoods.org) offers a 90-minute **"Make Way for Ducklings" tour** ($8 adults, $6 children, free for children under 5). The tour follows the path of the Mallard family described in Robert McCloskey's famous book and ends at the Public Garden. Reservations are required. Every year on Mother's Day, Historic Neighborhoods organizes the Ducklings Day Parade.

Children's Museum ★★ *Kids*   As you approach the Children's Museum, don't be surprised to see adults suddenly being dragged by the hand when their young companions realize how close they are and start running. You know that the museum is near when you see the 40-foot-high red-and-white milk bottle out front. It makes both children and adults look small in comparison—which is probably part of the point. No matter how old, everyone behaves like a little kid at this delightful museum.

Children under 11 are the museum's target audience. They can stick with their adults or wander on their own, learning, doing, and role-playing. The centerpiece of the renovated warehouse building is a two-story-high maze, the **New Balance Climb,** which incorporates motor skills and problem-solving. Other favorite hands-on exhibits include **Grandparents' Attic,** a souped-up version of playing dress-up at Grandma's; **Under the Dock,** an environmental exhibit that teaches about the Boston waterfront and allows youngsters to dress up in a crab suit; physical experiments (such as creating giant soap bubbles) in **Science Playground;** and **Boats Afloat,** which has an 800-gallon play tank and a replica of the bridge of a working boat. **Supermercado** is a marketplace that introduces Hispanic culture, and you can explore a Japanese house and subway train from Kyoto (Boston's sister city) and learn about young adults in **Teen Tokyo.** Children under 4 and their caregivers have a special room, **Playspace,** that's packed with toys and activities.

Call or surf ahead for information about traveling exhibitions, KidStage participatory plays, and special programs. And be sure to check out the excellent gift shop (as if you have a choice).

300 Congress St. (Museum Wharf). (✆ 617/426-8855. www.bostonkids.org. Admission $8 adults, $7 children 2–15 and seniors, $2 children age 1, free for children under 1; Fri 5–9pm $1 for all. Sat–Thurs 10am–5pm; Fri 10am–9pm. Closed Thanksgiving, Dec 25, and until noon Jan 1. T: Red Line to South Station. Walk north on Atlantic Ave. 1 block (past Federal Reserve Bank), turn right onto Congress St., walk 2 blocks (across bridge). Call for information about discounted parking.

Franklin Park Zoo *Kids*   The Franklin Park Zoo constantly becomes more enjoyable—for animals as well as people. From June to September, you can visit the popular, colorful **Butterfly Landing** enclosure. On the **Outback Trail,** you can see kangaroos, wallabies, emus, and cockatoos. **Serengeti Crossing** is home to zebras, ibex, ostriches, and wildebeests. Other installations house cheetahs, lions, snow leopards, and African wild dogs. The **African Tropical Forest** exhibit is a sprawling complex where you'll see more than 50 species of animals.

Impressions

And this is good old Boston,
The home of the bean and the cod,
Where the Lowells talk to the Cabots,
And the Cabots talk only to God.
      —John Collins Bossidy, toast at the Holy Cross College alumni dinner, 1910

As a family, the Bradlees had been around for close to three hundred
years, but well down the totem pole from the Lowells and the Cabots.
      —Former *Washington Post* executive editor Ben Bradlee,
                                                        A Good Life, 1995

This is the domain of the Western lowland gorillas, which appear to be roaming free in an approximation of their natural habitat. If you're traveling with animal-mad youngsters, the **Children's Zoo** is both entertaining and educational.

Schedule at least half a day for a visit to the zoo. Franklin Park is 40 minutes from downtown by public transportation, and the walk from the main gate and parking area to the entrance is fairly long, especially for those with little legs.

1 Franklin Park Rd. ⓒ 617/541-LION or 617/541-5466. www.zoonewengland.com. Admission $9.50 adults, $8 seniors, $5 children 2–15, free for children under 2. Apr–Sept Mon–Fri 10am–5pm, Sat–Sun and holidays 10am–6pm; Oct–Mar daily 10am–4pm. T: Orange Line to Forest Hills, then bus no. 16 to the main entrance. Call for driving directions.

Blue Hills Trailside Museum *(Kids)*   At the foot of Great Blue Hill, this museum is fun for all ages and especially popular with the under-10 set. It's at the 7,500-acre Blue Hills Reservation, a 20-minute drive south of Boston. Here you'll see replicas of the natural habitats found in the area, Native American displays, and live animal exhibits. Resident animals include owls, honeybees, otters, foxes, snakes, and turtles. Children can feed the ducks, deer, and turkeys. Other activities include hiking and climbing the lookout tower. On weekends, there's story time at 11am and natural-history programs at 1 and 2pm. Special events and family programs change with the seasons; call ahead to register.

1904 Canton Ave., Milton. ⓒ 617/333-0690. www.massaudubon.org. Admission $3 adults, $2 seniors, $1.50 children 3–15, free for children under 3 and Massachusetts Audubon Society members. Wed–Sun and Mon holidays 10am–5pm. By car, take I-93 south to Exit 2B (Rte. 138 north).

10 Organized Tours

ORIENTATION TOURS

GUIDED WALKING TOURS   Even if you usually prefer to explore on your own, consider a walking tour with **Boston By Foot** *(★★)*, 77 N. Washington St. (ⓒ **617/367-2345,** or 617/367-3766 for recorded information; www.bostonby foot.com). From May to October, the nonprofit educational corporation conducts historical and architectural tours that focus on particular neighborhoods or themes. The rigorously trained guides are volunteers who encourage questions. Buy tickets ($8–$10 per person) from the guide; reservations are not required. The 90-minute tours take place rain or shine.

Note: All excursions from Faneuil Hall start at the statue of Samuel Adams on Congress Street.

The **"Heart of the Freedom Trail"** tour starts at Faneuil Hall daily at 10am. Tours of **Beacon Hill** begin at the foot of the State House steps on Beacon Street weekdays at 5:30pm, Saturday at 10am, and Sunday at 2pm. **"Boston Underground"** looks at subterranean technology, including crypts, the subway, and the depression of the Central Artery. It starts at Faneuil Hall Sunday at 2pm. Other tours and meeting places are **Victorian Back Bay,** on the steps of Trinity Church, 10am Friday through Sunday; the **North End,** at Faneuil Hall, 2pm Friday and Saturday; and the **South End,** at Southwest Corridor Park, on Dartmouth Street opposite Back Bay Station, 10am Saturday and Sunday.

Once a month, a special tour ($10) covers a particular theme or area. Special theme tours—they include "Great Women of Boston," "Literary Landmarks," and a Chinatown tour—can be scheduled if there are enough requests. Off-season tours for groups only (minimum 10 people; $10 per person) are available.

The **Society for the Preservation of New England Antiquities** ★ (© 617/227-3956; www.spnea.org) offers a fascinating tour that describes and illustrates life in the mansions and garrets of Beacon Hill in 1810. "Magnificent and Modest," a 2-hour program, costs $10 and starts at the Harrison Gray Otis House, 141 Cambridge St., at 11am on Saturdays from mid-May to October. The price includes a tour of the Otis House, and reservations are recommended.

The **Historic Neighborhoods Foundation** (© 617/426-1885; www.historic-neighborhoods.org) offers 90-minute walking tours of various neighborhoods, including Beacon Hill, the North End, Chinatown, the Waterfront, and the Financial District. Schedules change with the season, and reservations are required. The programs highlight points of interest to visitors while covering history, architecture, and topographical development. Tours usually cost about $8 for adults, $6 for children; check ahead for schedules and meeting places.

The **Boston Park Rangers** (© 617/635-7383; www.ci.boston.ma.us/parks) offer free guided walking tours. The best-known focus is the **Emerald Necklace,** a loop of green spaces designed by pioneering American landscape architect Frederick Law Olmsted. They include Boston Common, the Public Garden, the Commonwealth Avenue Mall, the Muddy River in the Fenway, Olmsted Park, Jamaica Pond, the Arnold Arboretum, and Franklin Park. The full walk takes 6 hours; a typical offering is a tour of one of the sites. Call for schedules.

"DUCK" TOURS   The most unusual and enjoyable way to see Boston is with **Boston Duck Tours** ★★★ (© 800/226-7442 or 617/723-DUCK; www.bostonducktours.com). The tours, offered only April through November, are pricey but great fun. Sightseers board a "duck," a reconditioned World War II amphibious landing craft, at the Prudential Center or the Museum of Science. The 80-minute narrated tour begins with a quick but comprehensive jaunt around the city. Then the duck lumbers down a ramp, splashes into the Charles River, and goes for a spin around the basin.

Tickets, available at the Prudential Center, the Museum of Science, and Faneuil Hall, are $23 for adults, $20 for seniors and students, $14 for children 4 to 12, and 25¢ for children under 4. Tours run every 30 minutes from 9am to 30 minutes before sunset, and they usually sell out. You can buy tickets online or in person. Try to buy same-day tickets early in the day, or ask about the limited number of tickets available 2 days in advance. Reservations are only accepted for groups of 20 or more. No tours December through March.

Note: Planned construction near the Prudential Center may force the Duck Tour boarding area to relocate from Boylston Street; be sure to ask when you buy your tickets.

TROLLEY TOURS   The ticket-sellers who clamor for your business wherever tourists gather (notably in front of the aquarium and on Boston Common) will

Moments Photo Synthesis

Boston is such a shutterbug magnet that residents sometimes offer to snap a picture of a visiting family even before being asked. Arrange Junior and Sissy in the lap of one of the area's numerous portrait sculptures, or take a step back and capture the juxtaposition of a 19th-century steeple silhouetted against a 20th-century office tower.

Say "Cheese": At the bronze **teddy bear** on Boylston Street at Berkeley Street. Arm-in-arm or deep in thought with Mayor **James Michael Curley,** in the park on Union Street across North Street from Faneuil Hall. Pulling the cigar away from Celtics legend **Red Auerbach,** between the South Canopy of Quincy Market and the South Market building, Faneuil Hall Marketplace. Comparing your tiny sneakers to **Larry Bird's** clodhoppers or marathon legend **Bill Rodgers's** running shoes, captured in bronze right next to Red. Falling at the feet of a colonial hero: pedestals support **Benjamin Franklin** (School St., in front of Old City Hall), **Paul Revere** (Hanover St. at Clark St., across from St. Stephen's Church), and **George Washington** (in the Public Garden at the foot of the Commonwealth Avenue Mall). Perched on Mrs. Mallard (or one of her babies, if you fit) of *Make Way for Ducklings* fame, in the Public Garden near the corner of Beacon and Charles streets. Outdistancing the winner (or the runner-up) captured in *The Tortoise and Hare at Copley Square,* in front of Trinity Church. And at a spot so popular that the grass on the area favored by photographers had to be paved over, in front of **John Harvard,** Harvard Yard, Cambridge.

Say "Ooh": Always remember to look up for a quirky perspective. Capture a church against a backdrop of skyscrapers on **Tremont Street** (with the Boston Common Visitor Information Center at your back, turn left toward Park Street Church) or **Boylston Street** (in front of the Four Seasons Hotel, turn left toward the Arlington Street Church; across from Trinity Church, focus on the Hancock Tower). From any angle, the **Old State House** makes a striking contrast to its towering neighbors. Kill two birds with one stone: Pointing up at the **Paul Revere** statue on Hanover Street, you can lock in the **Old North Church** in the background, or walk around the statue for a new perspective on **St. Stephen's Church.** The **Old North Church** crops up all over the North End and Charlestown, as the **Hancock Tower** does throughout the Back Bay.

Say "Wow": Every **bridge** that crosses the river between Boston and Cambridge affords an excellent perspective. If your travels take you to the area around the Charles/MGH T stop, wander out onto the **Longfellow Bridge,** especially at twilight—the views of the river are splendid, and if you hit it just right, the moon appears to shine out of the Hancock Tower.

claim that no visit is complete without a day on a trolley. For many people, this is simply not true, but if you're unable to walk long distances or are traveling with children, it can be worth the money. Because Boston is so pedestrian-friendly, a trolley tour isn't the best choice for the able-bodied and unencumbered making a long visit. A narrated tour on a trolley (actually a bus chassis with a trolley body) can give you an overview before you focus on specific attractions, or you can use the all-day pass to hit as many places as possible in 8 hours or so. In some neighborhoods, notably the North End, the trolleys stop some distance from the attractions—don't believe a ticket-seller who tells you otherwise.

The business is extremely competitive, with various firms offering different stops in an effort to distinguish themselves from the rest. All cover the major attractions and offer informative narratives and anecdotes in their 90- to 120-minute tours; most offer free reboarding if you want to visit the attractions. Each tour is only as good as its guide, and quality varies widely—every few years a TV station or newspaper runs an "exposé" of the wacky information a tour guide is passing off as fact. Have a grain of salt ready. If you have time, you might even chat up guides in the waiting area and choose the one you like best.

Trolley tickets cost $18 to $24 for adults, and $12 or less for children. Boarding spots are at hotels, historic sites, and tourist information centers. There are busy waiting areas near the New England Aquarium, the Park Street T stop, and the corner of Boylston Street and Charles Street South. Each company paints its cars a different color. Orange-and-green **Old Town Trolleys** (© **617/269-7150;** www.trolleytours.com) are the most numerous. Minuteman Tours' **Boston Trolley Tours** (© **617/867-5539;** www.historictours.com) are blue; **Freedom Trail Trolleys** (© **800/343-1328** or 781/986-6100; www.bostontrolley.com) say "Gray Line" but are red; and **CityView Trolleys** (© **617/363-7899;** www.cityviewtrolleys.com) are silver. The **Discover Boston Trolley Tours** (© **617/742-1440;** www.discoverbostontours.com) vehicle is white; it offers tours translated into Japanese, Spanish, French, German, and Italian.

SIGHTSEEING CRUISES

Take to the water for a taste of Boston's rich maritime history or a daylong break from walking and driving. You can cruise around the harbor or go all the way to Provincetown. The **sightseeing cruise** ★★ season runs from **April through October,** with spring and fall offerings often restricted to weekends. Check websites for discount coupons before you leave home. If you're traveling in a large group, call ahead for information about reservations and discounted tickets. If you're prone to seasickness, check the size of the vessel for your tour before buying tickets; larger boats provide more cushioning and comfort than smaller ones.

Tip: Before taking a cruise just for the sake of taking a cruise, weigh the investment of time and money against your group's interests. Especially if kids are along, you might be better off with an excursion that targets a destination—the Charlestown Navy Yard (see the box titled "On the Cheap" below), the Boston Harbor Islands (see the box titled "A Vacation in the Islands" on p. 190), or Boston Light (see the box titled "Trip the Light Fantastic" on p. 185)—than with a "cruise to nowhere" with narration that the children are ignoring anyway.

⟮*Value* On the Cheap

You don't have to take a tour to take a cruise. The MBTA runs a ferry that connects Long Wharf and the Charlestown Navy Yard. It costs $1.25, is included in the MBTA Boston Visitor Pass, and makes a good final leg of the Freedom Trail.

⌒Finds Trip the Light Fantastic

North America's oldest lighthouse, **Boston Light** ★★, is the only one in the country that's still staffed (by the Coast Guard). Built on **Little Brewster Island** in 1716, it fell to the British in 1776 and was rebuilt in 1783. Excursions to the 102-foot lighthouse include a narrated cruise, 90 minutes to explore the island, and a chance to climb the spiral stairs to the top (you must be 50 in. tall). The 3½-hour tours leave from the Moakley Courthouse at Fan Pier and from the John F. Kennedy Library. From early June to mid-October, trips leave from Fan Pier Saturday at 10am and 2pm and Sunday at 2pm, and from the Kennedy Library Friday at 2pm. Between July 4th and Labor Day, there are additional departures from Fan Pier on Sunday at 10am and from the Kennedy Library Thursday and Friday at 10am. Tickets from Fan Pier cost $25 for adults, $20 for seniors, and $15 for children 6 to 12; they're free for children under 6. From the Kennedy Library (including library admission), they cost $29, $22, and $15, respectively. Only 32 people may take each tour; reservations (© **617/223-8666;** www.bostonislands.com) are strongly recommended.

The largest company is **Boston Harbor Cruises,** 1 Long Wharf (© **877/ 733-9425** or 617/227-4321; www.bostonharborcruises.com). Ninety-minute **historic sightseeing cruises,** which tour the Inner and Outer harbors, depart daily at 11am, 1pm, 3pm, and 6 or 7pm (the sunset cruise), with extra excursions at busy times. Tickets are $17 for adults, $15 for seniors, and $12 for children under 12. The 45-minute **USS *Constitution* cruise** takes you around the Inner Harbor and docks at the Charlestown Navy Yard so that you can go ashore and visit Old Ironsides. Tours leave Long Wharf hourly from 10:30am to 4:30pm, and on the hour from the navy yard from 11am to 5pm. The cruise is $11 for adults, $10 for seniors, and $8 for children. The same company offers service to **Georges Island,** where free water-taxi service to the rest of the Boston Harbor Islands is available (see the box titled "A Vacation in the Islands" on p. 190).

Another large operation, Massachusetts Bay Lines, operates the **Boston Steamship Company** (© **617/542-8000;** www.bostonsteamship.com), which offers 55-minute **harbor tours** from Memorial Day to Columbus Day. Cruises leave from Long Wharf on the hour from 11am to 6pm (there's no 6pm cruise in Sept and Oct); the price is $11 for adults, $8 for children and seniors. The 90-minute sunset cruise leaves at 7pm. Tickets are $17 for adults, $13 for children and seniors.

The **Charles Riverboat Company** (© **617/621-3001;** www.charlesriverboat. com) offers 55-minute narrated cruises around the **lower Charles River basin.** Boats leave the CambridgeSide Galleria mall seven times a day daily June through August, and weekends in April, May, and September. Tickets cost $9 for adults, $8 for seniors, and $6 for children 2 to 12. Call for schedules. The sunset cruise operates Thursday through Saturday, but only when there's enough demand. Tickets cost $10 for adults, $7 for seniors and children.

DAY TRIPS   Two companies serve **Provincetown** ★★★, at the tip of Cape Cod. On a day trip, you'll have time for world-class people-watching, strolling around the novelty shops and art galleries, lunching on seafood, and—if you're quick—a trip to the famous beaches. You'll have to forgo the hopping gay nightlife scene unless you've planned a longer excursion, however. (For in-depth coverage of Provincetown and other Cape Cod locales, consult *Frommer's Cape Cod, Nantucket & Martha's Vineyard* or *Frommer's New England*.)

Bay State Cruises (© 617/748-1428; http://boston-ptown.com) operates conventional and high-speed service to Provincetown. Trips leave from Commonwealth Pier at the World Trade Center, 200 Seaport Blvd. To get to the pier, take the $1.25 ferry (© 617/227-4321; www.mbta.com) from Lovejoy Wharf, behind North Station; the $10 water taxi (© 617/422-0392) from locations around the harbor; or a regular taxi (when you reserve your cruise, ask the clerk for the best way to reach the pier from your hotel).

MV *Provincetown II* sails Friday through Sunday from late June to early September. It leaves at 9:30am for the 3-hour trip to Provincetown, at the tip of Cape Cod. The return trip leaves at 3:30pm, giving you 3 hours for shopping and sightseeing in P-town. Same-day round-trip fares are $39 for adults, $29 for seniors and children 3 to 12. Bringing a bike costs $5 extra each way. **High-speed service** takes 90 minutes and operates 3 times a day from late May to September. The round-trip fare is $60 for adults and $50 for seniors, plus $5 each way for your bike. Reservations are recommended.

Boston Harbor Cruises, 1 Long Wharf (© 877/733-9425 or 617/227-4321; www.bostonharborcruises.com), operates catamarans that make the trip in just 90 minutes. They operate daily Memorial Day through Columbus Day, leaving Boston at 9am and Provincetown at 4pm, with extra runs on summer weekends. The round-trip fare is $55 for adults, $50 for seniors, and $45 for children under 12.

WHALE WATCHING

For whale-watching trips from Cape Ann, see the box titled "A Whale of an Adventure" on p. 272.

The **New England Aquarium** (© 617/973-5277 for information, 617/973-5206 for tickets; p. 186) runs **whale watches** 👁👁 daily from May through mid-October and on weekends in April and late October. You'll travel several miles out to sea to Stellwagen Bank, the feeding ground for the whales as they migrate from Newfoundland to Provincetown. Allow 3½ to 5 hours. Tickets are $28 for adults, $23 for seniors and college students, $20 for youths 12 to 18, and $18 for children 3 to 11. Children must be 3 years old and at least 30 inches tall. Reservations are strongly recommended; you can also buy tickets online, subject to a service charge.

With its onboard exhibits and vast experience, the aquarium offers the best whale watches in Boston. If they're booked, several other companies offer whale watches: **Boston Harbor Cruises** (© 617/227-4321; www.bostonharborcruises.com), which has a high-speed catamaran; Massachusetts Bay Lines' **Beantown Whale Watch** (© 617/542-8000; www.beantownwhalewatch.com); and, on weekends only, **A.C. Cruise Line** (© 617/261-6633; www.accruiseline.com).

SPECIALTY TOURS

BOSTON HISTORY COLLABORATIVE The evolving offerings of the non-profit **Boston History Collaborative** (© 617/350-0358; www.bostonhistorycollaborative.org) include several new heritage trails presented as guided and self-guided walking tours, longer excursions by bus and boat, and copiously documented websites.

Boston By Sea (www.bostonbysea.org) offers an entertaining but pricey 90-minute boat trip around the harbor. Subtitled "Living History in Story, Sites, and Songs," the excursion includes an account of the city's maritime legacy, video clips, and sea chanteys. Tickets cost $25 for adults, $22 for seniors, students, and children. Tours leave Long Wharf twice daily in warm weather and on spring and fall weekends. For schedules and reservations, contact **Massachusetts Bay Lines** (© 617/542-8000; www.massbaylines.com). A free 25-minute land-only version of the tour, led by a costumed guide, runs on summer Saturdays; call or surf ahead for schedules.

The History Collaborative organizes its **Boston Family History** information (www.bostonfamilyhistory.org) by ethnic group. The comprehensive website describes specialized walking tours and includes links to research tools.

The 20-mile **Literary Trail** (www.lit-trail.org) links sites in Boston, Cambridge, and Concord, exploring locations associated with authors and poets such as Emerson, Thoreau, Longfellow, and Louisa May Alcott, among others. You can pick up a guide at local bookstores or order it online. The trolley-tour version, offered on the second Saturday of every month, costs $30 for adults, $26 for children under 12

The **Innovation Odyssey** (www.innovationodyssey.com) covers locations in Boston and Cambridge associated with the area's rich legacy of scientific discovery and invention. Currently available as a weekly bus tour, it costs $25 for adults, $21 for seniors and students, and $15 for 10-year-olds (the tour isn't recommended for younger kids, and older ones pay the student price).

FOR HORROR-MOVIE FANS **Ghosts & Gravestones** covers burial grounds and other shiver-inducing areas in a trolley and on foot. Presented by **Minuteman Tours** (© 617/269-3626; www.ghostsandgravestones.com), the 2-hour tour starts at dusk on summer and fall weekends. It costs $35 for adults and $18 for children under 12. Reservations are required.

MORE SPECIAL-INTEREST TOURS Boston's busiest operator of theme tours is **Old Town Trolley** (© 617/269-3626; www.trolleytours.com). Schedules and offerings vary according to the season and level of visitor interest. Prices depend on what's included but are usually at least $22 for adults, a little less for seniors and children. Call ahead for details, reservations, and meeting places. At press time, options included **JFK's Boston** (with stops at John F. Kennedy's birthplace in Brookline and the presidential library), separate tours for **seafood** lovers and **chocolate** fanatics, a tour that stops at several **brewpubs,** and a December **Holiday Lights** tour.

11 Outdoor Pursuits

At press time, the **Metropolitan District Commission** (© 617/727-9547; www.state.ma.us/mdc), which runs many of the state's recreational areas, was imperiled by budget cuts. MDC's incredibly helpful website includes descriptions of properties and activities, and has a planning area to help you make the most of your time. If the website is inoperative, you should be redirected; if you aren't, visit the main state website (www.mass.gov) and click "Having Fun."

BEACHES

The beaches in Boston proper are not worth the trouble. Besides being bone-chilling, Boston Harbor water is subject to being declared unsafe for swimming. If you want to swim, book a hotel with a pool. If you want the sand-between-your-toes experience, add some time to your excursion to the North Shore or to Walden Pond in Concord. See chapter 11 or consult the MDC (see the introduction to this section) for information on suburban beaches.

BIKING

Even expert cyclists who feel comfortable with Boston's layout (a tiny group) will be better off in Cambridge, which has bike lanes, or on the area's many bike paths. State law requires that children under 12 wear helmets. Bicycles are forbidden on buses and the Green Line at all times, and during rush hours on the other parts of the subway system.

On summer Sundays from 11am to 7pm, a flat 1½-mile stretch of **Memorial Drive** ⟅ in Cambridge from Western Avenue to the Eliot Bridge (Central Sq. to west Cambridge) closes to cars. It's also popular with pedestrians and in-line skaters, and it can get quite crowded. The **Dr. Paul Dudley White Charles River Bike Path** ⟅⟅ is an 18-mile circuit that begins at Science Park (near the Museum of Science) and runs along both sides of the river to Watertown and back. You can enter and exit at many points along the way. Bikers share the path with joggers and in-line skaters, especially in Boston near the Esplanade and in Cambridge near Harvard Square. The **Metropolitan District Commission** (see the introduction to this section) maintains this path and the 5-mile **Pierre Lallement Bike Path,** in Southwest Corridor Park, which starts behind Copley Place and runs through the South End and Roxbury along the route of the MBTA Orange Line to Franklin Park. The 10½-mile **Minuteman Bikeway** ⟅ starts at Alewife station at the end of the Red Line in Cambridge. It runs through Arlington and Lexington to Bedford along an old railroad bed, and is a wonderful way to reach the historic sites in Lexington.

Rental shops require you to show a driver's license or passport and leave a deposit using a major credit card. Most charge around $5 an hour, with a minimum of at least 2 hours, or a flat daily rate of about $25. They include **Back Bay Bikes & Boards,** 336 Newbury St., near Mass. Ave. (© **617/247-2336;** www.backbaybicycles.com), and **Community Bicycle Supply,** 496 Tremont St., near East Berkeley Street (© **617/542-8623;** www.communitybicycle.com). Across the river, try **Cambridge Bicycle,** 259 Mass. Ave. (© **617/876-6555;** http://oldroads.com/cb.html), near MIT, or **Ata Cycle,** 1773 Mass. Ave. (© **617/ 354-0907;** www.atabike.com), near Porter Square. For additional information, contact **MassBike** (© **617/542-2453;** www.massbike.org).

GOLF

You won't get far in the suburbs without seeing a golf course, and given the sport's popularity, you won't be the only one looking. If possible, opt for the lower prices and smaller crowds you'll find on weekdays. The **Massachusetts Golf Association** (© **781/449-3000;** www.mgalinks.org) represents more than 310 golf courses around the state. It has a searchable online database and will send you a list of courses on request.

One of the best public courses in the area, **Newton Commonwealth Golf Course,** 212 Kenrick St., Newton (© **617/630-1971;** www.sterlinggolf.com), is a challenging 18-hole Donald Ross design. It's 5,305 yards from the blue tees, par is 70, and greens fees are $28 on weekdays and $35 on weekends.

Within the city limits is the legendary 6,009-yard **William J. Devine Golf Course,** in Franklin Park, Dorchester (© **617/265-4084;** www.sterlinggolf.com). As a Harvard student, Bobby Jones sharpened his game on the 18-hole, par-70 course, which emerged from a state of decrepitude in time to catch the golf boom of the 1990s. Greens fees are $25 on weekdays and $32 on weekends.

Less challenging but with more of a neighborhood feel is 9-hole, par-35 **Fresh Pond Golf Course,** 691 Huron Ave., Cambridge (© **617/349-6282;**

www.freshpondgolf.com). The 3,161-yard layout adjoins the Fresh Pond Reservoir, and there's water on four holes. Before a refurbishment in 2002 and 2003, it charged $17, or $27 to go around twice, on weekdays; $22 and $35, respectively on weekends.

GYMS

If your hotel doesn't have a health club, the concierge or front desk staff can recommend one nearby and possibly give you a pass good for free or discounted admission. Guests at the new **Ritz-Carlton, Boston Common,** have the use of the over-the-top facilities at the 100,000-square-foot Sports Club/LA (guests at the original Ritz pay $20), which is otherwise closed to nonmembers. Other hotels with good health clubs (see chapter 5) include the **Boston Harbor Hotel,** the **Four Seasons Hotel,** the **Hilton Boston Logan Airport,** and the **Royal Sonesta Hotel.**

The "Y" offers the best combination of facilities and value. The **Wang YMCA of Chinatown,** 8 Oak St. W., off Washington St. (© 617/426-2237), is close to downtown; the **Central Branch YMCA,** 316 Huntington Ave. (© 617/536-7800), is near Symphony Hall. A 1-day pass costs $10 and includes the use of the pool, gym, weight room, and fitness center. Closer to downtown, **Fitcorp** (© 617/375-5600; www.fitcorp.com) charges $20 for a guest pass that includes well-equipped facilities but not a pool. It has branches at 1 Beacon St. (© 617/248-9797), near Government Center; 133 Federal St. (© 617/542-1010), in the Financial District; and in the Prudential Center (© 617/262-2050).

HIKING

For information about hiking in state parks and forests, visit the Department of Environmental Management's website, **www.massparks.org**. The **Boston Harbor Islands** offer great hiking; it takes a half-day to circle the largest island, Peddocks. See the box, "A Vacation in the Islands" on p. 190.

The **Bay Circuit Trail** is a 200-mile corridor of open space that curves around Boston from Newburyport, near the New Hampshire border, to Kingston Bay, north of Plymouth. The ribbon of conservation land touches on 50 cities and towns; it comes closest to the areas covered in this book when it cuts through **Concord** along the north shore of Walden Pond (see chapter 11). For information, contact the nonprofit **Bay Circuit Alliance,** 3 Railroad St., Andover, MA 01810 (© 978/470-1982; www.serve.com/baycircuit).

ICE SKATING & IN-LINE SKATING

The skating rink at the Boston Common **Frog Pond** (© 617/635-2120) is an extremely popular cold-weather destination. It's an open surface with an ice-making system and a clubhouse. Admission is $3 for adults and free for children under 14; skate rental costs $7 for adults, $5 for kids. The rink gets unbelievably crowded on weekend afternoons, so try to go in the morning or on a weekday.

A favorite spot for in-line skaters is the **Esplanade,** between the Back Bay and the Charles River. It continues onto the bike path that runs to Watertown and back, but after you leave the Esplanade, the pavement isn't totally smooth, which can lead to mishaps. Your best bet is to wait for a Sunday in the summer, when **Memorial Drive** near Harvard Square in Cambridge closes to traffic from 11am to 7pm. It's a perfect surface. Unless you're confident of your ability and your knowledge of Boston traffic, stay off the streets.

To rent skates or blades, visit the **Beacon Hill Skate Shop,** 135 Charles St. S. (© 617/482-7400), not far from the Esplanade, or **Blades Board & Skate,**

Finds **A Vacation in the Islands**

Majestic ocean views, hiking trails, historic sites, rocky beaches, nature walks, campsites, and picnic areas abound in New England. To find them all together, take a 45-minute trip east (yes, east) of Boston to the **Boston Harbor Islands** (✆ 617/223-8666; www.bostonislands.com). Their unspoiled beauty makes a welcome break from the urban landscape, but they're not well known, even to many longtime Bostonians. There are 30 islands in the Outer Harbor, and at least a half dozen are open for exploring, camping, or swimming. Bring a sweater or jacket. Plan a day trip or even an overnight trip, but note that fresh water is available only on Georges Island, and management strongly suggests bringing your own.

Ferries run to the most popular, **Georges Island,** home of Fort Warren (1834), which held Confederate prisoners during the Civil War. You can investigate on your own or take a ranger-led tour. The island has a visitor center, refreshment area, fishing pier, picnic area, and wonderful view of Boston's skyline. Allow at least half a day, and longer if you plan to take the free water taxi to **Lovell, Gallops, Peddocks, Bumpkin,** or **Grape Island,** all of which have picnic areas and campsites. Lovell Island also has the remains of a fort (Fort Standish).

Boston Harbor Cruises (✆ 617/227-4321; www.bostonharborcruises. com) serves Georges Island from Long Wharf; the trip takes 45 minutes, and tickets are $10 for adults, $9 for seniors, and $7 for children 4 to 12. Cruises depart daily at 10am, noon, 2pm, and 4pm in the spring and fall, and daily on the hour from 10am to 5pm in the summer. In the off-season, check ahead for winter wildlife excursions (scheduled occasionally). Water taxis and admission to the islands are free.

Administered as a National Park Partnership, the Boston Harbor Islands National Recreation Area (www.nps.gov/boha) is the focus of a public-private project designed to make the islands more interesting and accessible. Visit the website, consult the staff at the **kiosk on Long Wharf,** or contact the **Friends of the Boston Harbor Islands** (✆ 617/740-4290; www.fbhi.org). The Friends coordinate a variety of cruises on and around the harbor throughout the summer and fall; check ahead for details.

349A Newbury St. (✆ 617/437-6300; www.blades.com), near Mass. Ave., or 38 John F. Kennedy St., Cambridge (✆ 617/491-4244), near Memorial Drive. Expect to pay about $15 a day. The **InLine Club of Boston's** website (www. sk8net.com) offers up-to-date event and safety information.

JOGGING
The **Dr. Paul Dudley White Charles River Bike Path** ★★ is also a jogging route. The 18-mile loop along the water is extremely popular because it's car-free (except at intersections), scenic, and generally safe. The bridges that connect Boston and Cambridge allow for circuits of various lengths, but be careful around

abutments, where you can't see far ahead. Don't jog at night, and try not to go alone. Visit the MDC website (see the introduction to this section) to view a map that gives distances. If the river's not convenient, the concierge or desk staff at your hotel might be able to provide a map with suggested jogging routes. As in any other city, stay out of park areas at night.

SAILING

Sailboats fill the Charles River basin all summer and skim across the Inner Harbor in all but the coldest weather. Your options during a short stay aren't especially cost-effective, but they are fun.

The best deal is with **Community Boating,** 21 David Mugar Way, on the Esplanade (© **617/523-1038;** www.community-boating.org). Visitors pay $100 for 2 days of unlimited use in the Charles River Basin, a gorgeous but congested patch of water between the Back Bay and Cambridge's Kendall Square. The oldest public sailing facility in the country offers lessons and boating programs for children and adults from April through November. The fleet includes 13- to 23-foot sailboats as well as Windsurfers and kayaks. The **Boston Sailing Center,** Lewis Wharf (© **617/227-4198;** www.bostonsailingcenter.com), offers lessons for sailors of all ability levels. The center is open year-round (even for "frostbite" racing in the winter). The least expensive 30-day "mini-membership" costs $350. Prices for chartering a boat with a captain start at $100 an hour, with a 2-hour minimum and a six-person maximum.

TENNIS

Public courts maintained by the **Metropolitan District Commission** (see the introduction to this section) are available throughout the city at no charge. To find the one nearest you, call the MDC, visit the website, or ask the concierge or desk staff at your hotel. Well-maintained courts that seldom get busy until after work can be found at several spots on the Southwest Corridor Park in the **South End** (there's a nice one near **West Newton St.**). The courts on **Boston Common** and in **Charlesbank Park,** overlooking the river next to the bridge to the Museum of Science, are more crowded during the day.

12 Spectator Sports

Boston's well-deserved reputation as a great sports town derives in part from the days when at least one professional team was one of the best in the world. In 2002, the New England Patriots (who play in suburban Foxboro) continued that tradition by winning the Super Bowl. Although the other pro teams haven't enjoyed that level of success recently, passions still run deep. That enthusiasm applies to some college sports as well, particularly hockey, in which the Division I schools are fierce rivals.

The **FleetCenter,** 150 Causeway St. (© **617/624-1518;** www.fleetcenter.com), is open for tours from Memorial Day to Labor Day. Call for schedules during your visit. Tickets are $6 for adults and $4 for seniors and children 6 to 17. On the fifth- and sixth-floor concourses, the **Sports Museum of New England** (© **617/624-1234** or 617/787-7678) celebrates local teams and athletes (especially the Celtics and Bruins, who play in the building). Always call ahead; there's no access during events. Tours usually start daily at 11am, noon, 1, 2, and 3pm. Admission is $6 for adults, $4 for seniors and children. *Note:* Visitors may not bring any bags, including backpacks and briefcases, into the arena.

BASEBALL

No other experience in sports matches watching the **Boston Red Sox** play at **Fenway Park** ✸✸✸, which they do from early April to early October, and later if they make the playoffs. The quirkiness of the oldest park in the major leagues (1912) and the fact that (at press time) the team last won the World Series in 1918 only add to the Fenway mystique.

Impressions

Boston's quirky little Fenway Park . . . has been the scene of so many heartbreaks and dashed hopes that it is to Beantowners what the Bridge of Sighs is to Venetians.

—Charles McGrath, *The New York Times Book Review,* 1999

A hand-operated scoreboard fronts the 37-foot left-field wall, or "Green Monster." Watch carefully during a pitching change—the left fielder from either team might suddenly disappear into a door in the wall to cool off. The seats are narrow, uncomfortable, and gratifyingly close to the field, and the concession items are more varied than they once were, though definitely not cheaper. But that's not why you're here. You're in an intensely green place that's older than your grandparents, inhaling a Fenway Frank and wishing for a home run—what could be better?

The Red Sox franchise changed hands in 2002, throwing plans to demolish most of Fenway Park into limbo. The new owners have invested in the existing structure, erecting new seating above the Green Monster and behind home plate, but their long-term plans are unknown. Nothing is official, except the sense that if you've been hoping to visit "sometime," you'd better get moving.

Practical concerns: Compared with its modern brethren, Fenway is tiny. Tickets (at least $18, the most expensive in the majors) go on sale in January; order early. Forced to choose between seats in a low-numbered grandstand section—say, 10 or below—and in the bleachers, go for the bleachers. They can get rowdy during night games, but the view is better from there than from the deep right-field corner. Throughout the season, a limited number of standing-room tickets go on sale the day of the game, and presold tickets sometimes are returned. It can't hurt to check, especially if the team isn't playing well.

The **Fenway Park ticket office** (✆ **617/267-1700** for tickets, or 617/482-4SOX for touch-tone ticketing; www.redsox.com) is at 4 Yawkey Way, near the corner of Brookline Avenue. Tickets for people with disabilities and in no-alcohol sections are available. Smoking is not allowed in the park. Games usually begin at 7pm on weeknights and 1pm on weekends. Take the MBTA Green Line B, C, or D to Kenmore, or D to Fenway.

BASKETBALL

Sixteen National Basketball Association championship banners hang from the ceiling of the FleetCenter, testimony to the glorious history of the **Boston Celtics.** Unfortunately, the most recent is from 1986. The Celtics play from early October to April or May; when a top contender is visiting, you might have trouble buying tickets. Prices are as low as $10 for some games and top out at $85 ($250 for floor seats). For information, call the FleetCenter (✆ **617/624-1000;** www.nba.com/celtics); for tickets, contact Ticketmaster (✆ **617/931-2000;** www.ticketmaster.com). To reach the FleetCenter, take the MBTA Green or Orange Line or commuter rail to North Station. *Note:* Spectators may not bring any bags, including backpacks and briefcases, into the arena.

> *Moments* **Play Ball!**
>
> **Fenway Park tours** (© 617/236-6666) include a walk on the warning track. From May to September, tours begin on weekdays only at 10am, 11am, noon, and 1pm. There are no tours on holidays or before day games. Admission is $5 for adults, $4 for seniors, and $3 for children under 16.

FOOTBALL

The **New England Patriots** (© 800/543-1776; www.patriots.com) were playing to standing-room-only crowds even before they won the Super Bowl in 2002 and moved to a snazzy new stadium. The Pats play from August through December or January at Gillette Stadium on Route 1 in Foxboro, about a 45-minute drive south of Boston. Tickets sell out well in advance, often as part of season-ticket packages. Call or check the website for information on individual ticket sales and public-transit options.

Boston College, another tough ticket, is New England's only Division I-A college team. The Eagles play at Alumni Stadium in Chestnut Hill (© 617/552-3000). The area's Division I-AA teams are **Harvard University,** Harvard Stadium, North Harvard Street, Allston (© 617/495-2211); and **Northeastern University,** Parsons Field, Kent Street, Brookline (© 617/373-4700).

GOLF TOURNAMENTS

The major tours have changed their schedules several times in recent years; at least one usually gets within an hour of downtown Boston. The **Senior PGA Tour** (www.pgatour.com) swings by every July, landing at Nashawtuc Country Club in Concord (© 978/369-3457; www.nashawtuc.com). Over Labor Day weekend in 2003, the **PGA Tour** (www.pgatour.com) visited the Tournament Players Club of Boston, which is actually in Norton (© 508/285-3200; www.thetpcofboston.com). Check ahead for exact dates and other information, including whether the **LPGA** (www.lpga.com) and the **Women's Senior Golf Tour** (www.wsgtour.com) will return to eastern Massachusetts. The *Globe* and *Herald* regularly list numerous amateur events for fun and charity.

HOCKEY

The **Boston Bruins,** one of the NHL's original six teams, are exciting but incredibly expensive to watch. Tickets for many games sell out early despite being among the priciest ($23–$77) in the league. For information, call the FleetCenter (© 617/624-1000; www.bostonbruins.com); for tickets, contact Ticketmaster (© 617/931-2000; www.ticketmaster.com). To reach the Fleet-Center, take the MBTA Green or Orange Line or commuter rail to North Station. *Note:* Spectators may not bring any bags, including backpacks and briefcases, into the arena.

Budget-minded fans who don't have their hearts set on seeing a pro game will be pleasantly surprised by the quality of local **college hockey** ✸. Even for sold-out games, standing-room tickets are usually available the night of the game. Women's games don't sell out. The local teams regularly hit the national rankings; they include **Boston College,** Conte Forum, Chestnut Hill (© 617/552-3000); **Boston University,** Walter Brown Arena, 285 Babcock St. (© 617/353-3838); **Harvard University,** Bright Hockey Center, North Harvard Street, Allston

---

Tips **Place Your Bets**

At press time, legislation was pending that would make slot machines legal in Massachusetts. If it has passed by the time you visit, you can expect to find wheels spinning and bells ringing at Suffolk Downs. Check with the track or with the front desk at your hotel for details.

(✆ **617/495-2211**); and **Northeastern University**, Matthews Arena, St. Botolph Street (✆ **617/373-4700**). These four are the Beanpot schools, whose men's teams play a tradition-steeped tournament on the first two Mondays of February at the FleetCenter.

HORSE RACING

Suffolk Downs 🎯, 111 Waldemar Ave., East Boston (✆ **617/567-3900**; www. suffolkdowns.com), is one of the best-run smaller tracks in the country. It's home to the Grade 2 Massachusetts Handicap, contested on the first Saturday in June. There are extensive simulcasting options during and after the live racing season, which usually runs from late September to early June. (With the transformation of New Hampshire's Rockingham Park into a harness-racing track, that may change.) The day's entries appear in the *Globe* and *Herald.* The track is off Route 1A, about 2 miles north of Logan Airport. The MBTA Blue Line has a Suffolk Downs station; wait for the shuttle bus or walk about 10 minutes to the track entrance.

THE MARATHON

Every year on Patriots Day (the 3rd Mon in Apr), the **Boston Marathon** 🎯🎯🎯 rules the roads from suburban Hopkinton to Copley Square in Boston. Cheering fans line the entire route. An especially nice place to watch is tree-shaded Commonwealth Avenue between Kenmore Square and Mass. Ave., but you'll be in a crowd wherever you stand, particularly near the finish line in front of the Boston Public Library. For information about qualifying, contact the **Boston Athletic Association** (✆ **617/236-1652**; www.bostonmarathon.org).

ROWING

In late October, the **Head of the Charles Regatta** 🎯 (✆ **617/868-6200**; www.hocr.org) attracts more rowers than any other crew event in the country. Some 4,000 oarsmen and oarswomen race against the clock for 4 miles from the Charles River basin to the Eliot Bridge in west Cambridge. Hundreds of thousands of spectators socialize and occasionally watch the action, which runs nonstop on Saturday afternoon and all day Sunday.

Spring crew racing is more exciting than the "Head" format; the course is 1¼ miles, and races last just 5 to 7 minutes. Men's and women's collegiate events take place on Saturday mornings in April and early May in the Charles River basin. You'll have a perfect view of the finish line from Memorial Drive between the MIT boathouse and the Hyatt Regency Cambridge. To find out who's racing, check the Friday *Globe* sports section.

SOCCER

The **Boston Breakers** (✆ **866/462-7325** or 781/292-1016; www.bostonbreakers. com) of the Women's United Soccer Association play at Boston University's Nickerson Field, off Commonwealth Avenue, April through August. Tickets cost $11 to $25 and are available through Ticketmaster (✆ **617/931-2000**; www. ticketmaster.com).

The **New England Revolution** (© **877/438-7387** or 508/543-0350; www. nerevolution.com) of Major League Soccer plays at Gillette Stadium on Route 1 in Foxboro from April through September. Tickets cost $16 to $32 and are available through Ticketmaster (© **617/931-2000;** www.ticketmaster.com).

(Kids) Scavenger Hunt Answers

The Freedom Trail scavenger hunt appears on p. 152.

- **Boston Common:** Eagles.
- **Massachusetts State House:** Another eagle, and a mighty big one.
- **En route to Park Street Church:** A dove holding an olive branch.
- **Old Granary Burying Ground:** The mythical creature is a dragon. The coat of arms shows three cocks and a hand—"hand-cocks," "Hancocks," get it?
- **King's Chapel Burying Ground:** A rabbit jumps across the top of a shield decorated with a griffin, a monster with a lion's body and an eagle's head and wings.
- **First Public School:** My dozen, all in the alphabet around the edge, are bird, cat, duck, fish, grasshopper, lobster, mouse, owl, pig, rooster, yak, and zebra.
- **Benjamin Franklin Statue:** A Democratic donkey and the footprints of a Republican elephant.
- **En route to Old South Meeting House:** Lion heads.
- **Old State House:** Another huge eagle. *Bonus:* More lions.
- **Faneuil Hall:** A little fish.
- **Paul Revere House:** Yet another eagle.
- **Old North Church:** Who would guess a city this cold would have so many lions?
- **Copp's Hill Burying Ground:** The first line of the not-very-comforting poem is "The worms destroy this body's skin."
- **Charlestown Navy Yard:** *Bonus:* Powder monkeys.
- **En route to the Bunker Hill Monument:** Plenty of fish. The weather vane, on the site of the long-gone Three Cranes Tavern, is a crane.

8

Boston Strolls

Walking is the best way to see Boston. The narrow, twisting streets that make driving such a headache are a treat for pedestrians, who are never far from something worth seeing. The central city is compact—walking quickly from one end to the other takes about an hour—and dotted with historically and architecturally interesting buildings and neighborhoods.

In this chapter you'll find a tour of Boston's **Back Bay** and one of **Harvard Square** in Cambridge, plus some pointers to help you check out the **Big Dig.** For information on Boston's most famous walking tour, the 3-mile **Freedom Trail** ★★★, see chapter 7.

Be sure to wear comfortable shoes, and if you're not inclined to pay designer prices for designer water, bring your own bottle and fill it with ice at your hotel. By the time it's ready for you, you'll be ready for it.

WALKING TOUR 1   THE BACK BAY

Start:	The Public Garden (T: Green Line to Arlington).
Finish:	Copley Square.
Time:	2 hours if you make good time, 3 if you detour to the Esplanade, and longer if you do a lot of shopping.
Best Time:	Any time before late afternoon.
Worst Time:	Late afternoon, when people and cars pack the streets. And don't attempt the detour on July 4. This walk is mostly outdoors, so if the weather is bad, you may find yourself in lots of shops. You decide whether that makes an overcast day a "best" or "worst" time.

The Back Bay is the youngest neighborhood in central Boston, the product of a massive landfill project that took place from 1835 to 1882. It's flat, symmetrical, logically designed—the names of the cross streets go in alphabetical order—and altogether anomalous in Boston's crazy-quilt geography.

Begin your walk in the:

❶ Public Garden

Before the Back Bay was filled in, the Charles River flowed right up to Charles Street, which separates Boston Common from the Public Garden. On the night of April 18, 1775, British troops bound for Lexington and Concord boarded boats to Cambridge ("two if by sea") at the foot of

the Common and set off across what's now the Public Garden.

Explore the lagoon, the trees and other flora, and the statuary. Take a ride on the **swan boats** if you like, and then make your way toward the corner of Charles and Beacon streets.

A short distance away, inside the Public Garden (listen for the cries of delighted children), you'll see a 35-foot strip of

Walking Tour 1: The Back Bay

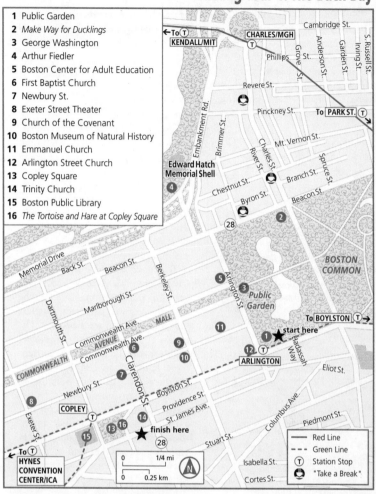

1 Public Garden
2 *Make Way for Ducklings*
3 George Washington
4 Arthur Fiedler
5 Boston Center for Adult Education
6 First Baptist Church
7 Newbury St.
8 Exeter Street Theater
9 Church of the Covenant
10 Boston Museum of Natural History
11 Emmanuel Church
12 Arlington Street Church
13 Copley Square
14 Trinity Church
15 Boston Public Library
16 *The Tortoise and Hare at Copley Square*

cobblestones topped with the bronze figures that immortalize Robert McCloskey's book:

② *Make Way for Ducklings*

Installed in 1987 and wildly popular since the moment they were unveiled, Nancy Schön's renderings of Mrs. Mallard and her eight babies are irresistible. Mrs. Mallard is 38 inches tall, making her back a bit higher than a tricycle seat, but that doesn't keep people of all ages from climbing on. If you don't know the story of the Mallards' perilous trip to meet Mr. Mallard at the lagoon, ask one of the parents or children you'll find here.

The city bought the site of the Public Garden from private interests in 1824. Planting began in 1837, but it wasn't until the late 1850s that Arlington Street was built and the land was permanently set aside. George F. Meacham executed the design.

Cross the lagoon using the little suspension bridge and look for the statue of:

③ George Washington

Unveiled in 1875, this was Boston's first equestrian statue. It stands 38 feet tall and is considered an excellent likeness of the first president of the

United States, an outstanding horse-man. The artist, Thomas Ball, was a Charlestown native who worked in Italy. Among his students was noted sculptor Daniel Chester French. Pass through the gate onto Arlington Street. Before you begin exploring in earnest, this is a good place to detour.

TAKE A BREAK
Turn right and walk up Arlington Street to Beacon Street. On your right across the busy intersection is **Cheers**, 84 Beacon St. (🕿 **617/227-9605**; www.cheersboston. com), originally the Bull & Finch Pub. The food is quite tasty, but two points bear remembering: The bar looks nothing like the set of the TV show (you'll find a replica at Faneuil Hall Marketplace), and the patrons generally consist of people from everywhere in the universe except Boston.

Alternatively, turn right on Beacon Street and walk 1 long block to Charles Street. You can pick up food to go at **Panificio**, 144 Charles St. (🕿 **617/227-4340**), or **Cafe Bella Vita**, 30 Charles St. (🕿 **617/720-4505**). This is also a promising place for a **shopping** break (see chapter 9).

When you've found something to eat, back-track along Beacon Street past Arlington Street to Embankment Road and turn right. Take the Arthur Fiedler Footbridge across Storrow Drive to the Esplanade, and unpack your food near the giant head of:

❹ Arthur Fiedler
Installed in 1985, this sculpture by Ralph Helmick consists of sheets of aluminum that eerily capture the coun-tenance of the legendary conductor of the Boston Pops, who died in 1979. The amphitheater to the right is the **Hatch Shell,** where the Pops perform free during the week leading up to and including July 4.

When you're ready, retrace your steps to the corner of Arlington Street and Common-wealth Avenue. This is the:

❺ Boston Center for Adult Education
Constructed in 1904 as a private home, this building, at 5 Common-wealth Ave., gained a huge ballroom in 1912. If the ornate ballroom is not in use for a class or a function (it's popular for weddings), you're welcome to have a look. The BCAE (🕿 **617/ 267-4430**; www.bcae.org), established in 1933, is the oldest continuing-edu-cation institution in the country.

You're now on the 8-block **Commonwealth Avenue Mall.** This graceful public promenade is the centerpiece of architect Arthur Gilman's design of the Back Bay. The mall is 100 feet wide (the entire street is 240 ft. wide) and stretches to Ken-more Square. The elegant Victorian mansions on either side—almost all divided into apartments or in commer-cial or educational use—are recognized as a great asset, but the attitude toward the apparently random collection of sculpture along the mall is hardly unanimous. Judge for yourself as you inspect the art, starting with **Alexan-der Hamilton** across Arlington Street from **George Washington.** The most moving sculpture is at Dartmouth Street. The **Vendome Memorial** hon-ors the memory of the nine firefighters who lost their lives in a blaze at the Hotel Vendome in 1972.

⟨ Fun Fact The Shape of Things to Come

The **First Baptist Church** is a fine building, but the design is notable mainly because its creators went on to much more famous projects. The architect, **H. H. Richardson,** is best known for nearby **Trinity Church.** The artist who created the frieze, which represents the sacraments, was **Frédéric Auguste Bartholdi,** who designed the **Statue of Liberty.**

Two blocks from the Public Garden, at 110 Commonwealth Ave., at the corner of Clarendon Street, is the:

❻ First Baptist Church

Built from 1870 to 1872 of Roxbury puddingstone, it originally housed the congregation of the Brattle Street Church (Unitarian), which had been downtown, near Faneuil Hall.

At Clarendon Street or Dartmouth Street, turn left and walk 1 block to:

❼ Newbury Street

Commonwealth Avenue is the architectural heart of the Back Bay, and Newbury Street is the commercial center. Take some time to roam around here (see chapter 9 for pointers), browsing in the galleries, window-shopping at the boutiques, and watching the chic shoppers.

At 26 Exeter St. is the building that was once the:

❽ Exeter Street Theater

Designed in 1884 as the First Spiritualist Temple, it was a movie house from 1914 to 1984. Once known for the crowds flocking to *The Rocky Horror Picture Show*, it's now the home of a TGI Friday's restaurant.

When you're ready to continue your stroll (or when your credit cards cry for mercy), head back toward the Public Garden and seek out three of Newbury Street's oldest buildings, starting with the:

❾ Church of the Covenant

This Gothic-revival edifice at 67 Newbury St. was completed in 1867 and designed by Richard Upjohn. The stained-glass windows are the work of Louis Comfort Tiffany.

Across the street, set back from the sidewalk at 234 Berkeley St., an opulent store occupies an opulent setting. Now the clothing emporium Louis Boston, this is the original home of the:

❿ Boston Museum of Natural History

A forerunner of the Museum of Science, it was built according to William Preston's French Academic design. The 1864 structure was originally two

stories high and has its original roof, preserved when the building gained a third floor.

Cross Newbury Street again and continue walking toward the Public Garden. On your left, at 15 Newbury St., is:

⓫ Emmanuel Church

The first building completed on Newbury Street, this Episcopal church ministers through the arts, so there might be a concert (classical to jazz, solo to orchestral) going on during your visit. Call ✆ 617/536-3355 to inquire.

Now you're almost back at the Public Garden. On your left is the original **Ritz-Carlton** (1927).

Turn right onto Arlington Street and walk 1 block. On your right, at 351 Boylston St., is the:

⓬ Arlington Street Church

This is the oldest church in the Back Bay, completed in 1861. An interesting blend of Georgian and Italianate details, it's the work of architect Arthur Gilman, who laid out this neighborhood. Here you'll find more Tiffany stained glass. Step inside to see the pulpit that was in use in 1788 when the congregation worshipped downtown on Federal Street.

Follow Boylston Street away from the Public Garden. You'll pass the famous FAO Schwarz toy store, with the huge bronze bear out front at the corner of Berkeley Street. Two blocks up is:

⓭ Copley Square

Enjoy the fountain and visit the farmers market (Tues and Fri afternoons July–Nov).

Overlooking the square is one of the most famous church buildings in the United States. This is:

⓮ Trinity Church

H. H. Richardson's Romanesque masterpiece, completed in 1877, is to your left. It's built on 4,502 pilings driven into the mud that was once the Back Bay. Brochures and guides are available to help you find your way around a building considered one of the finest examples of church architecture in the

---

> **Fun Fact   It's All French to Me**
>
> As you explore the Boston area, you'll keep hearing the name of sculptor **Daniel Chester French**. French (1850–1931) was responsible for the gorgeous doors on the Dartmouth Street side of the **Boston Public Library,** the statue of **John Harvard** in Harvard Yard, and the **Minute Man** statue near the North Bridge in Concord. If you're not a parochial Bostonian, you probably know him best as the sculptor of the seated Abraham Lincoln in the presidential memorial in Washington.

---

country. It's open daily from 8am to 6pm. Friday organ recitals begin at 12:15pm.

Across Dartmouth Street is the:

⑮ Boston Public Library

The work of architect Charles Follen McKim and many others, the Renaissance-revival building was completed in 1895 after 10 years of construction. Its design reflects the significant influence of the Bibliothèque Nationale in Paris. Wander up the steps to check out the building's impressive interior (see chapter 7 for more details). **Daniel Chester French** designed the doors.

Head across the street to Copley Square. In a sense, you've come full circle; as at the Public Garden, you'll see a playful and compelling sculpture:

⑯ *The Tortoise and Hare at Copley Square*

This is another work by Nancy Schön. Designed to signify the end of the **Boston Marathon** (the finish line is on Boylston St. between Exeter and Dartmouth sts.), it was unveiled for the 100th anniversary of the event in 1996.

From here you're in a good position to set out for any other part of town, or walk a little way in any direction and continue exploring. Copley Place and the Shops at Prudential Center are nearby, Newbury Street is 1 block over, and there's a Green Line T station at Boylston and Dartmouth streets.

WALKING TOUR 2	HARVARD SQUARE

Start:	Harvard Square (T: Red Line to Harvard).
Finish:	John F. Kennedy Park.
Time:	2 to 4 hours, depending on how much time you spend in shops and museums.
Best Time:	Almost any time during the day. The Harvard art museums are free on Saturday morning; the natural-history museums are free on Sunday morning year-round and on Wednesday from 3 to 5pm during the school year.
Worst Time:	The first full week of June. You might have trouble gaining admission to Harvard Yard during commencement festivities. The ceremony is Thursday morning; without a ticket, you won't be allowed in.

Popular impressions to the contrary, Cambridge is not exclusively Harvard. In fact, Harvard Square isn't even exclusively Harvard. During a walk around the area, you'll see historic buildings and sights, interesting museums, and notable architecture on and off the university's main campus.

Leave the T station by the main entrance (take the ramp to the turnstiles, then take the escalators) and emerge in the heart of:

① Harvard Square

Town and gown meet at this lively intersection, where you'll get a taste of

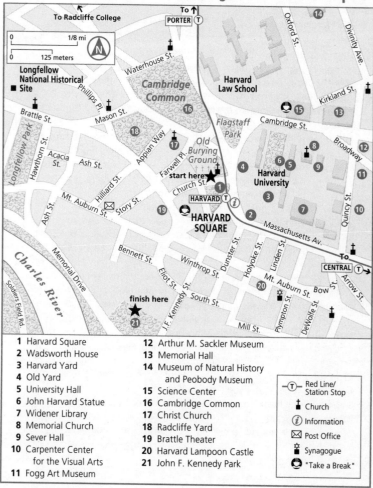

1 Harvard Square
2 Wadsworth House
3 Harvard Yard
4 Old Yard
5 University Hall
6 John Harvard Statue
7 Widener Library
8 Memorial Church
9 Sever Hall
10 Carpenter Center
  for the Visual Arts
11 Fogg Art Museum

12 Arthur M. Sackler Museum
13 Memorial Hall
14 Museum of Natural History
  and Peobody Museum
15 Science Center
16 Cambridge Common
17 Christ Church
18 Radcliffe Yard
19 Brattle Theater
20 Harvard Lampoon Castle
21 John F. Kennedy Park

— (T)— Red Line/
  Station Stop
✝ Church
(i) Information
✉ Post Office
✡ Synagogue
☕ "Take a Break"

the improbable mix of people drawn to the crossroads of Cambridge. To your right is the landmark **Out of Town News** kiosk. It stocks newspapers and magazines from all over the world and tons of souvenirs (beefed up when the rise of the Internet cut into the demand for nonvirtual journalism). At the booth in front of you, you can request information about the area. Step close to it so that you're out of the flow of pedestrian traffic, and look around.

The store across Mass. Ave. is the **Harvard Coop.** It rhymes with *hoop*—say "co-op" and risk being taken for a Yalie. On the far side of the intersection, at the corner of John F. Kennedy and Brattle streets, is a sign reading DEWEY CHEETHAM & HOWE (say it out loud) on the third floor of the brick building. National Public Radio's "Car Talk" originates here.

Turn around so that the Coop is at your back, and walk half a block, crossing Dunster Street. Across the way, at 1341 Mass. Ave., you'll see:

2 Wadsworth House
Most of the people waiting for the bus in front of this yellow wood building probably don't know that it was built

The Dirt on the Big Dig

Much as I'd love to outline a stop-by-stop tour of the **Big Dig** ✦✦✦, chances are good that it would be out of date before I even hit the "print" button. As the project proceeds, it changes almost daily, affecting the route of both streets and sidewalks. The schedule for 2004 includes the demolition of the elevated expressway, which promises to be fascinating.

You can visit the website (**www.bigdig.com**) to download a diagram and descriptions of a self-guided tour of the whole shebang that takes at least 2 hours. If you don't have that kind of time—or if you're interested but not *that* interested—then wait until you're going downtown anyway, and leave an extra half-hour or so for exploring.

Two important notes: **Be careful.** It sounds obvious, but despite abundant warning signs, at least one pedestrian and two motorists have fallen into construction ditches. Get a grip on the kids, and don't lean over or into anything. And **wear sturdy shoes**—there's gravel all over the place.

Every T stop near the harbor—**North Station, Haymarket, Aquarium, State,** and **South Station**—is close to or in the middle of the Big Dig. See the "Boston Transit" map on p. 63 to orient yourself. As you leave these stations, you'll see signs directing you around the construction. Many of the concrete barriers that enclose the work area have transparent panels attached to their top edges, allowing a clear view of the activity on the other side. The underpass from Blackstone Street to Cross Street, near Haymarket, is a good place for this. If something interesting is going on, you'll have plenty of company.

Tips: For the best chance of seeing work in progress, visit on a **weekday** during daylight hours. To get a sense of what's complete, check around on a **weekend,** especially early in the morning. And if you want to blend in, wear boots, jeans, and an **orange top** (T-shirt, sweatshirt, or vest).

---

in 1726 as a residence for Harvard's fourth president—but then, neither do most Harvard students. Now the headquarters of the alumni association, its biggest claim to fame is a classic: George Washington slept here.

Cross the street and go left. Follow the outside of the brick wall past one gate until you see another T exit. Turn right and use Johnston Gate to enter:

❸ Harvard Yard

This is the oldest part of "the Yard." It was a patch of grass with animals grazing on it when Harvard College was established in 1636 to train young men for the ministry. It wasn't much more when the Continental Army spent the winter of 1775–76 here. Harvard is the oldest college in the country, with the most competitive admissions process, and if you suggest aloud that it's not the best, you might encounter the attitude that inspired the saying, "You can always tell a Harvard man, but you can't tell him much."

Harvard, a private institution since 1865, includes the college and 10 graduate and professional schools. It owns more than 400 buildings in Boston and Cambridge; some of the most interesting surround this quad.

Fun Fact **Nothing but the Truth**

The likeness of **John Harvard** outside University Hall is known as the "Statue of Three Lies" because the inscription reads "John Harvard/Founder/1638." In fact, the college was founded in 1636; Harvard (one of many benefactors) didn't establish it, but donated money and his library; and this isn't John Harvard anyway. No portraits of him survive, so the model for this benevolent-looking bronze gentleman was, according to various accounts, either his nephew or a student.

The classroom and administration buildings and dormitories here make up the:

❹ Old Yard

To your right is **Massachusetts Hall.** Built in 1720, this National Historic Landmark is the university's oldest surviving building. First-year students share the building with the first-floor office of the university president (or perhaps it's the other way around), whom they traditionally invite upstairs for tea once a year. To your left, across from "Mass. Hall," is **Harvard Hall,** a classroom building constructed in 1765. Turn left and walk along Harvard Hall. You'll come to matching side-by-side buildings, **Hollis** and **Stoughton halls.** Hollis dates to 1763 (Stoughton "only" to 1805) and has been home to many students who went on to great fame, among them Ralph Waldo Emerson, Henry David Thoreau, and Charles Bulfinch. Almost hidden across the tiny lawn between these two buildings is **Holden Chapel,** a Georgian-style gem built in 1745. It has been an anatomy lab, a classroom building, and, of course, a chapel, and it is now home to the Harvard Glee Club.

Cross the Yard to the building opposite the gate where you entered. This is:

❺ University Hall

Designed by Charles Bulfinch and constructed of granite quarried in nearby Chelmsford, the 1813 structure is the college's main administration building. In 1969, students protesting the Vietnam War occupied it.

University Hall is best known as the backdrop of the:

❻ John Harvard Statue

This is one of the most photographed objects in the Boston area. Daniel Chester French designed it in 1884.

Walk around University Hall into the adjoining quad. This is still the Yard, but it's the **"New Yard,"** sometimes called **Tercentenary Theater** because the college's 300th-anniversary celebration was held here. Commencement and other university-wide ceremonies take place here.

On your right is:

❼ Widener Library

The centerpiece of the world's largest university library system was built in 1913 as a memorial to Harry Elkins Widener, Harvard class of 1907. Legend has it that he died when the *Titanic* sank in 1912 because he was unable to swim 50 yards to a lifeboat, and his mother donated $2 million for the library on the condition that every undergraduate prove his or her ability to swim 50 yards. Today the library holds more than 3 million volumes, including 3,500 rare volumes collected by Harry Elkins Widener, on 50 miles of shelves. Don't even think about swiping Harry's Gutenberg Bible. The last person to try, in 1969, gained access from above but couldn't climb out. With the 70-pound Bible in his knapsack, he fell six stories to the courtyard below.

Horace Trumbauer of Philadelphia designed the library. His primary design assistant was Julian Francis Abele, a student of architecture at the University of Pennsylvania and the first black graduate of L'Ecole des Beaux Arts in Paris. For security reasons, access to the lobby—which sits within view of the locked memorial room that holds Widener's collection—may be restricted. Check to see if you're allowed to take a peek, or just stop at the top of the outside staircase and enjoy the view.

Facing the library is:

8 Memorial Church

Built in 1931, it's topped with a tower and weather vane 197 feet tall. You're welcome to look around this Georgian revival–style edifice unless services are going on, or to attend them if they are. Morning prayers run daily from 8:45 to 9am, and the Sunday service is at 11am. Weddings and funerals also take place here. The entrance is on the left. On the south wall, toward the Yard, panels bear the names of Harvard alumni who died in the world wars, Korea, and Vietnam. One is Joseph P. Kennedy Jr., the president's brother, class of 1938.

With Memorial Church behind you, turn left toward:

9 Sever Hall

H. H. Richardson, architect of Boston's Trinity Church, designed this classroom building (1880). Notice the gorgeous brickwork that includes roll moldings around the doors, the fluted brick chimneys, and the arrangement of the windows.

Facing Sever Hall, turn right and go around to the back. The building on

your right is Emerson Hall, which appeared in the movie *Love Story* as Barrett Hall, named after the family of Ryan O'Neal's character. Cross this quad, and exit through the gate onto Quincy Street.

On your right on the other side of the street, at 24 Quincy St., is the:

10 Carpenter Center for the Visual Arts

Art exhibitions occupy the lobby, the Harvard Film Archive shows movies in the basement (pick up a schedule on the main floor), and the concrete-and-glass building is itself a work of art. Opened in 1963, it was designed by the Swiss-French architect Le Corbusier and the team of Sert, Jackson, and Gourley. It's the only Le Corbusier design in North America.

Just up Quincy Street, opposite the gate you used to leave the Yard, is the:

11 Fogg Art Museum

Founded in 1895, the museum has been at 32 Quincy St. since the building was completed in 1927. The Fogg's excellent collection of painting, sculpture, and decorative art runs from the Middle Ages to the present. See chapter 7 for a description of the Fogg, the Busch-Reisinger Museum, and the next stop on our walk.

Turn right as you leave the museum (or left if you're facing it) and cross Broadway to reach the:

12 Arthur M. Sackler Museum

The British architect James Stirling (who described this area as an "architectural zoo") designed the Sackler, at

---

Impressions

One emerged, as one still does, from the subway exit in the Square and faced an old red-brick wall behind which stretched, to my fond eye, what remains still the most beautiful campus in America, the Harvard Yard. If there is any one place in all America that mirrors better all American history, I do not know of it.
—Theodore H. White, *In Search of History,* 1978

Moments **Pssst . . . Check This Out**

As you cross Harvard Yard, stand with Memorial Church behind you and turn left toward **Sever Hall.** The front door is in a "whispering gallery." Stand on one side of the arch, station a friend or willing passerby on the opposite side, and speak softly into the facade. Someone standing next to you can't hear you, but the person at the other side of the arch can.

---

485 Broadway. It houses the university's spectacular collection of Asian art.

Continue on Quincy Street. As you cross Cambridge Street, watch out for confused drivers emerging from the underpass to your left. Covering the block between Cambridge and Kirkland streets is:

⑬ Memorial Hall

This imposing Victorian structure, known to students as "Mem Hall," was completed in 1874. Enter from Cambridge Street and investigate the hall of memorials, a transept where you can read the names of the Harvard men who died fighting for the Union during the Civil War—but not of their Confederate counterparts. (The name of Colonel Robert Gould Shaw—Matthew Broderick's character in the movie *Glory*—is halfway down on the right.) To the right is **Sanders Theatre,** prized as a performance space and lecture hall for its excellent acoustics and clear views. To the left is **Annenberg Hall.** It's a dining hall that's closed to visitors, but you might be able to sneak a look at the gorgeous stained-glass windows. Harvard graduates William Ware and Henry Van Brunt won a design competition for Memorial Hall, which was constructed for a total cost of $390,000 (most of it donated by alumni). The colorful tower is a replica of the original, which was destroyed by fire in 1956 and rebuilt in 1999.

Facing in the same direction you were when you entered, walk through the transept and exit onto Kirkland Street. Turn left and take the first right, onto Oxford Street. One block up on the right, at 26 Oxford St., you'll see an entrance to the:

⑭ Harvard Museum of Natural History

Adjoining the Peabody Museum of Archaeology & Ethnology at 11 Divinity Ave., the Museum of Natural History presents the collections and research of the university's Botanical Museum, Museum of Comparative Zoology, and Mineralogical Museum. See chapter 7 for a full description.

Leave through the back door of 11 Divinity Ave. and look around. Across the street at 6 Divinity Ave. is the **Semitic Museum** (*©* **617/495-4631**), where the second- and third-floor galleries hold displays of archaeological artifacts and photographs from the Near and Middle East. Horace Trumbauer, the architect of Widener Library, designed the building next door, 2 Divinity Ave. It's home to the Harvard-Yenching Institute, which promotes East Asian studies and facilitates scholar-exchange programs. For every person who can tell you that, there are several thousand who know this building for the pair of **Chinese stone lions** flanking the front door.

Turn right and return to Kirkland Street, then go right. At the intersection of Kirkland and Oxford streets, at Zero Oxford St., is the university's:

⑮ Science Center

The 10-story monolith is said to resemble a Polaroid camera (Edwin H. Land, founder of Cambridge-based Polaroid Corporation, was one of its main benefactors). The Spanish architect Josep Luis Sert designed the Science Center, which opened in 1972. Sert, the dean of the university's Graduate School of Design from 1953 to 1969, was a disciple of Le Corbusier (who designed the Carpenter Center for the Visual Arts). On the plaza between the Science Center and the Yard is the **Tanner Rock Fountain,** a group of 159 New England boulders arranged around a small fountain. Since 1985 this has been a favorite spot for students to relax and watch unsuspecting passersby get wet: The fountain sprays a fine mist, which begins slowly and gradually intensifies.

TAKE A BREAK
The **main level of the Science Center** is open to the public and has several options if you want a soft drink, gourmet coffee, or a sandwich. Go easy on the sweets, though, in anticipation of the next break.

Leave the Science Center near the fountain and turn right. Keeping the underpass on your left, follow the walkway for the equivalent of 1½ blocks as it curves around to the right. The Harvard Law School campus is on your right. You're back at Mass. Ave. Cross carefully to:

⑯ Cambridge Common
Memorials and plaques dot this well-used plot of greenery and bare earth. Follow the sidewalk along Mass. Ave. to the left, and after a block or so you'll walk near or over horseshoes embedded in the concrete. This is the path William Dawes, Paul Revere's fellow alarm-sounder, took from Boston to Lexington on April 18, 1775. Turn right onto Garden Street and continue following the Common for 1 block. On your right you'll see a monument

marking the place where General George Washington took control of the Continental Army on July 3, 1775. The elm under which he reputedly assumed command is no longer standing.

Cross Garden Street and backtrack to Zero Garden St. This is:
⑰ Christ Church
Peter Harrison of Newport, Rhode Island (also the architect of King's Chapel in Boston), designed the oldest church in Cambridge, which opened in 1760. Note the square wooden tower. Inside the vestibule you can still see bullet holes made by British muskets. At one time the church was used as the barracks for troops from Connecticut, who melted down the organ pipes to make ammunition. The graveyard on the Mass. Ave. side of the building, the **Old Burying Ground,** is the oldest in Cambridge, dating to 1635.

Facing the church, turn right and proceed on Garden Street to the first intersection. This is Appian Way. Turn left and take the first right into:
⑱ Radcliffe Yard
Radcliffe College was founded in 1879 as the "Harvard Annex" and named for Ann Radcliffe, Lady Mowlson, Harvard's first female benefactor. Undergraduate classes merged with Harvard's in 1943, Radcliffe graduates first received Harvard degrees in 1963, and Harvard officially assumed responsibility for educating undergraduate women in 1977. Radcliffe was an independent corporation until 1999; it's now the university's Radcliffe Institute for Advanced Study. After you've strolled around, return to

---

Fun Fact **Play It, Sam**
The **Brattle Theater,** one of the oldest independent movie houses in the country, started the *Casablanca* revival craze, which explains the name of the restaurant in the basement.

Appian Way and turn right. You'll emerge on Brattle Street.

The **Longfellow National Historic Site,** 105 Brattle St. (✆617/876-4491; see chapter 7), makes an interesting detour and adds about an hour to your walk. If you don't detour, turn left and continue walking along Brattle Street. There are excellent shops on both sides of the street.

TAKE A BREAK
Hi-Rise at the Blacksmith House, 56 Brattle St. (✆ 617/492-3003), a branch of a well-known local artisan bread company, handles the baking for this legendary house, made famous by a Longfellow poem. "Under the spreading chestnut tree," stuff yourself with delectable pastry.

Across the street, at 40 Brattle St., is the:

⑲ Brattle Theater

Opened in 1890 as Brattle Hall, it was founded by the Cambridge Social Union and used as a venue for cultural entertainment. It became a movie hall in 1953 and gained a reputation as Cambridge's center for art films.

You're now in the **Brattle Square** part of Harvard Square. You might see street performers, a protest, a speech, or more shopping opportunities. Cross Brattle Street at **WordsWorth Books,** bear right, and follow the curve of the building all the way around the corner to Mount Auburn Street. Stay on the left-hand side of the street as you cross John F. Kennedy Street, Dunster Street, Holyoke Street, and Linden Street. On your left between Dunster and Holyoke streets is **Holyoke Center,** an administration building designed by Josep Luis Sert that has commercial space on the ground floor.

The corner of Mount Auburn and Linden streets offers a good view of the:

⑳ Harvard Lampoon Castle

Constructed in 1909, designed by Wheelwright & Haven (architects of Boston's Horticultural Hall), and listed on the National Register of Historic Places, this is the home of Harvard's undergraduate humor magazine, the **Lampoon.** The main tower resembles a face, with windows as the eyes, nose, and mouth, topped by what looks like a miner's hat. The *Lampoon* and the daily student newspaper, the *Crimson,* share a long history of reciprocal pranks and vandalism. Elaborate security measures notwithstanding, *Crimson* editors occasionally make off with the bird that you might see atop the castle (it looks like a crane but is actually an ibis), and *Lampoon* staffers have absconded with the huge wooden president's chair from the *Crimson.*

You'll pass the *Crimson* on your right if you detour to the **Harvard Book Store** (turn left onto Plympton Street and follow it to the corner of Mass. Ave.). Otherwise, cross Mount Auburn Street and walk away from Holyoke Center on Holyoke Street or Dunster Street to get a sense of some of the rest of the campus.

Turn right on Winthrop Street or South Street, and proceed to Kennedy Street. Turn left, cross Kennedy Street at some point, and follow it toward the Charles River. On your right at Memorial Drive is:

㉑ John F. Kennedy Park

This lovely parcel of land was an empty plot near the MBTA train yard in the 1970s (the Red Line then ended at Harvard), when the search was on for a site for the Kennedy Library. Traffic concerns led to the library's being built in Dorchester, but the **Graduate School of Government** and this adjacent park bear the president's name. Walk away from the street to enjoy the fountain, which is engraved with excerpts from JFK's speeches. This is a great place to take a break and plan the rest of your day.

9

Shopping

If you turned straight to this chapter, you're in good company: Surveys of visitors to Boston consistently show that shopping is the most popular activity, beating museum-going by a comfortable margin.

Boston-area shopping represents a tempting blend of classic and contemporary. Boston and Cambridge boast tiny boutiques and sprawling malls, esoteric bookshops and national chain stores, classy galleries and snazzy secondhand-clothing outlets.

This chapter concentrates on only-in-Boston businesses, and includes many national (and international) names that are worth a visit. I'll point you to areas that are great for shop-hopping and toward specific destinations that are great for particular items.

1 The Shopping Scene

One of the best features of shopping in Massachusetts is that there's no sales tax on clothing priced below $175, or on food. Just about every store will ship your purchases home for a fee, but if it's part of a chain that operates in your home state, you'll probably have to pay that sales tax. Be sure to ask first. All other items are taxed at 5% (as are restaurant meals and takeout food).

In the major shopping areas, stores usually open at 10am and close at 6 or 7pm on weekdays and Saturday. On Sunday, most open at 11am or noon and close at 5 or 6pm, but some don't open at all. Closing time may be later on one night a week, usually Wednesday or Thursday. Malls keep their own hours (noted below), and some smaller shops open later. Days and hours can vary in winter. If a business sounds too good to pass up, call to make sure it's open before heading out.

GREAT SHOPPING AREAS

The area's premier shopping area is Boston's **Back Bay.** Dozens of classy galleries, shops, and boutiques make **Newbury Street** a world-famous destination. Nearby, the **Shops at Prudential Center** and **Copley Place** (linked by an enclosed walkway across Huntington Ave.) bookend a giant retail complex that includes the posh department stores **Neiman Marcus, Lord & Taylor,** and **Saks Fifth Avenue.** The adjacent **South End,** though less commercially dense, boasts a number of art galleries and quirky shops.

Another popular destination is **Faneuil Hall Marketplace.** The shops, boutiques, and pushcarts at Boston's busiest attraction sell everything from cosmetics to costume jewelry, sweaters to souvenirs.

If the hubbub at Faneuil Hall and in the Back Bay overwhelms you, stroll over to Beacon Hill. Picturesque **Charles Street,** at the foot of the hill, is a short but commercially dense street noted for its excellent gift shops and antiques dealers.

One of Boston's oldest shopping areas is **Downtown Crossing,** a traffic-free pedestrian mall along Washington, Winter, and Summer streets near Boston

Common. Here you'll find two major department stores (**Filene's** and **Macy's**), tons of smaller clothing and shoe stores, Swedish fashion phenomenon **H&M**, food and merchandise pushcarts, outlets of two major bookstore chains (**Barnes & Noble** and **Borders**), and the original **Filene's Basement** (see "Discount Shopping" later in this chapter).

Harvard Square in Cambridge, with its bookstores, boutiques, and T-shirt shops, is about 15 minutes from downtown Boston by subway. Despite the neighborhood association's efforts, chain stores have swept over "the Square." You'll find a mix of national and regional outlets, and more than a few persistent independent retailers.

For a less generic experience, stroll along shop-lined **Massachusetts Avenue** toward the next T stop (**Porter Sq.** to the north, **Central Sq.** to the southeast). Another neighborhood with a well-deserved reputation for variety is Brookline's **Coolidge Corner,** which is worth a trip (on the Green Line C train).

2 Shopping A to Z

Here I've singled out establishments that I especially like and neighborhoods that suit shoppers interested in particular types of merchandise. Addresses are in Boston unless otherwise indicated.

ANTIQUES & COLLECTIBLES

No antiques hound worthy of the name will leave Boston without an expedition along both sides of **Charles Street** from Cambridge Street to Beacon Street, and a detour to **River Street** (parallel to Charles, 1 block closer to the river). Also see the listing for the auction house **Skinner,** under "Art" below.

Boston Antique Cooperative I & II   Merchandise from Europe, Asia, and the United States fills these shops. They specialize in furniture and accessories, vintage photographs, jewelry, silver, and porcelain, but you might come across just about anything. 119 Charles St. ℂ **617/227-9810** or 617/227-9811. www.bostonantique co-op.com. T: Red Line to Charles/MGH.

Bromfield Pen Shop   This shop's selection of antique pens will thrill any collector. It also sells new pens, including Mont Blanc, Pelikan, Waterman, and Omas. Closed Sunday. 5 Bromfield St. ℂ **617/482-9053.** www.bromfieldpenshop.com. T: Red or Orange Line to Downtown Crossing.

Danish Country Antique Furniture   Owner James Kilroy specializes in Scandinavian furnishings dating from the 1700s onward. In this mahogany-intensive neighborhood, the light woods are a visual treat. You'll also see folk art, clocks, Royal Copenhagen porcelain, and antique Chinese furniture and home accessories. 138 Charles St. ℂ **617/227-1804.** T: Red Line to Charles/MGH.

Shreve, Crump & Low   "Shreve's," a Boston institution founded in 1796, is famous for its jewelry, china, silver, crystal, and watches. The antiques department specializes in 18th- and 19th-century American and English furnishings, British and American silver, and Chinese porcelain. 330 Boylston St. ℂ **800/225-7088** or 617/267-9100. T: Green Line to Arlington.

Upstairs Downstairs Antiques *Finds*   It's a cliché to say that antiques remind you of your grandmother's furniture. Here that's less trite because the merchandise displays are room arrangements that change with the seasons. From huge sideboards to delicate side tables to books and doilies, it's more evocative than a madeleine. 93 Charles St. ℂ **617/367-1950.** T: Red Line to Charles/MGH.

ART

The greatest concentration of galleries lines **Newbury Street** (at street level and above); budget some time for exploring. Browsers and questions are welcome. Most galleries are open Tuesday through Saturday or Sunday from 10 or 11am to 5:30 or 6pm. Exhibitions typically change once a month. For specifics, visit individual websites, pick up a copy of the free monthly *Gallery Guide* at businesses along Newbury Street, or check with the **Newbury Street League** (© 617/ 267-7961; www.newbury-st.com).

An excellent way to see artists at work is to visit during neighborhood **open studio** days. Artists' communities throughout the Boston area stage the weekend events once or twice a year. You might be asked for a contribution to a charity in exchange for a map of the studios. Check listings in the *Globe* and *Herald* or visit www.cityofboston.gov/arts for information.

Alpha Gallery   Directed by Joanna E. Fink, daughter of founder Alan Fink, the Alpha Gallery specializes in contemporary American paintings, sculpture, and works on paper, as well as modern master paintings and prints. 14 Newbury St., 2nd floor. © 617/536-4465. www.alphagallery.com. T: Green Line to Arlington.

Barbara Krakow Gallery   This prestigious gallery, established more than 30 years ago, specializes in paintings, sculpture, drawings, and prints created after 1945. Closed Sunday and Monday. 10 Newbury St., 5th floor. © 617/262-4490. www. barbarakrakowgallery.com. T: Green Line to Arlington.

Gallery NAGA   In the neo-Gothic Church of the Covenant, Gallery NAGA exhibits contemporary paintings, prints, sculpture, photography, studio furniture, and works in glass. A stop here is a must if you want to see holography (trust me, you do). Closed Sunday and Monday. 67 Newbury St. © 617/267-9060. www.gallerynaga.com. T: Green Line to Arlington.

Gargoyles, Grotesques & Chimeras *(Finds*   Gargoyles of all sizes decorate this intentionally gloomy space. You'll see plaster reproductions of details on famous cathedrals and other buildings, religious icons, nongargoyle home decorations, and haunting photographs that set the gothic mood. Hours vary; call ahead. 262 Newbury St. © 617/536-2362. T: Green Line B, C, or D to Hynes/ICA.

Haley & Steele   If you prefer traditional to contemporary, this is the place. The century-old business specializes in maritime, military, botanical, ornithological (think Audubon), and historical prints, as well as 19th-century oil paintings and British sporting prints. Closed Sunday. 91 Newbury St. © 617/536-6339. www.haleysteele.com. T: Green Line to Arlington.

International Poster Gallery *(Finds*   This extraordinary gallery's Italian vintage poster collection is the largest anywhere, and the thousands of other pieces include original posters from around the world. The accommodating staff will comb its databases (cyber and cerebral) to help you find the exact image you want. The theme of the works on display, such as skiing or (every summer) travel, changes three or four times a year. Prices start at $50, with most between $500 and $2,000. 205 Newbury St. © 617/375-0076. www.internationalposter.com. T: Green Line to Copley.

Nielsen Gallery   Owner Nina Nielsen personally selects the artists who exhibit in her gallery (which has been here for nearly 40 years), and she has great taste. You might see the work of a young, newly discovered talent or that of a more established artist. 179 Newbury St. © 617/266-4835. www.nielsengallery.com. T: Green Line to Copley.

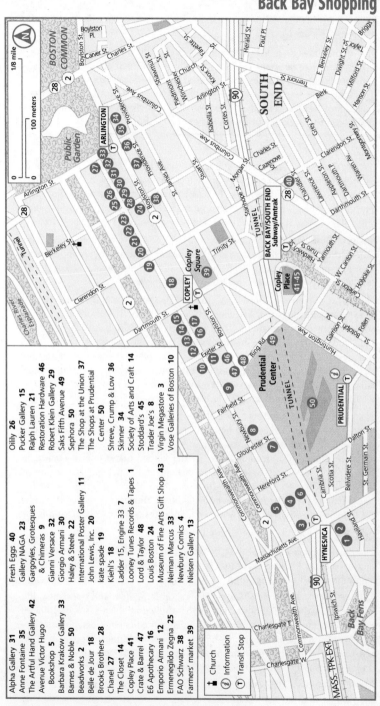

Alpha Gallery **31**
Anne Fontaine **35**
The Artful Hand Gallery **42**
Avenue Victor Hugo
 Bookshop **5**
Barbara Krakow Gallery **33**
Barnes & Noble **50**
Beadworks **2**
Belle de Jour **18**
Brooks Brothers **28**
Chanel **27**
The Closet **14**
Copley Place **41**
Crate & Barrel **47**
E6 Apothecary **16**
Emporio Armani **12**
Ermenegildo Zegna **25**
FAO Schwarz **38**
Farmers' market **39**

Fresh Eggs **40**
Gallery NAGA **23**
Gargoyles, Grotesques
 & Chimeras **9**
Gianni Versace **32**
Giorgio Armani **30**
Haley & Steele **22**
International Poster Gallery **11**
John Lewis, Inc. **20**
kate spade **19**
Kiehl's **18**
Ladder 15, Engine 33 **7**
Looney Tunes Records & Tapes **1**
Lord & Taylor **48**
Louis Boston **24**
Museum of Fine Arts Gift Shop **43**
Neiman Marcus **33**
Newbury Comics **4**
Nielsen Gallery **13**

Oilily **26**
Pucker Gallery **15**
Ralph Lauren **21**
Restoration Hardware **46**
Robert Klein Gallery **29**
Saks Fifth Avenue **49**
Sephora **50**
The Shop at the Union **37**
The Shops at Prudential
 Center **50**
Shreve, Crump & Low **36**
Skinner **34**
Society of Arts and Craft **14**
Stoddard's **45**
Trader Joe's **8**
Virgin Megastore **3**
Vose Galleries of Boston **10**

✝■ Church
ⓘ Information
Ⓣ Transit Stop

211

Finds   Fired Up

A good souvenir is something you'd never find anywhere else, and a **Boston Fire Department T-shirt** is a great one. They cost about $15 at most neighborhood firehouses. The handiest for out-of-towners are Engine 8, Ladder 1, on Hanover Street at Charter Street in the North End (off the Freedom Trail), and Ladder 15, Engine 33, on Boylston Street at Hereford Street in the Back Bay (near the Hynes Convention Center).

Pucker Gallery   The eclectic offerings at this 35-plus-year-old gallery include African, Asian, Inuit, and Israeli art; contemporary paintings, prints, drawings, porcelains, sculpture, and ceramics by regional and international artists; and excellent photographs. The staff is eager to discuss the art, which spreads over four floors. 171 Newbury St. © 617/267-9473. www.puckergallery.com. T: Green Line to Copley.

Robert Klein Gallery   For 19th- to 21st-century photography, head here. Among the dozens of artists represented are Diane Arbus, Robert Mapplethorpe, Man Ray, and Ansel Adams. Call ahead for hours. 38 Newbury St., 4th floor. © 617/ 267-7997. www.robertkleingallery.com. T: Green Line to Arlington.

Skinner   *Antiques Roadshow* fans, this one's for you. The show's rotating cast of appraisers includes staff members from New England's best-known auction house. Skinner mounts about 60 auctions a year in Boston (usually on weekends) and suburban Bolton. Visitors can bid or observe. You might see fine art, antiques, collectibles, jewelry, furniture, textiles, rugs, or even musical instruments. Call or check the website for information about buying a catalog, or just show up. Heritage on the Garden (Boylston and Arlington sts.), 63 Park Plaza. © 617/350- 5400. www.skinnerinc.com. T: Green Line to Arlington.

Vose Galleries of Boston   One of Vose's specialties is Hudson River School paintings—fitting, because the business and the mid-19th-century movement are about the same age. The Vose family (now in its 5th generation) runs the oldest continuously operating gallery in the United States, which opened in 1841. You'll see works of the Boston School and American Impressionists among the 18th-, 19th-, and early-20th-century American paintings, as well as contemporary pieces by American realists. Closed Sunday. 238 Newbury St. © 617/ 536-6176. www.vosegalleries.com. T: Green Line to Copley or Green Line B, C, or D to Hynes/ICA.

BOOKS

The Boston area is a book-lover's paradise. It's an important stop on most author tours; check the local papers or stop by any store that sells new books for details on **readings and book-signings.**

Avenue Victor Hugo Bookshop   This shop buys, sells, and trades new and used books and estate libraries. The thoughtfully assembled stock of 150,000 volumes is comprehensive; specialties include science fiction, biography, and history. You'll also find periodicals, with back issues of magazines that date to 1850, and a vast selection of general fiction. 353 Newbury St. © 617/266-7746. www.avenue victorhugobooks.com. T: Green Line B, C, or D to Hynes/ICA.

Barnes & Noble   The downtown branch of the national chain carries a large selection of local-interest titles and has a huge periodicals section. The similarly well-stocked Prudential Center location boasts both a lively pickup scene and plenty of kids' events. Barnes & Noble runs the bookstore operations at Boston

University and Harvard (see "College Merchandise" below). 395 Washington St. ✆ **617/426-5184.** www.barnesandnoble.com. T: Red or Orange Line to Downtown Crossing. Shops at Prudential Center, 800 Boylston St. ✆ **617/247-6959.** T: Green Line E to Prudential, Green Line to Copley, or Green Line B, C, or D to Hynes/ICA. 325 Harvard St., Brookline. ✆ **617/ 232-0594.** T: Green Line C to Coolidge Corner.

Borders Two levels of books and one of music, plus an in-house cafe, author appearances, and musical performances, make the sprawling Downtown Crossing store a popular destination. The comfy-cozy ambience of the Cambridge location makes it a good refuge when you've had enough of the mall. 10–24 School St. ✆ **617/557-7188.** www.bordersstores.com. T: Orange or Blue Line to State. CambridgeSide Galleria mall, Cambridge. ✆ **617/679-0887.** T: Green Line to Lechmere.

Brattle Book Shop Bibliophiles who start here might not get any other shopping done. This marvelous store near Macy's buys and sells used, rare, and out-of-print titles, and second-generation owner Kenneth Gloss does free appraisals. Be sure to check the carts out front for good deals on books of all ages. Closed Sunday. 9 West St. ✆ **800/447-9595** or 617/542-0210. www.brattlebookshop. com. T: Red or Green Line to Park St.

Brookline Booksmith The huge, varied selection makes this store a polymath's dream. The employees have excellent taste—look for their recommendations. Named the best bookstore in the country by *Publishers Weekly* in 1998, Brookline Booksmith boasts a great gift-and-card section and stages tons of events. 279 Harvard St., Brookline. ✆ **617/566-6660.** www.brooklinebooksmith.com. T: Green Line C to Coolidge Corner.

Curious George Goes to WordsWorth The younger sibling of the Harvard Square landmark stocks a superlative selection of children's books and gifts. Check downstairs for items that suit older kids. 1 John F. Kennedy St. ✆ **617/498-0062.** T: Red Line to Harvard.

Globe Corner Bookstore This overstuffed store (offspring of the dear departed original on the Freedom Trail) carries huge selections of travel guides and essays, maps, atlases, and globes. Check ahead for special events, such as the annual adventure-travel lecture series. 28 Church St., Cambridge. ✆ **617/497-6277.** www.globecorner.com. T: Red Line to Harvard.

Grolier Poetry Book Shop Shelves packed with poetry line this tiny space from floor to high, high ceiling. Grolier carries just what the name says: only poetry, and lots of it. 6 Plympton St., Cambridge. ✆ **617/547-4648.** T: Red Line to Harvard.

Harvard Book Store *Publishers Weekly*'s 2002 Bookseller of the Year attracts shoppers to its main level with an excellent scholarly selection and discounted bestsellers. The basement is the draw for those in the know: Prices on remainders are good, and used paperbacks (many bought for classes and hardly opened) are 50% off their original price. Check ahead for information on readings and other special events. 1256 Mass. Ave., Cambridge. ✆ **800/542-READ** outside 617, or 617/661-1515. www.harvard.com. T: Red Line to Harvard.

Rand McNally Map & Travel Store Armchair travelers who get as far as Faneuil Hall Marketplace can go 1 more block for guides, maps, games, software, travel accessories, and a great variety of globes. 84 State St. ✆ **617/720-1125.** www.randmcnally.com. T: Orange or Blue Line to State.

Schoenhof's Foreign Books The oldest foreign-language bookseller in the country stocks volumes for adults and children in more than 50 languages. It also carries dictionaries and language-learning materials for 700-plus languages and dialects, plus gift items. The multilingual staff arranges special orders at no extra charge. Closed Sunday. 76A Mt. Auburn St., Cambridge. © 617/547-8855. www. schoenhofs.com. T: Red Line to Harvard.

WordsWorth Books This sprawling store stocks more than 100,000 volumes, all (except textbooks) discounted at least 10%. It's a great place for browsing. If you prefer, the information desk staff will brainstorm with you until the database generates the title you want. 30 Brattle St., Cambridge. © 800/899-2202 or 617/354-5201. www.wordsworth.com. T: Red Line to Harvard.

COLLEGE MERCHANDISE

The big names are BU and Harvard (you'll see Boston College merchandise downtown, too), but why stop there? Look like an insider with a T-shirt from the **Emerson College Book Store,** 80 Boylston St. (© 617/728-7700; T: Green Line to Boylston); the **MIT Coop,** 3 Cambridge Center (© 617/499-3200; T: Red Line to Kendall/MIT); the **Northeastern University Bookstore,** 360 Huntington Ave. (© 617/373-2286; T: Green Line E to Northeastern); or the **Suffolk University Bookstore,** 148 Cambridge St., Beacon Hill (© 617/227-4085; T: Blue Line to Bowdoin).

Barnes & Noble at Boston University The BU crest, terrier mascot, or name appears on at least a floor's worth of clothing and just about any other item with room for a logo. The book selection is huge, and the author series brings writers to campus year-round. 660 Beacon St. © 617/267-8484. www.bkstore. com/bu. T: Green Line B, C, or D to Kenmore.

The Harvard Coop The Coop (rhymes with *hoop*), or Harvard Cooperative Society, is student-oriented but not a run-of-the-mill college bookstore. You'll find Harvard insignia merchandise, stationery, prints and posters, and music. As at BU, Barnes & Noble runs the book operation. 1400 Mass. Ave., Cambridge. © 617/499-2000. www.thecoop.com. T: Red Line to Harvard.

CRAFT GALLERIES

The Artful Hand Gallery The Artful Hand specializes, as you might guess, in handcrafted items. It shows and sells work by an excellent roster of artists. You'll see wonderful jewelry, ceramics, blown glass, wood pieces (including boxes), and sculpture, plus furniture, folk art, and books. Copley Place. © 617/262-9601. www.artfulhandgallery.com. T: Orange Line to Back Bay or Green Line to Copley.

Tips Craft Shows

New England is a hotbed of fine crafts, and the Boston area affords many opportunities to explore the latest trends in every medium and style you can imagine. Prominent artisans often have exclusive relationships with galleries; an excellent way to get an overview is to attend a show and sale. The best-known exhibitions, both in the Back Bay, are prestigious weekend events that benefit nonprofit organizations. **Crafts at the Castle** (© 617/523-6400, ext. 5987; www.artfulgift.com/catc) takes place in late November or early December at the Castle, an exhibition space on Columbus Avenue at Arlington Street; **CraftBoston** (© 617/232-7000; www.craft boston.org) takes place in mid-May at the Hynes Convention Center.

Society of Arts and Crafts   Contemporary American work, much created by New Englanders, is the focus at the oldest nonprofit craft organization in the country. The jewelry, furniture, home accessories, glass, and ceramics range from practical to purely decorative. 175 Newbury St. ✆ **617/266-1810.** www.societyofcrafts. org. T: Green Line to Copley.

CRAFT SUPPLIES

Paper Source   Gorgeous paper (writing and wrapping), cards, pens, ink, stamps, books, stickers, gifts, and custom invitations make these well-organized stores magnets for anyone with a thing for stationery stores. Be sure to check out the handmade paper from around the world. 1810 Mass. Ave., Cambridge. ✆ **617/497-1077.** www.paper-source.com. T: Red Line to Porter. 1361 Beacon St., Brookline. ✆ **617/264-2800.** T: Green Line C to Coolidge Corner.

Pearl Art & Craft Supplies   The Central Square branch of the national discount chain stocks everything you need to do it yourself, from pens and pencils to stamps and stencils to beads and fittings. 579 Mass. Ave., Cambridge. ✆ **617/547-6600.** www.pearlpaint.com. T: Red Line to Central.

DEPARTMENT STORES

Filene's   Filene's (say "Fie-*leen's*") is a full-service department store with all the usual trappings, plus a terrific cosmetics department. The original Filene's Basement (see "Discount Shopping" below) is still downstairs, under separate management. 426 Washington St. ✆ **617/357-2100.** www.filenes.com. T: Red or Orange Line to Downtown Crossing.

Lord & Taylor   Despite the strong New York association, Lord & Taylor is a Boston favorite for special-occasion outfits. Great seasonal sales, superb costume jewelry, and a wide selection of men's and women's sportswear make it a good stop even if you don't need something to wear to a wedding. 760 Boylston St. ✆ **617/262-6000.** www.lordandtaylor.com. T: Orange Line to Back Bay or Green Line to Copley.

Macy's   Across Summer Street from Filene's stands New England's largest store. It bears the hallmarks of the New York flagship, such as excellent selections of housewares, china, and silver. 450 Washington St. ✆ **617/357-3000.** www.macys.com. T: Red or Orange Line to Downtown Crossing.

Neiman Marcus   Here you'll find the trappings of true luxury, including exceptional cosmetics and unique accessories, at Texas-size prices. 5 Copley Place. ✆ **617/536-3660.** www.neimanmarcus.com. T: Orange Line to Back Bay or Green Line to Copley.

Saks Fifth Avenue   This is another classy New York name noted for its fashion and cosmetics. Don't forget to check out the shoe collections. If you aren't up for tangling with mall crowds, enter from Ring Road. Prudential Plaza, 786 Boylston St. ✆ **617/262-8500.** www.saksfifthavenue.com. T: Green Line to Copley or Orange Line to Back Bay.

DISCOUNT SHOPPING

DSW Shoe Warehouse   Here you'll find two large floors of discounted women's and men's shoes, boots, sandals, and sneakers. Check the clearance racks for the real deals. 385 Washington St. ✆ **617/556-0052.** www.dswshoe.com. T: Red or Orange Line to Downtown Crossing.

Eddie Bauer Outlet   Not what you might expect from an outlet—the prices aren't breathtaking, but the quality and selection are good. 500 Washington St. ✆ **617/423-4722.** www.eddiebaueroutlet.com. T: Red or Orange Line to Downtown Crossing.

Filene's Basement *Value* New England's most famous discount retailer opened in 1908 (it's now a subsidiary of the Midwestern chain Value City). Its celebrated automatic markdowns apply only at this location, the original. With the rise of competing chains, deals worth bragging about have become harder to find than they once were, but just as rewarding when you do. I happen to love that sort of thing, but if you don't, you might find that battling the no-holds-barred crowds isn't worth the payoff—the aisles are pretty wild at busy times.

The automatic-markdown policy (25% off the already-discounted price after 2 weeks on the selling floor, up to 75% after 4 weeks) applies to everything from lingerie to overcoats. The most ego-boosting quarries are designer and other top-quality clothes and shoes at a fraction of their original prices. Try to beat the lunchtime crowds, and check the papers for early opening times during special sales—notably the $249 wedding-dress blowout, at least twice a year. 426 Washington St. ℂ 617/542-2011. www.filenesbasement.com. T: Red or Orange Line to Downtown Crossing.

FASHION
Also see "Shoes & Boots" and "Vintage & Secondhand Clothing" later in this chapter.

ADULTS
Newbury Street is ground zero for high-end boutiques and if-you-have-to-ask-you-can't-afford-it designer shops. Bring your platinum card to **Chanel,** 15 Arlington St., in the Ritz-Carlton, Boston (ℂ **617/859-0055**); **Ermenegildo Zegna,** 39 Newbury St. (ℂ **617/424-6657**); **Gianni Versace,** 12 Newbury St. (ℂ **617/536-8300**); and **kate spade,** 117 Newbury St. (ℂ **617/262-2632**).

Anne Fontaine This is the first U.S. outlet for the designer's "perfect white blouse collection from Paris." I wanted to laugh, but then I saw for myself— almost every item *is* a perfect (for one reason or another) white blouse. Prices start at $80. Closed Sunday. Heritage on the Garden (Boylston and Arlington sts.), 318 Boylston St. ℂ 617/423-0366. www.annefontaine.com. T: Green Line to Arlington.

Belle de Jour A European-style lingerie boutique, Belle de Jour stops at nothing in its quest to bring high-end unmentionables (and sleepwear) to buttoned-up Bostonians. Closed Sunday. 164 Newbury St. ℂ 617/236-4554. www.belle-de-jour.com. T: Green Line to Copley.

Brooks Brothers Would-be "proper Bostonians" head here for blue blazers, gray flannels, seersucker suits, and less conservative business and casual wear for men and women. Brooks is the only place for exactly the right preppy shade of pink button-down oxford shirts—something I've never seen at the outlet stores. 46 Newbury St. ℂ 617/267-2600. www.brooksbrothers.com. T: Green Line to Arlington. 75 State St. ℂ 617/261-9990. T: Orange or Blue Line to State.

Dakini Come here for fleece in every form, from shearling-like jackets to velvety gloves, high-fashion women's separates to kids' pullovers. You'll see casual warm-weather fashions as well, but the locally made fleece clothing is the star of the show. Although it's not cheap, it's top quality, and the regular sales can make you feel both toasty and thrifty. 1704 Mass. Ave., Cambridge. ℂ 617/864-7661. www.dakini.com. T: Red Line to Porter.

Giorgio Armani Here you'll find Armani's sleek, sophisticated men's and women's clothing in a museum-like setting. If your taste (and budget) is less grand, head down the street to **Emporio Armani,** 210–214 Newbury St.

(© **617/262-7300;** T: Green Line to Copley). It carries sportswear, jeans, evening wear, and home accessories. 22 Newbury St. © **617/267-3200.** www.giorgio armani.com. T: Green Line to Arlington.

H&M   The Swedish discount-fashion juggernaut is a terrific place to look for cheap, stylish clothing and accessories for women, men, and kids. 350 Washington St. © **617/482-7001.** www.hm.com. T: Red or Orange Line to Downtown Crossing.

Louis Boston   Louis (pronounced "Louie's") enjoys a well-deserved reputation for offering cutting-edge New York style in a traditional Boston setting. The ultraprestigious store sells designer men's suits, handmade shirts, silk ties, and Italian shoes. The merchandise represents a mix of big names, emerging stars, and the celebrated house label, and the women's fashions are equally elegant. Also on the premises are an "apothecary" department, a full-service salon, and Café Louis, which serves lunch and dinner. 234 Berkeley St. © **800/225-5135** or 617/262-6100. www.louisboston.com. T: Green Line to Arlington.

Ralph Lauren   Just setting foot in this luxurious building is a trip—it feels like walking into a magazine ad. The Waspy fantasyland boasts three floors of fashion and accessories for you and your own mansion. 93–95 Newbury St. © **617/ 424-1124.** www.polo.com. T: Green Line to Arlington.

CHILDREN

Calliope *Finds*   The must-see window displays at this Harvard Square shop use stuffed animals, clothes, and toys to illustrate sayings and proverbs, often twisted into hilarious puns. The merchandise inside—clothing, shoes, accessories, and gifts, including a huge selection of plush animals—is equally delightful. 33 Brattle St., Cambridge. © **617/876-4149.** T: Red Line to Harvard.

Oilily   At this end of Newbury Street, even kids must be *au courant.* Lend a hand with a visit to the Boston branch of the chichi international chain, which specializes in brightly colored clothing and accessories. It stages several fashion shows a year; call ahead if you hope to catch one. There's also a women's store at 32 Newbury St. (© **617/247-2386**). 31 Newbury St. © **800/964-5459** or 617/247-9299. www.oililyusa.com. T: Green Line to Arlington.

Saturday's Child   Never mind the nursery rhyme—"Saturday's child works hard for a living," my foot. You won't want your little angel lifting a finger in these precious (in both senses of the word) outfits. You'll also find top-quality shoes, accessories, and toys. 1762 Mass. Ave., Cambridge. © **617/661-6402.** T: Red Line to Porter.

Varese Shoes   One window holds men's shoes, but that's not why you hear oohing and aahing all the way from the Freedom Trail (10 steps away). The other window is full of adorable Italian leather children's shoes. 285 Hanover St. © 617/523-6530. T: Green or Orange Line to Haymarket.

FOOD

Cardullo's Gourmet Shoppe   A veritable United Nations of fancy food, this Harvard Square landmark carries specialties (including beer, wine, and a huge variety of candy) from just about everywhere. If you can't afford the big-ticket items, order a tasty sandwich to go. 6 Brattle St., Cambridge. © 617/491-8888. T: Red Line to Harvard.

Dairy Fresh Candies *Finds*   This North End hole-in-the-wall is crammed with sweets and other delectables, from nuts and dried fruit to imported Italian specialties. Before sweet-tooth–oriented holidays (especially Easter), it's irresistible. There's also a fine gourmet-condiment selection. The store is too small for turning children loose, but they'll be happy they waited outside when you return with fuel for the Freedom Trail. 57 Salem St. © 800/336-5536 or 617/742-2639. www.dairyfreshcandies.com. T: Green or Orange Line to Haymarket.

Oliviers & Co.   This French chain operates just a handful of U.S. outlets, but scarcity isn't the only reason for foodies to check out this little shop. The stock is of the highest quality, and the atmosphere evokes a top-notch wine store (right down to suggestions of food pairings). 161 Newbury St. © 877/828-6620 or 617/859-8841. www.oliviers-co.com. T: Green Line to Copley.

Savenor's Supermarket   Long a Cambridge institution (and a Julia Child favorite), Savenor's moved to Beacon Hill in 1993. It's the perfect place to load up on provisions before a concert or movie on the nearby Esplanade. And it's *the* local purveyor of exotic meats—if you crave buffalo or rattlesnake, this is the place. 160 Charles St. © 617/723-6328. bestonblock@msn.com. T: Red Line to Charles/MGH.

Trader Joe's   This celebrated California-based retailer stocks a great selection of natural and organic products, wine, cheese, nuts, baked goods, and other edibles, at excellent prices. Get a preview from the website or just ask devotees—they can't shut up about it. The Cambridge location is a good place to stop for picnic provisions if you're driving. 899 Boylston St. © 617/262-6505. www.traderjoes. com. T: Green Line B, C, or D to Hynes/ICA. 1317 Beacon St., Brookline. © 617/278-9997. T: Green Line C to Coolidge Corner. 727 Memorial Dr., Cambridge. © 617/491-8582.

GIFTS & SOUVENIRS

Boston has dozens of shops and pushcarts that sell T-shirts, hats, and other souvenirs. At the stores listed here, you'll find gifts that say Boston without actually *saying* "Boston" all over them. Remember to check out museum shops for unique items, including crafts and games. Particularly good outlets include those at the **Museum of Fine Arts,** the **Museum of Science,** the **Isabella Stewart Gardner Museum,** the **Concord Museum,** and the **Peabody Essex Museum** in Salem.

Black Ink   The wacky wares defy categorization, but they all fit comfortably under the umbrella of "oh, cool." Rubber stamps, sleek office accessories, and fancy bath wares caught my eye recently; greeting cards and retro toys are equally appealing. 101 Charles St. © 617/723-3883. T: Red Line to Charles/MGH. 5 Brattle St., Cambridge. © 617/497-1221. T: Red Line to Harvard.

Joie de Vivre *Finds*   When I'm stumped for a present for a person who has everything, I head to this delightful little shop. Joie de Vivre's selection of gifts and toys for adults and sophisticated children is beyond compare. The kaleidoscope collection alone is worth the trip; you'll also find jewelry, note cards, puzzles, and even salt and pepper shakers. 1792 Mass. Ave., Cambridge. ℭ 617/864-8188. T: Red Line to Porter.

Museum of Fine Arts Gift Shop   For those without the time or inclination to visit the museum, the satellite shops carry posters, prints, cards and stationery, books, educational toys, scarves, mugs, T-shirts, and reproductions of jewelry in the museum's collections. You might even be inspired to pay a call on the real thing. Copley Place. ℭ 617/536-8818. T: Orange Line to Back Bay or Green Line to Copley. South Market Building, Faneuil Hall Marketplace. ℭ 617/720-1266. T: Green or Blue Line to Government Center.

The Shop at the Union   This large, crowded store carries a wide selection of high-quality home, garden, and personal accessories. You'll see jewelry, greeting cards, antiques, needlework, handmade children's clothes, toys, and confections. Most of the merchandise is manufactured by women or by woman-owned firms. And your spree is practically guilt-free: Proceeds benefit the human services programs of the Women's Educational and Industrial Union, a nonprofit educational and social-service organization founded in 1877. 356 Boylston St. ℭ 617/536-5651. www.weiu.org. T: Green Line to Arlington.

HOME & GARDEN

Abodeon   My notes say "groovy, retro, vintage"—was it the 20th-century furniture and home accessories? The classic kitchen equipment and tableware? The "stay tuned, *Laugh-In* will be right back" vibe? This place is great for browsing—and hey, it made me use the word "groovy." 1713 Mass. Ave., Cambridge. ℭ 617/497-0137. T: Red Line to Porter.

Cocoon   Sleek furnishings and accessories, mostly of natural materials—wood, glass, paper, metal, fiber, even stone—create a contemporary yet soothing atmosphere. The shop, near the Loews Boston Common movie theater, makes a good detour between the Back Bay and Downtown Crossing. Closed Sunday. 170 Tremont St. ℭ 617/728-9898. www.cocoonhome.com. T: Green Line to Boylston.

Crate & Barrel   This is wedding-present heaven, packed with contemporary and classic housewares. The merchandise, from juice glasses and linen napkins to top-of-the-line knives and roasting pans, suits every budget. The Boylston Street location (which also stocks the full line of housewares) and the Mass. Ave. store carry furniture and home accessories. South Market Building, Faneuil Hall Marketplace. ℭ 617/742-6025. www.crateandbarrel.com. T: Green or Blue Line to Government Center. 777 Boylston St. ℭ 617/262-8700. T: Green Line to Copley. 48 Brattle St., Cambridge. ℭ 617/876-6300. T: Red Line to Harvard. 1045 Mass. Ave., Cambridge. ℭ 617/547-3994. T: Red Line to Harvard.

Diptyque   I'm not a candle person, but even I admire the subtly scented offerings at this Parisian outpost. The shop carries other scented products, such as soaps and room sprays, but if you're looking for a hostess gift with off-the-charts snob appeal, you can't go wrong with a Diptyque candle ($40). 123 Newbury St. ℭ 617/351-2430. T: Green Line to Copley.

Fresh Eggs *(Finds)*   Venture into the South End for the latest in stylish home accessories, an irresistible assortment of classic designs and light-hearted touches. From kitchen gadgets to imported linens to tabletop accessories, everything is fun and functional. Closed Monday. 58 Clarendon St. ℭ 617/247-8150. T: Orange Line to Back Bay.

Koo De Kir   In the heart of 19th-century Beacon Hill, Koo De Kir is a splash of the 21st century. Owner Kristine Irving has a great eye, and her selection of contemporary home accessories, furniture, lighting, and sculpture ranges from classics-to-be to downright whimsical. 34 Charles St. ℂ 617/723-8111. www.koodekir. com. T: Red Line to Charles/MGH.

Restoration Hardware   This national chain specializes in old-fashioned style at new-fashioned prices. The merchandise runs more to home accessories, toys, and furniture than to hardware (although there's plenty of that, too) and makes for great browsing. 711 Boylston St. ℂ 617/578-0088. www.restorationhardware. com. T: Green Line to Copley.

Stoddard's   The oldest cutlery shop in the country (since 1800), Stoddard's is full of items that you don't know you need until you see them. You'll find scissors for just about any use, knives of all descriptions—including a spectacular selection of Swiss army knives—shaving brushes, binoculars, fishing tackle, and fly rods. 50 Temple Place. ℂ 617/426-4187. T: Red or Orange Line to Downtown Crossing. Copley Place. ℂ 617/536-8688. T: Orange Line to Back Bay or Green Line to Copley.

JEWELRY

For information on Boston's best-known jewelry emporium, **Shreve, Crump & Low,** see "Antiques & Collectibles" earlier in this chapter.

Beadworks   The jewelry at these shops will suit you exactly—you make it yourself. Prices for the dazzling variety of raw materials start at 5¢ a bead, fittings (hardware) are available, and you can assemble your finery at the in-store worktable. Beadworks also carries ready-made pieces and schedules jewelry-making workshops; check ahead for details. 167 Newbury St. ℂ 617/247-7227. www. beadworksboston.com. T: Green Line to Copley. 23 Church St., Cambridge. ℂ 617/868-9777. T: Red Line to Harvard.

High Gear Jewelry   Don't be put off by the sign saying that this eye-catching shop around the corner from the Paul Revere House (on the Freedom Trail) is a wholesale outlet. Retail shoppers are welcome to peruse the impressive selection of reasonably priced costume jewelry, watches, and hair accessories. 139 Richmond St. ℂ 617/523-5804. hgjewelry@aol.com. T: Green or Orange Line to Haymarket.

John Lewis, Inc. *Finds*   John Lewis's imaginative women's and men's jewelry— crafted on the premises—suits both traditional and trendy tastes. The wide selection of silver, gold, and platinum items and unusual colored stones makes the shop even more alluring. The pieces that mark you as a savvy Bostonian are earrings, necklaces, and bracelets made of hammered metal circles. Closed Sunday and Monday. 97 Newbury St. ℂ 617/266-6665. www.johnlewisinc.com. T: Green Line to Arlington.

MALLS & SHOPPING CENTERS

CambridgeSide Galleria   This three-level mall houses two large department stores—**Filene's** (ℂ 617/621-3800) and **Sears** (ℂ 617/252-3500)—and more than 100 specialty stores. Pleasant but quite generic, it might be the bargaining chip you need to lure your teenager to the nearby Museum of Science.

There's trendy sportswear at **Abercrombie & Fitch** (ℂ 617/494-1338), electronics at **Cambridge SoundWorks** (ℂ 617/225-3900) and the **Apple Store** (ℂ 617/225-0442), casual clothing at **J. Crew** (ℂ 617/225-2739), and music and appliances at **Best Buy** (ℂ 617/225-2004). The mall also has a branch of **Borders** (ℂ 617/679-0887), three restaurants, a food court, and seating along a pleasant canal.

Strollers and complimentary wheelchairs are available. Open Monday through Saturday from 10am to 9:30pm, Sunday from 11am to 7pm. 100 CambridgeSide Place, Cambridge. ✆ 617/621-8666. www.shopcambridgeside.com. T: Green Line to Lechmere, or Red Line to Kendall/MIT and free shuttle bus (every 10–20 min.). Garage parking from $1/hr.

Copley Place   Copley Place has set the standard for upscale shopping in Boston since 1985. Connected to the Westin and Marriott hotels and the Prudential Center, it's a crossroads for office workers, moviegoers, out-of-towners, and enthusiastic consumers. You can while away a couple of hours or a whole day shopping and dining here and at the adjacent Shops at Prudential Center (discussed later in this section) without ever going outdoors.

Some of Copley Place's 100-plus shops will be familiar from the mall at home, but this is emphatically not a suburban shopping complex that happens to be in the city. You'll see famous stores that don't have another branch in Boston: **Caswell-Massey** (✆ 617/437-9292), **Christian Dior** (✆ 617/927-7577), **Gucci** (✆ 617/247-3000), **Louis Vuitton** (✆ 617/437-6519), **Tiffany & Co.** (✆ 617/353-0222), and a suitably classy "anchor" department store, **Neiman Marcus** (✆ 617/536-3660). Also here are the **Artful Hand Gallery** (see "Craft Galleries" above), a **Museum of Fine Arts Gift Shop** (see "Gifts & Souvenirs" above), and a branch of **Stoddard's** (see "Home & Garden" above).

Open Monday through Saturday from 10am to 8pm, Sunday from noon to 6pm. Some stores have extended hours, and the theaters and some restaurants are open through late evening. 100 Huntington Ave. ✆ 617/369-5000. www.shopcopley place.com. T: Orange Line to Back Bay or Green Line to Copley. Discounted validated parking with purchase.

Faneuil Hall Marketplace   The original festival market is both wildly popular and widely imitated, and Faneuil Hall Marketplace changes constantly to appeal to visitors as well as locals wary of its touristy reputation. The original part of **Faneuil Hall** itself dates to 1742, and the lower floors preserve its retail roots. The **Quincy Market Colonnade,** in the central building, houses a gargantuan selection of food and confections. The bars and restaurants always seem to be crowded, and the shopping is terrific, if generic.

In and around the five buildings, the shops combine "only in Boston" with "only at every mall in the country." **Marketplace Center** and the ground floors of the **North Market and South Market buildings** have lots of chain outlets. Most of the unique offerings are under the Quincy Market canopies on the **pushcarts** piled high with crafts and gifts, and upstairs or downstairs in the market buildings. The only way to find what suits you is to explore.

Shop hours are Monday through Saturday from 10am to 9pm and Sunday from noon to 6pm. The Colonnade opens earlier, and most bars and restaurants close later. If you must drive, many businesses offer a discount at the 75 State

---

⟨Tips **Flying Lobsters**

Why go to the trouble of sending a postcard? Send a lobster instead. **James Hook & Co.,** 15 Northern Ave. at Atlantic Avenue (✆ **617/423-5500;** T: Red Line to South Station), and **Legal Sea Foods Fresh by Mail,** Logan Airport Terminal C (✆ **800/477-5342** or 617/569-4622; T: Blue Line to Airport), handle the overnight shipping.

St. Garage; there's also parking in the Government Center garage off Congress Street and the marketplace's crowded garage off Atlantic Avenue. Between North, Congress, and State sts. and I-93. © 617/338-2323. www.faneuilhallmarketplace.com. T: Green or Blue Line to Government Center or Orange Line to Haymarket.

The Shops at Prudential Center   The main level of the city's second-tallest tower holds this sprawling complex. In addition to **Lord & Taylor** (© 617/ 262-6000) and **Saks Fifth Avenue** (© 617/262-8500), there are more than 40 shops and boutiques, a large **Barnes & Noble** (see "Books" above), a food court, a "fashion court," a post office, and five restaurants, including Legal Sea Foods and California Pizza Kitchen. Vendors sell gifts, souvenirs, and novelty items off pushcarts in the arcades, the Greater Boston Convention & Visitors Bureau operates an **information booth,** and there's outdoor space in front if you need some fresh air. If you're planning a picnic, at ground level on Boylston Street is a **Star Market** supermarket (© 617/267-9721). **Restaurant Marché Mövenpick** (© 617/578-9700; www.marcheusa.com), near the Huntington Avenue and Belvidere Street entrances, is an enormous, frantic "food theater." It serves everything from salad and sushi to grilled meats and fresh baked goods at islands and stations where your meal or snack is cooked to order while you wait.

Hours are Monday through Saturday from 10am to 8pm, Sunday from 11am to 6pm. The restaurants and food court stay open later. 800 Boylston St. © 800/ SHOP-PRU. www.prudentialcenter.com. T: Green Line E to Prudential, Green Line to Copley, or Green Line B, C, or D to Hynes/ICA. Discounted validated parking with purchase.

MARKETS
Massachusetts farmers and growers under the auspices of the state **Department of Food and Agriculture** (© 617/227-3018) dispatch trucks filled with whatever's in season to the heart of the city from July through November. Depending on the time of year, you'll have your pick of berries, herbs, tomatoes, squash, pumpkins, apples, corn, and more, all fresh and reasonably priced. Stop by City Hall Plaza on Mondays and Wednesdays (T: Green or Blue Line to Government Center), or Copley Square on Tuesdays and Fridays (T: Green Line to Copley or Orange Line to Back Bay).

MUSIC
Disc Diggers   Disc Diggers boasts of carrying the largest selection of used CDs in New England. There's no way to check that, but it *looks* true. Definitely worth an excursion, maybe before a show at the nearby Somerville Theater or Johnny D's. 401 Highland Ave., Somerville. © 617/776-7560. www.discdiggers.com. T: Red Line to Davis.

Looney Tunes Records & Tapes   Where there are college students, there are pizza places, copy shops, and used-record (and CD) stores. These two Looney Tunes locations specialize in classical, jazz, and rock, and they have tons of other tunes at excellent prices. 1106 Boylston St. © 617/247-2238. T: Green Line B, C, or D to Hynes/ICA. 1001 Mass. Ave., Cambridge © 617/876-5624. T: Red Line to Harvard.

Newbury Comics   You'll find a wide selection of CDs, tapes, posters, and T-shirts—and, of course, comics—at the branches of this funky chain. The music is particularly cutting-edge, with lots of independent labels and imports. 332 Newbury St. © 617/236-4930. www.newbury.com. T: Green Line B, C, or D to Hynes/ICA. 1 Washington Mall, off State St. at Washington St. © 617/248-9992. T: Orange or Blue Line to State. 36 John F. Kennedy St., Cambridge © 617/491-0337. T: Red Line to Harvard.

Tower Records   The local branches of the mega-chain carry records, tapes, CDs, videos, periodicals, and books. Hot recordings draw crowds to the Boston store on Monday nights in anticipation of the official midnight release. 1349 Boylston St. ℂ 617/247-5900. www.towerrecords.com. T: Green Line B, C, or D to Hynes/ICA or Kenmore; 10-min. walk. 95 Mount Auburn St., Cambridge ℂ 617/876-3377. T: Red Line to Harvard.

Virgin Megastore   The entertainment preview system! The plasma-screen TVs! The interactive kiosks! The cafe! And oh, yeah, the music—a huge selection, as befits a 40,000-square-foot store, including a notable classical section. Virgin roared into Boston in 2002 and quickly established itself as a can't-miss destination for the limited-attention-span set. 360 Newbury St. (at Mass. Ave.). ℂ 617/896-0950. www.virginmega.com. T: Green Line B, C, or D to Hynes/ICA.

PERFUME & COSMETICS

Colonial Drug *Finds*   The perfume counter at this family business puts the "special" in "specialize." You can choose from more than 1,000 fragrances—plus cosmetics, soap, and countless other body-care products—with the help of the gracious staff members. They remain unflappable even during Harvard Square's equivalent of rush hour, Saturday afternoon. 49 Brattle St., Cambridge. ℂ 617/864-2222. T: Red Line to Harvard.

E6 Apothecary   This place is the exact opposite of scary department store cosmetic counters. The friendly staffers can guide you toward the right formula for your face, and they're equally helpful whether you're spending $5 or $500. E6 regularly adds new lines, and it carries many brands that are hard (or impossible) to find north of New York. 167 Newbury St. ℂ 800/664-6635 or 617/236-8138. www.e6apothecary.com. T: Green Line to Copley.

Kiehl's   Lots of trends originate in New York, but few of them develop this kind of cult following. Customers wax evangelical over the skin, hair, and body potions from Kiehl's ("since 1851"), which straddle the line between cosmetics and pharmaceuticals. 112 Newbury St. ℂ 617/247-1777. www.kiehls.com. T: Green Line to Copley.

Sephora   The European phenomenon is a *fashionista* magnet. Here you'll find an encyclopedic, international selection of manufacturers and products in a well-lit, well-organized space overflowing with testers. Everything is self-service, and the staff provides as much help as you want. Shops at Prudential Center, 800 Boylston St. ℂ 617/262-4200. www.sephora.com. T: Green Line E to Prudential, Green Line to Copley, or Green Line or B, C, or D to Hynes/ICA.

SHOES & BOOTS

Also see the listing for **DSW Shoe Warehouse** under "Discount Shopping" earlier in this chapter.

Berk's Shoes   "Trendy" is inadequate to describe the wares at this Harvard Square institution. College students and people who want to look like them come here to stock up on whatever's fashionable right this red-hot minute. 50 John F. Kennedy St. ℂ 617/492-9511. www.berkshoes.com. T: Red Line to Harvard.

Helen's Leather Shop   Homesick Texans visit Helen's just to gaze upon the boots. Many are handmade from exotic leathers, including ostrich, buffalo, and many varieties of snakeskin. The shop carries name brands such as Lucchese and Tony Lama, along with a large selection of other leather goods. 110 Charles St. ℂ 617/742-2077. www.helensleather.com. T: Red Line to Charles/MGH.

InVestments   InVestments carries women's shoes in sizes 9 to 14. If you're in this neglected demographic, you'll glory in the selection, which ranges from comfortable (Naturalizer) to sexy (Stuart Weitzman, Anne Klein), with plenty of options in between. 125 Newbury St., 4th floor. ℂ **888/371-SHOE** or 617/247-0202. www. designershoes.com. T: Green Line to Copley.

TOYS & GAMES
A number of businesses listed earlier in this chapter are good places to look for toys. They include most of the shops under "Gifts & Souvenirs," **Curious George Goes to WordsWorth** (see "Books") and **Calliope** (see "Fashion").

FAO Schwarz   The giant teddy bear out front is the first indication that you're in for a good time, and a teddy bear wouldn't steer you wrong. A branch of the famed New York emporium (and a survivor of the chain's bankruptcy filing), FAO Schwarz stocks top-quality toys, dolls, stuffed animals, games, books, and vehicles (motorized and not). 440 Boylston St. (aᵗ Berkeley St.). ℂ **617/262-5900.** www. fao.com. T: Green Line to Arlington.

The Games People Play   Just outside Harvard Square, this quarter-century-old business carries enough board games to outfit every country, summer, and beach house in New England. There are puzzles, playing cards, role-playing games, and chess and backgammon sets, too. 1100 Mass. Ave., Cambridge. ℂ **800/696-0711** or 617/492-0711. T: Red Line to Harvard.

Stellabella Toys   A large space that's both retro (lots of wooden toys) and modern (no guns), Stellabella is a welcoming destination for parents and kids alike. It carries everything from newborn trinkets to craft supplies and costumes for big kids, and the friendly staff can lend a hand if you need help maintaining your status as the cool aunt or uncle. 1360 Cambridge St., Cambridge. ℂ **617/491-6290.** T: Red Line to Central; 10-min. walk on Prospect St.

VINTAGE & SECONDHAND CLOTHING
The Closet   This is the not-very-secret weapon of many a chic shopper. One of Boston's best consignment shops, it offers "gently worn" designer clothing for women and men at drastically reduced prices. 175 Newbury St. ℂ **617/536-1919.** www.theclosetboston.com. T: Green Line to Copley.

The Garment District   You're hitting the clubs and you want to look cool, but you have almost no money. You'll be right at home among the shoppers here, paying great prices for a huge selection of contemporary and vintage clothing, costumes, and accessories. Merchandise on the first floor is sold (no kidding) by the pound. 200 Broadway, Cambridge. ℂ **617/876-5230.** www.garment-district. com. T: Red Line to Kendall/MIT.

Oona's   From funky accessories and costume jewelry to vintage dresses nice enough to get married in, Oona's carries an extensive selection of "experienced clothing" at good prices. The Harvard Square stalwart celebrated its 30th anniversary in 2003. 1210 Mass. Ave., Cambridge. ℂ **617/491-2654.** T: Red Line to Harvard.

10

Boston After Dark

Countless musicians, actors, and comedians went to college or got their start in the Boston area, and it's a great place to check out rising stars and promising unknowns. You might get an early look at the next Branford Marsalis, Denis Leary, Susan Tedeschi, or Yo-Yo Ma. And you'll certainly be able to enjoy the work of many established artists.

The nightlife scene is, to put it mildly, not exactly world-class—you can be home from a night on the town when your friends in New York are still drying their hair. Closing time for clubs is 2am, which means packing a lot into 4 hours or so.

The hottest news on the late-night scene is the **smoking ban** Boston imposed in 2003. It forbids smoking in all workplaces—including bars, clubs, and restaurants. The tobacco taboo may have spread to the rest of the state by the time you visit, but at press time, Cambridge still permitted puffing.

For up-to-date entertainment listings, consult the "Calendar" section of Thursday's *Boston Globe,* the "Scene" section of Friday's *Boston Herald,* and Sunday's arts sections of both papers. Three free publications, available at newspaper boxes around town, publish nightlife listings: the weekly *Boston Phoenix,* and the biweekly *Stuff@Night* (a *Phoenix* offshoot), and *Improper Bostonian.*

The *Phoenix* website (**www.boston phoenix.com**) archives the paper's season-preview issues; especially before a summer or fall visit, it's a worthwhile planning tool.

For more pointers on organizing your evening, turn to the "Suggested Evening Itineraries" box on p. 146.

⟨Value **Let's Make a Deal**

Yankee thrift gains artistic expression at the **BosTix** booths at Faneuil Hall Marketplace, on the south side of Faneuil Hall (T: Green or Blue Line to Government Center or Orange Line to Haymarket), and in Copley Square at the corner of Boylston and Dartmouth streets (T: Green Line to Copley or Orange Line to Back Bay). Same-day tickets to musical and theatrical performances are half price, subject to availability. Credit cards are not accepted, and there are no refunds or exchanges. Check the board or the website for the day's offerings.

BosTix (© **617/482-2849;** www.artsboston.org) also offers full-price advance tickets; discounts on more than 100 theater, music, and dance events; and tickets to museums, historic sites, and attractions in and around town. The booths, which are Ticketmaster outlets, also sell coupon books with discounted and two-for-one admission to many area museums and attractions. Open Tuesday through Saturday from 10am to 6pm (half-price tickets go on sale at 11am), and Sunday from 11am to 4pm. The Copley Square location is also open Monday from 10am to 6pm.

GETTING TICKETS

Some companies and venues sell tickets over the phone or the Internet; many will refer you to a ticket agency. The major agencies that serve Boston, **Ticketmaster** (© 617/931-2000; www.ticketmaster.com), **Next Ticketing** (© 617/423-NEXT; www.nextticketing.com), and **Tele-Charge** (© 800/447-7400 or TTY 888/889-8587; www.telecharge.com, click "Across the USA"), calculate service charges per ticket, not per order. To avoid the fee, visit the box office in person. If you wait until the day before or day of a performance, you'll sometimes have access to tickets that were held back for some reason and have just gone on sale.

1 The Performing Arts

CONCERT HALLS & AUDITORIUMS

The **Hatch Shell** on the Esplanade (© 617/727-9547, ext. 450) is an amphitheater best known for the Boston Pops' Fourth of July concerts. On many summer nights, free music and dance performances and films take over the stage, to the delight of crowds on the lawn. (T: Red Line to Charles/MGH, or Green Line to Arlington.)

Berklee Performance Center   The Berklee College of Music's theater features professional artists (many of them former Berklee students), instructors, and students. Offerings are heavy on jazz and folk, with plenty of other options. 136 Mass. Ave. © 617/747-8890. www.berkleebpc.com. T: Green Line B, C, or D to Hynes/ICA.

Boston Center for the Arts   Five performance spaces and an anything-goes booking policy make the BCA a leading venue for contemporary theater, music and dance performances, visual arts exhibitions, and poetry and prose readings. 539 Tremont St. © 617/426-7700 (events line) or 617/426-2787 (box office). www.bcaonline.org. T: Orange Line to Back Bay.

Emerson Majestic Theatre   A popular dance and music performance space, the gorgeous Emerson Majestic is the home stage of several small arts companies. The newly renovated 1903 theater also books Emerson College student productions. 219 Tremont St. © 617/824-8000 or 800/233-3123 (Tele-Charge). www.maj.org. T: Green Line to Boylston or Orange Line to Chinatown.

Jordan Hall   The New England Conservatory of Music's auditorium features students and professionals. It presents classical instrumental and vocal soloists, chamber music, and, occasionally, contemporary artists. 30 Gainsborough St. © 617/536-2412 or 617/262-1120, ext. 700 (concert line). www.newenglandconservatory.edu/jordanhall. T: Green Line E to Symphony, or Orange Line to Mass. Ave.

Sanders Theatre   A landmark space in Harvard's Memorial Hall, Sanders Theatre is a lecture hall and performance venue that books big names in classical, folk, and world music, as well as student performances. 45 Quincy St. (at Cambridge St.), Cambridge. © 617/496-2222. www.fas.harvard.edu/~memhall. T: Red Line to Harvard.

Symphony Hall   Acoustically perfect Symphony Hall, which celebrated its 100th anniversary in 2000, is the home of the **Boston Symphony Orchestra** and the **Boston Pops.** When they're away, top-notch classical and chamber music artists from elsewhere take over. 301 Mass. Ave. (at Huntington Ave.). © 617/266-1492 or 617/CONCERT (program information). SymphonyCharge © 888/266-1200 (from outside 617 area code) or 617/266-1200. www.bso.org. T: Green Line E to Symphony, or Orange Line to Mass. Ave.

Wang Theatre   Also known as the Wang Center, this Art Deco palace is home to **Boston Ballet,** and it books numerous and varied national companies. On some Monday evenings, it reverts to its roots as a movie theater and shows classic films on an enormous screen. 270 Tremont St. 📞 617/482-9393 or 800/447-7400 (Tele-Charge). www.wangcenter.org. T: Green Line to Boylston, or Orange Line to New England Medical Center.

CLASSICAL MUSIC

Boston Symphony Orchestra   The Boston Symphony, one of the world's greatest, was founded in 1881. The repertoire includes contemporary music, but classical is the BSO's calling card—you might want to schedule your trip to coincide with a particular performance, or with a visit by a celebrated guest artist. James Levine, who remains artistic director of New York City's Metropolitan Opera, replaces Seiji Ozawa as music director in fall 2004; until then, guest conductors (including Levine) will wield the baton.

The season runs from October to April, with performances most Tuesday, Thursday, and Saturday evenings; Friday afternoons; and some Friday evenings. Explanatory talks (included in the ticket price) begin 30 minutes before the curtain. If you couldn't get tickets in advance, check at the box office for returns from subscribers 2 hours before show time. A limited number of **rush tickets** (one per person) are available on the day of the performance for Tuesday and Thursday evening and Friday afternoon programs. Some Wednesday evening and Thursday morning rehearsals are open to the public. Symphony Hall, 301 Mass. Ave. (at Huntington Ave.). 📞 617/266-1492 or 617/CONCERT (program information). SymphonyCharge 📞 888/266-1200 (outside 617 area code) or 617/266-1200. www.bso.org. Tickets $25–$90. Rush tickets $8 (on sale Fri 9am; Tues, Thurs 5pm). Rehearsal tickets $15. T: Green Line E to Symphony, or Orange Line to Mass. Ave.

Boston Pops   From early May to early July, members of the Boston Symphony Orchestra lighten up. Tables and chairs replace the floor seats at Symphony Hall, and drinks and light refreshments are served. Under the direction of conductor Keith Lockhart, the Pops plays a range of music from light classical to show tunes to popular music (hence the name), often with celebrity guest stars. Performances are Tuesday through Sunday evenings. Special holiday performances in December ($20–$95) usually sell out well in advance, but it can't hurt to check; tickets go on sale in late October.

The regular season ends with a week of **free outdoor concerts at the Hatch Shell** on the Esplanade along the Charles River. It includes the traditional **Fourth of July concert.** Performing at Symphony Hall, 301 Mass. Ave. (at Huntington Ave.). 📞 617/266-1492 or 617/CONCERT (program information). SymphonyCharge 📞 888/266-1200 (outside 617 area code) or 617/266-1200. www.bso.org. Tickets $35–$55 for tables; $14–$35 for balcony seats. T: Green Line E to Symphony, or Orange Line to Mass. Ave.

Tips Music Under the Sky and Stars

Founded in 2001, the **Boston Landmarks Orchestra** (📞 617/520-2200; www.landmarksorchestra.org) schedules a series of free classical concerts in parks around town, including Boston Common, on weekend afternoons and evenings in July and August. The goal of the "greatest hits" repertoire is to demystify classical music and call attention to the historic settings.

Boston After Dark

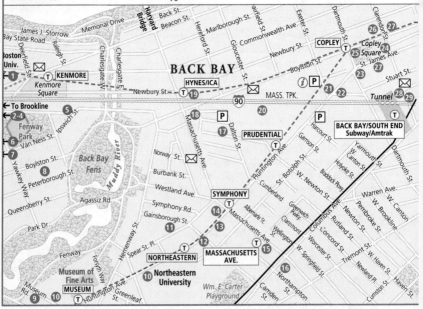

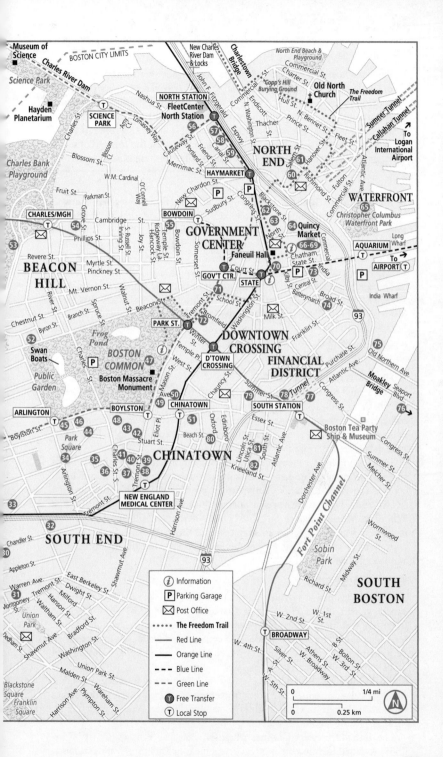

Tips   **A Major Music Festival in the Bucolic Berkshires**

When the Boston Symphony Orchestra goes on summer vacation, it goes to **Tanglewood** (© **413/637-5165,** or 617/266-1492 out of season; www. bso.org), in Lenox, Massachusetts, a 3-hour drive from Boston. Weekend concerts sell out in advance, but tickets to weeknight performances and Saturday morning rehearsals are usually available at the box office. If you can't get a seat inside, bring a blanket and picnic on the lawn. (Consult *Frommer's New England* for in-depth coverage of western Massachusetts.)

Handel & Haydn Society   The Handel & Haydn Society uses period instruments and techniques in its orchestral and choral performances, yet it's as cutting-edge as any other ensemble in town. Established in 1815, it's the oldest continuously performing arts organization in the country. The company prides itself on its creative programming of "historically informed" concerts, which it stages year-round, with most performances at Symphony Hall and Jordan Hall.

The society was the first American group to perform Handel's *Messiah,* in 1818, and has made it an annual holiday tradition since 1854 (the 2004 performances will celebrate the 150th anniversary). If you'll be in town in December, check for ticket availability as soon as you start planning your trip. 300 Mass. Ave. © **617/266-3605.** www.handelandhaydn.org. Tickets $21–$72. T: Green Line E to Symphony, or Orange Line to Mass. Ave.

ADDITIONAL OFFERINGS

The repertoire of the **Boston Lyric Opera** (© **617/542-6772,** 617/542-4912, or 800/447-7400 [Tele-Charge] for tickets; www.blo.org) includes classical and contemporary works. The season runs from October to March. Performances are at the Shubert Theatre, 265 Tremont St. Tickets cost $32 to $117; student rush tickets are half price.

Students and faculty members at two prestigious musical institutions perform frequently during the academic year; admission is usually free. For information, contact the **New England Conservatory of Music,** 290 Huntington Ave. (© **617/585-1100;** www.newenglandconservatory.edu), or Cambridge's **Longy School of Music,** 1 Follen St. (© **617/876-0956,** ext. 500; www.longy.edu). Also check listings when you arrive in town for the particulars of other student performances at area colleges; most are free or cheap, and the quality is often surprisingly high.

CONCERT SERIES

The biggest names in classical music, dance, theater, jazz, and world music appear as part of the **FleetBoston Celebrity Series** (© **617/482-2595,** or 617/482-6661 for Celebrity Charge; www.celebrityseries.org). It's a subscription series that also offers tickets to individual events, which go on sale in September. Performances take place at Symphony Hall, Jordan Hall, the Wang Theatre, and other venues.

World Music (© **617/876-4275;** www.worldmusic.org) showcases top-flight musicians, dance troupes, and other performers from around the world. Shows (60 a year) are at the Somerville Theater, the Berklee Performance Center, Sanders Theatre, and other venues.

The **Isabella Stewart Gardner Museum,** 280 The Fenway (© **617/734-1359;** www.gardnermuseum.org; T: Green Line E to Museum), features soloists, local students, chamber music, and sometimes jazz in the Tapestry Room. Performances are Saturday and Sunday at 1:30pm from late September to early May. Tickets (including museum admission) are $18 adults, $12 seniors, $10 students with ID, $5 children 5 to 17. Children under 5 not admitted. See chapter 7 for a full museum listing.

FREE (AND ALMOST FREE) CONCERTS

Radio stations sponsor free outdoor music all summer. Specifics change regularly, but you can count on hearing oldies, pop, jazz, and classical music at various convenient venues, including City Hall Plaza, Copley Square, and the Hatch Shell, at lunch, after work, and in the evening. Check the papers when you arrive, listen to a station that sounds good to you, or just follow the crowds.

Federal Reserve Bank of Boston   Local groups and artists perform jazz, classical, and contemporary music in the bank's ground-floor auditorium on selected Fridays at 12:30pm. You must have a photo ID to enter the building. 600 Atlantic Ave. ✆ 617/973-3453. www.bos.frb.org. T: Red Line to South Station.

Fridays at Trinity   This landmark church features 30-minute organ recitals by local and visiting artists on Friday at 12:15pm. Take advantage of the chance to look around the architectural showpiece. Trinity Church, Copley Sq. ✆ 617/536-0944, ext. 212. Donations accepted. T: Green Line to Copley, or Orange Line to Back Bay.

King's Chapel Noon Hour Recitals   Organ, instrumental, and vocal solos fill this historic building with music and make for a pleasant break along the Freedom Trail. Concerts are at 12:15pm Tuesday. 58 Tremont St. ✆ 617/227-2155. $2 donation requested. T: Red or Green Line to Park St.

ROCK & POP CONCERTS

FleetBoston Pavilion   One of the most pleasant venues in the area, this giant white tent encloses a 5,000-seat pavilion. It schedules pop, rock, country, rap, folk, and jazz on evenings from May through September. Check ahead for information about water transportation and shuttle service from South Station. 290 Northern Ave., Wharf 8, South Boston. ✆ 617/728-1600 or 617/931-2000 (Ticketmaster). www. fleetbostonpavilion.com.

FleetCenter   This state-of-the-art facility replaced legendary Boston Garden in 1995. It's the home of the Bruins (hockey), the Celtics (basketball), the circus (in Oct), ice shows (at least twice a year), and touring rock and pop artists of all stripes. Concerts are in the round or in the arena stage format. 1 FleetCenter (Causeway St.). ✆ 617/624-1000 (events line) or 617/931-2000 (Ticketmaster). www.fleetcenter. com. T: Orange or Green Line to North Station.

Orpheum Theater   Although it's old (the building went up in 1852) and cramped, the Orpheum offers an intimate setting for big-name performers. It books top local acts and national artists such as Elvis Costello, Tracy Chapman, Paul Simon, and the Pretenders. 1 Hamilton Place (off Tremont St., across from the Park St.

Impressions

Tonight I appear for the first time before a Boston audience—4,000 critics.
                                                    —Mark Twain, 1869
The New England conscience . . . does not stop you from doing what you shouldn't—it just stops you from enjoying it.
                                                    —Cleveland Amory, 1980

Church). ☏ **617/679-0810,** or 617/423-NEXT for tickets. http://boston.cc.com. T: Red or Green Line to Park St.

Tweeter Center for the Performing Arts   When a mainstream act's summer schedule says "Boston," that often means this bucolic setting about an hour south of town. A sheltered (it has a roof but no sides) auditorium surrounded by a lawn, the Tweeter Center features rock, alternative, folk, pop, country, reggae, and light classical artists. Shows are held rain or shine. 885 S. Main St. (Rte. 140), Mansfield. ☏ **508/339-2333** or 617/931-2000 (Ticketmaster). http://tweetercenter.com/boston.

DANCE

The best-known offering by Jose Mateo's **Ballet Theatre of Boston** (☏ **617/ 262-0961**) is *The Nutcracker,* performed throughout December at the Old Cambridge Baptist Church, 1151 Mass. Ave., Cambridge, or the Emerson Majestic Theatre, 219 Tremont St. Although Boston Ballet's production has more impressive sets, BTB's has a reputation as a good "starter" ballet. Tickets run $9 to $29.

Boston Ballet   Boston Ballet's reputation seems to jump a notch every time someone says, "So it's not just *The Nutcracker.*" The country's fourth-largest dance company performs the holiday staple from Thanksgiving to New Year's. During the rest of the season (Oct–May), it presents an eclectic mix of classic story ballets and contemporary works. Because the Wang was originally a movie theater, the pitch of the seats makes the top two balconies less than ideal for ballet—paying more for a better seat is a good investment. 19 Clarendon St. ☏ **617/695-6955** or 800/447-7400 (Tele-Charge). www.bostonballet.org. Performing at the Wang Theatre, 270 Tremont St. (box office Mon–Sat 10am–6pm). Tickets $15–$82. Student rush tickets (1 hr. before curtain) $13, except for The Nutcracker. T: Green Line to Boylston.

THEATER

Local and national companies, professional and amateur actors, and classic and experimental drama combine to make the local theater scene a lively one. Call ahead, or check the papers or BosTix (see "Let's Make a Deal" on p. 225) after you arrive.

Boston is one of the last cities for pre-Broadway tryouts, allowing an early look at a classic (or a classic flop) in the making. It's also a popular destination for touring companies of established hits. The promoter often is **Broadway in Boston** (☏ **617/880-2400;** www.broadwayinboston.com). You'll find most of the shows headed to or coming from Broadway in the Theater District, at the **Colonial Theatre,** 106 Boylston St. (☏ **617/426-9366**); the **Shubert Theatre,**

(*Finds* Dessert Alert

I don't want to boss you around; I'm here to suggest. So I *suggest* that after the theater, you run right over to **Finale.** It serves glorious desserts— fruit desserts, pastry desserts, dessert wines, and, best of all, chocolate desserts. It serves some real food, too. It's open all day, not just after the theater. Yes, it's a tad expensive. No, this is not a balanced meal. But the sweet tooths (sweet teeth?) who flock here don't want to hear it. Check it out near the Theater District at 1 Columbus Ave. (☏ **617/423-3184;** www.finaledesserts.com), in the pointy end of the Park Plaza Building, or at 30 Dunster St., Harvard Square (☏ **617/441-9797**).

Finds A Summer Theater Treat

The **Commonwealth Shakespeare Company** (© 617/747-4468; www. commonwealthshakespeare.org) performs free on Boston Common Tuesday through Sunday nights in July and early August. Bring a picnic and blanket, rent a chair ($5 or so) if you don't want to sit on the ground, and enjoy the sunset and a high-quality performance. The company is about half Equity actors, the sets are spectacular—and it's free!

---

265 Tremont St. (© **617/482-9393**); the **Wang Theatre,** 270 Tremont St. (© **617/482-9393**); and the **Wilbur Theater,** 246 Tremont St. (© **617/423-4008**).

The excellent local theater scene boasts the **Huntington Theatre Company,** which performs at the Boston University Theatre, 264 Huntington Ave. (© **617/266-0800;** www.huntington.org), and the **American Repertory Theatre,** or ART, which makes its home at Harvard University's **Loeb Drama Center,** 64 Brattle St., Cambridge (© **617/547-8300;** www.amrep.org). Both stage classic and contemporary productions; the ART is more likely to put on the work of a living playwright.

The **Lyric Stage,** 140 Clarendon St. (© **617/437-7172;** www.lyricstage. com), mounts contemporary and modern works in an intimate second-floor setting. The **Copley Theatre,** 225 Clarendon St. (© **617/266-7262**), stages revues, concerts, and one-person shows. The **Stuart Street Playhouse,** 200 Stuart St., in the Radisson Hotel Boston (© **617/426-4499**), often books one-person shows. **Jimmy Tingle's Off Broadway,** 255 Elm St., Davis Sq., Somerville (© **617/591-1616;** www.jimmytingle.com), is a 200-seat space where you'll often find the owner/comedian/actor/social critic performing.

The Loeb also features student productions. Other college options include Suffolk University's **C. Walsh Theatre,** 55 Temple St., Beacon Hill (© **617/573-8680**); various performance spaces at **MIT** (© **617/253-4720,** Theater Arts Hotline; web.mit.edu/arts) and **Boston University** (© **617/266-0800**); and Northeastern's **Blackman Theater,** 360 Huntington Ave. (© **617/373-2247**).

FAMILY THEATER/AUDIENCE PARTICIPATION

Charles Playhouse _Kids_   The off-Broadway sensation **Blue Man Group** began selling out as soon as it arrived on the Charles Playhouse's Stage I in 1995. Famous for reducing even the most eloquent theatergoer to one-syllable sputtering, the trio of cobalt-colored entertainers backed by a rock band uses music, percussion, food, and audience members in its overwhelming performance. It's not recommended for children under 8, but the older kids will love it. Shows are at 8pm Wednesday and Thursday; 7pm Friday; 4, 7, and 10pm Saturday; and 3 and 6pm Sunday (check ahead for extra performances during the holidays). Tickets are available at the box office and through Ticketmaster.

Shear Madness, on Stage II (downstairs), is the longest-running nonmusical play in theater history. Since January 1980, the zany "comic murder mystery" has turned the stage into a unisex hairdressing salon, and the show's never the same twice. One of the original audience-participation productions, the play changes at each performance as spectator-investigators question suspects, reconstruct events, and then name the murderer. Performances are Tuesday through

---

Tips **Got a Light? Not So Fast!**

In 2003, Boston banned smoking in all workplaces—including bars, night-clubs, restaurants. At press time, Cambridge still allowed public smoking, but a campaign to expand the ban to the entire state was in the works.

Friday at 8pm, Saturday at 6:30 and 9:30pm, and Sunday at 3 and 7:30pm. 74 Warrenton St. (C) 617/426-6912 (Blue Man Group) and 617/426-5225 (Shear Madness). www.blueman.com and www.shearmadness.com. Blue Man Group $53 and $43; Shear Madness $34. T: Green Line to Boylston.

Le Grand David and His Own Spectacular Magic Company *(Kids)*   Three generations of magicians make up this company, a nationally acclaimed troupe of illusionists that has delighted families since 1977. Le Grand David has received national attention for his sleight-of-hand and has performed at Easter parties at the White House. The 2-hour shows, directed by master magician Marco the Magi, take place on Sunday afternoon and Thursday evening at two theaters in Beverly, about 40 minutes from Boston by car. Cabot Street Cinema Theater, 286 Cabot St., Beverly; and Larcom Theatre, 13 Wallis St., Beverly. (C) 978/927-3677. lgdmagico@aol.com. Tickets $18 adults, $12 children under 12.

Puppet Showplace Theatre *(Kids)*   The Puppet Showplace stages programs of favorite fables, ethnic legends, and folktales and fairy tales from around the world. Professional puppeteers put on creative, engaging shows year-round in a lovely 100-seat theater. The theater displays historic puppets and puppet posters, offers puppet-making workshops, and sells toy puppets. Family performances take place on weekends, with shows for toddlers on weekdays. Adult-oriented "Puppets at Night" shows run at the theater and other local venues. Call for schedules and reservations. 32 Station St., Brookline. (C) 617/731-6400. www.puppetshowplace.org. Tickets $8.50 for children's shows, $12–$20 for adult shows. T: Green Line D to Brook-line Village.

2 The Club & Music Scene

The Boston-area club scene is multifaceted and constantly changing, and some-where out there is a good time for everyone, regardless of age, musical taste, or budget. Check the "Calendar" section of Thursday's *Globe,* the "Scene" section of Friday's *Herald,* the *Phoenix, Stuff@Night,* or the *Improper Bostonian* while you're making plans.

Many nightclubs are along **Lansdowne Street,** near Boston's **Kenmore Square,** and **Boylston Place,** off Boylston Street near Boston Common. The center of the local live-music universe is **Central Square** in Cambridge. That makes club-hopping easy, but it also means that students run wild on weekends. If you don't feel like dealing with swarms of teenagers and recent college grads, stick to slightly more upscale and isolated nightspots. If you do like teenagers, seek out a place where admission is 18- or 19-plus. Policies change regularly, sometimes from night to night, so call ahead. One component of the super-charged pool hall Jillian's Boston (p. 246) is **Atlas Dance,** 145 Ipswich St. ((C) 617/437-0300), a college-student magnet.

A night on the town in Boston and Cambridge is relatively brief: Most bars close by 1am, clubs close at 2am, and the T shuts down around 12:30am (except for Night Owl bus service till 2:30am on Fri and Sat nights). The drinking age is 21; a valid driver's license or passport is required as proof of age, and the law is strictly enforced, especially near college campuses.

COMEDY CLUBS

The Comedy Connection at Faneuil Hall   A large room with a clear view from every seat, the oldest original comedy club in town (established in 1978) draws top-notch talent from near and far. Big-name national acts lure enthusiastic crowds, and the openers are often just as funny but not as famous—yet. Shows usually start nightly at 8pm, plus Friday and Saturday at 10:15pm. The cover charge seldom tops $15 during the week but jumps for a big name appearing on a weekend. 245 Quincy Market Place (2nd floor, off the rotunda). ℭ **888/398-5100** or 617/248-9700. www.comedyconnectionboston.com. Cover $10–$40. T: Green or Blue Line to Government Center, or Orange Line to Haymarket. Validated parking available.

The Comedy Studio *Finds*   Nobody here is a sitcom star—yet. With a growing reputation for searching out undiscovered talent, the no-frills Comedy Studio draws connoisseurs, college students, and network scouts. It's not just setup-punchline-laugh, either; sketches and improv spice up the standup. Shows Thursday through Sunday at 8pm. At the Hong Kong restaurant, 1236 Mass. Ave., Cambridge. ℭ **617/661-6507.** www.thecomedystudio.com. Cover $7–$9. T: Red Line to Harvard.

Improv Asylum   The posters that catch your eye on the Freedom Trail might draw you back to the North End later for raucous improv and sketch comedy in a subterranean setting. Performances are Wednesday through Sunday evenings, and buying tickets in advance is recommended. 216 Hanover St. ℭ **617/263-6887.** www.improvasylum.com. Tickets $15–$20. T: Green or Orange Line to Haymarket.

DANCE CLUBS

Avalon   A cavernous multilevel space with a full concert stage, private booths and lounges, large dance floors, and a spectacular light show, Avalon is either great fun or sensory overload. It also books concerts, usually in the early evening (Steve Earle, John Mayer, and Ani DiFranco have played recently); when the stage is not in use, DJs take over.

Friday is **"Avaland,"** with national and international names in the DJ booth and costumed house dancers on the floor. On Saturday (suburbanites' night out), expect more mainstream dance hits. The dress code calls for jackets, shirts with collars, and no jeans or athletic wear. The crowd is slightly older than that at Axis. Open Thursday (international night) to Sunday (gay night) from 10pm to 2am. 15 Lansdowne St. ℭ **617/262-2424** or 617/423-NEXT (for tickets). www.avalonboston. com. Cover $5–$20. T: Green Line B, C, or D to Kenmore.

Tips **Cinderella Goes Clubbing**

The MBTA operates Night Owl bus service on Friday and Saturday nights until 2:30am. It runs on popular bus routes and on supplemental routes that parallel the subway lines. The fare is $1 in coins or a token. Municipal budget cutters regularly (but so far unsuccessfully) target the service, so check ahead before leaving the hotel without cab fare. For info and schedules, contact the MBTA (ℭ **800/392-6100** outside Mass. or 617/222-3200; www.mbta.com).

Axis   Progressive rock at bone-rattling volume and "creative dress"—break out the leather—attract a young crowd. There are special nights for alternative rock, house, techno, soul, and funk music, and for international DJs. Open Monday (gay night) through Saturday from 10pm to 2am. 13 Lansdowne St. ℂ **617/262-2437.** Cover $5–$10. T: Green Line B, C, or D to Kenmore.

The Big Easy   Buttoned-up Boston meets let-it-all-hang-out New Orleans—it could get ugly. Not here, in a large space with a balcony (great for people-watching), billiard room, dance floor, and live bands top local DJs playing anything from soul to alternative. The lower level is the **Sugar Shack;** at both, the crowd is on the young (collegiate and post-) side. No ripped jeans or athletic shoes. 1 Boylston Place. ℂ **617/351-7000.** www.bigeasyboston.com. Cover $8–$10. T: Green Line to Boylston.

The Roxy   This former hotel ballroom boasts excellent DJs and live music, a huge dance floor, a stage, and a balcony (perfect for checking out the action below). Occasional concerts and boxing cards take good advantage of the sight lines. Call for the latest schedule—offerings change regularly. No jeans or athletic shoes. Open 9pm (entertainment starts at 10pm) Thursday through Saturday, and some Wednesdays and Sundays. In the Tremont Boston hotel, 279 Tremont St. ℂ **617/338-7699.** www.roxyplex.com. Cover $10–$15. T: Green Line to Boylston.

Sophia's   One of the only places in Boston to hear Latin music (live and recorded), Sophia's attracts a lively international crowd and excellent dancers with three levels of entertainment and a seasonal rooftop deck. Be ready to move. Open Wednesday through Saturday until 2am; there's after-work entertainment Wednesday through Friday. No jeans or sneakers. 1270 Boylston St. ℂ **617/351-7001.** www.sophiasboston.net. Cover $10 after 9:30pm. T: Green Line B, C, or D to Hynes/ICA or Green Line D to Fenway; 10-min. walk.

ECLECTIC

Johnny D's Uptown Restaurant & Music Club *Finds*   This family-owned and -operated establishment is one of the best in the area. Live-music aficionados, you'll kick yourself if you don't at least check the lineup while you're in town. Johnny D's draws a congenial crowd for acts on international tours as well as acts that haven't been out of eastern Massachusetts. The music ranges from zydeco to rock, rockabilly to jazz, blues to ska. The veggie-friendly food's good, too; try the weekend brunch. This place is worth a long trip, but it's only two stops past Harvard Square on the Red Line (about a 15-min. ride at night). Open daily from 11:30am to 1am. Brunch starts at 9am on weekends; dinner runs from 4:30 to 9:30pm Tuesday through Saturday, with lighter fare until 11pm. 17 Holland St., Davis Sq., Somerville. ℂ **617/776-2004** or 617/776-9667 (concert line). www.johnnyds.com. Cover $2–$16, usually $5–$10. T: Red Line to Davis.

Kendall Café   This friendly neighborhood bar near the 1 Kendall Sq. office-retail complex typically showcases up-and-coming artists, with occasional appearances by national names (Kay Hanley played recently). Acoustic pop predominates; you might also hear rock, country, or blues in the tiny back room. Or just stay at the bar—you won't be able to see, but it's such a small place that you'll have no trouble hearing. Shows start between 8 and 9:30pm daily. 233 Cardinal Medeiros Ave., Cambridge. ℂ **617/661-0993.** www.thekendall.com. Cover $5–$10; no cover for bar only. T: Red Line to Kendall/MIT.

The Western Front   A 30-ish friend swears by this legendary reggae club for one reason: "You're never the oldest one there." A casual spot on a nondescript street south of Central Square, it attracts an integrated crowd for world-beat music, blues, and especially reggae. Sunday is dance-hall reggae night, and the infectious music makes every night dancing night. Open Wednesday through Sunday from 8pm to 2am; live entertainment begins at 9pm. 343 Western Ave., Cambridge. ✆ 617/492-7772. www.thewesternfrontclub.com. Cover $5–$10. T: Red Line to Central.

FOLK

Boston is one of the only cities where folk musicians consistently sell out larger venues that usually book rock and pop performers. If an artist you want to see is touring, check ahead for Boston-area dates. The annual **Boston Folk Festival** (✆ 617/287-6911; www.wumb.org/folkfest) is a 2-day event in mid-September on the UMass-Boston campus in Dorchester.

The music listings in the "Calendar" section of Thursday's *Globe* include information about **coffeehouses,** the main area outlets for folk. The streets around **Harvard Square** are another promising venue—Tracy Chapman is just one famous graduate of the scene.

Club Passim   Passim has launched more careers than the mass production of acoustic guitars—Joan Baez, Shawn Colvin, and Tom Rush started out here. In a basement on the street between buildings of the Harvard Coop, this legendary coffeehouse (which doesn't serve alcohol) enjoys an international reputation built on more than 30 years of nurturing new talent and showcasing established musicians. Patrons who have been regulars since day one mix with college students. There's live music nightly, and coffee and food until 10:30pm. Tuesday is open-mike night. Open Sunday through Thursday from 11am to 11pm, Friday and Saturday from 11am to 4am. Most shows start at 8pm. 47 Palmer St., Cambridge. ✆ 617/492-7679. www.clubpassim.org. Cover $5–$25; most shows $12 or less. T: Red Line to Harvard.

JAZZ & BLUES

If you're partial to these genres, consider timing your visit to coincide with the **Boston Globe** Jazz & Blues Festival (✆ 617/267-4301; www.boston.com/jazzfestival), usually scheduled for the third week of June. Constellations of jazz and blues stars (large and small) appear at events, some of them free, many of them outdoors. The festival wraps up with a free Sunday-afternoon program at the Hatch Shell.

Two restaurants that offer jazz along with excellent food are **Bob the Chef's Jazz Café** and **Les Zygomates** (see chapter 6).

On summer Fridays at 7pm, the free **Waterfront Jazz Series** (✆ 617/635-3911) brings amateurs and professionals to Christopher Columbus Park on the waterfront for a refreshing interlude of music and cool breezes. On summer Thursdays at 6pm, the **Boston Harbor Hotel** (✆ 617/491-2100; www.bhh.com) and the House of Blues sponsor free performances on the "Blues Barge," which floats in the water behind the hotel.

Cantab Lounge   Follow your ears to this friendly neighborhood bar, which attracts a lively three-generation crowd. When the door swings open at night, deafening music—usually blues, rock, folk, or bluegrass—spills out. If Little Joe Cook and the Thrillers are on the schedule, don't miss them. Downstairs is the Third Rail, which schedules poetry on Wednesday, improv on Thursday, and DJs on weekends. 738 Mass. Ave., Cambridge. ✆ 617/354-2685. Cover $3–$8. T: Red Line to Central.

House of Blues *Kids*   The original House of Blues, a blue clapboard house near Harvard Square, packs 'em in every evening and on Saturday afternoon. It attracts tourists, music buffs, and big names—Junior Brown, Michelle Shocked, Ike Turner, and Jason Mraz have played recently. And there's no telling when an audience member will turn out to be someone famous who winds up onstage jamming. The restaurant serves American fare with a Cajun accent from noon to 11pm Monday through Saturday, from 4:30 to 11pm on Sunday. The music hall is open until 1am Sunday through Wednesday, 2am Thursday through Saturday; most shows are 18-plus. Seatings for the Southern buffet at the **Sunday gospel brunch** are at 10am, noon, and 2pm; advance tickets ($27 adults, $14 children) are highly recommended. The music is live, the food is yummy, and kids just love it. Walk-ins pay just $14 but watch the action on closed-circuit TV. 96 Winthrop St., Cambridge. © 617/491-2583, or 617/497-2229 for tickets. Dining reservations (© 617/491-2100) accepted only for parties of 25 or more. www.hob.com. Cover $6–$30; no cover Sat 1pm matinee. Validated parking available. T: Red Line to Harvard.

Limbo   A see-and-be-seen scene, Limbo books jazz, blues, hip-hop, and soul. Live artists play on the lowest of the three levels nightly at 8 or 9pm; DJs spin on weekends after 10pm on the other two floors (otherwise a bar and restaurant). 49 Temple Pl. © 617/338-0280. www.limboboston.com. T: Red or Green Line to Park St., or Orange Line to Downtown Crossing.

Regattabar   The Regattabar's selection of local and international artists is often considered the best in the area—a title that Scullers Jazz Club (see below) is happy to dispute. Chick Corea, Irma Thomas, Joe Lovano, and Rebecca Parris have appeared recently. The large third-floor room holds about 200 and, unfortunately, sometimes gets a little noisy. Buy tickets in advance from Concertix (there's a $2.50 per ticket service charge), or try your luck at the door an hour before performance time. Open Tuesday through Saturday and some Sundays, with one or two performances per night. In the Charles Hotel, 1 Bennett St., Cambridge. © 617/661-5000. Concertix: 12 Arrow St., Cambridge. © 617/876-7777. www.regattabar.com. Tickets $12–$35. T: Red Line to Harvard.

Ryles Jazz Club   This popular spot books local, regional, and national acts. Hard-core fans turn out for a wide variety of first-rate jazz, R&B, world beat, and Latin in two rooms. Both levels offer excellent music and a friendly atmosphere. The Sunday jazz brunch runs from 10am to 3pm. Open Tuesday through Sunday; shows start at 9pm. 212 Hampshire St., Inman Sq., Cambridge. © 617/876-9330. www.rylesjazz.com. Cover $7–$15. T: Red Line to Central, 10-min. walk.

Scullers Jazz Club   Overlooking the Charles River, Scullers is a lovely, comfortable room with a top-notch sound system. It books acclaimed singers and instrumentalists—recent notables include Keely Smith, Abbey Lincoln, Nicholas Payton, and (quite a coup) Bobby Short. Patrons tend to be more hardcore than the crowds at the Regattabar, but it depends on who's performing. There are usually two shows a night Tuesday through Saturday; the box office is open Monday through Saturday from 11am to 6pm. Ask about dinner packages ($47–$75 per person), which include preferred seating and a three-course meal. In the Doubletree Guest Suites hotel, 400 Soldiers Field Rd. © 617/562-4111. www.scullersjazz.com. Tickets $12–$50. Validated parking available.

Wally's Cafe   This Boston institution, near a busy corner in the South End, opened in 1947. It draws a notably diverse crowd—black, white, straight, gay, affluent, indigent. Live music, by local ensembles, students and instructors from the Berklee College of Music, and (on occasion) internationally renowned musicians, starts every night at 9pm. Open daily until 2am, with food service until 9pm Monday through Saturday. 427 Mass. Ave. © 617/424-1408. www.wallys cafe.com. No cover; 1-drink minimum. T: Orange Line to Mass. Ave.

ROCK

Bill's Bar   Long known as the only real hangout on Lansdowne Street, Bill's made the transition from bar to live-music destination and kept its friendly atmosphere and great beer menu. It books locals and touring up-and-comers or DJs most nights at 9:30 or 10pm. This is still Lansdowne Street—expect a young crowd. There's reggae on Sunday and hip-hop on Tuesday. Open nightly from 9pm to 2am. 5½ Lansdowne St. © 617/421-9678. www.billsbar. com. Cover $5–$10. T: Green Line B, C, or D to Kenmore.

> **Tips   Rock of Ages**
>
> Bring an ID, bring an ID, bring an ID—you must be 21 to drink alcohol, and the law is strictly enforced. Even if you look older, most bouncers won't risk a fine or license suspension, especially at 18-plus shows.

Lizard Lounge   In the basement of the Cambridge Common restaurant, this cozy but not cramped room features well-known local rock and folk musicians who play right in the middle of the floor. The Lizard Lounge draws a postcollegiate-and-up crowd (Harvard Law School is next door). Shows Wednesday through Saturday at 10pm; Sunday is open-mike poetry jam night. 1667 Mass. Ave., Cambridge. © 617/547-0759. Cover $2–$7. T: Red Line to Harvard.

The Middle East   The best rock club in the area books an impressive variety of progressive and alternative artists in two rooms (upstairs and downstairs) every night. Showcasing top local talent as well as bands with local roots and international reputations—keep an eye out for the Mighty Mighty Bosstones— it's a popular hangout that gets crowded, hot, and *loud*. The Corner, a former bakery, features acoustic artists most of the time and belly dancers on Wednesday. There's also Middle Eastern food at **ZuZu** (© **617/492-9181**) and gallery space with rotating art exhibits. Some music shows are all ages (most are 18-plus); the age of the crowd varies with the performer. 472–480 Mass. Ave., Central Sq., Cambridge. © **617/864-EAST** or 617/931-2000 (Ticketmaster). www.mideastclub.com. Cover $7–$15. T: Red Line to Central.

Paradise Rock Club   Hard by the Boston University campus, the medium-size Paradise draws enthusiastic, student-intensive crowds for top local rock and alternative performers. You might also see national names (lately, Edwin McCain, Beth Orton, and the Wallflowers) who want a relatively small venue, and others who aren't ready to headline a big show on their own (Sister Hazel, the Donnas, the Soundtrack of Our Lives). Most shows are 18-plus. You must be 21 to drink alcohol, a policy that became iron-clad here after a months-long "vacation" courtesy of the Boston Licensing Board; don't forget your ID. 967 Commonwealth Ave. © **617/562-8800**, or 617/423-NEXT for tickets. http://boston.cc.com. T: Green Line B to Pleasant St.

Toad *(Value*   Essentially a bar with a stage, this smoky, claustrophobic space (the high ceiling helps a little) draws a savvy three-generation clientele attracted by the local big-name performers and no cover. Toad enjoys good acoustics but not much elbow room—a plus when restless musicians wander into the crowd. 1912 Mass. Ave., Cambridge. © **617/497-4950** (info line). T: Red Line to Porter.

Kids **Theme a Little Theme**

The **Hard Rock Cafe**, 131 Clarendon St. (© **617/424-ROCK;** www.hardrock.com), is a fun link in the fun chain—just ask the other tourists in line with you. The two-level space boasts a guitar-shaped bar and stained-glass windows that glorify rock stars. You'll see memorabilia of Jimi Hendrix, Elvis Presley, Madonna, local favorites Aerosmith and the Cars, and others. The kid-friendly menu features salads, burgers, and sandwiches, including the legendary "pig sandwich."

T.T. the Bear's Place   This no-frills spot generally attracts a young crowd, but 30-somethings will feel comfortable, too. Bookings range from cutting-edge alternative rock and roots music to ska and funk shows to up-and-coming pop acts. New bands predominate early in the week, with more established artists on weekends. Open Sunday and Monday from 7pm to midnight, Tuesday through Saturday from 6pm to 1am. 10 Brookline St., Cambridge. © **617/492-0082** or 617/492-BEAR (concert line). www.ttthebears.com. Cover $3–$15, usually less than $10. T: Red Line to Central.

3 The Bar Scene

Bostonians had some quibbles with the TV show *Cheers*, but no one complained that the concept of a neighborhood bar where the regulars practically lived was implausible. From the Littlest Bar (a closet-size downtown watering hole) to the original Cheers bar (formerly the Bull & Finch), the neighborhood bar occupies a vital niche. It tends to be a fairly insular scene—as a stranger, don't assume that you'll get a warm welcome. This is one area where you can and probably should judge a book by its cover: If you peek in and see people who look like you and your friends, give it a whirl.

BARS & LOUNGES

The Bay Tower   An elegant 33rd-floor lounge, the Bay Tower affords a mesmerizing view of the harbor, the airport, and Faneuil Hall Marketplace directly below. There's dancing to live music Monday through Saturday (piano on weeknights, jazz quartet Fri–Sat). No denim or athletic shoes. See chapter 6 for restaurant listing. 60 State St. © **617/723-1666.** www.baytower.com. T: Orange or Blue Line to State.

Casablanca   Students and professors jam this legendary Harvard Square watering hole, especially on weekends. You'll find excellent food (see chapter 6), an excellent jukebox, and excellent eavesdropping. 40 Brattle St., Cambridge. © **617/ 876-0999.** T: Red Line to Harvard.

Cheers (Beacon Hill)   If you're out to impersonate a native, try not to be shocked when you enter "the *Cheers* bar" and the inside looks nothing like the bar on the TV show. (A spin-off in Faneuil Hall Marketplace fills that niche—see the listing below.) Formerly the Bull & Finch Pub, it really is a neighborhood bar, but it's far better known for attracting legions of out-of-towners, who find good pub grub, drinks, and plenty of souvenirs. There's food from 11am to 12:15pm, and a kids' menu ($4–$5). 84 Beacon St. © **617/227-9605.** www.cheers boston.com. T: Green Line to Arlington.

Cheers (Faneuil Hall Marketplace)   Blatantly but good-naturedly courting fans of the sitcom, this bar's interior is an exact replica of the *Cheers* TV set. It serves pub fare until 11:45pm and schedules DJs on weekend nights. Memorabilia on display includes Sam Malone's Red Sox jacket. Go ahead, you know you want to. Quincy Market Building, South Canopy, Faneuil Hall Marketplace. (C) 617/227-0150. www.cheersboston.com. T: Green or Blue Line to Government Center, or Orange Line to Haymarket.

DeLux Cafe Ultracool but never obnoxious about it, the DeLux is one of the classiest dives around. The funky decor, selection of microbrews, and veggie-friendly ethnic menu attract a cross-section of the neighborhood, from off-duty chefs to yuppies. I'm writing this before the smoking ban; by the time you visit, the posters, photos, and postcards on the walls may actually be visible all night. 100 Chandler St. (C) 617/338-5258. T: Orange Line to Back Bay.

The Fours One of Boston's best and best-known sports bars, the Fours is about one football field away from the FleetCenter. Festooned with sports memorabilia and TVs, it's a madhouse before Celtics and Bruins games—and a promising place to pick up an extra ticket. 166 Canal St. (C) 617/720-4455. T: Green or Orange Line to North Station.

The Good Life Downtown At this 1950s-style lounge and restaurant, the roar of the crowd often drowns out the Sinatra music playing in the background. Two blocks from Downtown Crossing, it's also popular with office workers who flock here for the burgers. There's live jazz Sunday through Wednesday. 28 Kingston St. (C) 617/451-2622. www.the-goodlife-us.com. T: Red or Orange Line to Downtown Crossing.

Green Street Grill This Central Square hangout isn't the entertaining dive it once was, but it still draws a savvy crowd for live blues, rock, and jazz. Blues and jazz aficionados will find perhaps the best jukebox on the planet, and there's also excellent food (see chapter 6). 280 Green St., Cambridge. (C) 617/876-1655. www.green streetgrill.com. T: Red Line to Central.

Grendel's Den A vestige of pre-franchise Harvard Square, this cozy subterranean space is *the* place to celebrate turning 21. Recent grads and grad students dominate, but Grendel's has been so popular for so long that it also gets its share of Gen Y's parents. The food is tasty, with loads of vegetarian dishes, and the fireplace enhances the comfy atmosphere. 89 Winthrop St., Cambridge. (C) 617/491-1160. www.grendelsden.com. T: Red Line to Harvard.

Harvard Gardens A Beacon Hill standby, Harvard Gardens is a neighborhood favorite. In this neighborhood, that means students, yuppies, and medical professionals (Mass. General Hospital is across the street). It's more lounge than tavern, with plenty of beers on tap, great margaritas, and food until 11pm (midnight on weekends). 320 Cambridge St. (C) 617/523-2727. T: Red Line to Charles/MGH.

The Place Is it a Financial District hangout? A sports bar on (pardon the expression) steroids, with flat-screen TVs all over? An after-work destination for bankers and lawyers and the men and women who love them? Yes, yes, and yes. 2 Broad St. (C) 617/523-2081. www.theplaceboston.com. Cover $5 Thurs–Sat after 9pm. T: Orange or Blue Line to State.

The Purple Shamrock Across the street from Faneuil Hall Marketplace, the Purple Shamrock packs in wall-to-wall 20-somethings. This is a rowdy, fun place that schedules DJs and cover bands. Dress code: No tank tops on men. 1 Union St. (C) 617/227-2060. www.irishconnection.com. Cover $3–$6 Thurs–Sat. T: Green or Blue Line to Government Center, or Orange Line to Haymarket.

Radius   The high-tech bar at this hot, *haute* restaurant offers almost every-thing the dining room does—the chic crowd, the noise, the perfect martinis—without the sky-high food bill. 8 High St. ☎ 617/426-1234. T: Red Line to South Station.

Saint   A subterranean den of luxury, Saint radiates possibly the coolest vibe in town. Despite management's insistence on referring to it as a "nitery" (huh?), the line of Euro-chic would-be patrons stretches down Exeter Street on weekend nights. The cavernous three-room lounge includes some areas that are open only to members, who pay $10,000 for the privilege. In the Copley Square Hotel, 190 Exeter St. ☎ 617/236-1134. www.saintnitery.com. T: Green Line to Copley.

Top of the Hub   Boasting a panoramic view of greater Boston, Top of the Hub is 52 stories above the city; the view is especially beautiful at sunset. There is music and dancing nightly. Dress is casual but neat (no jeans). Open until 1am Sunday through Wednesday, 2am Thursday through Saturday. You must have a photo ID to enter the building. Prudential Center, 800 Boylston St. ☎ 617/536-1775. www.selectrestaurants.com. T: Green Line E to Prudential.

Via Matta   The chic Italian restaurant's equally stylish bar and divine wine list make this a perfect place to recharge after an afternoon of hard work—or hard shopping (Newbury St. is 3 blocks away). 79 Park Plaza (Arlington St. and Columbus Ave.). ☎ 617/422-0008. www.viamattarestaurant.com. T: Green Line to Arlington.

Whiskey Park   New York wannabes congregate outside the Boston incarna-tion of the posh chain that's cropping up around the country. A dark, plush space with wood and copper accents, Whiskey Park packs in the black-clad 20-somethings who line up outside to seek admission. Be sure to check out the space-age restrooms (on the lower level). In the Boston Park Plaza Hotel, 64 Arlington St. ☎ 617/542-1482. www.midnightoilbars.com. T: Green Line to Arlington.

BREWPUBS

Boston Beer Works   Across the street from Fenway Park, this cavernous space is frantic before and after Red Sox games. Don't plan to be able to hear anything your friends are saying. It has a full food menu and 14 brews on tap, including excellent bitters and ales. Especially good are the cask-conditioned offerings, seasoned in wood until they're as smooth as fine wine. The sweet-potato fries make a terrific snack. There's a branch near the **FleetCenter,** 110 Canal St. (☎ 617/896-2337), that's not as large but equally loud. Open daily from 11:30am to 1am. 61 Brookline Ave. ☎ 617/536-2337. T: Green Line B, C, or D to Kenmore.

John Harvard's Brew House   This subterranean Harvard Square hangout pumps out terrific English-style brews in a clublike setting (try to find the sports

---

Tips   Bowled Over

At press time, the hottest nightlife destination in town was, of all things, a bowling alley. **Kings,** 10 Scotia St. (☎ 617/266-2695; www.backbaykings. com), is a 25,000-foot complex in a former movie theater. It has 20 bowl-ing lanes (4 of them private), an eight-table billiards room, and a restau-rant and lounge. In the works was a branch of the Cambridge restaurant **Jasper White's Summer Shack** (p. 138). Scotia Street is off Dalton Street, across from the Hynes Convention Center.

figures in the stained-glass windows) and prides itself on its food. The beer selection changes regularly; it includes at least one selection from each "family" (ambers, porters, seasonals, and more), all brewed on the premises. Order a sampler if you can't decide. Open daily from 11:30am to 1:30am, with food service until 11:30pm. 33 Dunster St., Cambridge. ℭ 617/868-3585. www.johnharvards.com. T: Red Line to Harvard.

HOTEL BARS & LOUNGES

Many popular nightspots are associated with hotels and restaurants (see chapters 5 and 6); the following are particularly agreeable, albeit expensive, places to while away an hour or three.

The Atrium   The floor-to-ceiling windows of this ground-floor room across the street from Faneuil Hall Marketplace allow for great people-watching. The Atrium also offers champagne by the glass, live piano music on weeknights, and cushy furnishings that encourage lingering. Open daily until midnight. In the Millennium Bostonian Hotel, 40 North St. ℭ 617/523-3600. T: Green or Blue Line to Government Center, or Orange Line to State.

Bar 10   Cushy seating, sleek decor, huge windows, Mediterranean bistro cuisine, and French doors that open off the lobby lend an air of being away from it all yet in the middle of everything. Open daily until midnight. In the Westin Copley Place Boston, 10 Huntington Ave. ℭ 617/424-7446. T: Green Line to Copley, or Orange Line to Back Bay.

Boston Harbor Hotel   You have two appealing options on the ground floor. **Intrigue,** which looks like a comfortable living room, serves food all day, and boasts a harbor view; the **Rowes Wharf Bar,** which makes a serious martini, has a businesslike atmosphere. Rowes Wharf (entrance on Atlantic Ave.). ℭ 617/439-7000. T: Red Line to South Station.

Bristol Lounge   This is a perfect choice after the theater, after work, or after anything else. An elegant room with soft lounge chairs, a fireplace, and fresh flowers, it features a fabulous Viennese Dessert Buffet on weekend nights. There's live jazz every evening. An eclectic menu is available until 11:30pm (12:30am Fri–Sat). In the Four Seasons Hotel, 200 Boylston St. ℭ 617/351-2037. T: Green Line to Arlington.

Oak Bar   This paneled, high-ceilinged room feels like an old-fashioned men's club—but one that welcomes women. The lighting is muted, the leather seating soft and welcoming, and the raw bar picture-perfect. There's live entertainment on weekends. Proper dress (no jeans or sneakers) is required. Open Sunday through Thursday until midnight, Friday and Saturday until 1am. In the Fairmont Copley Plaza Hotel, 138 St. James Ave. ℭ 617/267-5300. T: Green Line to Copley, or Orange Line to Back Bay.

IRISH BARS

The Black Rose   Purists might sneer at the Black Rose's touristy location, but performers don't. Sing along with the authentic entertainment at this jam-packed pub and restaurant at the edge of Faneuil Hall Marketplace. You might be able to make out the tune on a fiddle over the din. 160 State St. ℭ 617/742-2286. www.irishconnection.com. Cover $3–$5. T: Orange or Blue Line to State.

The Burren   The expatriate Irish community seems to find the Burren an antidote to homesickness, and you will, too. There's traditional music in the smoky front room, acoustic rock in the large back room, and good food. *Movie moment:* If you saw the 1998 romantic comedy *Next Stop Wonderland,* you'll recognize the bar as the place where Hope Davis met her loser blind dates. 247 Elm St., Somerville. ✆ 617/776-6896. Cover (back room only) $5–$10. T: Red Line to Davis.

The Grand Canal No, it's not Italian. This is an atmospheric pub and restaurant with an excellent beer selection, good food, a 12-foot TV screen, and music Thursday through Saturday nights. (By the way, the canal connects Dublin to the Shannon River.) 57 Canal St. ✆ 617/523-1112. www.somerspubs.com. Cover $5 for music. T: Green or Orange Line to Haymarket or North Station.

Mr. Dooley's Boston Tavern Sometimes an expertly poured Guinness is all you need. If one of the nicest bartenders in the city pours it, and you enjoy it in an authentically decorated room, so much the better. This Financial District spot offers a wide selection of imported beers on tap, live music, and pub favorites at lunch and dinner. 77 Broad St. ✆ 617/338-5656. www.somerspubs.com. Cover (Fri–Sat only) $3–$5. T: Orange Line to State or Blue Line to Aquarium.

GAY & LESBIAN CLUBS & BARS

In addition to the clubs listed here, some mainstream clubs schedule a weekly gay night. On Sunday, **Avalon** (p. 235) plays host to the largest gathering of gay men in town. On Saturday, women congregate at the **Ekco Lounge,** 41 Essex St., in Chinatown (✆ 617/338-8283). For up-to-date listings, check *Bay Windows,* the *Improper Bostonian,* and the monthly *Phoenix* supplement "One in 10."

Club Café This trendy South End spot draws a chic crowd of men and women for conversation (the noise level is reasonable), dining, live music in the front room, and video entertainment in the back room. Thursday is the busiest night. Open daily until 1am; the kitchen serves lunch weekdays, Sunday brunch, and dinner nightly. 209 Columbus Ave. ✆ 617/536-0966. T: Green Line to Arlington, or Orange Line to Back Bay.

Fritz This popular South End hangout is a neighborhood favorite. The friendly crowd bonds over sports—there's even a satellite dish. In the Chandler Inn Hotel, 26 Chandler St. ✆ 617/482-4428. T: Orange Line to Back Bay.

Jacques The only drag venue in town, Jacques draws a friendly crowd of gay and straight patrons who mix with the "girls" and sometimes engage in a shocking activity—that's right, disco dancing. The eclectic entertainment includes live music (on weekends), performance artists, and, of course, drag shows. Open daily from noon to midnight. 79 Broadway, Bay Village. ✆ 617/426-8902. T: Green Line to Arlington.

Man-Ray The area's best goth scene is at Man-Ray, which has regular fetish nights and an appropriately gloomy atmosphere. Thursday is "Campus" night, when the crowd is 19-plus and mostly men; the Friday dress code calls for gothic or fetish attire. Open Wednesday until 1am, Thursday through Saturday until 2am. 21 Brookline St., Cambridge. ✆ 617/864-0400. www.manrayclub.com. Cover $6–$10. T: Red Line to Central.

Paradise Not to be confused with the Boston rock club (well, you can, but it won't be quite the same experience), the Paradise attracts an all-ages male crowd. There's a male stripper every evening. Thursday is college night. Open Sunday through Wednesday until 1am, Thursday through Saturday until 2am. 180 Mass. Ave., Cambridge. ✆ 617/494-0700. www.paradisecambridge.com. T: Red Line to Central, 10-min. walk.

4 More Entertainment

COFFEE & TEA

As in most other American cities, you won't get far without seeing a Starbucks. I'll submit to the passive-aggressive counter routine if it ends in a frozen drink, but for coffee, tea, and hanging out, there are plenty of less generic options. Many are in the North End (see chapter 6); other favorites are listed here. At all of them, hours are long, and loitering is encouraged—these are good places to bring your journal.

Algiers Café & Restaurant Middle Eastern food and music, plain and flavored coffees, and the legendary atmosphere make this a classic Harvard Square hangout. Your "quick" snack or drink (try the mint coffee) might turn into a longer stay, as the sociologist in you studies the resident and would-be intellectuals. This is a good spot to eavesdrop while you sample terrific soups, sandwiches, homemade sausages, falafel, and hummus. 40 Brattle St. © 617/492-1557. T: Red Line to Harvard.

BeanTowne Coffee House A splash of the bohemian in a buttoned-up office-retail complex, this is a good stop before or after a film at the Kendall Square Cinema. There's only one problem—it's too popular. If a table empties, move in fast. 1 Kendall Sq., Cambridge. © 617/621-7900. T: Red Line to Kendall.

Someday Café If *Friends* featured real people of all ages, they might hang out here, near the Somerville Theater. The coffee and tea selections are impressive, and there's great lemonade in summer, cider in winter, and brownies all the time. 51 Davis Sq., Somerville. © 617/623-3323. T: Red Line to Davis.

Tealuxe The selection of 100-plus teas (dispensed by unfortunately named "tea-tenders") makes Tealuxe a magnet for connoisseurs. The Harvard Square location is the original in the chain, which is thriving on a combination of hard-to-find selections and comfortable atmosphere. 108 Newbury St. © 617/927-0400. www.tealuxe.com. T: Green Line to Arlington. Zero Brattle St., Cambridge. © 617/441-0077. T: Red Line to Harvard.

1369 Coffee House A long, narrow room with a colorful clientele, the 1369 offers excellent baked goods, a dazzling selection of teas and flavored coffees, and great people-watching. The namesake original location is at 1369 Cambridge St., Inman Square (© 617/576-1369). 757 Mass. Ave., Central Sq., Cambridge. © 617/576-4600. T: Red Line to Central.

Trident Booksellers & Café This Back Bay institution offers a view of the funkier end of Newbury Street, a browsing-friendly book selection, occasional author events, and a casual, New Age-y atmosphere. The draw for the digital set is free Wi-Fi access throughout the premises. Open until midnight daily. 338 Newbury St. © 617/267-8688. T: Green Line B, C, or D to Hynes/ICA.

POOL PLUS

Plenty of bars have pool tables, but at Boston's relatively upscale billiards palaces, drinking is what you do while you're playing pool, rather than the other way around.

Boston Billiard Club A large, clubby space decorated with brass sconces and a mahogany bar, this club has 55 tables, tasty bar food, and full liquor service. If you don't want to wait for a table, ask about reserving a private room ($9–$17/hr.). Open daily from noon to 2am. On Monday, free lessons run from

7:30 to 9pm. 126 Brookline Ave. © 617/536-POOL. www.bostonbilliardclub.com. Weekend evenings $12 an hr. for 2 players, $2 an hr. for each extra person. Daytime and weeknight discounts. T: Green Line B, C, or D to Kenmore or D to Fenway.

Flat Top Johnny's   A spacious but loud room with a bar and 12 red-topped tables, Flat Top Johnny's has a funky neighborhood feel despite being in a rather sterile office-retail complex. Open daily from 3pm to 1am. 1 Kendall Sq., Cambridge. © 617/494-9565. www.flattopjohnnys.com. Sun–Thurs $10 an hr., Fri–Sat $12 an hr. T: Red Line to Kendall/MIT.

Jillian's Boston *Kids*   The owners of Jillian's revived Boston's interest in pool and continue to make the most of advances in entertainment technology. The 70,000-square-foot complex, which anchors the Lansdowne Street strip, contains a 52-table pool parlor, virtual bowling, blackjack tables (for fun, not profit), and tons of interactive games and sports. The 250-game video midway includes classic arcade games. There are dartboards, a table tennis area, foosball, a dance club, five full bars, and a restaurant. If you can't scare up some fun here, check your pulse. Open Monday through Saturday from 11am to 2am, Sunday from noon to 2am. Children under 18 accompanied by an adult are admitted before 7pm. 145 Ipswich St. © 617/437-0300. www.jilliansboston.com. $12 an hr. for 1–2 people, $14 for 3 or more. Valet parking available Wed–Sun after 6pm, except during Red Sox games. T: Green Line B, C, or D to Kenmore.

The Rack   Across the street from Faneuil Hall Marketplace, this enormous space is more nightspot than pool hall. It courts the after-work crowd with 22 tournament-size tables, two bars, and a lounge. You can order food from 11am to 1am and maybe do a little star-gazing—pro athletes turn up periodically. In good weather, the action spills onto the patio. 24 Clinton St. (at North St.). © 617/725-1051. www.therackboston.com. $7 an hr. before 4:30pm, $14 an hr. after 4:30pm. T: Green or Blue Line to Government Center, or Orange Line to Haymarket.

FILMS

Free Friday Flicks at the Hatch Shell (© 617/727-9547, ext. 450) are family films shown on a large screen in the amphitheater on the Esplanade. On the lawn in front of the Hatch Shell, hundreds of people picnic until the sky grows dark and the credits roll. In the last few years, the films have tended toward recent releases (no big thrill for anyone with a VCR), but a few classics usually crop up, and the movie is only part of the experience.

Tip: Bring sweaters in case the breeze off the river grows chilly.

True revival houses—they feature lectures and live performances in addition to foreign and classic films—include the **Brattle Theater,** 40 Brattle St., Cambridge (© 617/876-6837; www.brattlefilm.org), and the **Coolidge Corner Theater,** 290 Harvard St., Brookline (© 617/734-2500; www.coolidge.org/Coolidge). Classic and foreign films are the tip of the iceberg at the quirky **Harvard Film Archive,** 24 Quincy St., Cambridge (© 617/495-4700; www.harvardfilmarchive.org), which also shows student films.

For first-run independent and foreign films, head to the **Kendall Square Cinema,** 1 Kendall Sq., Cambridge (© 617/494-9800). The best movie theater in the immediate Boston area, it offers discounted parking in the adjoining garage. Second-run current releases at discount prices are the usual fare at the **Somerville Theater,** 55 Davis Sq. (© 617/625-5700), which sometimes schedules concerts, too. A promising newcomer that screens only mainstream releases is the 19-screen **Loews Boston Common,** 175 Tremont St. (© 617/4423-3499), which has stadium seating and digital sound.

LECTURES & READINGS

The Thursday *Globe* "Calendar" section is the best place to check for listings of lectures, readings, and talks on a wide variety of subjects, often at local colleges and libraries. Many are free or charge a small fee. Most of the bookstores listed in chapter 9 sponsor author readings; check their websites or in-store displays, or call ahead.

5 Late-Night Bites

To be frank, Boston's late-night scene needs to climb a couple of notches to reach pathetic, and Cambridge's wee-hour diversions are even skimpier. The only plus is that just about every cab driver out cruising knows how to reach the places that are still open.

Near the Theater District and Chinatown, the **News,** 150 Kneeland St. (© **617/426-6397**), is open until 5am during the week and round the clock on weekends. Besides the entertaining patrons, diversions include abundant periodicals, flat-screen TVs, and Internet access. A number of **Chinatown** restaurants (see chapter 6) don't close until 3 or 4am. Asking for "cold tea" might—*might*—get you a teapot full of beer. The hottest scene is at **Ginza Japanese Restaurant,** 14 Hudson St. (© **617/338-2261**). In the North End, **Caffe Pompei,** 280 Hanover St. (© **617/523-9438**), draws European club-hoppers and neighborhood shift workers until 3:30am. And if you have a car, make like a college student and road-trip to the **International House of Pancakes** at 1850 Soldiers Field Rd. in Brighton (© **617/787-0533**). It's open 24 hours daily.

11

Side Trips from Boston

In addition to being (in Oliver Wendell Holmes's words) "the hub of the solar system," Boston is the hub of a network of delightful excursions. The destinations in this chapter—**Lexington** and **Concord**, the **North Shore** and **Cape Ann**, and **Plymouth**—make fascinating, manageable day trips and offer enough diversions to fill several days.

Like Boston, the suburbs are home to many attractions that rely heavily on aid from the state government, which is battling a budget crisis. Admission fees in this chapter are current at press time, but establishments that rely heavily on state funding may cost a bit more by the time you visit. If you're on a tight budget, call ahead.

1 Lexington & Concord

The shooting stage of the Revolutionary War began here, and parts of the towns still look much as they did in April 1775, when the fight for independence began. Start your visit in **Lexington**, where colonists and British troops first clashed. On the border with **Concord**, spend some time at **Minute Man National Historical Park**, investigating the battle that raged there. Decide for yourself where the "shot heard round the world" rang out—bearing in mind that **Ralph Waldo Emerson**, who wrote those words, lived in Concord. Emerson's house and **Louisa May Alcott's** family home (also in Concord) are just two of the fascinating destinations in this area.

Some attractions close from November to March or mid-April, opening after **Patriots Day**, the third Monday in April. Information about both towns is available from the **Greater Merrimack Valley Convention & Visitors Bureau,** 9 Central St., Suite 201, Lowell, MA 01852 (© **800/443-3332** or 978/459-6150; www.merrimackvalley.org).

LEXINGTON ⊕
6 miles NW of Cambridge, 9 miles NW of Boston

A country village turned prosperous suburb, Lexington takes great pride in its history. It's a pleasant town with some engaging destinations, but it lacks the atmosphere and abundant attractions of nearby Concord. Being sure to leave time for a tour of the Buckman Tavern, you can schedule as little as a couple of

---

Tips **Poetry in Motion**

Before you set out for Lexington and Concord, you might want to read *Paul Revere's Ride,* Henry Wadsworth Longfellow's classic but historically questionable poem that dramatically chronicles the events of April 18 and 19, 1775.

> **Tips** The Liberty Ride
>
> Lexington's **Liberty Ride** (© 781/862-0500, ext. 702; www.ci.lexington.ma.
> us/Visiting/libertyride.htm) is a narrated tour that runs between the
> downtown attractions, the National Heritage Museum, and the Lexington
> end of Minute Man National Historical Park. It operates from April
> through October; the fare (good for a full day) is $10 for adults, $5 for
> children 6 to 18, free for children under 6. There's free parking at the
> museum and the park visitor center, and your ticket entitles you to dis-
> counts at local businesses.

hours to explore downtown Lexington, possibly en route to Concord; a visit can
also fill a half or full day. The town contains part of **Minute Man National Historical Park** (see "Exploring the Area" in the "Concord" section later in this
chapter), which is definitely worth a visit.

British troops marched from Boston to Lexington late on April 18, 1775 (no
need to memorize the date; you'll hear it everywhere). Tipped off, patriots Paul
Revere and William Dawes rode ahead to sound the warning. Members of the
local militia, known as "Minutemen" for their ability to assemble quickly, were
waiting at the **Buckman Tavern.** John Hancock and Samuel Adams, leaders of
the revolutionary movement, were sleeping (or trying to) at the nearby **Hancock-
Clarke House.** The warning came around midnight, followed about 5 hours
later by some 700 British troops, en route to Concord, where they planned to
destroy the rebels' military supplies. Ordered to disperse, the colonists—fewer
than 100, and some accounts say 77—stood their ground. Nobody knows who
started the shooting, but when it was over, eight militia members lay dead,
including a drummer boy, and 10 were wounded.

ESSENTIALS

GETTING THERE   From downtown Boston, take Storrow or Memorial
Drive to Route 2. Take Route 2 from Cambridge through Belmont, exit at
Route 4/225, and follow signs to the center of Lexington. Or take Route 128
(I-95) to Exit 31A and follow the signs. Massachusetts (or Mass.) Ave.—the
same street as the one in Boston and Cambridge—runs through Lexington.
There's metered parking on the street and in several municipal lots.

The **MBTA** (© 617/222-3200; www.mbta.com) runs bus routes nos. 62
(Bedford) and 76 (Hanscom) to Lexington from Alewife station, the last stop on
the Red Line. The one-way fare is 75¢, and the trip takes about 25 minutes.
Buses leave every hour during the day and every half-hour during rush periods,
Monday through Saturday, with no service on Sunday. They pass the Munroe
Tavern and the National Heritage Museum, if you prefer not to walk from the
center of town.

VISITOR INFORMATION   The **Chamber of Commerce Visitor Center,**
1875 Mass. Ave., Lexington, MA 02420 (© 781/862-2480; www.lexington
chamber.org), distributes sketch maps and information.

SEEING THE SIGHTS
Minute Man National Historical Park is in Lexington, Concord, and Lincoln
(see "Concord" later in this chapter).

Start your visit to Lexington at the **visitor center,** on the town common or "Battle Green." It's open daily from 9am to 5pm (10am–4pm Nov to mid-Apr). A **diorama** and accompanying narrative illustrate the Battle of Lexington. The *Minuteman* Statue on the Green is of Captain John Parker, who commanded the militia. When the British confronted his troops, Parker called: "Stand your ground. Don't fire unless fired upon, but if they mean to have a war, let it begin here!" Allow about 30 minutes to look around the visitor center and the Green.

Three important destinations in Lexington were among the country's first **"historic houses"** when restoration of them began in the 1920s. The **Lexington Historical Society** (© **781/862-1703;** www.lexingtonhistory.org) operates all three. Currently headquartered in the Munroe Tavern, the society is in the process of restoring a building on Depot Square (downtown, off Mass. Ave. near the Battle Green) that will hold exhibits, offices, and a gift shop.

The **Buckman Tavern** 🎇🎇, 1 Bedford St. (© **781/862-5598**), built around 1710, is the only building still on the Green that was there on April 19, 1775. If time is short and you have to pick just one house to visit, this is the one. The interior has been restored to approximate its appearance the day of the battle. The Minutemen gathered here to await word of British troop movements, and they brought their wounded here after the conflict. The tour, by costumed guides, is educational and entertaining.

Within easy walking distance, the **Hancock-Clarke House,** 36 Hancock St. (© **781/861-0928**), is where Samuel Adams and John Hancock were staying when Paul Revere arrived. They fled to nearby Woburn. The 1698 house, furnished in colonial style, contains Lexington Historical Society's museum.

The British took over the **Munroe Tavern** 🎇, 1332 Mass. Ave. (about 1 mile from the Green), to use as their headquarters and, after the battle, as their field hospital. The building (1690) holds many fascinating artifacts. The furniture, carefully preserved by the Munroe family, includes the table and chair President George Washington used when he dined here in 1789. The historically accurate gardens in the rear (free admission) are beautifully planted and maintained.

All three houses are open for guided tours Monday through Saturday from 10am to 5pm and Sunday from 1 to 5pm, April through October. The Buckman Tavern is also open in late March and November. Admission for adults is $5 for one house, $8 for two, and $12 for all three; for seniors, $5 for one house, $7 for two, and $11 for all three; and for children 6 to 16, $3 for one house, $5 for two, and $7 for three. The last tour starts 30 minutes before closing time; tours take 30 to 45 minutes. Call for information about group tours, which are offered by appointment.

The fascinating exhibits at the **National Heritage Museum** 🎇, 33 Marrett Rd., Route 2A, at Mass. Ave. (© **781/861-6559** or 781/861-9638; www.monh. org), explore history through popular culture. The museum (formerly the Museum of Our National Heritage) makes an entertaining complement to the colonial focus of the rest of the town. The installations in the six exhibition spaces change regularly; you can start with another dose of the Revolution, the permanent exhibit **Lexington Alarm'd.** Other topics have ranged from George Washington to circus posters to U.S. Route 1. The museum schedules lectures, concerts, and family programs, and the cafe in the atrium serves lunch daily. Admission is free. The museum is open Monday through Saturday from 10am to 5pm, Sunday from noon to 5pm; it's closed January 1, Thanksgiving, and December 25. The Scottish Rite of Freemasonry sponsors the museum.

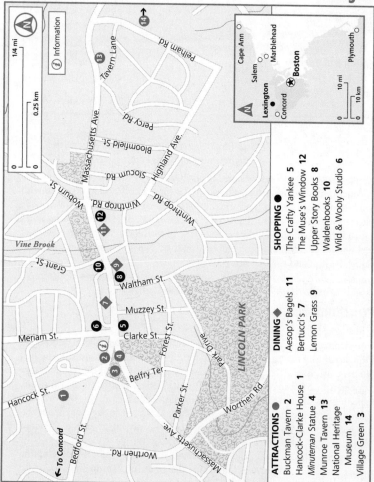

SHOPPING ●
The Crafty Yankee **5**
The Muse's Window **12**
Upper Story Books **8**
Waldenbooks **10**
Wild & Wooly Studio **6**

DINING ◆
Aesop's Bagels **11**
Bertucci's **7**
Lemon Grass **9**

ATTRACTIONS ●
Buckman Tavern **2**
Hancock-Clarke House **1**
Minuteman Statue **4**
Munroe Tavern **13**
National Heritage
Museum **14**
Village Green **3**

SHOPPING

A stroll along **Mass. Ave.** near the center of town won't disappoint. Start at **The Muse's Window,** 1656 Mass. Ave. (© **781/274-6873**), an excellent crafts gallery. As you head back toward the Green, check out **Waldenbooks,** 1713 Mass. Ave. (© **781/862-7870**); **Upper Story Books,** 1730 Mass. Ave. (© **781/862-0999**); and the **Crafty Yankee,** 1838 Mass. Ave. (© **781/861-1219**). One of the best-known yarn shops in eastern Massachusetts is **Wild & Woolly Studio,** 7A Meriam St., off Mass. Ave. (© **781/861-7717**).

DINING

The cafe at the **National Heritage Museum** (see above) is a popular spot for lunch. **Bertucci's,** 1777 Mass. Ave. (© **781/860-9000**), is a branch of the family-friendly pizzeria chain. **Aesop's Bagels,** 1666 Mass. Ave. (© **781/674-2990**), is a good place to pick up a light meal. **Copacafe Grand Cafe & Bar,**

Impressions

Listen, my children, and you shall hear
Of the midnight ride of Paul Revere,
On the eighteenth of April, in Seventy-five;
Hardly a man is now alive
Who remembers that famous day and year . . .

—Henry Wadsworth Longfellow, "Paul Revere's Ride," 1863

1727 Mass. Ave. (✆ **978/862-6622**), serves tasty food, luscious pastries, and excellent coffee daily from early morning through evening.

Lemon Grass THAI   A welcome break: The only revolution going on here is in Americans' culinary habits. The space is a former coffee shop disguised with bamboo decorations and the aroma of Asian spices. You might start with satay (skewers of meat served with delectable peanut sauce) or chicken coconut soup, with a kick of pepper and plenty of poultry. Entrees include a tasty rendition of traditional pad Thai and excellent curry dishes. The accommodating staff will adjust the heat and spice to suit your taste.

1710 Mass. Ave. ✆ 781/862-3530. Main courses $7–$9 at lunch, $8–$16 at dinner. AE, DISC, MC, V. Mon–Fri 11:30am–3pm; Mon–Thurs 5–9:30pm; Fri–Sat 5–10pm; Sun 4–9pm.

CONCORD ★★★
18 miles NW of Boston, 15 miles NW of Cambridge, 6 miles W of Lexington

Concord (say "conquered") revels in its legacy as a center of groundbreaking thought and its role in the country's political and intellectual history. The first official battle of the Revolutionary War took place in 1775 at the North Bridge (now part of Minute Man National Historical Park); less than a century later, Concord was an important literary and intellectual center. A visit can easily fill a day; if your interests are specialized or time is short, a half-day excursion is reasonable. For an excellent overview of town history, start at the **Concord Museum.**

After just a little time in this lovely town, you might find yourself adopting the local attitude toward two famous residents: **Ralph Waldo Emerson,** who comes across as a respected uncle figure, and **Henry David Thoreau,** everyone's favorite eccentric cousin. The contemplative writers wandered the countryside and did much of their work in Concord, forming the nucleus of a group of important writers who settled in the town. By the mid–19th century, Concord was the center of the Transcendentalist movement; sightseers can tour the former **homes of Emerson, Thoreau, Nathaniel Hawthorne,** and **Louisa May Alcott.** Lovers of literature can visit their graves at **Sleepy Hollow Cemetery.**

ESSENTIALS
GETTING THERE   From Lexington, take Route 2A west from Mass. Ave. (Route 4/225) at the National Heritage Museum; follow the BATTLE ROAD signs. From Boston and Cambridge, take Route 2 into Lincoln and stay in the right lane. Where the main road makes a sharp left, go straight onto Cambridge Turnpike. Signs that point to HISTORIC CONCORD lead downtown. To go straight to Walden Pond, use the left lane, take what's now Route 2/2A another mile or so, and turn left onto Route 126. There's parking throughout town and at the attractions.

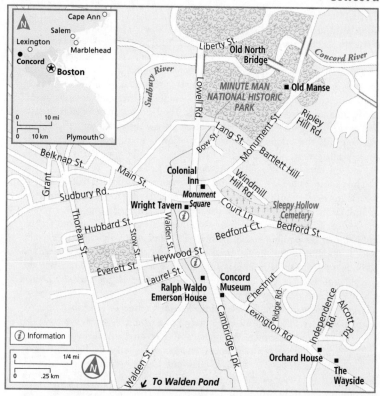

The **commuter rail** (© 617/222-3200; www.mbta.com) takes about 45 minutes from North Station in Boston, with a stop at Porter Square in Cambridge. The round-trip fare is $8. There is no bus service from Boston to Concord. The station is about ¾ miles over flat terrain from the town center.

VISITOR INFORMATION The **Chamber of Commerce,** 100 Main St., Suite 310-2, Concord, MA 01742 (© **978/369-3120;** www.concordmachamber. org), maintains a visitor center at 58 Main St., behind Middlesex Savings Bank, 1 block south of Monument Square. It's open daily 9:30am to 4:30pm from April through October, when guided walking tours are available on weekends. Weekday and group tours are available by appointment. The chamber office is open year-round Monday through Friday from 9am to 2pm. The community (www.concordma.com) and town (www.concordnet.org) websites also include visitor information.

⌐Tips Row, Row, Row Your Boat

Pretend you're Henry David Thoreau and take to the Concord River. The **South Bridge Boathouse,** 496 Main St. (© **978/369-9438**), ⁷⁄₁₀ mile west of the town center, will rent you a canoe for about $11 an hour on weekends, less on weekdays.

EXPLORING THE AREA

Minute Man National Historical Park ★★ *Kids*   This 900-acre park pre-
serves the scene of the first Revolutionary War battle at Concord on (all together
now) April 19, 1775. After the skirmish at Lexington, the British continued to
Concord in search of stockpiled arms (which militia members had already
moved). Warned of the advance, the colonists prepared to confront the troops.
The Minutemen crossed the North Bridge, evading the regulars standing guard,
and waited on a hilltop for reinforcements. The British searched nearby homes
and burned any guns they found. The colonials saw the smoke and, mistakenly
thinking that the troops were torching the town, attacked the soldiers at the
bridge. The gunfire that ensued is remembered as "the shot heard round the
world," the opening salvo of the Revolution.

The park is open daily, year-round. A visit can take as little as half an hour—
for a jaunt to the North Bridge—or as long as half a day (or more), if you stop
at both visitor centers and perhaps participate in a ranger-led program. To reach
the bridge (a reproduction), follow Monument Street out of Concord Center
until you see the parking lot on the right. Park and walk a short distance to the
bridge, stopping along the unpaved path to read the narratives and hear the
audio presentations. On one side of the bridge is a plaque commemorating the
British soldiers who died in the Revolutionary War; on the other is Daniel
Chester French's *Minuteman* statue.

You can also start at the **North Bridge Visitor Center** ✪, 174 Liberty St., off
Monument Street (© **978/369-6993**; www.nps.gov/mima), which overlooks the
Concord River and the bridge. A diorama and video program illustrate the battle,
and exhibits include uniforms, weapons, and tools of colonial and British soldiers.
Park rangers are on duty if you have questions. Outside, picnicking is allowed,
and the scenery is lovely, especially in the fall. The center is open daily from 9am
to 5pm (until 4pm in winter), and is closed January 1 and December 25.

At the Lexington end of the park is the **Minute Man Visitor Center** ✪, off
Route 2A, about ½ mile west of I-95 Exit 30B (© **781/862-7753**; www.
nps.gov/mima). The park includes the first 4 miles of the Battle Road, the route
the defeated British troops took as they left Concord. At the visitor center, you'll
see a fascinating multimedia program about the Revolution, informational displays, and a 40-foot mural illustrating the battle. On summer weekends, rangers
lead tours of the park (call ahead for times). The **Battle Road Trail,** a 5½-mile
interpretive path, carries pedestrian, wheelchair, and bicycle traffic. Panels and
granite markers display information about the military, social, and natural history of the area and point the way along the trail. Open daily from 9am to 5pm
(until 4pm in winter); call ahead from December through March, when open
days and hours are subject to change. Closed January 1 and December 25.

Walden Pond State Reservation ★★   The conservation movement started
here, in a small wooden structure where a misunderstood social activist moved

---

Impressions

By the rude bridge that arched the flood,
Their flag to April's breeze unfurled,
Here once the embattled farmers stood,
And fired the shot heard round the world.
                        —Ralph Waldo Emerson, *Concord Hymn,* 1836

to "live deliberately." A pile of stones marks the site of the cabin where Henry David Thoreau lived from 1845 to 1847. Today the picturesque park is an extremely popular destination for walking (a path circles the pond), swimming, and fishing. Although crowded, it's well preserved and insulated from development, making it less difficult than you might expect to imagine Thoreau's experience. Call for the schedule of ranger-led interpretive programs. No dogs or bikes are allowed. From Memorial Day to Labor Day, the park charges a daily parking fee ($5) and the lot still fills early every day—call before setting out, because the rangers turn away visitors if the park has reached capacity (1,000).

915 Walden St. (Rte. 126). © 978/369-3254. www.state.ma.us/dem/parks/wldn.htm. From Concord Center, take Walden St. (Rte. 126) south, cross Rte. 2, and follow signs to the parking lot.

Museums & Literary Sites

Concord Museum 🟉🟉 *Kids*   Just when you're (understandably) suspecting that everything interesting in this area started on April 18, 1775, and ended the next day, this superb museum sets you straight. It's a great place to start your visit to the town.

The **History Galleries** 🟉🟉 explore the question "Why Concord?" Artifacts, murals, films, maps, documents, and other presentations illustrate the town's changing roles. It has been a Native American settlement, Revolutionary War battleground, 19th-century intellectual center, and focal point of the 20th-century historic preservation movement. Items on display include archaeological artifacts, silver from colonial churches, a fascinating collection of embroidery samplers, and rooms furnished with period furniture and textiles. Explanatory text places the exhibits in context. One of the **lanterns** that signaled Paul Revere from the steeple of the Old North Church is on display. You'll also see the contents of Ralph Waldo Emerson's study, arranged the way it was at his death in 1882, and a large collection of Henry David Thoreau's belongings.

Pick up a **family activity pack** 🟉 as you enter, and use the games and reproduction artifacts (including a quill pen and powder horn) to give the kids a hands-on feel for life in the past. The museum also offers changing exhibits in the New Wing, special events such as "tea and tour" (call for reservations), and an outstanding gift shop.

200 Lexington Rd. (at Cambridge Tpk.). © 978/369-9609 (recorded info) or 978/369-9763. www.concord museum.org. Admission $7 adults, $6 seniors and students, $3 children under 16, $16 families. June–Aug daily 9am–5pm; Apr–May and Sept–Dec Mon–Sat 9am–5pm, Sun noon–5pm; Jan–Mar Mon–Sat 11am–4pm, Sun 1–4pm. Closed Easter, Thanksgiving, Dec 25. Parking allowed on road. Follow Lexington Rd. out of Concord Center and bear right at museum onto Cambridge Tpk.; entrance is on left.

The Old Manse 🟉   The engaging history of this home touches on the military and the literary, but it's mostly the story of a family. The Rev. William Emerson built the Old Manse in 1770 and watched the Battle of Concord from the yard. He died during the Revolutionary War, and for almost 170 years the house was home to his widow, her second husband, their descendants, and two famous friends. Nathaniel Hawthorne and his bride, Sophia Peabody, moved in after their marriage in 1842 and stayed for 3 years. As a wedding present, Henry David Thoreau sowed a vegetable garden; today, a re-creation of that garden is part of a self-guided tour of the grounds. This is also where William's grandson Ralph Waldo Emerson wrote the essay "Nature." Today you'll see mementos and memorabilia of the Emerson and Ripley families and of the Hawthornes, who scratched notes on two windows with Sophia's diamond ring.

269 Monument St. (at North Bridge). © **978/369-3909**. www.thetrustees.org. Guided tour $7.50 adults, $6.50 seniors and students, $5 children 6–12, $22 families. Mid-Apr to Oct Mon–Sat 10am–5pm, Sun and holidays noon–5pm (last tour at 4:30). Closed Nov to mid-Apr. From Concord Center, follow Monument St. to North Bridge parking lot (on right); Old Manse is on left.

Orchard House ★★★ *Kids*   *Little Women* (1868), Louisa May Alcott's best-known and most popular work, was written and set at Orchard House. (Most of the events took place a decade or two earlier—Louisa was in her mid-30s when *Little Women* was first published.) Seeing the Alcotts' home brings the author and her family to life for legions of female visitors and their pleasantly surprised male companions. Fans won't want to miss the excellent tour, copiously illustrated with heirlooms. Serious buffs can check ahead for information on holiday programs and many other special events, some of which require reservations.

Note: Call before visiting; an extensive preservation project was under way at press time and may be continuing when you're here.

Louisa's father, Amos Bronson Alcott, was a writer, educator, and philosopher, and the leader of the Transcendentalist movement. He created Orchard House by joining and restoring two homes on 12 acres of land that he bought in 1857. The family lived here from 1858 to 1877, socializing in the same circles as Emerson, Thoreau, and Hawthorne.

Other family members served as the models for the characters in *Little Women.* Anna ("Meg"), the eldest, was an amateur actress, and May ("Amy") was a talented artist. Elizabeth ("Beth"), a gifted musician, died before the family moved to this house. Their mother, the social activist Abigail May Alcott, frequently assumed the role of family breadwinner—Bronson, Louisa wrote in her journal, had "no gift for money making."

399 Lexington Rd. © **978/369-4118**. www.louisamayalcott.org. Guided tours $8 adults, $7 seniors and students, $5 children 6–17, $20 families. Apr–Oct Mon–Sat 10am–4:30pm, Sun 1–4:30pm; Nov–Mar Mon–Fri 11am–3pm, Sat 10am–4:30pm, Sun 1–4:30pm. Closed Jan 1–15, Easter, Thanksgiving, Dec 25. Follow Lexington Rd. out of Concord Center and bear left at Concord Museum; house is on the left. Overflow parking lot is across the street.

Ralph Waldo Emerson House   This house offers an instructive look at the days when a philosopher could attain the status we now associate with rock stars. Emerson, also an essayist and poet, lived here from 1835 until his death, in 1882. He moved here after marrying his second wife, Lydia Jackson, whom he called Lydian; she called him Mr. Emerson, as the staff still does. The tour gives a good look at his personal side and at the fashionably ornate interior decoration of the time. You'll see original furnishings and some of Emerson's personal effects. (The contents of his study at the time of his death are in the Concord Museum.)

28 Cambridge Tpk. © **978/369-2236**. Guided tours $6 adults, $4 seniors and students. Call to arrange group tours (10 people or more). Mid-Apr to Oct Thurs–Sat 10am–4:30pm, Sun 2–4:30pm. Closed Nov to mid-Apr. Follow Cambridge Tpk. out of Concord Center; just before Concord Museum, house is on right.

Sleepy Hollow Cemetery ★   Follow the signs for AUTHOR'S RIDGE and climb the hill to the graves of some of the town's literary lights, including the Alcotts, Emerson, Hawthorne, and Thoreau. Emerson's grave bears no religious symbols; it's an uncarved quartz boulder. Thoreau's grave is nearby; at his funeral in 1862, his old friend Emerson concluded his eulogy with these words: ". . . wherever there is knowledge, wherever there is virtue, wherever there is beauty, he will find a home."

Entrance on Rte. 62 W. © **978/318-3233**. www.concordnet.org. Daily 7am–dusk, weather permitting. Call ahead for wheelchair access. No buses allowed.

> **Fun Fact Military Intelligence**
>
> Veterans' graves in Sleepy Hollow Cemetery often bear small American flags or other symbols, especially around holidays such as Memorial Day and Veterans Day. Of the famous occupants of Author's Ridge, only Louisa May Alcott (a Union Army nurse during the Civil War) qualifies.

The Wayside ⚐ The Wayside was Nathaniel Hawthorne's home from 1852 until his death, in 1864. The Alcotts also lived here (the girls called it "the yellow house"), as did Harriett Lothrop, who wrote the *Five Little Peppers* books under the pen name Margaret Sidney and owned most of the current furnishings. The Wayside is part of Minute Man National Historical Park, and the fascinating 45-minute ranger tour illuminates the occupants' lives and the house's crazy-quilt architecture. The exhibit in the barn (free admission) consists of audio presentations and figures of Hawthorne, Louisa May and Bronson Alcott, and Sidney.

455 Lexington Rd. (C) 978/369-6975. www.nps.gov/mima/wayside. Guided tours $4 adults, free for children under 17. May–Oct Thurs–Tues 10am–4:30pm. Closed Nov–Apr. Follow Lexington Rd. out of Concord Center past Concord Museum and Orchard House. Park across the street.

NEARBY SIGHTS

DeCordova Museum and Sculpture Park ⚐⚐ Indoors and out, the DeCordova shows the work of American contemporary and modern artists, with an emphasis on living New England residents. The main building, on a leafy hilltop, overlooks a pond and the area's only outdoor public sculpture park. The museum also has a roof garden, and a sculpture terrace that displays the work of one sculptor per year. The prestigious **DeCordova Annual Exhibition,** from June through September, is a group show of recent work by a select group of New England artists. Picnicking is allowed in the sculpture park; bring your lunch or buy it at the cafe (open Wed–Sun 11am–3pm). Free guided tours of the main galleries start at 2pm Wednesday and Sunday, year-round; sculpture-park tours run May through October on weekends at 1pm. Be sure to check out the **Store @ DeCordova,** the excellent gift shop.

51 Sandy Pond Rd., Lincoln. (C) 781/259-8355. www.decordova.org. Museum: $6 adults; $4 seniors, students, and children 6–12. Tues–Sun and some Mon holidays 11am–5pm. Sculpture park: Free admission. Daily daylight hours. Closed Jan 1, July 4, Thanksgiving, Dec 25. From Rte. 2 E., take Rte. 126 to Baker Bridge Rd. (1st left after Walden Pond). When it ends, go right onto Sandy Pond Rd.; museum is on left. From Rte. 2 W., take I-95 to Exit 28B, follow Trapelo Rd. 2½ miles to Sandy Pond Rd., then follow signs.

Gropius House ⚐ Architect Walter Gropius (1883–1969), founder of the Bauhaus school of design, built this home for his family in 1938. Having taken a job at the Harvard Graduate School of Design, he worked with Marcel Breuer to design the hilltop house, now maintained by the Society for the Preservation of New England Antiquities. He used traditional materials such as clapboard, brick, and fieldstone, with components then seldom seen in domestic architecture, including glass blocks and welded steel. Breuer designed many of the furnishings, which were made for the family at the Bauhaus. Decorated as it was in the last decade of Gropius's life, the house affords a revealing look at his life, career, and philosophy. Call for information on special tours and workshops.

68 Baker Bridge Rd., Lincoln. (C) 781/259-8098. www.spnea.org. Guided tours $8 adults, $4 students with ID. Tours on the hour June–Oct 15 Wed–Sun 11am–4pm; Oct 16–May Sat–Sun 11am–4pm. Take Rte. 2 to Rte.

126 south to left on Baker Bridge Rd.; house is on the right. From I-95, Exit 28B, follow Trapelo Rd. to Sandy Pond Rd., go left onto Baker Bridge Rd.; house is on the left.

SHOPPING

Downtown Concord, off **Monument Square,** is a terrific shopping destination. Here you'll find the **Concord Toy Shop,** 4 Walden St. (© **978/369-2553**); the **Grasshopper Shop,** 36 Main St. (© **978/369-8295**), which carries women's clothing and accessories; jewelry and art at **Catseye,** 48 Monument Sq. (© **978/ 369-8377**); and the **Concord Bookshop,** 65 Main St. (© **978/371-2672**). The compact shopping district in **West Concord,** along Route 62, boasts the old-fashioned **West Concord 5 & 10,** 106 Commonwealth Ave. (© **978/369-9011**), which carries everything from light bulbs to lace.

ACCOMMODATIONS & DINING

Consider taking a **picnic** to the North Bridge, Walden Pond, or another spot that catches your eye. Stock up at **Nashoba Brook Bakery** (see entry below) or downtown at the **Cheese Shop,** 25–31 Walden St. (© **978/369-5778**).

Colonial Inn ☆   The main building of the Colonial Inn has overlooked Monument Square since 1716. Like many historic inns, it's not luxurious, but it is comfortable, centrally located—and possibly home to a ghost. Additions since it became a hotel in 1889 have left the inn large enough to offer modern conveniences (including wireless Internet access) and small enough to feel friendly. It's popular with local businesspeople as well as vacationers, especially during foliage season. The 12 original guest rooms—one of which (no. 24) supposedly is haunted—are in great demand. Reserve early if you want to stay in the main inn, which is decorated (surprise, surprise) in colonial style. Rooms in the Prescott wing are a bit larger and have country-style decor. Three freestanding buildings hold one-, two-, and three-bedroom suites suitable for long-term stays.

The dining options are pleasant, though hardly exciting—you're here for the atmosphere, not the cuisine. The inn has two lounges that serve light meals; ask for a table on the porch, and you'll have a front-row seat for the action on Monument Square. The lovely restaurant serves salads, sandwiches, and pasta at lunch, and traditional American fare at dinner. Afternoon tea ($22) is served Wednesday through Sunday; reservations (© **978/369-2373**) are required.

48 Monument Sq., Concord, MA 01742. © **800/370-9200** or 978/369-9200. Fax 978/369-2170. www.concordscolonialinn.com. 55 units (some w/shower only). Apr–Oct $195–$225 main inn; $159–$189 Prescott wing. Nov–Mar $165 main inn; $145 Prescott wing. AE, DC, DISC, MC, V. **Amenities:** Restaurant (American); 2 lounges; bar with live jazz and blues on weekends; bike rental; concierge; tour desk; business center; babysitting; laundry service; dry cleaning; executive-level rooms. *In room:* A/C, TV, wireless Internet access, coffeemaker, hair dryer, iron.

Nashoba Brook Bakery & Café ☆ AMERICAN   The enticing variety of fresh artisan breads, baked goods, pastries, and made-from-scratch soups, salads, and sandwiches makes this airy cafe a popular destination throughout the day. It offers a good break from the sightseeing circuit. The industrial-looking building off West Concord's main street backs up to little Nashoba Brook, which is visible through the glass back wall. Order and pick up at the counter, and then grab a seat along the window or near the children's play area. You can also order takeout—this is great picnic food—or a loaf of crusty bread. See chapter 6 for information about the branch in Boston's **South End.**

152 Commonwealth Ave., West Concord. © **978/318-1999**. www.slowrise.com. Sandwiches $5–$6; salads $6–$8 per lb. MC, V. Mon–Fri 6am–6:30pm, Sat–Sun 8am–5pm. From Concord Center, follow Main St. (Rte. 62) west, across Rte. 2; bear right at traffic light in front of train station and go 3 blocks.

2 The North Shore & Cape Ann

The areas north of Boston abound with historic sights and gorgeous ocean vistas. Cape Ann is a rocky peninsula so enchantingly beautiful that when you hear the slogan "Massachusetts's *Other* Cape," you might forget what the first one was. Cape Ann and Cape Cod do share some attributes—scenery, shopping, seafood, and traffic. Its proximity to Boston and smaller manageable scale make Cape Ann a wonderful day trip as well as a good choice for a longer stay.

The **Cape Ann Chamber of Commerce** information center (see "Gloucester" later in this section) is a good resource. The **North of Boston Convention & Visitors Bureau,** 17 Peabody Sq., Peabody, MA 01960 (© **800/742-5306** or 978/977-7760; www.northofboston.org), publishes a visitor guide that covers 34 municipalities, including Salem, Marblehead, and Cape Ann. It also coordinates **ArtsNorth** (www.artsnorth.org), which lists cultural venues throughout the area.

MARBLEHEAD ✶✶✶
15 miles NE of Boston

Like an attractive person with a great personality, Marblehead has it all. Scenery, history, architecture, and shopping combine to make it one of the area's most popular day trips for both locals and visitors. It's even polite—many speed-limit signs say PLEASE. Marblehead is also a good place to spend a night or more. Allow at least a full morning, but be flexible, because you might want to hang around.

One of the most picturesque neighborhoods in New England is **Old Town** ✶✶✶, where narrow, twisting streets lead down to the magnificent harbor that helps make this the self-proclaimed "Yachting Capital of America." As

---

Tips North of Boston: Road Tips

The drive from Boston to Cape Ann on I-93 and Route 128 takes about an hour. A more leisurely excursion on Routes 1A, 129, 114, and 127 allows you to explore Marblehead and Salem. You can also follow Route 1 to I-95 and 128, but don't attempt it during rush hour. To go straight to Gloucester and Rockport—or to start there and work back—take I-93 north out of Boston. Where it turns into I-95 (signs point to New Hampshire and Maine), stay left and take Route 128 to the end. The last exit, no. 9, puts you in East Gloucester. To take Route 1A, leave downtown Boston through the Callahan Tunnel, which is in the middle of the Big Dig. If you miss the tunnel and wind up on I-93, follow signs to Route 1 and pick up Route 1A in Revere.

If you can, drive a car to explore north of the city. Public transportation in this area is good, but it doesn't go everywhere, and in many towns the train station is some distance from the attractions. For the full day-trip experience, try to visit on a spring, summer, or fall weekday; traffic is brutal on warm weekends. Many areas are practically ghost towns November through March, but all have enough of a year-round community to make an off-season excursion worthwhile.

Finds **For the Birds**

Marblehead Neck, an upscale neighborhood across the causeway from Devereux Beach, is home to an **Audubon bird sanctuary.** Turn east on Ocean Avenue south of downtown, and follow it less than a mile until you see a small sign to the left at Risley Avenue. Park in the small lot and follow the path into the sanctuary. To return to Marblehead proper, continue on Ocean Avenue, which becomes Harbor Avenue and forms a loop. En route, at the end of "the Neck," you can park near the decommissioned lighthouse and take in a breathtaking view.

---

you walk around Old Town, you'll see plaques on the houses bearing the date of construction, as well as the names of the builder and original occupant—a history lesson without studying. Many of the houses have stood since before the Revolutionary War, when Marblehead was a center of merchant shipping. Two historic homes are open for tours (see "Exploring the Town" below).

ESSENTIALS

GETTING THERE   By car, take Route 1A north through Revere and Lynn; bear right at the signs for Nahant and Swampscott. Follow Lynn Shore Drive through Swampscott to Route 129, which runs into town. Or take I-93 or Route 1 to Route 128, then follow Route 114 through Salem into Marblehead. Parking is tough, especially in Old Town—grab the first spot you see.

MBTA (© **617/222-3200;** www.mbta.com) bus no. 441/442 runs from Haymarket (Orange or Green Line) to downtown Marblehead. During rush periods on weekdays, the no. 448/449 connects Marblehead to Downtown Crossing. The trip takes about an hour, and the one-way fare is $2.75.

VISITOR INFORMATION   The **Marblehead Chamber of Commerce,** 62 Pleasant St., P.O. Box 76, Marblehead, MA 01945 (© **781/631-2868;** www. marbleheadchamber.org), is open weekdays from 9am to 5pm. The **information booth** (© **781/639-8469**) on Pleasant Street near Spring Street is open daily from late May to October, Friday through Sunday from 10am to 6pm; call ahead for varying hours the rest of the week. The chamber publishes a visitor guide and map that includes a calendar of events; ask for a business directory or check the website if you want a description of a walking tour. Another website to check out is www.visitmarblehead.com.

SPECIAL EVENTS   Sailing regattas take place in the outer harbor all summer, and **Race Week** in mid to late July attracts enthusiasts from all over the country. The **Christmas Walk,** on the first weekend in December, incorporates music, arts and crafts, shopping, and Santa Claus, who arrives by lobster boat.

EXPLORING THE TOWN

Marblehead is a wonderful place for aimless wandering; to add some structure, consult the walking tour described in the chamber of commerce's business directory. Whatever else you do, be sure to spend some time in **Crocker Park** ★★, on the harbor off Front Street. Especially in the warmer months, when boats jam the water nearly as far as the eye can see, the view is breathtaking. There are benches and a swing, and picnicking is allowed. The view from **Fort Sewall,** at the other end of Front Street, is equally mesmerizing.

Marblehead

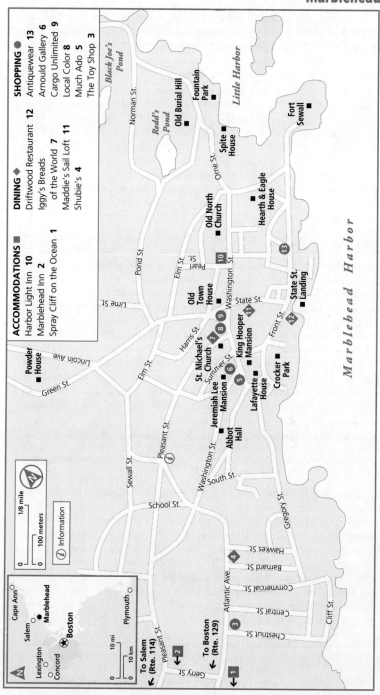

ACCOMMODATIONS ■
Harbor Light Inn **10**
Marblehead Inn **2**
Spray Cliff on the Ocean **1**

DINING ◆
Driftwood Restaurant **12**
Iggy's Breads
 of the World **7**
Maddie's Sail Loft **11**
Shubie's **4**

SHOPPING ●
Antiquewear **13**
Arnould Gallery **6**
Cargo Unlimited **9**
Local Color **8**
Much Ado **5**
The Toy Shop **3**

Marblehead Harbor

Little Harbor

Black Joe's Pond

Redd's Pond

Old Burial Hill

Fountain
Park

Spite
House

Fort
Sewall

Hearth & Eagle
House

Old North
Church

State St.
Landing

Old Town
House

St. Michael's
Church

King Hooper
Mansion

Jeremiah Lee
Mansion

Crocker
Park

Lafayette
House

Abbot
Hall

Powder
House

Norman St.
Orne St.
Pond St.
Elm St.
Pearl St.
Washington St.
State St.
Front St.
Lime St.
Harris St.
Summer St.
Lincoln Ave.
Green St.
Elm St.
Pleasant St.
Sewall St.
Washington St.
South St.
School St.
Gregory St.
Hawkes St.
Barnard St.
Commercial St.
Central St.
Cliff St.
Chestnut St.
Atlantic Ave.
pleasant St.
Gerry St.

To Salem
(Rte. 114)

To Boston
(Rte. 129)

Cape Ann
Salem
Marblehead
Lexington
Concord
Boston
Plymouth

10 mi
10 km

1/8 mile
100 meters

N

i Information

Just inland, the **Lafayette House** is at the corner of Hooper and Union streets. A corner of the private home was chopped off to make room for the passage of the Marquis de Lafayette's carriage when he visited the town in 1824. In Market Square on Washington Street, near the corner of State Street, is the **Old Town House,** in use for meetings and gatherings since 1727.

Abbot Hall   A 5-minute stop here (look for the clock tower) is just the ticket if you want to be able say you did some sightseeing. The town offices and historical commission share Abbot Hall with Archibald M. Willard's famous painting *The Spirit of '76* 🐦, on display in the Selectmen's Meeting Room. The thrill of recognizing the ubiquitous drummer, drummer boy, and fife player is the main reason to stop here. Cases in the halls contain objects and artifacts from the Marblehead Historical Society's collections.

Washington Sq. 🕿 781/631-0528. Free admission. Nov–Apr Mon–Tues and Thurs 8am–5pm, Wed 7:30am–7:30pm, Fri 8am–1pm; May–Oct Mon–Tues and Thurs 8am–5pm, Wed 7:30am–7:30pm, Fri 8am–5pm, Sat 9am–6pm, Sun 11am–6pm. From the historic district, follow Washington St. up the hill.

Jeremiah Lee Mansion 🐦🐦   The prospect of seeing original hand-painted wallpaper in an 18th-century home is reason enough to visit this house, built in 1768 for a wealthy merchant and considered an outstanding example of pre-Revolutionary Georgian architecture. Original rococo carving and other details complement historically accurate room arrangements, and ongoing restoration and interpretation by the Marblehead Historical Society place the 18th- and 19th-century furnishings and artifacts in context. The friendly guides welcome questions and are well versed in the history of the home. The lawn and gardens are open to the public.

The historical society's headquarters, across the street, house the **J.O.J. Frost Folk Art Gallery** and a changing exhibition gallery. Frost, a noted primitivist painter, was a Marblehead native. The society occasionally offers **candlelight tours** of the house and sponsors **walking tours** of Marblehead in July, August, and September. Call ahead to see if your schedules match.

🕿 781/631-1768. www.marbleheadhistory.org. Mansion: 161 Washington St. Guided tours $5 adults, $4.50 seniors and students. June to mid-Oct Tues–Sat 10am–4pm, Sun 1–4pm. Closed mid-Oct to May. Historical Society: 170 Washington St. Free admission. Tues–Sat 10am–4pm. Follow Washington St. until it curves right and heads uphill toward Abbot Hall; mansion is on right.

King Hooper Mansion   Shipping tycoon Robert Hooper got his nickname because he treated his sailors so well, but it's easy to think he was called King because he lived like royalty. Around the corner from the home of Jeremiah Lee (whose sister was the 2nd of Hooper's 4 wives), the 1728 King Hooper Mansion gained a Georgian addition in 1745. The period furnishings, although not original, give a sense of the life of an 18th-century merchant prince, from the wine cellar to the third-floor ballroom. The building houses the headquarters of the **Marblehead Arts Association,** which stages monthly exhibits and runs a gift shop that sells members' work. The mansion has a lovely garden; enter through the gate at the right of the house.

(Fun Fact Architectural Details

On the hill between the Jeremiah Lee Mansion and Abbot Hall, notice the private homes at 185, 181, and 175 Washington St. They are other good examples of the architecture of the pre-Revolutionary period.

8 Hooper St. ⓒ **781/631-2608.** Donation requested for tour. Mon–Sat 10am–4pm, Sun 1–5pm. Call ahead; no tours during private parties. Where Washington St. curves at the foot of hill near Lee mansion, look for the colorful sign.

SHOPPING

Marblehead is a legendary (or notorious, if you're on a budget) shopping desti-nation. Shops, boutiques, and galleries abound in **Old Town** and on **Atlantic Avenue** and the east end of **Pleasant Street.** The most unusual shop in town, **Antiquewear,** 82 Front St., near the town pier (ⓒ **781/639-0070;** http://users. primushost.com/~antiquew), sells 19th-century buttons ingeniously fashioned into jewelry. Other good stops include **Local Color,** 1 Pleasant St. (ⓒ **781/ 631-7166**), a quirky gift shop; **Cargo Unlimited,** 82 Washington St. (ⓒ **781/ 631-1112;** www.cargounlimited.com), for home furnishings and accessories; an excellent antiquarian bookstore, **Much Ado,** 108 Washington St. (ⓒ **781/ 639-0400;** www.muchadobooks.com); **Arnould Gallery and Framery,** 111 Washington St. (ⓒ **781/631-6366**); and **Toy Shop,** 44–48 Atlantic Ave. (ⓒ **781/631-9900**).

ACCOMMODATIONS

This is B&B heaven. Space precludes listing the numerous small inns and bed-and-breakfasts, but the accommodations listings of the **Marblehead Chamber of Commerce,** 62 Pleasant St., P.O. Box 76, Marblehead, MA 01945 (ⓒ **781/ 631-2868;** www.marbleheadchamber.org), include many of them. Check the website, call or write for a visitor guide, or consult one of the agencies listed in chapter 5.

Harbor Light Inn ★★   A stone's throw from the Old Town House, two Fed-eral-era mansions make up this gracious inn. From the wood floors to the 1729 beams (in a 3rd-floor room) to the swimming pool, it's both historic and relax-ing. Rooms are comfortably furnished in period style, with some lovely antiques; most have canopy or four-poster beds. Eleven hold working fireplaces, and five of those have double Jacuzzis. VCRs and free video rentals are available. The best rooms, on the top floor at the back of the building, away from the street, have gorgeous harbor views. Undeniably romantic, the inn also attracts business trav-elers (often for meetings) during the week.

58 Washington St., Marblehead, MA 01945. ⓒ **781/631-2186.** Fax 781/631-2216. www.harborlightinn. com. 21 units (some w/shower only). $125–$245 double; $195–$295 suite. Rates include breakfast, after-noon refreshments, and use of bikes. Corporate rate available midweek. 2-night minimum stay weekends, 3-night minimum holiday and high-season weekends. AE, MC, V. Free parking. **Amenities:** Heated outdoor pool; access to nearby health club ($5); airport shuttle. *In room:* A/C, TV/VCR, dataport, hair dryer, iron, safe, robes.

Marblehead Inn ★   This three-story Victorian mansion just outside the his-toric district is an all-suite inn. It's not as convenient and romantic as the Har-bor Light Inn, but it offers better amenities and a more family-friendly atmosphere. Each attractively decorated unit contains a living room, bedroom, and workstation. This is a good choice for businesspeople making an extended stay, as well as families, who can make good use of the kitchenette (the inn sup-plies breakfast provisions). Most suites have Jacuzzis, and some have working fireplaces and small patios. The 1872 building has been an inn since 1923, and it once played host to Amelia Earhart.

264 Pleasant St. (Rte. 114), Marblehead, MA 01945. ⓒ **800/399-5843** or 781/639-9999. Fax 781/639-9996. www.marbleheadinn.com. 10 units (2 w/shower only). $149–$199 double. Extra person $25. Children under 10 stay free in parent's room. Rates include continental breakfast. Winter discounts, corporate and long-term

rates available. 2-night minimum stay busy weekends, 3-night minimum holiday weekends. AE, MC, V. Free parking. *In room:* A/C, TV/VCR, dataport, kitchenette, fridge, coffeemaker, hair dryer.

Spray Cliff on the Ocean ⟨⟩

Spray Cliff, a three-story Victorian Tudor built in 1910 on a cliff overlooking the ocean, is 5 minutes from town and a world away. It books honeymooners, vacationers in search of isolation, and some mid-week business travelers who want a minimum of distractions. The most desirable of the large, sunny rooms are the five that face the water. Three rooms have fireplaces, and all are luxuriously decorated in contemporary style with down comforters and bright accents, including fresh flowers. Roger and Sally Plauché have run their romantic inn on a quiet residential street 1 minute from the beach since 1994.

25 Spray Ave., Marblehead, MA 01945. ⓒ **800/626-1530** or 781/631-6789. Fax 781/639-4563. www.spray cliff.com. 7 units (some w/shower only). May–Oct $200–$250 double. Extra person $25. Rates include continental breakfast, evening refreshments, and use of bikes. Off-season discounts available. 2-night minimum stay weekends, 3-night minimum busy holiday weekends. AE, MC, V. Free parking. Take Atlantic Ave. (Rte. 129) to traffic light at Clifton Ave. and turn east (right driving north, left driving south); parking area is at end of street. No children accepted. *In room:* No phone.

DINING

At a number of places in Old Town, you can stock up for a picnic along the water. **Shubie's,** 32 Atlantic Ave. (ⓒ **781/631-0149**), carries a good selection of specialty foods. **Iggy's Bread of the World** ⟨⟩, 5 Pleasant St. (ⓒ **781/639-4717**), serves fabulous gourmet baked goods and coffee. It also has a small seating area, but really, go outside.

Driftwood Restaurant ⟨⟩ DINER/SEAFOOD

At the foot of State Street next to Clark Landing (the town pier) is an honest-to-goodness local hangout. Join the crowd at a table or the counter for generous portions of breakfast (served all day) or lunch. Try pancakes or hash, chowder or a seafood roll—a hot dog bun filled with, say, fried clams or lobster salad). The house specialty, served on weekends and holidays, is fried dough, which is exactly as delicious and indigestible as it sounds.

63 Front St. ⓒ **781/631-1145**. Main courses $3–$11; breakfast items less than $6. No credit cards. Summer daily 6:30am–5pm; winter daily 6:30am–2pm.

Maddie's Sail Loft SEAFOOD

Less than a block from the harbor, Maddie's is a friendly tavern that serves good steaks as well as excellent fresh seafood. The strong drinks are another attraction, especially during the summer boating season; this (or, alas, one of the private yacht clubs) is the place to search for that cute sailor you saw down by the water. There's live jazz on Thursday nights and a lively local scene year-round.

15 State St. ⓒ **781/631-9824**. Main courses $9–$16. No credit cards. Mon–Sat 11:45am–2pm and 5–10pm; Sun 11:45am–4pm. Bar open until 11:30pm.

SALEM ⟨⟩⟨⟩

17 miles NE of Boston, 4 miles NW of Marblehead

Settled in 1626, 4 years before Boston, Salem later enjoyed international renown as a center of merchant shipping, but today it's famous around the world because of a 7-month episode in 1692. The witchcraft trial hysteria led to 20 deaths, 3-plus centuries of notoriety, countless lessons on the evils of prejudice, and innumerable bad puns ("Stop by for a spell" is a favorite slogan).

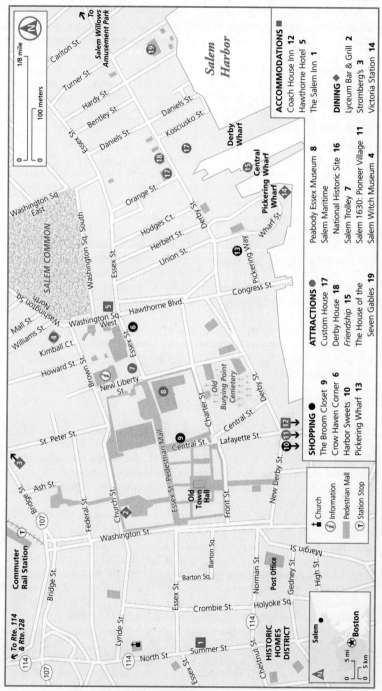

Salem

ACCOMMODATIONS ■
Coach House Inn **12**
Hawthorne Hotel **5**
The Salem Inn **1**

DINING ◆
Lyceum Bar & Grill **2**
Stromberg's **3**
Victoria Station **14**

ATTRACTIONS ●
Custom House **17**
Derby House **18**
Friendship **15**
The House of the
Seven Gables **19**

Peabody Essex Museum **8**
Salem Maritime
National Historic Site **16**
Salem Trolley **7**
Salem 1630: Pioneer Village **11**
Salem Witch Museum **4**

SHOPPING ●
The Broom Closet **9**
Crow Haven Corner **6**
Harbor Sweets **10**
Pickering Wharf **13**

✝ Church
ⓘ Information
▨ Pedestrian Mall
Ⓣ Station Stop

Salem Harbor

*Salem Willows
Amusement Park*

SALEM COMMON

HISTORIC
HOMES
DISTRICT

Commuter
Rail Station

To Rte. 114
& Rte. 128

Salem ●
★ Boston

Unable to live down the association, and never forgetting the victims, Salem embraces its reputation. The high school sports teams are the Witches, and the *Salem Evening News* logo is a silhouette of a sorceress. The city abounds with witch-associated attractions, plus nearly as many reminders of Salem's seagoing legacy. Most are historically accurate, but you'll also see a fair number of goofy souvenirs and opportunistic tourist traps. An excellent antidote to the latter is the newly expanded **Peabody Essex Museum.** Salem is a family-friendly destination that's worth at least a half-day visit (perhaps after a stop in Marblehead) and can easily fill a day.

ESSENTIALS

GETTING THERE   By car from Marblehead, follow Route 114 west. From Boston, take Route 1A north to Salem, being careful in Lynn, where the road turns left and immediately right. You can also take I-93 or Route 1 to Route 128 and then Route 114 into downtown Salem. There's metered street parking, and a reasonably priced municipal garage across the street from the National Park Service Regional Visitor Center.

From Boston, the **MBTA** (*©* 617/222-3200; www.mbta.com) operates commuter trains from North Station and bus no. 450 from Haymarket (Orange or Green Line). The train is more comfortable than the bus but runs less frequently. It takes 30 to 35 minutes; the round-trip fare is $6. The station is about 5 blocks from the downtown area. The one-way fare for the 35- to 55-minute bus trip is $2.75.

VISITOR INFORMATION   A good place to start is the **National Park Service Regional Visitor Center,** 2 New Liberty St. (*©* 978/740-1650; www.nps.gov/sama), open daily from 9am to 5pm. Exhibits highlight early settlement, maritime history, and the leather and textiles industries. The center distributes brochures and pamphlets, including one that describes a **walking tour** of the historic district, and has an auditorium where a free film on Essex County provides an overview.

The city's Office of Tourism & Cultural Affairs, **Destination Salem,** 59 Wharf St., Salem, MA 01970 (*©* 877/SALEM-MA or 978/744-3663; www.salem.org), and the Salem Chamber of Commerce collaborate on a free visitor guide that includes a good map. The **Salem Chamber of Commerce,** 63 Wharf St., Salem, MA 01970 (*©* 978/744-0004; www.salem-chamber.org), maintains a large rack of brochures and pamphlets at its office on the first floor of Old Town Hall. It's open weekdays from 9am to 5pm. Salem has an excellent community website (www.salemweb.com) that includes a city guide.

GETTING AROUND   In the congested downtown area, **walking** is the way to go, but you might not want to hoof it to all the sights, especially if it's hot. At the Essex Street side of the visitor center, you can board the **Salem Trolley** (*©* 978/744-5469; www.salemtrolley.com) for a 1-hour narrated tour, and you can reboard as often as you like at any of the 15 stops. It's a good deal if you're spending the day and don't want to keep moving the car or carrying leg-weary children. The trolley operates from 10am to 5pm (last tour at 4) daily April through October, and weekends in March and November. Tickets ($10 adults, $9 seniors, $5 children 5 to 12, $25 families) are good all day; they're available onboard and at the Trolley Depot shop on the Essex Street pedestrian mall at Central Street.

SPECIAL EVENTS   The city's 3-week Halloween celebration, **Haunted Happenings** *ⓡⓡ*, includes parades, parties, tours, and a ceremony on the big day.

During **Heritage Days,** a weeklong event in mid-August, the city celebrates its multicultural history with musical and theatrical performances, a parade, and fireworks. Contact Destination Salem (see "Visitor Information" above) for details.

EXPLORING THE TOWN

The historic district extends well inland from the waterfront. Many 18th-century houses, some with original furnishings, still stand. Ship captains lived near the water at the east end of downtown, in relatively small houses crowded close together. The captains' employers, the shipping company owners, built their homes away from the water (and the accompanying aromas). Many of them lived on **Chestnut Street** ★★, now a National Historic Landmark. Residents along the grand thoroughfare must, by legal agreement, adhere to colonial style in their decorating and furnishings. Ask at the visitor center for the pamphlet that describes a walking tour of the historic district.

By car or trolley, the **Salem Willows** (© 978/745-0251; www.salem willows.com) amusements are 5 minutes away; many signs point the way. The strip of rides and snack bars has a honky-tonk air, and the waterfront park is a good place to bring a picnic and wander along the shore. There's no admission fee; meter parking is available. To enjoy the great view without the arcades and rides, have lunch one peninsula over at **Winter Island Park.**

The House of the Seven Gables ★ *Kids*   Nathaniel Hawthorne's cousin lived here, and stories and legends of the house and its inhabitants inspired his 1851 book of the same name. If you haven't read the eerie novel, don't let that keep you away—begin your visit with the audiovisual program, which tells the story. The house, built by Captain John Turner in 1668, holds six rooms of period furniture, including pieces referred to in the book, and a secret staircase. Tours include a visit to Hawthorne's birthplace (built before 1750 and moved to the grounds) and describe what life was like for the house's 18th-century inhabitants. The costumed guides can get a little silly as they mug for young visitors, but they're well versed in the history of the buildings and artifacts, and eager to answer questions. Also on the grounds, overlooking Salem Harbor, are period gardens, the **Retire Beckett House** (1655), the **Hooper-Hathaway House** (1682), and a **counting house** (1830).

Under the same management, **Salem 1630: Pioneer Village,** Forest River Park, West Avenue off Route 114/1A, is a re-creation of a Puritan village just 4 years after European settlement. Costumed interpreters lead tours around the unpaved village (wear sneakers), demonstrate crafts, and tend farm animals. A popular destination for school and day-camp field trips, the village is open to the public only in July and August (Mon–Sat 10am–5pm, Sun noon–5pm).

54 Turner St. © 978/744-0991. www.7gables.org. Guided tour of house and grounds $10 adults, $9 seniors, $6.50 children 5–12, free for children under 5. Salem 1630 admission $7.50 adults, $6.50 seniors, $4.50 children 5–12. Tour and Salem 1630 admission $16 adults, $14 seniors, $10.50 children 5–12. Surcharges may apply for special exhibitions. Nov–June daily 10am–5pm; July–Oct daily 10am–7pm. Closed 1st 3 weeks of Jan, Thanksgiving, Dec 25. From downtown, follow Derby St. east 3 blocks past Derby Wharf.

Peabody Essex Museum ★★ *Kids*   The Peabody Essex Museum is a treasure trove of art and cultural history peeking out from under a pointy black hat. Though sometimes overshadowed by Salem's every-witch-way reputation, the museum's encyclopedic collections offer an engaging look at nearly 4 centuries in a fascinating seaport (yes, including the witchcraft trials). A huge expansion project completed in 2003 created new galleries and even added an 18th-century

Qing dynasty house that was shipped from China and reassembled. The new wing, designed by Moshe Safdie, allows the museum to display a significant proportion of its holdings for the first time.

The permanent collections blend "the natural and artificial curiosities" that Salem's sea captains and merchants brought back from around the world to the Peabody Museum (1799) with the local and domestic artifacts of the Essex Institute (1821), the county historical society. The displays help you understand the significance of each artifact, and interpretive materials (including interactive and hands-on activities) let children get involved. You might see objects related to the history of the port of Salem (including gorgeous furniture), the whaling trade, the witchcraft trials, East Asian art, and the practical arts and crafts of East Asian, Pacific Island, and Native American peoples. Portraits of area residents include Charles Osgood's omnipresent rendering of Nathaniel Hawthorne. Temporary exhibitions during the lifespan of this book include **Luxury & Innovation: Furniture Masterworks of John & Thomas Seymour** (Nov 2003–Feb 2004) and **Behind the Painted Smile: Image, Reality & the Japanese Geisha** (Feb–Apr 2004).

Sign up for a fascinating tour of one or more of the museum's 10 historic houses. Besides the newly acquired Chinese house, the sites include the meticulously restored 1804 **Gardner-Pingree House** ★★, a magnificent Federal mansion where a notorious murder was committed in 1830. You can also take a gallery tour or select from about a dozen pamphlets that describe self-guided tours. The museum cafe serves lunch daily.

East India Sq. ⓒ 800/745-4054 or 978/745-9500. www.pem.org. Admission $10 adults, $8 seniors and students, free for children under 17. Surcharges may apply for special exhibitions. Apr–Oct Mon–Sat 10am–5pm, Sun noon–5pm; Nov–Mar Tues–Sat 10am–5pm, Sun noon–5pm. Closed Jan 1, Thanksgiving, Dec 25. Take Hawthorne Blvd. to Essex St., following signs for visitor center. Enter on Essex St. or New Liberty St.

Salem Maritime National Historic Site ★ *Kids* An entertaining introduction to Salem's seagoing history, this complex includes an exciting attraction: a real live ship. The *Friendship* ★★ is a full-size replica of a 1797 East Indiaman merchant vessel, a three-masted 171-footer that disappeared during the War of 1812. The tall ship is a faithful replica with some concessions to the modern era, such as diesel engines and accessibility for people with disabilities. The **guided ranger tour** includes a tour of the ship.

With the decline of merchant shipping in the early 19th century, Salem's wharves fell into disrepair. In 1938, the National Park Service took over a small piece of the waterfront, **Derby Wharf.** It's now a finger of parkland extending into the harbor, part of the 9 acres dotted with explanatory markers that make up the historic site.

On adjacent **Central Wharf** is a warehouse, built around 1800, that houses the orientation center. Tours, which vary seasonally, expand on Salem's maritime history. Yours might include the **Derby House** (1762), a wedding gift to shipping magnate Elias Hasket Derby from his father, and the **Custom House** (1819). Legend (myth, really) has it that Nathaniel Hawthorne was working here when he found an embroidered scarlet "A." If you prefer to explore on your own, you can see the free film at the orientation center and wander around **Derby Wharf,** the **West India Goods Store,** the **Bonded Warehouse,** the **Scale House,** and Central Wharf.

174 Derby St. ⓒ 978/740-1660. www.nps.gov/sama. Free admission. Guided tours $5 adults, $3 seniors and children 6–15. Daily 9am–5pm. Closed Jan 1, Thanksgiving, Dec 25. Take Derby St. east; just past Pickering Wharf, Derby Wharf is on the right.

Fun Fact **A Face in the Crowd**

On the traffic island across from the entrance to the **Salem Witch Museum** is a statue that's easily mistaken for a witch. It's really **Roger Conant,** who founded Salem in 1626.

Salem Witch Museum ★★ (Kids)   This is one of the most memorable attractions in eastern Massachusetts—it's both interesting and scary. The main draw of the museum (a former church) is a three-dimensional audiovisual presentation with life-size figures. The show takes place in a huge room lined with displays that are lighted in sequence. The 30-minute narration tells the story of the witchcraft trials and the accompanying hysteria. The well-researched presentation tells the story accurately, if somewhat overdramatically. One of the victims was crushed to death by rocks piled on a board on his chest—smaller kids might need a reminder that he's not real. The narration is available translated into French, German, Italian, Japanese, and Spanish. There's also a small exhibit that traces the history of witches, witchcraft, and witch hunts.

19½ Washington Sq., on Rte. 1A. © **978/744-1692.** www.salemwitchmuseum.com. Admission $7 adults, $6 seniors, $4.50 children 6–14. Daily July–Aug 10am–7pm; Sept–June 10am–5pm. Closed Jan 1, Thanksgiving, Dec 25. Follow Hawthorne Blvd. to the northwest corner of Salem Common.

SHOPPING

Pickering Wharf (© 978/740-6990; www.pickeringwharf.com), at the corner of Derby and Congress streets, is a waterfront complex of shops, boutiques, restaurants, and condos. It's popular for strolling, snacking, and shopping, and the central location makes it a local landmark.

Several shops specialize in witchcraft accessories. Bear in mind that Salem is home to many practicing witches who take their beliefs very seriously. The **Broom Closet,** 3–5 Central St. (© **978/741-3669**), and **Crow Haven Corner,** 125 Essex St. (© **978/745-8763**), stock everything from crystals to clothing.

ACCOMMODATIONS

The busiest and most expensive time of year is Halloween week; reserve well in advance.

Coach House Inn   Built in 1879 for a ship's captain, this inn is in a historic district 2 blocks from the harbor and just a mile from downtown. It's a 20-minute walk or 5-minute drive from the center of town. Besides sightseers, it books travelers with business at nearby Salem State College. The three-story mansion was renovated in 2001. The good-size rooms are elegantly furnished in traditional style. All have high ceilings, and most have (nonworking) fireplaces. Breakfast arrives at your door in a basket—a nice perk if dining-room chitchat isn't your thing.

284 Lafayette St. (Rtes. 1A and 114), Salem, MA 01970. © **800/688-8689** or 978/744-4092. Fax 978/745-8031. www.coachhousesalem.com. 11 units, 9 w/bathroom (2 w/shower only). $80–$98 double with shared bathroom; $95–$155 double with private bathroom; $160–$198 suite. Rates include continental breakfast. Minimum 2- or 3-night stay weekends and holidays. AE, DISC, MC, V. Free parking. *In room:* A/C, TV, coffeemaker.

Hawthorne Hotel ★ (Kids)   This historic hotel, built in 1925, is both convenient and comfortable. The only full-service hotel downtown, it books both vacationers and business travelers, and it's popular for functions. The six-story

---

Finds The Confection Collection

Shops throughout New England sell the chocolate confections of **Harbor Sweets** ⚝⚝, Palmer Cove, 85 Leavitt St., off Lafayette Street (© **978/745-7648**). The retail store overlooks the floor of the factory. The deliriously good sweets are expensive, but candy bars and small assortments are available. Closed Sunday.

---

building is centrally located and well maintained, with a traditional atmosphere. A recent $1 million renovation refurnished the guest rooms, which are attractively furnished and adequate in size. The best units, on the Salem Common (north) side of the building, have better views than rooms that face the street. Whatever direction you face, ask to be as high up as possible, because the neighborhood is busy. If you're traveling with children, ask about "Family Fun" packages, which include discounted tickets to area museums.

18 Washington Sq. (at Salem Common), Salem, MA 01970. © 800/729-7829 or 978/744-4080. Fax 978/745-9842. www.hawthornehotel.com. 89 units (some w/shower only). $104–$204 double; $204–$309 suite. Extra person $12. Children under 16 stay free in parent's room. Off-season discounts, senior discount, and weekend and other packages available. 2-night minimum stay May–Oct weekends. AE, DC, DISC, MC, V. Limited self-parking. Small pets accepted; $15 charge. **Amenities:** Restaurant (American); tavern; exercise room; access to nearby heath club ($5–$8); concierge; airport shuttle; room service until 10pm; laundry service; same-day dry cleaning. Rooms for travelers with disabilities are available. *In room:* A/C, TV, dataport, hair dryer, iron.

Salem Inn ⚝⚝   The Salem Inn occupies the comfortable niche between too-big hotel and too-small B&B. Its clientele includes honeymooners as well as sightseers and families, and the variety of rooms means that the innkeepers can make a good match of guest and accommodations. The inn consists of three properties. The 1834 West House and the 1854 Curwen House, former homes of ship captains, are listed on the National Register of Historic Places. The best units are the honeymoon and family suites (which have kitchenettes) in the 1874 Peabody House. Guest rooms are large and tastefully decorated; some rooms have fireplaces, canopy beds, and whirlpool baths. Guests of all three houses can relax in the peaceful rose garden at the rear of the main building.

7 Summer St. (Rte. 114), Salem, MA 01970. © 800/446-2995 or 978/741-0680. Fax 978/744-8924. www.saleminnma.com. 42 units (some w/shower only). Nov–Sept $119–$149 double; $169–$229 suite. Oct $180–$210 double; $220–$285 suite. Rates include continental breakfast. Extra person $15–$25. Minimum stay 2–3 nights during special events and holidays. AE, DC, DISC, MC, V. Free parking. Pets accepted with prior arrangement. *In room:* A/C, TV, coffeemaker, hair dryer, iron.

DINING

Pickering Wharf has a food court as well as a link in the **Victoria Station** chain (© **978/744-7644**), where the deck has a great view of the marina. The cafe at the **Peabody Essex Museum** (see above) serves lunch.

Lyceum Bar & Grill ⚝⚝ CONTEMPORARY AMERICAN   The elegance of the Lyceum's high-ceilinged front rooms and glass-walled back rooms matches the quality of the food, which attracts local businesspeople and out-of-towners. Grilling is a favorite cooking technique—try the signature grilled marinated portobellas. They're available as an appetizer and scattered throughout the menu—for example, in delectable pasta with chicken, red peppers, and Swiss chard in wine sauce. Beef tenderloin comes with garlic mashed potatoes and brandy-and-peppercorn mushroom sauce. Try to save room for one of the traditional yet sophisticated desserts—the brownie sundae is out of this world.

43 Church St. (at Washington St.). © **978/745-7665.** www.lyceumsalem.com. Reservations recommended. Main courses $7–$12 at lunch, $15–$27 at dinner. AE, DISC, MC, V. Mon–Fri 11:30am–3pm; Sun brunch 11am–3pm; daily 5:30–10pm. Validated parking available.

Stromberg's ★ *Kids* SEAFOOD   For generous portions of well-prepared seafood and a view of the water, seek out this popular spot at the foot of the bridge to Beverly, which draws both locals and out-of-towners. You won't care that Beverly Harbor isn't the most exciting spot, especially if it's summer and you're out on the deck. The fish and clam chowders are excellent, daily specials are numerous, and there are more chicken, beef, and pasta options than you might expect. Crustacean lovers in the mood to splurge will fall for the world-class lobster roll.

2 Bridge St. (Rte. 1A). © **978/744-1863.** www.strombergs.com. Reservations recommended at dinner. Main courses $6–$11 at lunch, $11–$18 at dinner; children's menu $5. AE, DISC, MC, V. Sun and Tues–Thurs 11am–9pm; Fri–Sat 11am–10pm.

A DETOUR TO ESSEX

If you approach or leave Cape Ann on Route 128, head west on Route 133 to **Essex.** It's a beautiful little town known for Essex clams, salt marshes, a long tradition of shipbuilding, an incredible number of antiques shops, and one celebrated restaurant.

Legend has it that **Woodman's of Essex** ★★★, Main Street (© **800/649-1773** or 978/768-6451; www.woodmans.com), was the birthplace of the fried clam in 1916. Today the thriving family business is a great spot to join legions of locals and visitors from around the world for lobster "in the rough," chowder, steamers, corn on the cob, onion rings, and (you guessed it) superb fried clams. Expect the line to be long, but it moves quickly and offers a good view of the regimented commotion in the food-preparation area. Eat in a booth, upstairs on the deck, or out back at a picnic table. Credit cards aren't accepted, but there's an ATM on the premises. You'll want to be well fed before you set off to explore the numerous antiques shops along Main Street. Open daily in the summer from 11am to 10pm; winter, Sunday to Thursday from 11am to 8pm, Friday and Saturday 11am to 9pm.

A DETOUR TO A CASTLE

South of downtown Gloucester on Route 127, you'll see signs for Magnolia and the **Hammond Castle Museum,** 80 Hesperus Ave. (© **978/283-7673;** www.hammondcastle.org). Eccentric inventor John Hays Hammond Jr. designed the medieval castle, which was constructed of Rockport granite and cost more than $6 million when it was built from 1926 to 1929. Guided tours aren't offered, so you're on your own with a pamphlet to direct you—not the most fulfilling way to explore such a peculiar place. Still, if the medieval era appeals to you, you'll definitely enjoy a visit. The castle has 85-foot towers, battlements, stained-glass windows, a great hall 60 feet high, and an enclosed "outdoor" pool and courtyard

---

Fun Fact **Party Line**

Alexander Graham Bell made the first long-distance telephone call from the building that now holds the Lyceum Bar & Grill.

Kids A Whale of an Adventure

The depletion of New England's fishing grounds has led to the rise of another important seagoing industry, **whale watching** ★★. The waters off the coast of Massachusetts are prime territory, and Gloucester is a center of cruises. Stellwagen Bank, which runs from Gloucester to Provincetown about 27 miles east of Boston, is a rich feeding ground for the magnificent mammals. Species spotted in the area are mainly humpback, finback, and minke whales, who dine on sand eels and other fish that gather along the ridge. The whales often perform for their audience by jumping out of the water, and dolphins occasionally join the show. Naturalists onboard narrate the trip for the companies listed here, pointing out the whales and describing birds and fish that cross your path.

Whale watching is not particularly time- or cost-effective, especially if restless children are along, but it's so popular for a reason: The payoff is, literally and figuratively, huge. This is an "only in New England" experience that kids (and adults) will remember for a long time.

The season runs May through October. Dress warmly—it's much cooler at sea than on land. Wear a hat and rubber-soled shoes, and take sunglasses, sunscreen, a hat, and a camera with plenty of film. If you're prone to motion sickness, take precautions, because you'll be at sea for 4 to 6 hours. If you plan to take Dramamine, take it before you depart.

This is an extremely competitive business—they'd deny it, but the companies are virtually indistinguishable. Most guarantee sightings, offer a morning and an afternoon cruise as well as deep-sea fishing excursions, honor other firms' coupons, and offer AAA and AARP discounts. Check the local marinas for sailing times, prices ($29–$31 for adults, less for seniors and children), and reservations, which are strongly recommended.

In downtown Gloucester, **Cape Ann Whale Watch** (© **800/877-5110** or 978/283-5110; www.caww.com) is the oldest and best-known operation. Also downtown are **Capt. Bill's Whale Watch** (© **800/33-WHALE** or 978/283-6995; www.captainbillswhalewatch.com) and **Seven Seas Whale Watch** (© **888/238-1776** or 978/283-1776; www. 7seas-whalewatch.com). At the Cape Ann Marina, off Route 133, is **Yankee Whale Watch** (© **800/WHALING** or 978/283-0313; www.yankee whalewatch.com).

lined with foliage, trees, and medieval artifacts (including the whole wooden front of a butcher shop). Many 12th-, 13th-, and 14th-century furnishings, tapestries, paintings, and architectural fragments fill the rooms. Admission is $8 for adults, $6 for seniors and students, $5 for children 4 to 12, free for children under 4. It's open weekends year-round from 10am to 3pm, plus June through December Monday through Friday from 10am to 6pm; call ahead in fall and winter to double-check hours before setting out.

GLOUCESTER ✦✦

33 miles NE of Boston, 16 miles NE of Salem

The ocean has been Gloucester's lifeblood since long before the first European settlement in 1623. The French explorer Samuel de Champlain called the harbor "Le Beauport" when he came across it in 1604, some 600 years after the Vikings. Its configuration and proximity to good fishing gave it the reputation it enjoys to this day. If you read or saw *The Perfect Storm,* you'll have a sense of what to expect.

Gloucester (which rhymes with "roster") is a working city, not a cutesy tourist town, with one of the last surviving commercial fishing fleets in New England, an internationally celebrated artists' colony, a large Portuguese-American community, and just enough historic attractions. Allow at least half a day, perhaps combined with a visit to the tourist magnet of Rockport; a full day would be better, especially if you plan a cruise or whale watch.

ESSENTIALS

GETTING THERE   From Salem, follow Route 1A across the bridge to Beverly, pick up Route 127, and take it through Manchester (near, not on, the water) to Gloucester. From Boston, the quickest path is I-93 or Route 1 to Route 128, which runs directly to Gloucester. Route 128 is mostly inland; to take in more scenery, leave Route 128 at Manchester and continue to Gloucester on Route 127. There's street parking (metered and not), and a free lot on the causeway to Rocky Neck.

The **commuter rail** (© **617/222-3200;** www.mbta.com) runs from Boston's North Station. The trip takes about an hour; the round-trip fare is $9. The station is across town from downtown, so allow time for getting to the waterfront area. The **Cape Ann Transportation Authority,** or CATA (© **978/283-7916;** www.canntran.com), runs buses from town to town on Cape Ann and operates special routes during the summer.

VISITOR INFORMATION   The **Gloucester Tourism Office,** 22 Poplar St., Gloucester, MA 01930 (© **800/649-6839** or 978/281-8865; www.gloucester ma.com), operates the excellent Visitors Welcoming Center at Stage Fort Park, off Route 127 at Route 133. It's open during the summer daily from 9am to 5pm. The **Cape Ann Chamber of Commerce,** 33 Commercial St., Gloucester, MA 01930 (© **800/321-0133** or 978/283-1601; www.capeannvacations. com), is open year-round (summer weekdays 8am–6pm, Sat 10am–6pm, Sun 10am–4pm; winter weekdays 8am–5pm) and has a helpful staff. It also operates a seasonal information booth on Rogers Street at Harbor Loop. Call or write for the chamber's four-color map and brochure.

⌒ Moments Down to the Sea

On Stacy Boulevard west of downtown Gloucester is a reminder of the sea's danger. Leonard Craske's bronze statue of the **Gloucester Fisherman,** known as "The Man at the Wheel," bears the inscription "They That Go Down to the Sea in Ships 1623–1923." About a ¼ mile west is a memorial to the women and children who waited at home. As you take in the glorious view, consider this: More than 10,000 fishermen lost their lives during the city's first 300 years.

SPECIAL EVENTS   Gloucester holds summer festivals and street fairs at the drop of a hat. They honor everything from clams to schooners—check while you're planning to see what's up while you'll be in town. The best-known event is **St. Peter's Fiesta,** a colorful 4-day celebration at the end of June. The Italian-American fishing colony's festival has more in common with a carnival midway than a religious observation, but it's great fun. There are parades, games, music, food, sporting events, and, on Sunday, the blessing of the fleet.

EXPLORING THE TOWN

Business isn't nearly what it once was, but fishing is still Gloucester's leading industry (as your nose will tell you). Tourism is a very close second, and the city is an exceptionally welcoming destination—residents seem genuinely happy to see out-of-towners and to offer directions and insider info. The **"Gloucester Maritime Trail"** brochure, available at visitor centers, describes four excellent self-guided tours.

Stage Fort Park, off Route 127 at Route 133, offers an excellent view of the harbor and has a busy snack bar (summer only). It's a good spot for picnicking, swimming, or playing on the cannons in the Revolutionary War fort.

To reach **East Gloucester,** follow signs as you leave downtown, or go directly from Route 128, Exit 9. On East Main Street, you'll see signs for the world-famous **Rocky Neck Art Colony** ⊛⊛, the oldest continuously operating art colony in the country. Park in the lot on the tiny causeway and head west along Rocky Neck Avenue, which abounds with studios, galleries, restaurants, and people. The draw is the presence of working artists, not just shops that happen to sell art. Most galleries are open daily in the summer, 10am to 10pm.

The prestigious **North Shore Arts Association,** 197 E. Main St. (© **978/ 283-1857;** www.cape-ann.com/nsaa), was founded in 1922 to showcase local artists' work. The exhibits are worth a visit before or after your excursion across the causeway. The building is open late May through Columbus Day, Monday through Saturday from 10am to 5pm, Sunday noon to 5pm. Admission is free.

Also in East Gloucester, the **Gloucester Stage Company,** 267 E. Main St. (© **978/281-4099;** www.cape-ann.com/stageco.html), is one of the best repertory troupes in New England. Founder and artistic director Israel Horovitz, a

---

⟮Moments *The Perfect Storm*

Sebastian Junger's best-selling book *The Perfect Storm,* a thrilling but tragic nonfiction account of the "no-name" hurricane of 1991, became a blockbuster movie in 2000. Even before that, fans of the book were arriving in Gloucester and asking to be pointed toward the neighborhood tavern that costars in both accounts. The **Crow's Nest,** 334 Main St. (© **978/ 281-2965**), a bit east of downtown, is a no-frills place with a horseshoe-shaped bar and a crowd of regulars who seem amused that their favorite hangout is a tourist attraction. The Crow's Nest plays a major role in Junger's story, but its ceilings aren't high enough for it to be a movie set—so the crew built an exact replica nearby. If you admired the movie's wardrobe design, check out the shirts and caps at **Cape Pond Ice,** 104 Commercial St., near the Chamber of Commerce (© **978/283-0174;** www.cape pondice.com).

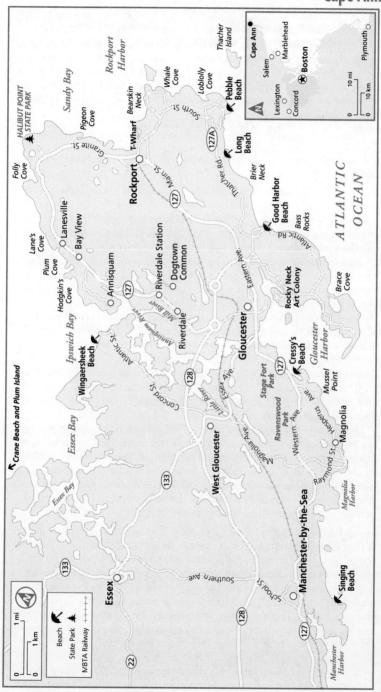

Cape Ann

Thacher Island

Cape Ann
Salem
Marblehead
Lexington
Concord
Boston
Plymouth

10 mi
10 km

Rockport Harbor

Sandy Bay

Whale Cove

Loblolly Cove

Pebble Beach

HALIBUT POINT STATE PARK

Bearskin Neck

South St.

127A

Folly Cove

Pigeon Cove

Granite St.

T-Wharf

Long Beach

Brier Neck

Rockport

Main St.

127

Thatcher Rd.

Good Harbor Beach

Bass Rocks

Atlantic Rd.

ATLANTIC OCEAN

Lane's Cove

Lanesville

Bay View

Plum Cove

Hodgkin's Cove

Annisquam

127

Riverdale Station

Dogtown Common

Eastern Ave.

Rocky Neck Art Colony

Brace Cove

Mill River

Annisquam River

Riverdale

Gloucester

Ipswich Bay

Wingaersheek Beach

Atlantic St.

128

Cressy's Beach

127

Gloucester Harbor

Mussel Point

Crane Beach and Plum Island

Essex Bay

Concord St.

Little River

Essex Ave.

Stage Fort Park

Ravenswood Park

Western Ave.

Hesperus Ave.

Magnolia

West Gloucester

Magnolia Ave.

Raymond St.

Magnolia Harbor

Essex Bay

133

133

Essex

Southern Ave.

Manchester-by-the-Sea

School St.

Singing Beach

22

128

127

Manchester Harbor

1 mi
1 km

Beach
State Park
MBTA Railway

Finds Come and Get It!

The schooner **Adventure** (© 978/281-8079; www.schooner-adventure.org) serves breakfast on summer Sundays from 9:30am to 1pm. The hearty meal includes typical American breakfast items, plus whatever the volunteer cooks decide to add. This is a great way to check out the ship, fuel up for sightseeing, and mingle with the locals. Adults pay $8, children $5; reservations are recommended.

---

prizewinning playwright and screenwriter, schedules six plays a season (June to mid-September).

NARRATED CRUISES   For information on whale watches, see the box "A Whale of an Adventure" (p. 272).

Moby Duck Tours (© 978/281-3825; www.mobyduck.com) are 55-minute sightseeing expeditions that travel on land (20 min.) before plunging into the water (35 min.). They're just the right length for kids, who delight in the transition from street to sea. The amphibious vehicles leave from **Harbor Loop** downtown. Tickets (cash only) cost $16 for adults, $14 for seniors, and $10 for children under 12. They operate daily from Memorial Day to Labor Day, and on weekends in September.

Also at Harbor Loop, you can tour the two-masted schooner **Adventure** (© 978/281-8079; www.schooner-adventure.org), a 121-foot fishing vessel built in Essex in 1926 and undergoing extensive restoration. It doesn't move, so it's not as thrilling as the *Thomas E. Lannon* (discussed next), but it's quicker and cheaper and can be much more interesting, depending on what's being worked on. The "living museum," a National Historic Landmark, is open to visitors from Memorial Day to Labor Day, Thursday through Sunday from 10am to 4pm. The suggested donation is $5 for adults and $4 for children.

The schooner **Thomas E. Lannon** (© 978/281-6634; www.schooner.org) is a gorgeous reproduction of a Gloucester fishing vessel. The 65-foot tall ship sails from Seven Seas Wharf downtown; 2-hour excursions ($30 for adults, $25 for seniors, $20 for children under 17) leave about four times daily from mid-June to mid-October, less often on weekends from mid-May to mid-June. Reservations are recommended. The company also offers music and dining cruises, including lobster bakes on Friday, and "storytelling sails."

Beauport (Sleeper-McCann House)   The Society for the Preservation of New England Antiquities, which operates Beauport, describes it as a "fantasy house," and that's putting it mildly. Interior designer Henry Davis Sleeper used his summer home as a retreat and a repository for his vast collections of American and European decorative arts and antiques. From 1907 to 1934, he decorated the 40 rooms, 26 of which are open to the public, to illustrate literary and historical themes. The entertaining tour concentrates more on the house and rooms in general than on the countless objects on display. You'll see architectural details rescued from other buildings, magnificent arrangements of colored glassware, an early American kitchen, the "Red Indian Room" (with a majestic view of the harbor), and "Strawberry Hill," the master bedroom. Check ahead to see if there's a special event (afternoon tea, specialty tour, or evening concert) while you're in town. Note that the house is closed on summer weekends.

75 Eastern Point Blvd. ℂ **978/283-0800**. www.spnea.org. Guided tour $10 adults, $9 seniors, $5 students and children 6–12. Tours on the hr. May 15 to mid-Sept Mon–Fri 10am–4pm; mid-Sept to Oct 15 daily 10am–4pm. Closed Oct 16–May 14 and summer weekends. Take E. Main St. to Eastern Point Blvd. (a private road), continue ½ mile to house, park on left.

Cape Ann Historical Museum 🏛   This meticulously curated museum makes an excellent introduction to Cape Ann's history and artists. It devotes an entire gallery to the extraordinary work of **Fitz Hugh Lane** 🏛🏛🏛, the Luminist painter whose light-flooded canvases show off the best of his native Gloucester. The nation's largest collection of his paintings and drawings is here. Other galleries feature works on paper by 20th-century artists such as Maurice Prendergast and Milton Avery, work by other contemporary artists, and granite-quarrying tools and equipment. There's also an outdoor sculpture court. On display in the maritime and fisheries galleries are entire vessels (including one about the size of a station wagon that crossed the Atlantic), exhibits on the fishing industry, ship models, and historic photographs and models of the Gloucester waterfront. The **Capt. Elias Davis House** (1804), decorated and furnished in Federal style with furniture, silver, and porcelains, is part of the museum.

27 Pleasant St. ℂ **978/283-0455**. www.cape-ann.com/historical-museum. Admission $5 adults, $4.50 seniors, $3.50 students, free for children under 6. Mar–Jan Tues–Sat 10am–5pm. Closed Feb. Follow Main St. west through downtown and turn right onto Pleasant St.; the museum is 1 block up on right. Metered parking on street or in lot across street.

SHOPPING

Rocky Neck (see "Exploring the Town" above) offers great browsing. Downtown, **Main Street** between Pleasant and Washington streets is a good destination. Agreeable stops include **Mystery Train,** 178 Main St. (ℂ **978/281-8911;** www.mystrain.com), which carries a huge variety of used LPs, CDs, tapes, and videos; **Ménage Gallery,** 134 Main St. (ℂ **978/283-6030**), which shows work by artists and artisans, including gorgeous furniture; and the **Dogtown Book Shop,** 2 Duncan St. (ℂ **978/281-5599**), noted for its used and antiquarian selection.

ACCOMMODATIONS

Gloucester abounds with B&Bs; for guidance, check with the Cape Ann Chamber of Commerce or consult one of the agencies listed in chapter 5.

Atlantis Oceanfront Motor Inn   This motor inn with an outdoor pool sits across the street from the water, affording stunning views from every window. It doesn't have the resort feel of the neighboring Bass Rocks Ocean Inn, but the views are the same. The well-maintained guest rooms are decorated in comfortable, contemporary style. The good-size rooms all have a terrace or balcony and a small table and chairs. Second-floor accommodations are slightly preferable because the view is a little better.

125 Atlantic Rd., Gloucester, MA 01930. ℂ **800/732-6313** or 978/283-0014. Fax 978/281-8994. www. atlantismotorinn.com. 40 units (some w/shower only). Late June to Labor Day $140–$170 double; spring and fall $90–$140 double. Extra person $8. Off-season packages available. AE, MC, V. Closed Nov to mid-Apr. Minimum 2-night stay spring and fall weekends, 3-night stay holiday and summer weekends. Follow Rte. 128 to the end (Exit 9, East Gloucester), turn left onto Bass Ave. (Rte. 127A), and follow it ½ mile. Turn right and follow Atlantic Rd. **Amenities:** Coffee shop (breakfast only); heated outdoor pool. *In room:* A/C, TV.

Best Western Bass Rocks Ocean Inn   A family operation since 1946, the Bass Rocks Ocean Inn offers gorgeous ocean views, a heated pool, and modern accommodations in a traditional setting. Across the road from the rocky shore,

North Shore Beaches

North of Boston, sandy beaches complement the predominantly rocky coastline. Things to know: The water is *cold* (optimistic locals say "refreshing"). And parking can be scarce, especially on weekends, and pricey—as much as $15 per car. If you can't set out early, wait until midafternoon and hope that the people who arrived in the morning have had their fill. During the summer, lifeguards are on duty from 9am to 5pm at larger public beaches. Surfing is generally permitted outside of those hours. The beaches listed here all have bathhouses and snack bars. Swimming or not, watch out for greenhead flies in July and August. They don't sting—they take little bites of flesh. Bring or buy insect repellent.

The best-known North Shore beach is **Singing Beach** 🏖🏖, off Masconomo Street in Manchester-by-the-Sea. Because it's accessible by public transportation, it attracts the most diverse crowd—carless singles, local families, and other beach bunnies of all ages. They walk ½ mile on Beach Street from the train station to find sparkling sand and lively surf. Take the commuter rail (© **617/222-3200**; www.mbta.com) from Boston's North Station.

Nearly as famous and popular is **Crane Beach** 🏖, off Argilla Road in Ipswich, part of a 1,400-acre barrier beach reservation. Fragile dunes and a white sand beach lead down to Ipswich Bay. The surf is calmer than that at less sheltered Singing Beach, but it's still quite chilly. Pick up Argilla Road south of Ipswich Center near the intersection of Routes 1A and 133. Also on Ipswich Bay is Gloucester's **Wingaersheek Beach** 🏖, on Atlantic Street off Route 133. It has its own exit (no. 13) off Route 128, about 15 minutes away on winding roads with low speed limits. When you finally arrive, you'll find beautiful white sand, a glorious view, and more dunes. Because these beaches are harder to get to, they attract more locals—but also lots of day-tripping families. At the east end of Route 133, the beaches and snack bar in Gloucester's easily accessible **Stage Fort Park** are popular local hangouts.

the sprawling comfortable two-story motel contains spacious guest rooms. A Colonial Revival mansion built in 1899 and known as the "wedding-cake house" holds the office and public areas, including a billiard room and a library. The inn has more of a resort feel than the neighboring Atlantis. Each guest room has sliding glass doors that open onto a balcony or patio, and a king bed or two double beds. Second-floor rooms have slightly better views. In the afternoon, the staff serves coffee, tea, lemonade, and chocolate-chip cookies.

107 Atlantic Rd., Gloucester, MA 01930. © **800/528-1234** or 978/283-7600. Fax 978/281-6489. www.bestwestern.com/bassrocksoceaninn. 48 units. Late June to Labor Day $150–$250 double; spring and fall $125–$210 double. Extra person $8. Children under 12 stay free in parent's room. Rollaway or crib $12. Rates include continental breakfast, afternoon refreshments, and use of bikes. Minimum 3-night stay summer weekends, some spring and fall weekends. Closed Nov to late Apr. AE, DC, DISC, MC, V. Follow Rte. 128 to the end (Exit 9, East Gloucester), turn left onto Bass Ave. (Rte. 127A), and follow it ½ mile. Turn right and follow Atlantic Rd. **Amenities:** Heated outdoor pool; game room. *In room:* A/C, TV, dataport, fridge, coffeemaker, hair dryer, iron.

DINING

See "A Detour to Essex" on p. 271, for information about the celebrated **Woodman's of Essex,** which is about 20 minutes from downtown Gloucester. The Stage Fort Park snack bar, the **Cupboard** (☎ **978/281-1908**), serves excellent fried seafood and blue-plate specials. If you're in town just for a day, consider sticking around for dinner at the **Franklin Cape Ann,** 118 Main St. (☎ **978/283-7888**). The upscale bistro cuisine is excellent, and it's served daily from 5pm to midnight (but unfortunately not at lunchtime).

Boulevard Oceanview Restaurant ⭐ PORTUGUESE/SEAFOOD This is a friendly, unassuming neighborhood place in a high-tourist-traffic location. Across the street from the waterfront promenade just west of downtown, it's a dinerlike spot with water views from the front windows and the small deck. It serves ultrafresh seafood (crane your neck and you can almost see the processing plants) and lunch-counter sandwiches. Try "Seafood Portuguese style"—shrimp *a la plancha* (in irresistible lemon-butter sauce) and *sao* style (in garlic and wine sauce), and several unusual casseroles. The hostess and I were chatting about where to send visitors to eat in Gloucester when a waitress chimed in: "Send 'em here, dear," she said. "It's the best food they'll ever eat." Even if that's not strictly true, it's good to know an employee thinks so.

25 Western Ave. (Stacy Blvd.). ☎ **978/281-2949.** Reservations recommended at dinner in summer. Sandwiches $4–$9; main courses $7–$17; lobster priced daily. DISC, MC, V. Summer daily 11am–10pm; winter daily 11am–9:30pm.

The Gull Restaurant ⭐⭐ (Kids) SEAFOOD/AMERICAN Floor-to-ceiling windows show off the Annisquam River from almost every seat at the Gull. The big, friendly restaurant is known for prime rib as well as seafood. It draws locals, visitors, boaters, and families for large portions at reasonable prices. The seafood chowder is famous (with good reason), appetizers tend toward bar food, and the french fries are terrific. Fish is available in just about any variety and style. Ask about daily specials, which run from simple lobster (market price) to sophisticated fish and meat dishes. At lunch, there's an extensive sandwich menu.

75 Essex Ave. (Rte. 133), at Cape Ann Marina. ☎ **978/281-6060.** Reservations recommended for parties of 8 or more. Main courses $5–$13 at lunch, $8–$22 at dinner; breakfast items less than $8. DISC, MC, V. Daily late Apr to late Oct 6am–9pm. Closed late Oct to late Apr. Take Rte. 133 west from intersection with Rte. 127, or take Rte. 133 east from Rte. 128.

Halibut Point Restaurant SEAFOOD/AMERICAN A local legend for its chowders and burgers, Halibut Point is a friendly tavern that serves generous portions of good food. The "Halibut Point Special"—$12 for a cup of chowder, a burger, and a beer—hits the high points. Although the clam chowder is terrific, spicy Italian fish chowder is so good that some people come to Gloucester just for that. There's also a raw bar. Main courses are simple (mostly sandwiches) at lunch and more elaborate at dinner. Be sure to check the specials board—you didn't come all this way to a fishing port not to have fresh fish, did you?

289 Main St. ☎ **978/281-1900.** Main courses $5–$11 at lunch, $9–$16 at dinner. AE, DISC, MC, V. Daily 11:30am–11pm.

ROCKPORT

40 miles NE of Boston, 7 miles N of Gloucester

This lovely little town at the tip of Cape Ann was settled in 1690. Over the years it has been an active fishing port, a center of granite excavation and cutting, and a thriving summer community whose specialty appears to be selling fudge and refrigerator magnets to out-of-towners. Rockport is an entertaining half-day trip, perhaps combined with a visit to Gloucester.

There's more to Rockport than just gift shops. It's home to a lovely state park, and it's popular with photographers, painters, jewelry designers, and sculptors. Winslow Homer, Fitz Hugh Lane, and Childe Hassam are among the famous artists who have captured the local color. At times, especially on summer weekends, you'll be hard pressed to find much local color in this tourist-weary destination. But for every year-round resident who seems genuinely startled when legions of people with cameras around their necks descend on Rockport each June, there are dozens who are proud to show off their town.

ESSENTIALS

GETTING THERE   Rockport is north of Gloucester along Route 127 or 127A. At the end of Route 128, turn left at the signs for Rockport to take 127, which is shorter but more commercial. To take 127A, which runs along the east coast of Cape Ann, continue on Route 128 until you see the sign for East Gloucester and turn left. Parking is next to impossible, especially on summer Saturday afternoons. Make one loop around downtown, and then head to the free parking lot on Upper Main Street (Route 127). The shuttle bus to downtown costs $1.

The **commuter rail** (© 617/222-3200; www.mbta.com) runs from Boston's North Station. The trip takes 60 to 70 minutes, and the round-trip fare is $10. The station is about 6 blocks from the downtown waterfront. The **Cape Ann Transportation Authority,** or CATA (© 978/283-7916), runs buses from town to town on Cape Ann.

VISITOR INFORMATION   The **Rockport Chamber of Commerce and Board of Trade,** 3 Main St. (© 888/726-3922 or 978/546-6575; www.rockportusa.com), is open daily in summer from 9am to 5pm, and winter weekdays from 10am to 4pm. The chamber operates an information booth on Upper Main Street (Rte. 127) from mid-May to October. It's about a mile from the town line and a mile from downtown—look for the WELCOME TO ROCKPORT sign on the right as you head north. At either location, ask for the pamphlet *Rockport: A Walking Guide,* which contains a good map and descriptions of three short walking tours. Out of season, especially January through mid-April, Rockport is pretty but somewhat desolate, though some businesses stay open and keep reduced hours.

SPECIAL EVENTS   The **Rockport Chamber Music Festival** (© 978/546-7391; www.rcmf.org) takes place over several weeks in June and early July at the Rockport Art Association, 12 Main St. In addition to performances and family concerts, events include lectures and discussions. The annual **Christmas pageant,** on Main Street in early December, is a crowded, kid-friendly event with carol singing and live animals.

EXPLORING THE TOWN

The most famous sight in Rockport has something of an "Emperor's New Clothes" aura—it's a wooden fish warehouse on the town wharf, or T-Wharf, in the harbor. The barn-red shack known as **Motif No. 1** is the most frequently painted and photographed object in a town filled with lovely buildings and surrounded by breathtaking rocky coastline. The color certainly catches the eye in the neutrals of the seascape, but you might find yourself wondering what the big deal is. Originally constructed in 1884 and destroyed during the blizzard of 1978,

Motif No. 1 was rebuilt using donations from residents and tourists. It stands on the same pier, duplicated in every detail, and reinforced to withstand storms.

Nearby is a phenomenon whose popularity is easier to explain. **Bearskin Neck,** named after an unfortunate ursine visitor who drowned and washed ashore in 1800, has perhaps the highest concentration of gift shops anywhere. It's a narrow peninsula with one main street (South Rd.) and several alleys crammed with galleries, snack bars, antiques shops, and ancient houses. The peninsula ends in a plaza with a magnificent water view.

Throughout the town, more than 2 dozen **art galleries** 🎨 display the works of local and nationally known artists. The **Rockport Art Association,** 12 Main St. (© **978/546-6604;** www.rockportusa.com/RAA), sponsors major exhibitions and special shows. It's open daily year-round.

To get a sense of the power of the sea, take Route 127 north of town to the tip of Cape Ann. Turn right on Gott Avenue to reach **Halibut Point State Park** 🎨🎨 (© **978/546-2997;** www.state.ma.us/dem/parks/halb.htm). The park is a great place to wander around and admire the scenery. On a clear day, you can see Maine. It has a staffed visitor center, walking trails, and tidal pools. Swimming in the water-filled quarries is absolutely forbidden. You can climb around on giant boulders on the rocky beach, or climb to the top of the World War II observation tower. Guided quarry tours and stone-splitting demonstrations take place on summer Saturdays at 10am. November through April, there's a guided bird walk on the first Saturday of the month at 9am. The park is open daily, year-round, from dawn to dusk; parking costs $2 from Memorial Day to Columbus Day.

If the mansions of Gloucester are too plush for you, or if you want some recycling tips, visit the **Paper House,** 52 Pigeon Hill St., Pigeon Cove (© **978/546-2629;** www.rockportusa.com/attractions). It was built in 1922 entirely out of 100,000 newspapers—walls, furniture, and even a piano. Every item is made from papers of a different period. It's open daily April through October from 10am to 5pm. Admission is $1.50 for adults, $1 for children. Follow Route 127 north out of downtown about 1½ miles until you see signs at Curtis Street pointing to the left.

SHOPPING

Bearskin Neck is the obvious place to start. Dozens of little shops stock clothes, gifts, toys, jewelry, souvenirs, inexpensive novelties, and expensive handmade crafts and paintings. Another enjoyable stroll is along **Main** and **Mount Pleasant streets.** Good stops include the nonprofit **Toad Hall Bookstore,** 47 Main St. (© **978/546-7323**); **New England Goods,** 57 Main St. (© **978/546-9677**), where the stock is exclusively local; and **Willoughby's,** 20 Main St. (© **978/546-9820**), a women's clothing and accessories shop.

Two of my favorite stops are retro delights. Downtown, you can watch taffy being made at **Tuck's Candy Factory,** 7 Dock Sq. (© **800/569-2767** or 978/546-6352), a local landmark since the 1920s. Near the train station, **Crackerjacks,** 27 Whistlestop Mall, off Railroad Avenue (© **978/546-1616**), is an old-fashioned variety store with a great crafts department.

ACCOMMODATIONS

When Rockport is busy, it's very busy—and when it's not, it's practically empty. Make summer reservations well in advance, or cross your fingers and call the Rockport Chamber of Commerce to ask about cancellations.

Captain's Bounty Motor Inn   This modern, well-maintained motor inn is on the water. In fact, it's almost *in* the water, and nearly as close to the center of town as to the harbor. Each recently redecorated room in the three-story building overlooks the water and has its own balcony and sliding glass door. Rooms are spacious and soundproofed, with good cross-ventilation but no air-conditioning. The best units are on the adults-only top floor. Although it's hardly plush and the pricing structure is a bit peculiar (note the charge for children), you can't beat the location. Kitchenette units are available.

1 Beach St., Rockport, MA 01966. ℂ **978/546-9557.** www.cape-ann.com/capt-bounty. 24 units. Mid-June to early Sept $120 double, $135 efficiency, $150 efficiency suite; spring and fall $83–$95 double, $87–$100 efficiency, $95–$105 efficiency suite. Extra adult $10; $5 for each child over 5. All rates based on double occupancy. Minimum 2-night stay weekends, 3-night stay holiday weekends. DISC, MC, V. Closed Nov–Apr. *In room:* TV, coffeemaker.

Peg Leg Inn   The Peg Leg Inn consists of two Early American houses with front porches, attractive living rooms, and well-kept flower-bordered lawns that run down to the ocean's edge. It's not luxurious, but it is convenient and comfortable. Vacationing couples make up much of the clientele; families will probably be more comfortable at a more relaxed establishment (such as the Sandy Bay Motor Inn, listed next). Rooms are good-size and neatly furnished in colonial style. The best units open onto excellent ocean views. Breakfast is served in the main building's dining room. Guests may use the sandy beach across the road.

2 King St., Rockport, MA 01966. ℂ **800/346-2352** or 978/546-2352. www.pegleginn.com. 16 units (1 w/shower only). Mid-June to Labor Day, holiday and fall weekends $115–$160 double, $200 2-bedroom unit. Extra person $15. Rates include continental breakfast. Off-season discounts available. Minimum 2-night stay summer weekends, 3-night stay holiday weekends. AE, MC, V. Closed Nov–Mar. **Amenities:** Access to nearby health club ($10); bike rental. Rooms for travelers with disabilities are available. *In room:* TV. No phones.

Sandy Bay Motor Inn ⚘   About ½ mile from downtown Rockport, this modern motor inn offers comfortable accommodations and a variety of recreational facilities at a good price. One of the largest lodgings in town, it's a sprawling two-story complex with attractively landscaped grounds on a hill next to Route 127, which is busy during the day but not at night. Still, units that face away from the unattractive road are preferable. Guest rooms are large and conventionally furnished—nothing fancy, but well maintained and large enough to hold a cot. There are six two-bedroom units; if you don't need that much space, you can book an efficiency and eat some meals in.

173 Main St. (Rte. 127), Rockport, MA 01966. ℂ **800/437-7155** or 978/546-7155. www.sandybay motorinn.com. 79 units (some w/shower only). Mid-June to early Sept $115–$160 double; spring and fall $96–$125 double; winter $80–$110 double. Extra adult $10. Each child $4. Cot $6. Minimum 2-night stay summer weekends. AE, MC, V. Pets accepted; $50 deposit. **Amenities:** Restaurant (breakfast only); heated indoor pool; putting green; 2 outdoor tennis courts; whirlpool; saunas. Rooms for travelers with disabilities are available. *In room:* A/C, TV.

DINING

Rockport is a "dry" community—no alcoholic beverages can be sold or served—but you can bring your own bottle, usually subject to a corking fee.

The birthplace of the fried clam, **Woodman's of Essex** (see "A Detour to Essex" on p. 271), is about half an hour from Rockport.

Off Bearskin Neck, the **Portside Chowder House,** 7 Tuna Wharf (ℂ **978/ 546-7045;** www.portsidechowderhouse.com) serves Southern barbecue—no, seriously, it serves delicious fresh chowder, fresh seafood, salads, and sandwiches. It's a tasty way to start a picnic.

Brackett's Oceanview Restaurant SEAFOOD/AMERICAN   The dining room at Brackett's has a gorgeous view of the water you glimpsed between buildings as you walked along Main Street. The nautical decor suits the seafood-intensive menu, which offers enough variety to make this a good choice for families—burgers are always available. The service is friendly, and the fresh seafood is quite good, if not particularly adventurous. Try the moist, plump codfish cakes if you're looking for a traditional New England dish, or go for something with Cajun spices for variety. The most exciting offerings are on the extensive dessert menu, where anything homemade is a great choice.

29 Main St. $\mathcal{C}$ 978/546-2797. www.bracketts.com. Reservations recommended at dinner. Main courses $7–$20 at lunch, $10–$26 at dinner. AE, DC, DISC, MC, V. Mid-Apr to Memorial Day Wed–Sun 11:30am–8pm; Memorial Day to Oct Sun–Fri 11:30am–8pm, Sat 11:30am–9pm. Closed Nov to mid-Apr.

The Greenery ✦ SEAFOOD/AMERICAN   The Greenery could get away with serving so-so food because of its great location at the head of Bearskin Neck—but it doesn't. The cafe at the front serves delicious light fare to stay or to go; the dining rooms, at the back, boast great views of the harbor. The food ranges from tasty quiche at lunch to lobster at dinner to steamers and fresh-caught fish anytime. As in any town with working fishermen, check out the daily specials. The salad bar is available on its own or with many entrees. All baking is done in-house, which explains the lines at the front counter for muffins and pastries. When the restaurant is busy, the cheerful service tends to drag. This is a good place to launch a picnic lunch on the beach, and an equally good spot for lingering over coffee and dessert and watching the action around the harbor.

15 Dock Sq. $\mathcal{C}$ 978/546-9593. www.thegreeneryrestaurant.com. Reservations recommended at dinner. Main courses $7–$12 at lunch, $10–$22 at dinner; breakfast items $2–$7. AE, DC, DISC, MC, V. Apr–Oct Mon–Fri 8am–11pm, Sat–Sun 7am–11pm; off season daily 8am–8pm (off-season hr. may vary; call ahead).

My Place By-the-Sea SEAFOOD   The lure of My Place By-the-Sea is its location at the very end of Bearskin Neck, where you'll find Rockport's only outdoor oceanfront deck. The two decks and shaded patio afford excellent views of Sandy Bay. The menu is reliable, with many options dictated by the daily catch. The baked fish and seafood pasta entrees are good choices, and you can also have chicken or beef.

68 South Rd., Bearskin Neck. $\mathcal{C}$ 978/546-9667. www.myplacebythesea.com. Reservations recommended at dinner; accepted same day after noon. Main courses $7–$14 at lunch, $20–$29 at dinner. AE, DC, DISC, MC, V. Apr–Nov daily 11:30am–9:30pm. Closed Dec–Mar.

3 Plymouth ✦✦

40 miles SE of Boston

Everyone educated in the United States knows at least a little about Plymouth—about how the Pilgrims, fleeing religious persecution, left Europe on the *Mayflower* and landed at Plymouth Rock in December 1620. Many also know that the Pilgrims endured disease and privation, and that just 51 people from the original group of 102 celebrated the first Thanksgiving in 1621 with Squanto, a Pawtuxet Indian associated with the Wampanoags, and his cohorts.

What you won't know until you visit is how small everything was. The *Mayflower* (a replica) seems perilously tiny, and when you contemplate how dangerous life was at the time, it's hard not to marvel at the settlers' accomplishments. One of their descendants' accomplishments is this: Plymouth is in many ways a model destination, where the 17th century coexists with the 21st, and most historic attractions are both educational and fun. Tourists positively jam the downtown area in the summer, but the year-round population is so large that Plymouth feels more like the working community it is than like a warm-weather day-trip destination. It's a manageable one-day excursion from Boston, particularly enjoyable if you're traveling with children. It also makes a good stop between Boston and Cape Cod.

ESSENTIALS

GETTING THERE   By car, follow the Southeast Expressway (I-93) south from Boston to Route 3. Take Exit 6A and then Route 44 east, and follow signs to the historic attractions. The trip from Boston takes 45 to 60 minutes if it's not rush hour. Take Exit 5 to the **Regional Information Complex** for maps, brochures, and information. To go directly to **Plimoth Plantation,** take Exit 4. There's metered parking throughout town.

The **commuter rail** (© 617/222-3200; www.mbta.com) serves Cordage Park, on Route 3A north of downtown, from Boston's South Station four times a day on weekdays and three times a day on weekends (at other times, service is to nearby Kingston). The round-trip fare is $10. The **Plymouth Area Link** bus (© 508/222-6106; www.gatra.org/pal.htm) runs between the train station and downtown. The fare is 75¢.

Plymouth and Brockton **buses** (© 617/773-9401 or 508/746-0378; www.p-b.com) take about an hour from South Station. They run more often and cost more than the train: $9 one-way, $17 round-trip.

VISITOR INFORMATION   If you haven't visited the Regional Information Complex, pick up a map at the **visitor center** (© 508/747-7525), open seasonally at 130 Water St., across from the town pier. To plan ahead, contact **Destination Plymouth** (Plymouth Visitor Information), 170 Water St., Suite 10C, Plymouth, MA 02360 (© 800/USA-1620 or 508/747-7533; www.visitplymouth.com). The **Plymouth County Convention & Visitors Bureau,** 32 Court St., Plymouth, MA 02360 (© 508/747-0100; www.plymouth-1620.com), publishes a vacation guide.

GETTING AROUND   The downtown attractions are easily accessible on foot. A shallow hill slopes from the center of town to the waterfront.

Plymouth Rock Trolley Company (© 800/698-56636 or 508/747-4161; www.plymouthrocktrolley.com) offers a 40-minute narrated tour and unlimited reboarding daily from Memorial Day to October and weekends through Thanksgiving. It serves marked stops downtown every 20 minutes and stops at Plimoth Plantation once an hour in the summer. Tickets are $10 for adults, $9 for seniors and AAA members, $8 for children 3 to 12.

SEEING THE SIGHTS

The logical place to begin (good luck talking children out of it) is where the Pilgrims first set foot—at **Plymouth Rock** 🐝🐝. The rock, accepted as the landing place of the *Mayflower* passengers, was originally 15 feet long and 3 feet wide. It was moved on the eve of the Revolution and several times thereafter. In 1867, it assumed its present permanent position at tide level. The Colonial Dames of America commissioned the portico around the rock, designed by McKim, Mead & White and erected in 1920. The rock itself isn't much to look at, but the

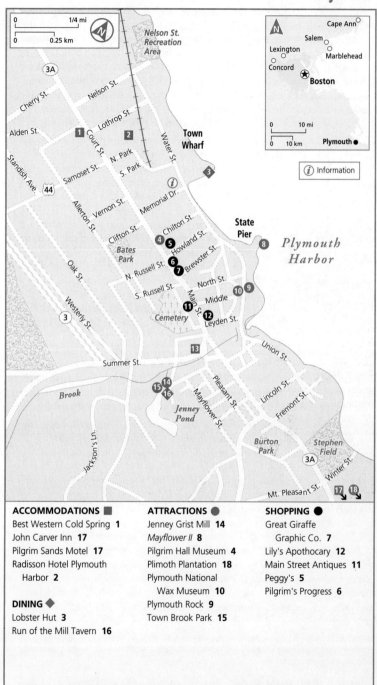

Plymouth

Town Wharf

State Pier

Plymouth Harbor

Boston

Cape Ann
Salem
Marblehead
Lexington
Concord

Plymouth ●

(i) Information

Nelson St. Recreation Area

Bates Park

Cemetery

Brook

Jenney Pond

Burton Park

Stephen Field

ACCOMMODATIONS ■
Best Western Cold Spring **1**
John Carver Inn **17**
Pilgrim Sands Motel **17**
Radisson Hotel Plymouth
　Harbor **2**

DINING ◆
Lobster Hut **3**
Run of the Mill Tavern **16**

ATTRACTIONS ●
Jenney Grist Mill **14**
Mayflower II **8**
Pilgrim Hall Museum **4**
Plimoth Plantation **18**
Plymouth National
　Wax Museum **10**
Plymouth Rock **9**
Town Brook Park **15**

SHOPPING ●
Great Giraffe
　Graphic Co. **7**
Lily's Apothocary **12**
Main Street Antiques **11**
Peggy's **5**
Pilgrim's Progress **6**

accompanying descriptions are interesting, and the atmosphere is curiously inspiring.

To get away from the bustle of the waterfront, make your way to **Town Brook Park,** at Jenney Pond, across Summer Street from the John Carver Inn. Ducks and geese live in the pond, and there's room to run around. Here you'll find the **Jenney Grist Mill,** 6 Spring Lane (© 508/747-4544; www.jenneygristmill. com). You can see a replica of a 1636 water-powered mill, which operates daily from April through November, and take a self-guided tour. Admission is free except during corn-grinding exhibitions, when visitors over 5 years old pay $2.

GUIDED TOURS   To put yourself in the Pilgrims' footsteps, take a **Colonial Lantern Tour** (© 800/698-5636 or 508/747-4161; www.lanterntours.com). Participants carry pierced-tin lanterns on a 90-minute walking tour of the original settlement under the direction of a knowledgeable guide. It might seem a bit hokey at first, but it's fascinating. Tours run nightly from April to Thanksgiving. The standard history tour begins at 7:30pm; the "Ghostly Haunts & Legends" tour starts at 9pm. Tickets are $15 for adults and $12 for children 5 to 12; free for children under 5; check the meeting place when you call for reservations. The company also offers special tours for Halloween and Thanksgiving.

Narrated cruises run from April or May to November. **Splashdown Amphibious Tours** (© 800/225-4000 or 508/747-7658; www.ducktours plymouth.com) takes you around town on land and water. The kid-friendly 1-hour excursions (half on land, half on water) leave from Harbor Place, near the Governor Bradford motel, on Water Street—and wind up in the harbor. They cost $18 for adults, $10 for children ages 3 to 12, and $3 for children under 3. **Capt. John Boats,** Town Wharf (© 800/242-2469 or 508/747-2400; www.captjohn.com), offers several tours. The most eye-catching option is the *Pilgrim Belle* paddle wheeler (© 508/747-2400). Its 75-minute narrated tours of the harbor ($10 adults, $8 seniors, $7 children under 12) leave from State Pier. Dining and entertainment cruises and whale watches are also available.

Mayflower II (Kids)   Berthed a few steps from Plymouth Rock, the *Mayflower II* is a full-scale reproduction of the type of ship that brought the Pilgrims from England to America in 1620. Even though it's full-scale, the 106½-foot vessel, constructed in England from 1955 to 1957, is remarkably small. Although little technical information about the original *Mayflower* survives, William A. Baker, designer of the *Mayflower II,* incorporated the few references in Governor Bradford's account of the voyage with other research to re-create the ship as authentically as possible.

Costumed guides provide interesting first-person narratives about the vessel and voyage, and other interpreters provide a contemporary perspective. Displays describe and illustrate the journey and the Pilgrims' experience, including 17th-century navigation techniques, and the history of the *Mayflower II.* Plimoth Plantation (listed later in this section), which is 3 miles south of the ship, owns and maintains the vessel. Alongside it are museum shops that replicate early Pilgrim dwellings.

State Pier. © 508/746-1622. www.plimoth.org. Admission $8 adults, $6 children 6–12. *Mayflower II* and Plimoth Plantation admission $22 adults, $20 seniors and students, $14 children 6–12. Free for children under 6. Apr–Nov daily 9am–5pm.

Pilgrim Hall Museum (Kids)   This is a great place to get a sense of the day-to-day lives of Plymouth's first European residents. Many original possessions of the early Pilgrims and their descendants are on display, including one of Myles

Standish's swords, Governor Bradford's Bible, and an uncomfortable chair (you can sit in a replica) that belonged to William Brewster. Regularly changing exhibits explore aspects of the settlers' lives, such as home construction or the history of prominent families. Among the permanent exhibits is the skeleton of the *Sparrow-Hawk,* a ship wrecked on Cape Cod in 1626 that lay buried in the sand until 1863. (It's even smaller than the *Mayflower II.*) Through May 2004 you can see the temporary exhibit **Bringing Up Baby: 300 Years of Childhood in the Old Colony.** Built in 1824, the Pilgrim Hall Museum is the oldest public museum in the United States.

75 Court St. Ⓒ **508/746-1620.** www.pilgrimhall.org. Admission $5 adults, $4.50 seniors and AAA members, $3 children 5–17, $15 families. Feb–Dec daily 9:30am–4:30pm. Closed Dec 25 and all of Jan. From Plymouth Rock, walk north on Water St. and up the hill on Chilton St.

Plimoth Plantation ★★ *Kids*   Allow at least half a day to explore this re-creation of the 1627 Pilgrim village, which children and adults find equally interesting. Enter by the hilltop fort that protects the village and walk down the hill to the farm area, visiting homes and gardens constructed with careful attention to historic detail. Once you get over the feeling that the whole operation is a bit strange (we heard someone mention Pompeii), talking to the Pilgrims is great fun. They're actors who, in speech, dress, and manner, assume the personalities of members of the original community. You can watch them framing a house, splitting wood, shearing sheep, preserving foodstuffs, or cooking a pot of fish stew over an open hearth, all as it was done in the 1600s, and using only the tools and cookware available then. Sometimes you can join the activities—perhaps planting, harvesting, witnessing a trial, or visiting a wedding party. Wear comfortable shoes, because you'll be walking a lot, and the plantation isn't paved.

The plantation is as accurate as research can make it. The planners combined accounts of the original colony with archaeological research, old records, and the history written by the Pilgrims' leader, William Bradford (who often used the spelling "Plimoth"). There are daily militia drills with matchlock muskets that are fired to demonstrate the community's defense system. In fact, little defense was needed because the Native Americans were friendly. Local tribes included the Wampanoags, who are represented near the village at **Hobbamock's Homesite** (included in plantation admission). Members of the museum staff show off native foodstuffs, agricultural practices, and crafts.

At the main entrance are two modern buildings with an interesting orientation show, exhibits, a gift shop, a bookstore, and a cafeteria. There's also a picnic area. Call or surf ahead for information about the numerous special events, lectures, tours, workshops, theme dinners, and children's and family programs offered throughout the season.

Rte. 3. Ⓒ **508/746-1622.** www.plimoth.org. Admission $20 adults, $12 children 6–12. Plimoth Plantation and *Mayflower II* admission $22 adults, $20 seniors and students, $14 children 6–12. Free for children under 6. Apr–Nov daily 9am–5pm. From Rte. 3, take Exit 4, Plimoth Plantation Hwy.

Plymouth National Wax Museum ★★ *Kids*   Adults who visited this entertaining museum as children can still tell you all about the Pilgrims. The galleries hold more than 180 life-size figures arranged in scenes. Dramatic soundtracks tell the story of the move to Holland to escape persecution in England, the harrowing trip across the ocean, the first Thanksgiving, and even the tale of Myles Standish, Priscilla Mullins, and John Alden. This museum is a must if children are in your party, and adults will enjoy it, too. On the hill outside is a monument at the gravesite of the Pilgrims who died during the settlement's first winter.

16 Carver St. ℂ **508/746-6468.** Admission $6 adults, $5.50 seniors, $2.75 children 5–12, free for children under 5 accompanied by parents. Daily Mar–May and Nov 9am–5pm; June and Sept–Oct 9am–7pm; July–Aug 9am–9pm. Closed Dec–Feb. From Plymouth Rock, turn around and walk up the hill or the steps.

SHOPPING

Water Street, along the harbor, boasts an inexhaustible supply of souvenir shops. A less kitschy destination, just up the hill, is Route 3A, known as Court, Main, and Warren Street as it runs through town. **Lily's Apothecary,** 6 Main St. extension, in the old post office (ℂ **508/747-7546;** www.lilysapothecary.com), carries a big-city-style selection of skin- and hair-care products for women and men. **Main Street Antiques,** 46 Main St. (ℂ **508/747-8887**), is home to dozens of dealers; **Pilgrim's Progress,** 13 Court St. (ℂ **508/746-6033**), carries women's and men's clothing and accessories; and **Great Giraffe Graphic Co.,** 11 Court St. (ℂ **508/830-1990**), is an entertaining card and gift shop. Plymouth also has a pawnshop, **Peggy's,** 37 Court St. (ℂ **508/746-1952**), that sells jewelry, electronic equipment, and power tools.

ACCOMMODATIONS

On busy summer weekends, it's not unusual for every room in town to be taken. Make reservations well in advance. Whenever you travel, don't book a room without checking for special packages and offers. Just about every establishment in town participates in a **Destination Plymouth** (ℂ **800/USA-1620;** www. visit-plymouth.com) program that piles on deals and discounts in an effort to turn day-trippers into overnight guests.

The **Radisson Hotel Plymouth Harbor,** 180 Water St. (ℂ **800/333-3333** or 508/747-4900), is the only chain hotel downtown. The 175-unit hotel, on a hill across the street from the waterfront, offers all the usual chain amenities, including a swimming pool in the atrium lobby. Doubles in high season run $180 to $225.

Best Western Cold Spring ⭐ Convenient to downtown and the historic sights, this pleasant, fastidiously maintained motel and the adjacent cottages surround nicely landscaped lawns. A $2 million project completed in 2001 updated the existing accommodations and added 30 units, and in 2003, the outdoor pool opened. Rooms are pleasantly decorated and big enough for a family to spread out; if the adults want some privacy, book a two-bedroom cottage. The location, a bit removed from the water, makes the Cold Spring a good deal. The two-story complex is 1 long block inland, set back from the street in a quiet part of town.

188 Court St. (Rte. 3A), Plymouth, MA 02360. ℂ **800/678-8667** or 508/746-2222. Fax 508/746-2744. www. bwcoldspring.com. 58 units (some w/shower only), 2 two-bedroom cottages. $99–$159 double; $139–$199 suite; $109–$159 cottage. Extra person $10. Rollaway $10. Crib $5. Children under 12 stay free in parent's room. Rates include continental breakfast. Packages and off-season discounts available. AE, DC, DISC, MC, V. Closed Dec–Mar. **Amenities:** Outdoor pool. Rooms for travelers with disabilities are available. *In room:* A/C, TV, dataport, coffeemaker, hair dryer, iron.

John Carver Inn *(Kids)* A three-story colonial-style building with a landmark portico, this hotel offers comfortable, modern accommodations and plenty of amenities, including two swimming pools. The indoor "theme pool," a big hit with families, has a large water slide and a Pilgrim ship model. Business features, including meeting space, make this the Sheraton's main competition for corporate travelers. The good-size guest rooms are regularly renovated and decorated in colonial style. The best units are the lavishly appointed two-room suites, with two TVs and private Jacuzzis; "four-poster" rooms contain king beds and sleeper sofas. The inn is within walking distance of the main attractions on the edge of the downtown business district.

25 Summer St., Plymouth, MA 02360. ℂ **800/274-1620** or 508/746-7100. Fax 508/746-8299. www.john carverinn.com. 85 units. Mid-Apr to mid-June and mid-Oct to Nov $109–$179 double, $219–$229 suite; mid-June to mid-Oct $139–$209 double, $249–$269 suite; Dec to mid-Apr $99–$159 double, $209–$219 suite. Extra person $20. Rollaway $20. Cribs free. Children under 19 stay free in parent's room. Packages and senior and AAA discounts available. AE, DC, DISC, MC, V. **Amenities:** Restaurant (American/seafood); outdoor and indoor pools; room service; laundry service; dry cleaning. Rooms for travelers with disabilities are available. *In room:* A/C, TV, dataport.

Pilgrim Sands Motel 🌟🌟 *Kids*   This attractive motel sits on its own beach 3 miles south of town, within walking distance of Plimoth Plantation. If you want to avoid the bustle of downtown and still be near the water, it's an excellent choice. If you don't care for ocean swimming, the motel has both an indoor and an outdoor pool. The good-size guest rooms are tastefully furnished and well maintained. Most have two double or queen beds, and they're divided into sections (separated by doors) for smokers and nonsmokers. If you can swing it, book a beachfront room—the view is worth the money, especially when the surf is rough.

150 Warren Ave. (Rte. 3A), Plymouth, MA 02360. ℂ **800/729-7263** or 508/747-0900. Fax 508/746-8066. www.pilgrimsands.com. 64 units. Summer $130–$170 double; spring and early fall $100–$135 double; Apr and late fall $85–$105 double; Dec–Mar $75–$90 double; $140–$275 suite year-round. Extra person $6–$8 (suite $10–$15). Minimum 2-night stay holiday weekends. Rates may be higher on holiday weekends. AE, DC, DISC, MC, V. **Amenities:** Coffee shop; indoor and outdoor pools; Jacuzzi; private beach. Rooms for travelers with disabilities are available. *In room:* A/C, TV, dataport, fridge, hair dryer.

DINING

Plimoth Plantation (see above) has a cafeteria and a picnic area, and occasionally schedules theme dinners.

Lobster Hut 🌟 SEAFOOD   The Lobster Hut is a busy self-service restaurant with a great view. It's popular with both locals and sightseers. Order and pick up at the counter, and then head to an indoor table or out onto the large deck that overlooks the action on the bay. To start, try clam chowder or lobster bisque. The seafood rolls (hot dog buns with your choice of filling) are excellent. The many fried seafood options include clams, scallops, shrimp, and haddock. There are also boiled and steamed items, burgers, chicken tenders—and lobster, of course. Beer and wine are served, but only with meals.

25 Town Wharf. ℂ **508/746-2270.** Reservations not accepted. Luncheon specials $5–$8; main courses $6–$14; sandwiches $3–$7; lobster priced daily. MC, V. Summer daily 11am–9pm; winter daily 11am–7pm. Closed Jan.

Run of the Mill Tavern 🌟 AMERICAN   This friendly restaurant sits 3 blocks inland, across from Town Brook Park. You won't mind not having a water view—the food is tasty and reasonably priced, and the comfortable wood-paneled tavern is a popular hangout. The unconventional clam chowder, made with red potatoes, is fantastic. Other appetizers include nachos, potato skins, buffalo wings, and mushrooms. Entrees are well-prepared versions of familiar meat, chicken, and fish dishes, plus sandwiches, burgers, and fresh seafood specials (fried, broiled, or baked).

Jenney Grist Mill Village, off Summer St. ℂ **508/830-1262.** Reservations not accepted. Main courses $6–$12; children's menu $3–$4. AE, DC, DISC, MC, V. Sun–Thurs 11:30am–10pm; Fri–Sat 11:30am–11pm. Bar closes at 1am.

Appendix:
Boston in Depth

Boston embodies contrasts and contradictions—blueblood and blue collar, Yankee and Irish, Brahmin banker and budget-conscious graduate student. It's home to the country's first public school and to a problematic educational system. A proud seaport, it's reclaiming its harbor from crippling pollution. It's a one-time hotbed of abolitionism with an intractable reputation for racism. It's a magnet for college students from all over the world and others engaged in intellectual pursuits, yet the traditional, parochial obsessions are "sports, politics, and revenge."

Boston is a living landmark that bears many marks of its colonial heritage, but where it's theoretically possible (this is an observation, not a suggestion) to spend days without going near anything built before 1960, or even going outdoors. How did it get this way?

1 Boston Today

The turn of the century found Boston where it had been at the turn of the other 3 centuries of its existence: in the middle of a transformation. As the 1700s dawned, the town was growing into one of the colonies' most important commercial centers; 100 years later, flush with post-Revolutionary prosperity, it was growing into a city. The end of the 19th century saw the rise of the "Athens of America" and the rich cultural tradition that endures today in the Museum of Fine Arts, the Boston Symphony Orchestra, and the Boston Public Library, among other institutions.

Today you'll find a metropolis of 589,141 at the heart of the Greater Boston area, which encompasses 83 cities and towns and some 4 million people. The hospitals and medical centers are among the best in the world, and the ongoing health-care revolution is a hot topic. Education and tourism are pillars of the local economy, which has mirrored national trends (positive and negative) in unemployment statistics. Though hardly recession-proof, the banking, financial services, and insurance industries are important components as well. The heart of downtown is in the midst of an unprecedented—in technique as well as budget—highway reconstruction. The crime rate, while not at the historically low levels that brought national attention to the "Boston miracle" of the late 1990s, remains relatively low.

WELCOME HOME As they have for more than a century, immigrants flock to the Boston area, where Irish, eastern European Jews, Italians, Portuguese, African Americans, Latinos, West Indians, and, most recently, Asians have made their homes and made their mark. Between 1990 and 2000, the city's Asian population nearly doubled, and the Latino population grew by more than one-third.

One pastime that traditionally united many immigrants was rooting for the city's professional sports teams—an easy task when success seemed to come easily, but less of a common denominator now. Football fans still exclaim over the 2002 Super Bowl champion New England Patriots, who play in a distant suburb.

Mentioning the Red Sox remains the best opener if you want to strike up a conversation. Although Boston is still a sports town, the glory days of Boston Garden are but a rumor to many current fans. That's good news for visitors, who might find that tickets to the Celtics and Bruins (who now play at the FleetCenter) are no longer so hard to come by.

CONSTRUCTION AHEAD   The most prominent feature of downtown Boston, today and for the immediate future, is not an architectural masterpiece or a natural wonder but an enormous construction site. The Central Artery (I-93) is being "depressed"—as are many of the people who travel into and through the city every day—in a massive project that's expected to cost nearly $15 billion. The **Big Dig** is so big that it even has its own website (www.bigdig.com). Since the project began in 1988, its ultimate goals have been not only to hide the interstate underground and turn the land that it had occupied into green space and smaller surface roads, but also to link the Massachusetts Turnpike (I-90) directly to Logan Airport through the Ted Williams Tunnel. The opening of the tunnel in 1995 was the project's first easily visible milestone. The most visible is the Leonard P. Zakim Bunker Hill Bridge, the eye-catching white span over the Charles River, which opened to northbound traffic in 2003. The Big Dig's target completion date is early 2005, and although the site is currently a giant eyesore, other parts of the city are pretty enough to help make up for it.

When the project is finished, Boston will, in a sense, have come full circle. The worst of the traffic will be hidden away, the pedestrians who originally owned the city will once again have easy access to the harbor, and the center of commerce will open onto the waterfront as it did 3 centuries ago.

2 History 101

Permanently settled in 1630 by representatives of the Massachusetts Bay Company, Boston was named for the hometown of some of the Puritans who left England to seek religious freedom in the New World. They met with little of the usual strife with the natives, members of the small, Algonquian-speaking Massachuset tribe that roamed the area. The natives might have used the peninsula they called Shawmut (possibly derived from "Mushau-womuk," or "unclaimed land") as a burial place. They grew corn on some harbor islands, but made their permanent homes farther inland.

In 1632, the little peninsula became the capital of the Massachusetts Bay Colony, and over the next decade the population increased rapidly during the great Puritan migration. Thanks to its excellent location on a deep, sheltered harbor, Boston quickly became a center of shipbuilding, fishing, and trading.

Dateline

- 1614 Captain John Smith maps the New England coast, names the Charles River after King Charles I of England, and calls the area "a paradise."
- 1621 A party of 11 led by Myles Standish explores Boston Harbor, visits with the Massachuset Indians, and returns to Plymouth.
- ca. 1624 William Blackstone settles on the Shawmut peninsula (on Beacon Hill) with 200 books and a Brahma bull.
- 1630 John Winthrop leads settlers to present-day Charlestown. Seeking better water, they push on to Shawmut, which they call Trimountain. On September 7, they name it Boston in honor of the English hometown of many Puritans. On October 19, 108 voters attend the first town meeting.
- 1632 Boston becomes the capital of Massachusetts.

continues

The only thing more important than commerce was religion, and the Puritans exerted such a strong influence that their legacy survives to this day. A concrete reminder is Harvard College's original (1636) mission: preparing young men to be ministers. In 1659, the town fathers officially banned Christmas (the town children apparently had second thoughts—records show that the holiday was back in favor by the 1680s). Another early example of puritanical stuffiness was recorded in 1673. One Captain Kemble was sentenced to confinement in the stocks for 2 hours because he had kissed his wife on their front steps—on a Sunday. He had been away for 3 years.

THE ROAD TO REVOLUTION

In 1684, the Crown revoked the colony's charter, and the inhabitants came under tighter British control. Laws increasing taxes and restricting trading activities gradually led to trouble. The situation came to a head after the French and Indian War (known in Europe as the Seven Years' War) ended in 1763.

Having helped fight for the British, the notoriously independent-minded colonists were outraged when the Crown expected them to help pay off the war debt. The Sugar Act of 1764 imposed tariffs on sugar, wine, and coffee, mostly affecting those engaged in trade; the 1765 Stamp Act taxed everything printed, from legal documents to playing cards, affecting virtually everyone. Boycotts, demonstrations, and riots ensued. The repeal of the Stamp Act in 1766 was too little, too late—the revolutionary slogan "No taxation without representation" had already taken hold.

The Townshend Acts of 1767 imposed taxes on paper, glass, and tea, sparking more unrest. The following year, British troops occupied Boston.

- **1635** Boston Latin School, America's first public school, opens.
- **1636** Harvard College is founded.
- **1638** America's first printing press is established in Cambridge.
- **1639** The country's first post office opens in Richard Fairbank's home.
- **1660** Unrepentant Quaker Mary Dyer is hanged on the Common.
- **1704** America's first regularly published newspaper, the *Boston News Letter*, is founded.
- **1721** First smallpox inoculations are administered, over the violent objections of many residents.
- **1764** "Taxation without representation" is denounced in reaction to the Sugar Act.
- **1770** On March 5, five colonists are killed outside what is now the Old State House, an incident soon known as the Boston Massacre.
- **1773** On December 16, during the Boston Tea Party, colonists dump 342 chests of tea into the harbor from three British ships.
- **1774** The "Intolerable Acts," which include the closure of the port of Boston and the quartering of British troops in colonists' homes, go into effect.
- **1775** On April 18, Paul Revere and William Dawes spread the word that the British are marching toward Lexington and Concord. The next day, "the shot heard round the world" is fired. On June 17, the British win the Battle of Bunker Hill but suffer heavy casualties.
- **1776** On March 17, royal troops evacuate by ship. On July 18, the Declaration of Independence is read from the balcony of the Old State House.
- **1790s** The China trade helps bring great prosperity to Boston.
- **1825** The first city census lists 58,277 people.
- **1831** William Lloyd Garrison publishes the first issue of the *Liberator*, a newspaper dedicated to emancipation.
- **1839** Boston University is founded.
- **1846** Doctors at Massachusetts General Hospital perform the first operation under general anesthesia (the removal of a jaw tumor).

Perhaps inevitably, tension led to violence. In the Boston Massacre of 1770, five colonists were killed in a scuffle with the redcoats. The first to die was a former slave named Crispus Attucks; another was 17-year-old Samuel Maverick. The site, represented by a circle of cobblestones, sits on what is now State Street, and the colonists' graves are nearby.

TEA & NO SYMPATHY

Parliament repealed the Townshend Acts but kept the tea tax and, in 1773, granted the nearly bankrupt East India Company a monopoly on the tea trade with the colonies. The idea was to undercut the price of smuggled tea, but the colonists weren't swayed. In December, three British ships sat at anchor in Boston Harbor, waiting for their cargo of tea to be unloaded. Before that could happen, the rabble-rousing Sons of Liberty, some poorly disguised as Indians, boarded the ships and dumped 342 chests of tea into the harbor. The Boston Tea Party became a rallying point for both sides.

The British responded by closing the port until the tea was paid for and forcing Bostonians to house the soldiers who began to flood the community. They soon numbered 4,000 in a town of 16,000. Mutual distrust ran high—Paul Revere wrote of helping form "a committee for the purpose of watching the movements of the British troops." When the royal commander in Boston, General Gage, learned that the patriots were accumulating arms and ammunition, he dispatched men to destroy the stockpiles.

A NEW WORLD ORDER

Troops marched from Boston toward Lexington and Concord late on April 18, 1775. William Dawes and Revere, who alerted the colonists to the British advance on their famous "midnight ride," sounded the warning to the local militia companies, the Minutemen,

1861 Massachusetts Institute of Technology is founded.

1863 Boston College is founded. In Charleston, S.C., the 54th Massachusetts Colored Regiment of the Union Army suffers heavy casualties in an unsuccessful attempt to capture Fort Wagner.

1870 Museum of Fine Arts is founded.

1872 The Great Fire burns 65 acres and 800 buildings, and kills 33 people.

1876 Boston University professor Alexander Graham Bell invents the telephone.

1878 Girls Latin School opens.

1881 Boston Symphony Orchestra is founded.

1895 Boston Public Library opens on Copley Square.

1897 The first Boston Marathon is run. The first subway in America opens—a 1¾-mile stretch beneath Boylston Street.

1910 John F. "Honey Fitz" Fitzgerald is elected mayor.

1913 James Michael Curley is elected mayor for the first time.

1918 The Red Sox celebrate their World Series victory; a championship drought—of 86 years, and counting—begins.

1919 A storage tank at the corner of Foster and Commercial streets ruptures. Two million gallons of raw molasses spill into the streets of the North End, killing 21 people and injuring 150.

1930s The Great Depression devastates what remains of New England's industrial base.

1938 Guest conductor Nadia Boulanger becomes the first woman to lead the Boston Symphony Orchestra.

1940s World War II and the accompanying industrial frenzy restore some vitality to the economy, particularly the shipyards.

1942 A fire at the Cocoanut Grove nightclub kills 491 people.

1946 Boston's 1st Congressional District sends John F. Kennedy to Congress.

continues

who mobilized for the impending confrontation. The next day, some 700 British soldiers under Major John Pitcairn emerged victorious from a skirmish in Lexington. Later that day, they were routed at Concord and forced to retreat to Charlestown.

It took the redcoats almost an entire day to make the trip (along the route now marked "Battle Road"), which you can do in a car in about half an hour. Thanks in no small part to Henry Wadsworth Longfellow's 1861 poem "Paul Revere's Ride" ("Listen my children and you shall hear / Of the midnight ride of Paul Revere"), Lexington and Concord are closely associated with the beginning of the Revolution. In the early stages, military activity left its mark all over eastern Massachusetts, particularly in Cambridge. Royalist sympathizers, or Tories, were concentrated so heavily along one stretch of Brattle Street that it was called "Tory Row." When the tide began to turn, George Washington made his headquarters on the same street (in a house later occupied by Longfellow that's now a National Park Service site). On nearby Cambridge Common is the spot where Washington took command of the Continental Army on July 3, 1775.

The British won the Battle of Bunker Hill (actually fought on Breed's Hill) in Charlestown on June 17, 1775, but at the cost of half their forces. They abandoned Boston the following March 17. On July 4, 1776, the Continental Congress adopted the Declaration of Independence. Although many Bostonians fought in the 6-year war that followed, no more battles were fought in Boston.

COMMERCE & CULTURE

After the war, Boston again became a center of business. Fishing, whaling, and trade with the Far East dominated the economy. Exotic spices and fruits, textiles, and porcelain were familiar luxuries in Boston and nearby Salem.

- **1954** Doctors at Peter Bent Brigham Hospital perform the first successful human-to-human organ transplant (of a kidney).
- **1957** The Boston Celtics win the first of their 16 NBA championships.
- **1958** The Freedom Trail is mapped out and painted.
- **1959** Construction of the Prudential Center begins—and with it, the transformation of the skyline.
- **1962** Scollay Square is razed to make room for Government Center. Doctors at Massachusetts General Hospital carry out the first successful reattachment of a human limb, a 12-year-old boy's right arm.
- **1966** Massachusetts Attorney General Edward Brooke, a Republican, becomes the first black elected to the U.S. Senate in the 20th century.
- **1969** Students protesting the Vietnam War occupy University Hall at Harvard.
- **1974** Twenty years after the U.S. Supreme Court made school segregation illegal, school busing begins citywide, sparking unrest in Roxbury and Charlestown.
- **1976** The restored Faneuil Hall Marketplace opens.
- **1988** The Central Artery/Third Harbor Tunnel Project, better known as the Big Dig, is approved.
- **1990s** The murder rate plummets, the economy booms, and Boston again becomes a "hot" city.
- **1993** Thomas Menino is elected mayor, becoming the first Italian-American to hold the office.
- **1995** The New England Holocaust Memorial is dedicated. The FleetCenter opens, replacing Boston Garden as the home of the Celtics (basketball) and Bruins (hockey). The first complete piece of the Big Dig, the Ted Williams Tunnel, opens.
- **1999** Busing quietly ends, not with a riot but with a court order.
- **2000** Engineers announce that Big Dig construction is half complete.
- **2001** The 2000 Census shows Boston with a population of 589,141—49.5% of which is white. On September 11, both planes that hit the World Trade Center originate in Boston.

The influential merchant families became known as Boston Brahmins. They spearheaded the cultural renaissance that continued long after the effects of the War of 1812 ravaged international shipping, and banking and manufacturing rose in importance. Boston took a back seat to New York and Philadelphia in size and influence, but the "Athens of America" became known for fine art and architecture, including the luxurious homes on Beacon Hill, and a flourishing intellectual community.

2002 The New England Patriots win the Super Bowl, breaking a drought that dates to 1986 (the Celtics' most recent NBA championship).

2003 Boston bans smoking in all workplaces. The Leonard P. Zakim Bunker Hill Bridge, the signature of the Big Dig and 21st-century Boston, opens to traffic.

2004 The Democratic National Convention takes place at the FleetCenter. Demolition of the elevated Central Artery begins.

In 1822, Boston became a city. From 1824 to 1826, Mayor Josiah Quincy oversaw the landfill project that moved the waterfront away from Faneuil Hall. The market building constructed at that time, which still stands, was named in his honor. The undertaking was one of many, all over the city, in which hills were lopped off and deposited in the water, transforming the coastline and skyline. For example, the filling of the Mill Pond, now the area around North Station, began in 1807 and in 25 years consumed the summits of Copp's and Beacon hills.

In the 19th century the city tripled in area, creating badly needed space. The largest project, started in 1835 and completed in 1882, was the filling of the Back Bay, the body of mud flats and marshes that gave its name to the present-day neighborhood. Beginning in 1857, much of the fill came by railroad from suburban Needham.

By the mid-1800s, Ralph Waldo Emerson, Oliver Wendell Holmes, Henry Wadsworth Longfellow, Nathaniel Hawthorne, Bronson Alcott, Louisa May Alcott, John Greenleaf Whittier, Walt Whitman, Henry David Thoreau, and even Charles Dickens (briefly) and Mark Twain (more briefly) had appeared on the local literary scene. William Lloyd Garrison published the weekly *Liberator* newspaper, a powerful voice in the antislavery and social reform movements. Boston became an important stop on the Underground Railroad, the secret network the abolitionists developed to smuggle runaway slaves into Canada.

LOCAL GLORY

During the Civil War (1861–65), abolitionist sentiment was the order of the day—to such a degree that the rolls listing the war dead in Harvard's Memorial Hall include only members of the Union Army. Massachusetts' contributions to the war effort included enormous quantities of firearms, shoes, blankets, tents, and men.

The famed black abolitionist Frederick Douglass, a former member of the Massachusetts Anti-Slavery Society, helped recruit the 54th and 55th Massachusetts Colored Regiments. The movie *Glory* tells the story of the 54th, the first army unit made up of free black soldiers, and its white commander, Colonel Robert Gould Shaw. The regiment's memorial, a gorgeous bas-relief by Augustus Saint-Gaudens, stands on Boston Common opposite the State House.

A CAPITAL CITY

The railroad boom of the 1820s and 1830s and the flood of immigration that began soon afterward had made New England an industrial center. Then as now,

Boston was the region's unofficial capital. Thousands of immigrants from Ireland settled in the city, the first ethnic group to do so in great numbers since the French Huguenots in the early 18th century. Signs reading NO IRISH NEED APPLY became scarce as the new arrivals gained political power, and the first Irish mayor was elected in 1885.

By this time, the class split in society was a chasm, with the influx of immigrants who swelled the ranks of the local working class adding to the social tension. The Irish led the way and were followed by eastern European Jewish, Italian, and Portuguese immigrants, who had their own neighborhoods, churches, schools, newspapers, and livelihoods that intersected only occasionally with "proper" society.

Even as the upper crust was sowing seeds that would wind up enriching everyone—the Boston Symphony, the Boston Public Library, and the Museum of Fine Arts were established in the second half of the 19th century—it was engaging in prudish behavior that gained Boston a reputation for making snobbery an art form. In 1878 the censorious Watch and Ward Society was founded (as the New England Society for the Suppression of Vice), and the phrase "banned in Boston" soon made its way into the American vocabulary. In 1889, the private St. Botolph Club removed John Singer Sargent's portrait of Isabella Stewart Gardner from public view (it's now at the museum that bears her name) because her dress was too tight.

The Boston Brahmins could keep their new neighbors out of many areas of their lives, but not politics. The forebears of the Kennedy clan had appeared on the scene—John F. "Honey Fitz" Fitzgerald, Rose Kennedy's father, was elected mayor in 1910—and the city was changing.

World War II bolstered Boston's Depression-ravaged industrial economy, and the war's end touched off an economic transformation. Shipping declined, along with New England's textile, shoe, and glass industries, at the same time that students on the G.I. Bill poured into area colleges and universities. The rise of high technology led to new construction, changing the look of the city yet again. The 1960s saw the beginning of a building boom that continues to this day (after a lull during the recession of the late 1980s).

THE LATE 20TH CENTURY

The mid-1970s brought the Boston busing crisis, sparked by a court-ordered school desegregation plan enacted in 1974 that touched off riots, violence, and a white boycott. Because of "white flight," Boston is now what urban planners call a "doughnut city." It has a relatively large black population (23.8% of Boston residents are black, compared with 11% of the U.S. population) surrounded by many lily-white suburbs. The 2000 Census showed that Boston had become a "majority minority" city, with whites making up less than 50% of the population for the first time. The city has battled its reputation for racism with varying degrees of success. One of the most integrated neighborhoods, Jamaica Plain, is linked to one of the least integrated, Charlestown—but only by the Orange Line of the subway. The school system has yet to fully recover from the traumatic experience of busing, but every year it sends thousands of students on to the institutions of higher learning that continue to be Boston's greatest claim to fame.

The economic boom of the 1990s made a lot of noise in the Boston area, home to many high-tech businesses, financial-services firms, and venture capitalists. The bust that followed took its toll, but some sectors of the economy remained relatively strong. Visitors will quickly realize that one such sector is construction, which benefited from ongoing development and the enormous highway construction project known as the Big Dig.

To get a sense of what Boston is (and is not) like, hit the streets. The puritanical Bostonian is virtually extinct, but you can still uncover traces of the groups, institutions, and events that have shaped history to make Boston the complex city you see today.

Index

See also Accommodations and Restaurant indexes, below.

FROMMER'S® COMPLETE TRAVEL GUIDES

Alaska
Alaska Cruises & Ports of Call
Amsterdam
Argentina & Chile
Arizona
Atlanta
Australia
Austria
Bahamas
Barcelona, Madrid & Seville
Beijing
Belgium, Holland & Luxembourg
Bermuda
Boston
Brazil
British Columbia & the Canadian
    Rockies
Budapest & the Best of Hungary
California
Canada
Cancún, Cozumel & the Yucatán
Cape Cod, Nantucket & Martha's
    Vineyard
Caribbean
Caribbean Cruises & Ports of Call
Caribbean Ports of Call
Carolinas & Georgia
Chicago
China
Colorado
Costa Rica
Denmark
Denver, Boulder & Colorado
    Springs
England
Europe
European Cruises & Ports of Call
Florida

France
Germany
Great Britain
Greece
Greek Islands
Hawaii
Hong Kong
Honolulu, Waikiki & Oahu
Ireland
Israel
Italy
Jamaica
Japan
Las Vegas
London
Los Angeles
Maryland & Delaware
Maui
Mexico
Montana & Wyoming
Montréal & Québec City
Munich & the Bavarian Alps
Nashville & Memphis
Nepal
New England
New Mexico
New Orleans
New York City
New Zealand
Northern Italy
Nova Scotia, New Brunswick &
    Prince Edward Island
Oregon
Paris
Philadelphia & the Amish Country
Portugal
Prague & the Best of the Czech
    Republic

Provence & the Riviera
Puerto Rico
Rome
San Antonio & Austin
San Diego
San Francisco
Santa Fe, Taos & Albuquerque
Scandinavia
Scotland
Seattle & Portland
Shanghai
Singapore & Malaysia
South Africa
South America
South Florida
South Pacific
Southeast Asia
Spain
Sweden
Switzerland
Texas
Thailand
Tokyo
Toronto
Tuscany & Umbria
USA
Utah
Vancouver & Victoria
Vermont, New Hampshire &
    Maine
Vienna & the Danube Valley
Virgin Islands
Virginia
Walt Disney World® & Orlando
Washington, D.C.
Washington State

FROMMER'S® DOLLAR-A-DAY GUIDES

Australia from $50 a Day
California from $70 a Day
Caribbean from $70 a Day
England from $75 a Day
Europe from $70 a Day

Florida from $70 a Day
Hawaii from $80 a Day
Ireland from $60 a Day
Italy from $70 a Day
London from $85 a Day

New York from $90 a Day
Paris from $80 a Day
San Francisco from $70 a Day
Washington, D.C. from $80 a Day

FROMMER'S® PORTABLE GUIDES

Acapulco, Ixtapa & Zihuatanejo
Amsterdam
Aruba
Australia's Great Barrier Reef
Bahamas
Berlin
Big Island of Hawaii
Boston
California Wine Country
Cancún
Charleston & Savannah
Chicago
Disneyland®
Dublin
Florence

Frankfurt
Hong Kong
Houston
Las Vegas
London
Los Angeles
Los Cabos & Baja
Maine Coast
Maui
Miami
New Orleans
New York City
Paris
Phoenix & Scottsdale

Portland
Puerto Rico
Puerto Vallarta, Manzanillo &
    Guadalajara
Rio de Janeiro
San Diego
San Francisco
Seattle
Sydney
Tampa & St. Petersburg
Vancouver
Venice
Virgin Islands
Washington, D.C.

FROMMER'S® NATIONAL PARK GUIDES

Banff & Jasper
Family Vacations in the National
    Parks
Grand Canyon

National Parks of the American
    West
Rocky Mountain

Yellowstone & Grand Teton
Yosemite & Sequoia/ Kings Canyon
Zion & Bryce Canyon

FROMMER'S® MEMORABLE WALKS

Chicago
London

New York
Paris

San Francisco
Washington, D.C.

FROMMER'S® GREAT OUTDOOR GUIDES

Arizona & New Mexico
New England

Northern California
Southern New England

Vermont & New Hampshire

SUZY GERSHMAN'S BORN TO SHOP GUIDES

Born to Shop: France
Born to Shop: Hong Kong,
   Shanghai & Beijing

Born to Shop: Italy
Born to Shop: London

Born to Shop: New York
Born to Shop: Paris

FROMMER'S® IRREVERENT GUIDES

Amsterdam
Boston
Chicago
Las Vegas
London

Los Angeles
Manhattan
New Orleans
Paris
Rome

San Francisco
Seattle & Portland
Vancouver
Walt Disney World®
Washington, D.C.

FROMMER'S® BEST-LOVED DRIVING TOURS

Britain
California
Florida
France

Germany
Ireland
Italy
New England

Northern Italy
Scotland
Spain
Tuscany & Umbria

HANGING OUT™ GUIDES

Hanging Out in England
Hanging Out in Europe

Hanging Out in France
Hanging Out in Ireland

Hanging Out in Italy
Hanging Out in Spain

THE UNOFFICIAL GUIDES®

Bed & Breakfasts and Country
   Inns in:
   California
   Great Lakes States
   Mid-Atlantic
   New England
   Northwest
   Rockies
   Southeast
   Southwest
Best RV & Tent Campgrounds in:
   California & the West
   Florida & the Southeast
   Great Lakes States
   Mid-Atlantic
   Northeast
   Northwest & Central Plains

   Southwest & South Central
      Plains
   U.S.A.
Beyond Disney
Branson, Missouri
California with Kids
Chicago
Cruises
Disneyland®
Florida with Kids
Golf Vacations in the Eastern U.S.
Great Smoky & Blue Ridge Region
Inside Disney
Hawaii
Las Vegas
London

Mid-Atlantic with Kids
Mini Las Vegas
Mini-Mickey
New England and New York with
   Kids
New Orleans
New York City
Paris
San Francisco
Skiing in the West
Southeast with Kids
Walt Disney World®
Walt Disney World® for Grown-ups
Walt Disney World® with Kids
Washington, D.C.
World's Best Diving Vacations

SPECIAL-INTEREST TITLES

Frommer's Adventure Guide to Australia &
   New Zealand
Frommer's Adventure Guide to Central America
Frommer's Adventure Guide to India & Pakistan
Frommer's Adventure Guide to South America
Frommer's Adventure Guide to Southeast Asia
Frommer's Adventure Guide to Southern Africa
Frommer's Britain's Best Bed & Breakfasts and
   Country Inns
Frommer's Caribbean Hideaways
Frommer's Exploring America by RV
Frommer's Fly Safe, Fly Smart
Frommer's France's Best Bed & Breakfasts and
   Country Inns
Frommer's Gay & Lesbian Europe

Frommer's Italy's Best Bed & Breakfasts and
   Country Inns
Frommer's New York City with Kids
Frommer's Ottawa with Kids
Frommer's Road Atlas Britain
Frommer's Road Atlas Europe
Frommer's Road Atlas France
Frommer's Toronto with Kids
Frommer's Vancouver with Kids
Frommer's Washington, D.C., with Kids
Israel Past & Present
The New York Times' Guide to Unforgettable
   Weekends
Places Rated Almanac
Retirement Places Rated